Lund Studies in International History 6

Göran Rystad

Ambiguous Imperialism

American Foreign Policy and Domestic Politics at the Turn of the Century

☸ ESSELTE STUDIUM

For my parents

Contents

Acknowledgments

I would like to take this opportunity to thank the institutions, organizations, and individuals who aided me, directly or indirectly, in this work.

The American Council of Learned Societies awarded me a Research Fellowship in 1963—1964 and again in 1970. In 1966—1967 I was Research Fellow at the Charles Warren Center for Studies in American History at Harvard University. The excellent facilities at the Center and even more its stimulating scholarly atmosphere made my stay there a most rewarding experience. I would like to extend my thanks to Professor Oscar Handlin, Director of the Center at the time, and to members of the Administrative Committee, Professors Bernard Bailyn, Donald Fleming, Frank Freidel, and Ernest R. May.

For generous financial aid I am most grateful to *Wallenbergsstiftelsen* and above all to *Statens Humanistiska Forskningsråd,* which also made the publication of this study possible.

I began this book as an ACLS Fellow in 1963. I had the good fortune to become associated with Professors Robert H. Ferrell of Indiana University and Irvin G. Wyllie of the University of Wisconsin. I owe much to debates and discussions with them, over the years. They have followed the progress of my work with interest, and their friendship and encouragement has been invaluable. Professor Ferrell has also had the fortitude to read my entire manuscript and his suggestions have improved it in many ways. I further extend my thanks to Mrs. Lila Ferrell and Mrs. Harriet Wyllie for all their hospitality and kindness.

I have numerous obligations to libraries, librarians, archives, and archivists. I am especially indebted to the staffs of Indiana University's Lilly Library, the Wisconsin State Historical Society, and the Charles Warren Center at Harvard University, where a major part of the work was carried out. Of great assistance were also the staffs of Widener Library and Houghton Library at Harvard, the Massachusetts Historical Society, New York Public Library, Pennsylvania Historical Society, Indiana University Library, Indiana State Library, Indiana State Historical Society, the University of Wisconsin Library, Stanford University Library, the University of North Carolina Library, Washington University Library, and especially the Library of Congress.

I was also helped in many ways by many friends, including Richard and Mac Showman, James and Louise Ferguson, Justus and Ely Hanks, Victor and Virginia Hanson, Al and Siv Mott, Alf Erlandsson and Britt Kjölstad, who all not only facilitated my work but also made my visits to the United States most enjoyable and rewarding.

To many other friends and colleagues, too numerous to mention, who in various ways have helped me in my work, I can only express the hope that they will consider the results worthwhile.

I am indebted to my wife, Birgitta, in many ways, but here I will mention only her help in preparing the bibliography and the name index. Mr. Leif Eliasson, my daughters, Margareta and Åsa, and my son, Johan, have assisted with proofreading. I am indebted to Mrs. Gillian Nilsson for her help with the translation, and the manuscript was excellently typed by Mrs. Siv Axenholt.

Introduction

On May 1 1898 an American squadron under the command of Commodore Dewey annihilated the renowned but completely obsolete Pacific Fleet of Spain laying at anchor in the harbor of Manila in the Philippine Islands.

The event has been considered a turning point in American history. In the subsequent peace treaty, Cuba was made independent but became in reality an American protectorate. Puerto Rico became American. And, what was even more important, the Philippine Islands became an American colony. The United States had taken her place as a world power. Her traditional isolation in the Western hemisphere had been broken.

In itself expansion was nothing new in American history. But the former expansion had been in sparsely populated, directly contiguous territories, part of the American continent, which had been settled and cultivated by Americans and which gradually were accepted as states on equal terms with the others in the Union. What happened at the turn of the century was different. Now it was a question of thickly populated, foreign possessions, divided from the American continent by vast expanses of water.

There had been signs during the last decades of the 19th century of an awakening interest in this direction and of an increased self-awareness in the dynamic power that was growing at so violent a rate. Ideas of distant colonies and coaling stations for support of the navy had been expressed increasingly often, in conjunction with notions of the United States being destined to play an active part in the affairs of the world. But the great change came after the Spanish-American war, which broke out at the beginning of 1898. The consequences of this conflict mark the definite turning point in America's position in international affairs.

*

11

One of the most popular and most widely embraced ideas among historians is that both war and territorial expansion usually stem from economic factors. The need for raw materials and consumer markets is often pushed into the foreground, as are the efforts of financial interests to find profitable investments. Imperialism, even if it is defined in different ways, is usually thought of as being caused by economic forces and is explained in such terms. This view of the Spanish-American war and its consequences is common. At the turn of the century it entered into the contemporary debate. In his famous book, *Imperialism: A Study*, published in 1902, J. A. Hobson used the conflict in question as a typical example.

The American drive for foreign acquisitions he explained as depending on "a sudden demand for foreign markets for manufactures and for investment," bottoming in the rapid growth of industry in the country and a subsequent lack of domestic investment prospects for the profits of the trusts and big business.[1] Lenin also described the Spanish-American conflict as an imperialistic war, of the kind that he analyzed in his classic work, *Imperialism: The Highest Stage of Capitalism* (1917).[2]

The influential Charles A. Beard used to a very large extent economic causal explantions and interpretations and it is not surprising that he saw the Spanish-American war largely in this light. Beard wrote that references to fate, historical coincidences, the course of events or the gifts of the gods said nothing about the background to the American annexation of the Philippines. It should be seen instead in the context of American moves in the Far East throughout the 19th century. In his book, *The Idea of National Interest: An Analytical Study in American Foreign Policy* (1934) Beard claimed that, although strategic considerations and power politics had a role to play, it was the economic interests that were decisive.[3] Beard differentiated between an agrarian expansionism, which tried to acquire contiguous territories for settlement, cultivation and incorporation into the Union, and commercial expansionism, with marketing demand as its driving force. The latter, he wrote, was supported by the Republican party and had a decisive influence on policy at the turn of the century.

During the first decades of the 20th century the explanations of the war against Spain—and the consequent imperialist policy of expansion—lay mainly on the economic plane, until at the beginning of the 1930's this view began to seem unsatisfactory and new factors were introduced into the debate. In 1932 Marcus M. Wilkerson published a study which asserted that America went to war because McKinley and Congress gave way to a jingoist opinion that had been whipped up by the uncontrolled agitation of the popular press, led by the New York *World* and *Journal*.[4] Studies by Joseph E. Wisan and George W. Auxier appeared to support this theory.[5]

The new understanding of the importance of opinion-molding for political decision processes added a new dimension to the debate and to some extent cleared the way for the decisive change in the view of the war with Spain and the new foreign policy, a change which emerged with the studies published by Julius W. Pratt in the middle of the 1930's. In 1934 the article, "American Business and the Spanish-American War" appeared[6] and two years later the important study, *Expansionists of 1898: The Acquisition of Hawaii and the Spanish Islands*.[7] Pratt had examined a wide range of material: financial journals and newspapers, minutes and reports from chambers of commerce, letters, official statements and private notes made by businessmen, bankers and industrial magnates, all for the purpose of establishing as precisely as possible the attitudes of the business world and industry towards the war. An overwhelming proportion of his material indicated that these groups were negative to the war and did everything in their power to prevent it. Nor was there any interest in these quarters for territorial expansion prior to the conflict.

The opinion that propagated so zealously for war in 1898, he believed was driven by idealistic, humanitarian and nationalist arguments and the groups and individuals that tried to influence the decision process in favor of intervention were not businessmen, but economists, sociologists and historians. Once Spain had been defeated, business and financial interests began to realize what opportunities the victory had opened up, with the result that they became increasingly committed to a policy of expansion. Business interests were not the driving force.

Pratt's views had a widespread influence. His main thesis about the negative or passive role of finance and the business world in the process leading to the American intervention and the necessity of differentiating between factors leading to the outbreak of war and those that lay behind the subsequent annexations was quickly accepted and is to be found in some form in the majority of later studies, irrespective of how they otherwise interpret developments. Thus Dexter Perkins declared that the actions of the American government, the intervention in Cuba and the following acquisitions of new territories, were to be traced not to economic pressure but to a change in the national mood.[8] Thomas A. Bailey emphasized that before the outbreak of war big business functioned as a brake on "the jingoistic spirit".[9] Samuel Flagg Bemis also rejected what he

13

described as the "legend" that American business strove for intervention.[10] To Bemis the acquisition of the Philippines, the climax of American expansion, was "a great national aberration." In *Ideals and Self Interest in America's Foreign Relations* (1953) Robert E. Osgood also denied that America was drawn into the war by businessmen looking for new markets and investment opportunities.[11] It was an idealistic crusade, but the war and the victory increased the national self-assertiveness as well as a general sense of national power and destiny. In *Dream and Reality: Aspects of American Foreign Policy* (1959) Louis J. Halle argued that in 1898 the nation "lost its sobriety and abandoned itself to glory." It was "a people's war into which our government was swept by public opinion." A decision to attach the Philippines to the United States did not exist "until it was found that they virtually were attached already." By that time there was no acceptable alternative to keeping them.[12]

In an article, "Manifest Destiny and the Philippines" (1952), Richard Hofstadter explained the outbreak of war as being caused by what he called America's psychic crisis of the 1890's, a general feeling of frustration and uncertainty, connected with economic crises and social unrest.[13] The intervention in Cuba became a kind of crusade, he maintained, releasing excess energy and aggressions. Jingoism and idealistic fervor were different ways of responding to frustrations. The situation was then exploited by a small group of influential imperialists.

Pratt's outlook was shared also by other historians such as Selig Adler,[14] Howard K. Beale,[15] Foster Rhea Dulles,[16] Oscar Handlin[17] and William E. Leuchtenburg.[17a] Thus the Pratt interpretation was widely accepted and even when the interpretations diverged in other respects there was belief that the war was not provoked by economic interests but that on the contrary, business opposed American intervention.

The first direct attack on the Pratt theory was not until more than twenty years later. In 1958 Nancy Leonore O'Connor published an article, "The Spanish American War: A Re-evaluation of Its Causes," claiming that Pratt's results were based on insufficient and not wholly representative material, and that business and economic considerations were much more involved in the war and the new policy than Pratt and his successors had thought.[18]

In an article published in 1960, "American Continentalism: An Idea of

14

Expansion, 1845—1910," Charles Vevier stressed the continuity in American expansionist ideas and tried to minimize the change in 1898.[19]

One historian who has consistently asserted the importance of business interests in the shaping of American foreign policy at different periods is William Appleman Williams. He has put forward this view in works such as *The Tragedy of American Diplomacy, 1750—1955* (1959)[20] and *The Contours of American History* (1961).[21] Williams has devoted a comprehensive special study to the expansionist policy of the 1890's, *The Roots of the Modern American Empire. A Study of the Growth and Shaping of Social Consciousness in a Marketplace Society* (1969).[22] One of the chapters is entitled "Onward to War for the Free American Marketplace." The words reveal an essential part of Williams' view of the driving forces of American foreign policy. His is an economic interpretation, characterized by emphasis on the expansionist outlook of the agrarian majority of the nation. Agrarian businessmen had a fervent interest in extension of freedom and global extension of export markets and exercised increasing pressure for expansion, demanding among other things intervention to free Cuba. The farmer became important in shaping an assertive expansionist foreign policy, prompted by his "export-dominated relationship with the world marketplace."

The renaissance of the economic interpretation of America's emergence as a Great Power has been mainly the work by students of William A. Williams. In 1963 Walter LaFeber published *The New Empire: An Interpretation of American Expansion, 1866—1898.*[23] In his search for the driving forces of "the New Departure" LaFeber emphasized that the American business community saw foreign markets, above all in Latin America and Asia, as a solution to the crisis that had descended upon them in 1893. Pressure was brought to bear on the State Department and later on Congress and the administration to use diplomatic and other means to support American business interests in, among other places, the Far East.

In the same year, 1963, Thomas J. McCormick published an article, entitled "Insular Imperialism and The Open Door: The China Market and the Spanish-American War," followed in 1967 by, *China Market: America's Quest for Informal Empire, 1893—1901.*[24] The importance of American business interests for the Open Door policy and their relation to expansionism already had been stressed by Charles S. Campbell, Jr. in an article published in 1949, "American Business Interests and the Open Door."[25] This line of investigation was taken up by McCormick who analyzed the increased American economic attention to the Far East and not least the China Market, stressing the connection between the Cuba crisis and the expansion in the Far East. He focused his interest on "the business community and its political and intellectual allies" and saw the business-oriented community as "the chief shapers of expansionism in the 1890's." Like Williams, McCormick centered attention on "free-trade imperialists" but did not include the agrarian interests in his study.

China policy, emphasized by McCormick, has been illuminated in two other recent studies, Paul A. Varg, *The Making of a Myth: The United States and China, 1897—1912,*[26] and Marilyn Blatt Young, *The Rhetoric of Empire: American China Policy, 1895—1901.*[27] McCormick's, Varg's, and Young's works, each valuable, differ in many respects, demonstrating how complex the question is and how differently it can appear, depending on the focus. As implied by the title of his book Varg denies the substance and reality of American economic interests in China at the time. Marilyn Young's approach is similar to that of Richard Hofstadter in that she regards the explosive foreign policy at the turn of the century as a result of a century of domestic development in America. The violent rate of urbanization and industrialization, combined with the flow of immigrants, produced divisions in society, tendencies toward disorganization and disintegration. The deep depression after 1893 created uncertainty, both among the people and especially the middle-class. Nativism and nationalism appeared to be ways of channeling frustration, either toward the ill-assimilated masses of immigrants or foreign powers. The result was "a national neurosis" which was "acted out in the fantastic fervor that preceded, and perhaps made inevitable, the war." The imperialist spirit was born out of the anxiety and frustration of the nineties.

In his *American Neo-Colonialism: Its Emergence in the Philippines and Asia* (1970), William J. Pomeroy refuted talk of American expansion after the Spanish-American war as being an "aberration."[28] On the contrary, he remarked, it was an expression of imperialism as defined by Lenin. The reason its character has not been recognized was that American imperialism has not been exposed as a system in the same way as its European counterparts. This in turn was due to the fact that there are "variations in the formula of imperialism," reflecting peculiar historical circumstances. According to Pomeroy the events after the Spanish-American war meant emergence of American Neo-Colonialism. Another recent study by Philip S. Foner, *The Spanish-Cuban-American War and the Birth of American Imperialism,* I—II (1972) also comes down clearly and categorically in favor of the idea that both the war and annexations showed

16

the same conscious policy, which was rooted in the rise of monopoly capitalism and its drive for markets."[29]

If modern studies have presented an economic interpretation of the war with Spain and American expansion at the turn of the century, with business interest and market demand seen as driving forces, the analyses given by Pratt, Bailey, Perkins, Osgood, etc., are still generally accepted. In his *Imperial Democracy: The Emergence of America as a Great Power* (1961) Ernest R. May stressed that "for the people as for the government, war with monarchical, Catholic, Latin Spain had no purpose except to relieve emotion." He saw the subsequent policy of annexation more as a result of an opinion released by the war, rather than as the consequence of a conscious policy with a defined purpose. This expansionist opinion encompassed elements such as "piety, superstition, patriotism and greed."[30] Broadly similar interpretations appear in books by Harold U. Faulkner,[31] Frank Freidel,[32] Margaret Leech,[33] H. Wayne Morgan,[34] Richard W. Van Alstyne[35] and others. It is also the way the development is presented in textbooks such as Robert H. Ferrell, *American Diplomacy: A History* (3d ed. 1975),[36] Alexander De Conde, *A History of American Foreign Policy* (1963)[37] Richard W. Leopold, *The Growth of American Foreign Policy* (1962),[38] Daniel M. Smith, *The American Diplomatic Experience* (1972)[39] and others. Of the more extensive recent special studies David Healy's *US Expansionism: The Imperialist Urge in the 1890s* (1970) centers on a small group of expansionists.[40] Healy also attempts a synthesis, and his interpretation does not differ from Ernest May.

In some respects a different view is presented by John A. S. Grenville and George Berkeley Young in their stimulating book *Politics, Strategy, and American Diplomacy: Studies in Foreign Policy, 1873—1917* (1966).[41] They agree with Morgan in refuting the general view of William McKinley as a weak president. More important is that they question that McKinley capitulated to the pressure of jingoists. McKinley went to war because he believed "the dictates of civilization and humanity" impelled the United States to act, and because the president considered it in the long-term interest of the country. Acquisition of the Philippines was not "a great aberration." Grenville and Young do not emphasize business interests and economic considerations, but reasons of strategy and national security.

Despite the many studies devoted to America's emergence as a great power at the turn of the century a generally accepted interpretation has not emerged. One weakness of the "economic interpretation" of American expansionism is failure to find evidence showing that business interests really decisively influenced the decision making process shaping the expansionist foreign policy. Alternative explanations have similar difficulties. There is need for further investigation.

*

However much historians disagree, they usually unite in believing that the declaration of war, the intervention in 1898, became possible because of a war psychosis. This applies irrespective of whether one sees President McKinley as passive and unwilling, forced by an opinion he could not resist, or as a leader with a clearly defined purpose. It is equally obvious that this opinion was not characterized by ideas of expansion or annexation. The opinion certainly did not include a military intervention for the purpose of territorial expansion. A crusade was desired, not a war of conquest.

But we cannot expect to grasp American expansionism, its implications and its roots in opinion and politics by studying the outbreak of war and its background. The essential area of study is the subsequent peace and its aftermath. It was not the intervention and the war against Spain that led to the new departure, America's emergence as a great power in the international arena. It was the consequences of the war: the rise of expansionism and the policy of annexation. The war acted as a catalyst.

How then could the crusade turn into a war of conquest? It is plain that when the peace treaty was signed in the autumn of 1898 it was a matter of bipartisan policy, as the war had been. Expansion played no part ni the campaigns and elections that autumn. The party-political polarization of the issue had not yet started. There had always been expansionists, and their numbers increased with success. They were publicists, strategists, economists, politicians, and their arguments varied: economic-commercial, power-political, strategic. Businessmen then saw opportunities for market expansion with the help of the newly-acquired territories. But this was not enough. The decisive factor was that public opinion that had forced a declaration of war "not out of realistic calculation of national advantage but largely as an idealistic crusade to free the Cubans from Spain's imperial shackles," as Robert E. Osgood put is, now backed annexation."[42] Expansionist propaganda after the peace overwhelmingly resembled the arguments used to motivate the war. There was little talk of economy, power politics, or strategy, but of humanity and idealism. Territorial acquisitions were presented not as war gains but as areas and peoples that America had a moral duty to take care of and protect, through responsibility of the

18

victor. By formulating the problem in this way, in humanitarian and moral terms, an opinion favorable to annexations was created.

If like Osgood one can say that America displayed a facility for "acquiring an empire in a fit of absentmindedness,"[43] or as May expressed it, "had greatness thrust upon it,"[44] awareness of what happened was not far behind, and the new policy and its consequences became an issue, starting an intense debate. It is the period from the signing of the peace treaty up to the turn of the century that must be analyzed closely. This can help to answer the question why the new policy was never pursued, why hesitation and restraint came to dominate the American attitude to continued territorial expansion at the beginning of this century.

*

The present study is not primarily concerned with conduct of foreign affairs as a whole, nor with all the problems related to the shaping of American foreign policy on the decision-making level. The study is focused on the domestic environment, on factors involving public opinion and party politics. It works from the idea that domestic circumstances are influenced by and in their turn influence foreign policy. The study concentrates on the presidential election of 1900.

In few American campaigns has a foreign policy issue played so prominent a role. Did it influence the outcome? The problem is complicated. It is also related to the converse question of how foreign policy can have been affected by being made an issue in the election campaign in this way and drawn into party politics. How was the issue formulated by the two parties? How was it exploited in the campaign at different levels and for different voters? To what extent were the positions of the parties influenced by strategic and tactical party considerations and what were the consequences of this? The problem can be formulated as the inter-relationship between domestic politics and foreign policy.

Those opposing the new foreign policy spoke of "imperialism" and this concept was used in the Democratic election propaganda of 1900. The Republicans in turn denied the validity of the term and claimed that it was only a question of "expansion." Distinctions were constantly made between "imperialism" and "expansion," but these distinctions were unclear and varied depending on whether made by supporters or opponents of the new foreign policy.

Some later writers also use the terms "imperialism" and "expansion" in different ways and with the one excluding the other. The result is debatable,

19

and in the present study "expansion" and "expansionism" are preferred, while "imperialism" is usually used only either in referring to a contemporary debate in which the content is immediately apparent, or as a subordinate concept referring primarily to territorial expansion of a colonial type.

*

Opinions are sharply divided on American expansionism at the turn of the century, its background, driving forces and implications. One reason is the complex nature of the movement. People in favor of expansion were motivated differently and held different ideas as to the organization of the newly acquired territories. The variables were economic interests, strategic and power-policy considerations, religious and humanitarian idealism, racial theories and Social Darwinism, all combined in varying proportions in different groups and individuals. Misleading interpretations and generalizations arise easily, especially as representativeness of the material used is often dubious. Sources are all too often insubstantial and simplifications conspicuous.

The expansionist mood was diverse and expressed itself in different ways. The heated debate produced concepts of National Interest, not only varying in perceptions of the present but based on conflicting interpretations of the past. Another reason for lack of consensus as to the nature and the driving force of American expansionism at this period is the confusion of arguments, motives, ideas, the lack of consistency and amazing unawareness of consequences of positions held, that characterized so much of the contemporary debate. Not only do we meet deliberate agitatorial and propagandist shifts in the concepts, but it is plain that the individuals involved were themselves confused and uncertain.

It is necessary to analyze the prevailing contemporary arguments and policy positions in order to establish the structure of expansionism as revealed in political objectives and motives. Only then is a meaningful discussion possible of the use of the issue in the context of domestic politics.

The debate between supporters and opponents of the new expansionism was charged with emotion. It was conducted with vague, undefined concepts and ideas, which sometimes gave the struggle an air of unreality. Arguments and standpoints put forward often showed a remarkable lack of rationality. In fact the issue fulfills to an extremely high degree the criteria set up by modern opinion researchers as likely to lead to irrational thinking: vagueness, the consequences of actions remote and difficult to assess, a debate full of abstract terms. These researchers also point out that the more the public's interest is directed toward an issue, the more likely it is to give rise to irrational opinions. All these factors apply to the fight over the new foreign policy at the turn of the century. These features became especially apparent when the political parties took up the issue.

By focusing analysis on a concrete issue, we can see more easily where the dividing lines lie, what was really meant by the rhetoric that blossomed in different quarters, what consequences people were prepared to take. The violent fight over the Puerto Rican tariff bill in the spring of 1900 was just such an issue. Here the problem was reduced to its essence and concerned the fundamental question of whether the United States should or could have colonial possessions. It was the prelude to the important Insular Cases in 1900.

A little-studied area is the importance of foreign policy issues in party politics at state level. How and to what effect were such antagonisms exploited? The problem touches another essential question concerning the domestic environment of the foreign policy process, namely the extent to which controversies engage the general public, the man in the street. If we restrict ourselves to the voters, the problem can be formulated in terms of how far foreign policy controversies had any significance in domestic politics that consisted of campaigns and elections at state level. To illuminate these questions, an intensive study has been made of the pre-convention campaign in Indiana, considered by both parties to be a pivotal state in the coming election. The study takes up questions hitherto neglected, concerning the relationship between foreign and domestic policies.

Was imperialism a "genuine" or an "artificial" issue in the campaign of 1900? Did the confrontation which the Democratic leadership sought by declaring imperialism to be the "paramount," "burning" issue, in fact represent a real clash between standpoints held by rank and file Democrats and Republicans respectively, or was it just a tactical device? To establish the differences it is essential to get behind the National Conventions at which the platforms were adopted and positions locked. Chapter 4 provides an analysis of the different Democratic and Republican pre-convention state party platforms in 1900. The intention is to reveal not only points on which the parties differed or agreed on foreign policy issues, above all territorial expansion, but also to study if possible the regional variations. The next stage is to follow the process by which the Democratic party finally came to enter the campaign with a program where foreign policy was in the center and with the fight against imperialism the main content of the campaign.

When studying the development of American expansionism, it is imperative to take a close look at the party political side of the question. Modern election studies have established that the single most important factor in deciding the attitude to a given question is party identification.

The party emerges as an opinion molder of the first degree, not primarily by information or propaganda but through a process of identification. This is effective not least in the case of voters whose information level and grasp of the questions is low. For many voters with strong party identification, which means a large group, the question is settled when the party has decided its standpoint, that is, when a party doctrine has been formed. After this, the inclination of the voter to identify with and defend this standpoint is so strong that it often neutralizes other influences. Once the party line had been settled by adoption of the platform at Kansas City it had immediate effects, clearly shown in the press opinion, where the Democratic newspapers adjusted to the party line in preparation for the campaign.

Formation of party doctrines is not only important for development of public opinion, however, but directly influences both the party's representatives in Congress and the party press. Keeping all this in mind, it becomes a matter of importance to investigate how and when the party positions were formed.

Another matter of special interest is to study developments after the Democratic National Convention, the effect of the party's decisive anti-imperialist platform. Voters with strong party identification or lacking convictions on the controversial issue of expansion created no problem. But how did pro-expansionist Democrats and convinced anti-imperialist Republicans, Independents or Gold Democrats react?

Chapters 6 and 7 present a study of developments, once the front lines had been drawn, of how party identification functioned and how different groups of voters tried to solve problems of conflicting loyalties in different ways. Persons aflicted by such conflicting loyalties: their attitude to the party, the party's standpoint on expansionism and their own opinion on this question, all reacted in full accord with the patterns revealed by modern opinion research and psychology. There was obviously an inclination toward consistency and the persons concerned tried to reduce the dissonance. The usual way of doing this was to change the cognitions that most easily lent themselves to change. An opinion could be changed if party identification was strong and conviction on the issue less firm. In the converse case the dissonance could lead to a change of party, which happened in prominent cases. But consonance could be achieved by a reorganization of priorities, a denial of the importance of the issue compared to others. Distortion of the party's position was another method of reducing dissonance.

Chapters 7 and 8 contain an investigation of the strategy and tactics of the parties in using the issue of expansion in the campaign, not least how the main actors, William Jennings Bryan and the Republican vice-presidential candidate, Theodore Roosevelt, varied their message and their arguments regionally and in time. Attention is paid to the key states, Indiana and New York, the main battle grounds of the campaign. The final chapter is an attempt to analyze the importance of the paramount issue for the outcome of the election, together with the long-term effect on American foreign policy of the question of territorial expansion.

As a result of the policy of expansion becoming drawn into party politics, the opinion that had made the annexations possible was split. The intensive election campaign meant that the "humanitarian-idealistic" picture put forward in the expansionist propaganda was subjected to a critical examination. It could not stand up to such an examination; the hollowness of many of the arguments was revealed. This meant that expansionism lost the broad support of public opinion that was a requisite for an active policy. At the same time the protracted and bloody war in the Philippines led to many formerly convinced expansionists having second thoughts. To this can be added the fact that it was not to be long before territorial expansion lost its appeal to businessmen. They came to realize that empires of the accepted type were obsolete phenomena, that territorial annexations were as unnecessary as they were costly and hazardous.

CHAPTER I

The Structure of American Expansionism at the Turn of the Century

The Objects of Policy: Continentalism, Hemispherism, Globalism

1

In the bitter struggle between expansionists and anti-imperialists in America following the Spanish-American War, the expansionists often insisted that they were only continuing the tradition of expansionism that had characterized American foreign policy ever since the foundation of the Union. The anti-imperialists indignantly rejected this argument. In their view there lay an impassable gulf between traditional expansionism and the new imperialism. The earlier form of expansion had involved only the North American continent and only contiguous territory, completely or partially uninhabited, intended for cultivation and settlement by Americans, to be incorporated into the Union States, each on equal terms with the others. This kind of expansionism was usually called *continentalism*. It was also what was meant by the celebrated term Manifest Destiny. The manifest destiny doctrine had gained many adherents during the 1830's and 1840's. Its message was that it was the clear and inevitable lot of the United States to absorb all of North America. Manifest destiny also came to refer not least to the annexation of land suitable for a system of slavery. This expansionism, largely championed by adherents of the Democratic party, was regarded with distrust in the northeastern states, as a threat to the balance of power in the Union. By following the doctrine of continental manifest destiny, the United States acquired Texas, Oregon and the southwestern regions including California.

Years ago Charles A. Beard stressed that American expansionism during the nineteenth century comprised two quite different types of land acquisition, represented by two wholly separate groups and based on different conceptions of national interest. One was continentalism, striving for annexation of neighboring territories, which could be settled and cultivated. It was an agrarian expansion, inaugurated under Jefferson, pursued by the

25

Democrats during the whole of the nineteenth century. The other form of expansionism was overseas annexation. It developed as a parallel movement to the industrialization of America, aiming not at acquisition of land for cultivation, but at acquisition of naval bases and coaling stations, island trade centers and spheres of control. The goal was new markets for trade and investment.[1]

This dualistic view of American expansion is clearly oversimplified. The agrarian expansionism at the end of the nineteenth century also had commercial aims. But it is quite clear that manifest destiny expansionism, continentalism, was basically of an agrarian nature. When, after 1898 and above all in the presidential election campaign of 1900, the political parties disagreed on foreign policy, the Democrats mainly adopted the well-tried continentalist point of view. They declared in favor of this type of expansion, but rejected the new type that the McKinley administration had introduced and which they described as imperialism. The Democratic presidential candidate, William Jennings Bryan, summed up their attitude quite clearly in his letter of acceptance: "The Democratic Party does not oppose expansion when expansion enlarges the area of the republic and incorporates land which can be settled by American citizens, or adds to our population people who are willing to become citizens and are capable of discharging their duties as such." However, neither Bryan nor the rest of the Democrats, nor most of the other anti-imperialists, opposed acquisition of naval bases and coaling stations for the benefit of American foreign trade. They all agreed that the United States ought to obtain these facilities in the Philippines. But they strongly objected to annexation of the entire group of islands. For Bryan and many of those who shared his views, this was a question of ideology, and they denied that the Constitution permitted American rule over any people "without the consent of the governed." The New York *World* put the situation more bluntly: "The flag raised by Rear-Admiral Dewey in Manila is there to stay. There is no occasion for hysterics to assure this fact. ... But Manila is not the Philippines. Its possession and retention fortunately do not impose upon us the government and care of 1400 islands, with their seven millions of barbarians. We have the juice of the orange without the rind and pulp."[2] The same tone was heard in many quarters, as in *The American Grocer*: "It is not necessary in order to secure commerce to own territory, for nations buy, as do individuals, in the cheapest market; but it is necessary to have coaling and naval stations the world over."[3]

The truth is that the division of opinion among Americans at the turn of the century was not quite as Beard saw it. Indeed the situation was complex. Neither the *World* nor the *Grocer* saw the problem of expansion from the point of view of the Constitution, or ideology. They represented what can be called *informalism*, since their goal was sometimes designated "the informal empire." The consistent informalists often joined the genuine anti-imperialists in criticizing the new expansionism. They protested on practical and rational, not ideological grounds. Informalists often advocated a dynamic commercial-economic expansionism, but their analysis of the problem led them to the conclusion that the usual imperialistic type of territorial expansion was obsolete and produced more disadvantages than advantages. Their idea was that more efficient results could be achieved by economic control of an informal empire than by old-fashioned empire-building or indeed any form of expensive and politically troublesome territorial annexation. History proved them right and the rapid collapse of American territorial imperialism can to some extent be attributed to the fact that their views gained ground. The ease with which this change of opinion was accomplished was partly because informalism was really a common denominator for most expansionists, even though they differed on how far they were prepared to go. Few of them saw the building of an extensive colonial empire as a goal. What they wanted was a system of bases, strategic and commercial, which would safeguard the United States position as a great power and ensure control of the markets of the world.[4]

2

Another outlook of the time was what might be called *hemispherism*, which also had a long history in American politics. The term is used here to denote a form of expansionism which can best be described as continentalism plus the Caribbean Sea. It came to the fore under Seward and Grant. As late as 1895, Henry Cabot Lodge, soon to be one of the foremost advocates of imperialism, expressed the idea of hemispherism when he said, "From Rio Grande to the Arctic Ocean there should be but one flag and one country." He did not consider expansion further to the south desirable— neither the people nor the land would be "desirable additions to the United States." At the same time he was anxious to have one of the islands in the Caribbean as a naval base and thought it would be necessary for the United States to acquire Cuba after the Isthmian Canal was built.[5] Lodge also wanted to see Hawaii under American control, partly to protect the projected canal, also "for the sake of our commercial supremacy in the Pacific."⁶

A leading expansionist with sympathies for hemispherism was e.g. Albert Shaw, editor of the *American Monthly Review of Reviews.* "Our chief destiny lies in our own hemisphere," he wrote in a letter to Andrew Carnegie, who in this respect was of the same opinion as Shaw, although he was at the same time emerging as an active anti-imperialist. Shaw also explained that an annexation of Nicaragua (for the building of a canal between the Atlantic and the Pacific) would be worth more than all the islands of both the Indies.⁷ Hemispherism was formulated even more distinctly in an article by H. O. Money in the *Arena,* with the title "Expansion—Past and Prospective."⁸ The writer rejected overseas expansion absolutely and was an uncompromising opponent to the annexation of the Philippines. But, he said, "... there is an expansion that confines itself to this hemisphere—that keeps within the limits of the so-called Monroe (or, rather, American) doctrine. In this expansion the United States assumes the hegemony of all the United States and takes the responsibility of settling without conventions with other Powers all purely American questions. Both Continental territory and West Indian and Caribbean islands are included within its bounds." Money also recommended the annexation of Cuba.

Senator Henry Moore Teller of Colorado, a prominent silver Republican, was another of the men who declared themselves as convinced hemispherists. He backed President Cleveland in the Venezuela boundary dispute with Great Britain and attacked him in the controversy over the annexation of Hawaii. In that debate he gave an excellent formulation of this brand of expansionism:

"I am in favor of the annexation of those islands (Hawaii). I am in favor of the annexation of Cuba; I am in favor of the annexation of the great country lying to the north of us. I expect in a few years to see the American flag floating from the extreme north to the line of our sister Republics on the South. I expect to see it floating over the isles of the sea—not only these, but in the Great Gulf and in the West India sea."⁹

The Teller amendment, which pledged the United States to make Cuba independent, did not mean that Teller had changed his mind. The Senator, like many other expansionists, felt that an independent Cuba would eventually ask for annexation.¹⁰

The difference between continentalists and hemispherists was not all

28

that great. In one sense it was only a question of a geographical expansion of a not too revolutionizing nature. There is, however, a further important aspect. As Frederick Merk emphasized, the theory of consent was an important element in the continentalist doctrine.[11] In itself this could also be taken over by the hemispherists and that was in fact what happened to a large extent. But another problem was also involved. Continentalism was an expansion aiming at the areas that had or could be expected to get a population that would someday qualify for equal statehood in the Union. Many expansionists were not willing to follow this logical conclusion when it was a question of the inhabitants of, for example, Cuba and Puerto Rico, who were numerous and from a racial point of view heterogeneous. Andrew Carnegie, the financial backer of the anti-imperialist movement, was in favor of acquiring not only Canada, but also Puerto Rico and Cuba, if the inhabitants of the islands agreed. Nor was the thought of such a development foreign to other leading anti-imperialists, such as George F. Hoar and Carl Schurz. It should be pointed out that most hemispherists also accepted the annexation of Hawaii. The arguments they used were partly the same as those brought out in connection with the Caribbean islands. As far as Cuba was concerned, the situation was complicated by the fact that Congress had pledged itself, through the Teller Resolution, to respect the independence of the islands. But many Americans and primarily the genuine imperialists of course, considered that this promise to Cuba had been hasty in the extreme. Thus Albert J. Beveridge proclaimed that "Cuba is a mere extension of our Atlantic coast-line, commanding the ocean entrance to the Mississippi and the Isthmian Canal." Even a man such as Richard Olney, Secretary of State in Cleveland's second administration, was a hemispherist. He considered American expansion in the Caribbean Sea, with annexation of Cuba, a proper and desirable policy, while he sharply criticized expansion in the Pacific, in particular acquisition of the Philippines. Like many others, he can be described as an informalist on hemispherist territory.

3

A third position at the turn of the century was *globalism*, properly a genuine, conscious imperialism, unrestricted by anything other than practical considerations in either geographical location and extent of the expansion area or the way in which the annexed regions were to be governed. The term does not in itself imply a desire for world supremacy or establishment of American colonies all over the world. The majority of men that could be described as globalists did not see the building of an empire as an end in itself and had no particular interest in a colonial empire of the British type. They were primarily interested in territorial expansion as a means of acquiring strategic bases, which could safeguard America's position as a great power and supply the country with markets for raw materials, American products and investment. A more extreme form of expansionist dreams naturally existed, as when Josiah Strong predicted in 1885 that the American branch of the Anglo-Saxon race would "move down upon Mexico, down open Central and South America, out upon the islands of the sea, over upon Africa and beyond." But in general "the new imperialism" had a different outlook.

In an article called "Expansion not Imperialism," published in the pro-expansionist journal *Outlook* and probably written by its editor Lyman Abbot, the difference between a continentalist and an expansionist—what is here called a globalist—was said to be that, whereas the latter "believes that American ideas and institutions are good for the whole world," the former thinks that they are only suitable for the North American continent. According to the *Outlook* this did not mean that the latter was an imperialist and the former a democrat, but that the expansionist was a more radical, optimistic, enthusiastic democrat. It should be added, that the expansion expressed in the *Outlook* was consistently idealistic—it was a question of spreading the Pax Americana, giving other peoples the opportunity of sharing the blessings of American civilization and freedom. Other globalists among the editors of periodicals were Albert Shaw, editor of the respected *Review of Reviews,* and Horatio Bridge of *the Overland Monthly.*[12]

Globalists usually denied that there was any fundamental difference between the traditional American form of expansion and the new form. During the Presidential election campaign of 1900, Theodore Roosevelt often defended the new expansion when speaking in the West and South by arguing that the Republicans were only completing what the Democrats had started under Jefferson and Jackson, that the annexation of Louisiana was in principle no different from the acquisition of the Philippines. The attacks made on the policy by the Democrats were therefore unfounded.[13] The young Beveridge, perhaps the most enthusiastic apostle of imperialism, made a celebrated speech in the autumn of 1898, which has gone down in history under the title, "The March of the Flag." He said, among other

30

things: "And now, obeying the same voice that Jefferson heard and obeyed, that Seward heard and obeyed, William McKinley plants the flag over the islands of the seas, outposts of commerce, citadels of national security, and the march of the flag goes on!" He refuted the argument that American expansion should be restricted to contiguous territory as in former times: "Distance and oceans are no arguments ... Steam joins us; electricity joins us—the very elements are in league with our destiny. Cuba not contiguous! Hawaii and the Philippines not contiguous! Our navy will make them contiguous. Dewey and Sampson and Schley have made them contiguous, and American speed, American guns, American heart and brain and nerve will keep them contiguous forever ..." The same idea was expressed in the expansionist Jacksonville *Times-Union*: "Steam and electricity have so shortened distance that the remotest isles of the Pacific are not really so far from Philadelphia as California and Alaska once were, and Porto Rico is as near as once was Charleston."[14]

The globalists enthusiastically supported the policy of annexation after the Spanish-American War. "We don't want more States. We want more land for the people. We ought to have all the West Indies, Iceland, and Greenland, and there would be no objection to additional islands in the Pacific," wrote Murat Halstead of Cincinnati enthusiastically to President McKinley.[15]

Many widely varying motives were produced in favor of expansion, but the American consul-general in Shanghai, John Goodnow, went to the heart of the matter and spoke for many globalists when he declared before the peace treaty had been signed: "We should hold the Philippine islands, the Caroline islands and the Ladrone islands, also Cuba and Porto Rico. It does not matter whether we call them war indemnity or what. We need them in our business."

For many globalists navalism was an important motive, and the influence of Captain Alfred T. Mahan should not be underestimated, particularly his influence on the little group of determined expansionists who were his faithful disciples and who through the posts they held could affect the course of decision-making and of foreign policy: John Hay, Theodore Roosevelt, Henry Cabot Lodge among others.[16] Another of the most active globalists was Whitelaw Reid, editor of the New York *Tribune*, friend of both John Hay and McKinley and appointed by the President to the Peace Commission in Paris. Reid also rejected the arguments of the continentalists: "Can a nation with safety set such limits to its development? When a tree stops growing, our foresters tell us, it is ripe for the ax."

The controversy over expansionism did not only concern and in a way did not primarily concern the geographical extent of expansion. What was more essential was the nature of annexation, the relation the new areas were to have with the United States.

The problem of government organization gave rise to a passionate debate, and the fight between anti-imperialists and expansionists largely revolved around this aspect of the questions. The old manifest destiny expansionism—that is continentalism—had not really produced this problem, since there it was a matter of contiguous territory, intended for settlement by Americans and gradual absorption into the Union. Integration and incorporation were self-evident goals.

Constitutional arguments were one of the anti-imperialists' favorite weapons and played a prominent part in the attempts to prevent ratification of the peace treaty with Spain. Senator Vest of Missouri introduced a resolution, which declared that the Constitution of the United States did not empower the federal Government to acquire areas to be retained and ruled as colonies: "all territory acquired by the government, except such small amount as may be necessary for coaling stations, must be acquired and governed with the purpose of ultimately organizing such territory into States suitable for admission into the Union."[17]

Nor did genuine globalists have problems over where they stood on this issue. Convinced expansionists, imperialists, naturally realized that expansion on any scale implied that new areas became colonies, that inhabitants in no way automatically became American citizens, that the Constitution did not automatically extend to all territory where the American flag was flown.

Even so, there were complications here, too. The great majority of expansionists must have held a position somewhere in the middle, between the integrationists and the colonialists. Many of them disliked the word "colony" and emphasized humanitarian reasons for annexation, but could not at the same time conceive of accepting the consequences that incorporation would bring. They usually spoke vaguely of "the greatest possible degree of self-government" or "self-government as soon as the people concerned have shown that they are mature enough and as far as their capacity permits." Such phrases were also used by the colonialists. The difference was that for the convinced imperialists it was a question of practical solutions, where the important thing was to ensure a free hand.

The motto of the anti-imperialists and, during the 1900 presidential election campaign, of the entire Democratic party was that "the constitution follows the Flag." The debate was very confused, the lack of logic which marked many of the arguments was shown quite plainly when many newspapers and individuals that earlier had accepted the administration's expansion policy and praised the McKinley regime for the annexation of Puerto Rico and the Philippines, also spoke up in favor of extension of the Constitution to all territory belonging to the United States.[18]

The problem came to a head when a bill was introduced in the spring of 1900, proposing a tariff between Puerto Rico and the United States. In the violent fight that followed, a large part of the Republican press went over to the opposition.[19]

One of the individuals who fought for a colonial system was, not unexpectedly, Whitelaw Reid of the *Tribune*. He stated that "We have ample constitutional power to acquire and govern new territory absolutely at will, according to our sense of right and duty, whether as dependencies, as colonies, or as a protectorate." His arguments were to the point: if Americans could not hold the Philippines as a colony, then they could not hold the islands at all. It was, of course, unthinkable that they should open their doors to "Chinese or half-breed or what not", who would compete with American labor.[20] They had to have the right to establish tariffs, otherwise the protectionist system would break down. Anyone contemplating letting these people into the Senate and the House of Representatives would be "the most imbecile of all the offspring of time." If there was any risk that the American people would be unable to restrain themselves from so acting, then it would be better to ask some civilized nation "with more common sense and less sentimentality and gush" to take over the newly acquired territories.[21]

Reid made this speech shortly after the treaty with Spain had received the consent of the Senate, following a long and intense debate. The constitutional arguments had played a very prominent part in the debate and the defence against the attacks of the integrationists had been led primarily by Senator Orville Platt of Connecticut. Like other imperialists such as Roosevelt, Beveridge and Lodge, Reid rejected the constitutional arguments put forward by the anti-imperialists, and described them as "a crazy extension of the doctrine." "The rule of liberty, that all just government derives its authority from the consent of the governed, applies only to *those* who are capable of self-government," claimed Beveridge.[22] To be sure this was a risky argument, since it implied that the situation might change if it could be proved that the Filipinos were ready for self-government. But Beveridge did not think there was any likelihood of this, since he saw a race that lacked the fundamental qualities required and was thus incapable of ever reaching that level of development. Lodge argued on exactly the same lines as Reid: the Philippines should be held "as a possession of the United States, not incorporated in our body politic nor brought within our tariff."[23]

Different people's interpretations of constitutional law usually concurred with their attitudes toward expansionism. The theoretical side of the matter was ambiguous. Precedents pointed in different directions, so everyone could find points in support of an opinion. The attitude of the colonialists at its simplest was that territories could be acquired by the federal government for "any purpose which may seem desirable," and that Congress had the full right to legislate for these new areas, e.g., as far as taxes and tariffs were concerned, even if the territories had not been incorporated and were therefore not covered by the Constitution.

Motives: National Interest, Duty, Destiny

1

American expansionism displays an extremely rich flora of motives, more or less central, often combined or interwoven. By motive is meant here both perception and evaluations. One main group of motives can be distinguished, in which all the arguments deal with some aspect of *National Interest*. These motives are mainly of an economic-commercial nature, or concerned with international politics or strategy. The other main group comprises all the motives that do not fall into these categories. Their common factor is that they are usually either veiled in moral and idealistic terms, or are based on a perception of reality colored by deterministic ideas about human development. *Duty* and *destiny* are key-words in this sphere, and the arguments range from cultural and religious to racial considerations.

Commercial expansion covered a motive generally recognized as attractive. The depression that had afflicted the United States during the 1890's had left deep scars. Both in the farming districts and in industry, the general opinion was that the crisis had been the result of over-capacity and over-production and that the only hope lay in new markets for American products and capital—in expansion. This conviction was as rooted in the agrarian South and West as in the industrial Northeast and became a theme in almost all that was said and written on the subject of expansion. This interest in foreign markets was nothing new. It had existed before the Civil War and had steadily increased after 1865. The *Commercial and Financial Journal* expressed it succinctly in 1885: the time was at hand when America's large surplus production "must be employed in extending American interests in other countries—or not at all."[24] But it was the panic of 1893 and the consequent financial crisis that gave currency to these ideas.

"The output of factories working at full capacity is much greater than the domestic market can possibly consume, and it seems to be conceded that every year we shall be confronted with an increasing surplus of manufactured goods for sale in foreign markets if American operatives and artisans are to be kept employed the year round," wrote Frederic Emory in the spring of 1898 in an analysis of America's foreign trade.[25] The problem was equally serious for farmers and in his March of the Flag speech Beveridge pounded it out: "Today we are raising more than we can consume. Today, we are making more than we can use. Today our industrial society is congested; there is more workers than there is work; there is more capital than there is investment."[26]

And the self-evident solution to all these problems was said to be the acquisition of new markets and for many this meant territorial expansion, at least to the extent that was necessary for maintaining control over the new markets.

Despite the lyrical descriptions by men such as Beveridge of the natural resources of the Philippines, the commercial interest in the islands was based on quite a different aspect, their presumed usefulness as a gateway into the enormous Chinese market. Dewey's victory at Manila was significant in the context of activities of the European powers in China, more and more disturbing for American interests. In an article with the eloquent title "Expansion Unavoidable," published in *Harper's Weekly* in 1900, R. Van Bergen argued that territorial expansion was essential if America was to compete in the Chinese market. Without a nearby base, they would be helpless.[27]

Charles Denby, United States minister to China until 1898, had worked hard to further American commercial and manufacturing interests there. After his return home, he stressed the importance of the Chinese market and helped build an opinion for commitment in the Far East. He combined crass economic points of view with idealistic arguments, in a way that was

35

characteristic of the expansionist debate. Sometimes the combination of missionary zeal and profit produced bizarre effects: "Fancy what would happen to the cotton trade if every Chinese wore a shirt: well, the missionaries are teaching them to wear shirts." Denby described the missionary as "the forerunner of commerce."[28] The hopes roused by the thought of the opportunities offered by the Chinese market were wildly exaggerated. Hay's Open Door policy was greeted with enthusiasm. His actions were in no way as significant as they were made out to be, but served to heighten the feeling that China—and the Asian market as a whole—was a necessary and worthwhile venture. Quite unrealistic expectations about the possibility of exporting cotton textiles to China produced a strong wave of expansionism in the Southern states. And this was where the Philippines became important: "With the Philippines as a three-quarter way house, forming a superb trading station, the bulk of this trade should come to this country."[29]

All sorts of apostles appeared. The influential economic writer Charles A. Conant, considered commercial expansion necessary for survival of the USA. Conant was Washington correspondent of the New York *Commercial Bulletin* and wrote on international monetary affairs for the *Banker's Magazine*. Originally a Gold Democrat, he had become an ardent supporter of the Republican administration on the foreign policy issue.

What he thought important was not so much markets for surplus production or markets for raw materials, as markets for investment of America's excess of capital. According to Conant, America was in the same situation as the other highly-developed, industrial countries, hence the rivalry between them; inexorable and unavoidable conflicts would follow, as a result of tensions and antagonisms of world politics.

In 1900 Conant published a collection of essays on this theme, under the title, "*The United States in the Orient*."[30] The essays had appeared during the two previous years as articles in the *North American Review, Forum*, and *Atlantic Monthly*.

Perhaps the most interesting ones were those that had appeared in the *Forum* in July and August 1900 under the title, "*The United States as a World Power*." There Conant based his arguments on the premiss that: "The time has come when intensity of the struggle for new markets and for opportunities for investments has forced the great commercial nations, by the instinct of self-preservation, to demand that the field of competition be kept open, even by exercise, if necessary, of paramount military force." The United States now had to enter into this struggle, whether she wished it or not, by the conditions of her industrial development. It was this point which made their foothold in the Philippines important as a lever for keeping the door to China open and for sharing in the development of Asia. Conant went on to declare:

"It is this struggle between the great political powers of the world for bolstering up national economic power which constitutes the cardinal fact of modern diplomacy. The issue involved is sometimes obscured by motives which seem to be purely national and political, rather than economic; but the controlling fact is coming home more and more to statesmen, even of the least advanced countries, that the real basis of national power is capacity for competitive production. Henceforth therefore, the aim of national leaders promises more and more to become the finding and keeping of markets and fields for investment.

It is precisely because certain states seem to fear this competition, and desire not only to deprive it of all conditions of equality, but to exclude its influence completely from undeveloped countries, that intervention is justified by those states which represent in the truest sense the political and social ideals of Western civilization.

The United States enters upon the conflict for world empire with a great advantage over the democracies of antiquity and over the smaller nations of Western Europe. The movement towards concentration of political power and the elimination of small governments has been advancing with rapid strides during the last two centuries.

The United States is following in the Orient the same process of absorbing new territory which began with the organization of the Northwest Territory, the purchase of Louisiana, and the acquisition of Florida from its Spanish masters, and was continued by the absorption of the republic of Texas, the conquest of California, and, finally, the expulsion of Spain from Cuba and Porto Rico. While Russia advances with giant strides in Central Asia, the great Republic of the West is pursuing a similar destiny, and is tending to put herself upon an equal plane for the contest."[31]

A speech made by Chauncey Depew at the Republican Party Convention in 1900 provided a typical example of the arguments used by commercial-economic expansionists. Depew posed the question of why there was war in South Africa, why the walls of Peking were being stormed, why troops were on the march in Asia and Africa, and why armies from foreign countries and empires were to be found there? He supplied the answer: because production in civilized countries was greater than the countries could consume and because this overproduction led to stagnation and poverty. "The American people now produce $2,000,000,000 worth more than they can consume, and we have met the emergency, and by the statesmanship of William McKinley, and by the valor of Roosevelt and his associates, we have our market in Cuba, we have our market i Puerto Rico, we have our market in the Philippines, we have our market in Hawaii, and we stand in the presence of 800,000,000 of people, with the Pacific as an American lake, and the American artisans producing better and cheaper goods than any country in the world."[32] A financier, Depew primarily had the industrial over-production in mind, but in these years there was an equally important agrarian expansionism.[33]

Especially after the victory over Spain, the economic-commercial arguments became important to the expansionists. It nevertheless should be pointed out that there was a consensus on the necessity of new markets. Industrial magnates and financiers such as Carnegie, Charles Francis Adams, Jr., Henry Lee Higginson, and many others among the most rigid anti-imperialists, and in the election campaign of 1900 the Democrats—all emphatically declared their support of commercial expansion. This at the same time as they adopted a strongly anti-imperialistic platform.[34] There was no contradiction. What the group of agrarians that dominated the Democratic party, the farm businessmen, wanted was a free global market-place for American products and they did not consider that this required annexation of areas to be governed as colonies.[35]

2

Economic-commercial motives were often combined with arguments concerning the politics of power. Rivalry between the great powers was often looked upon as nothing more or less than pure economic competition. Conant announced in his article in *Forum* in July 1900 that the goal of the nation's leaders must to an ever-greater extent be to gain and retain markets and areas for investment. The necessity of military and naval strength became obvious when it was a question of "seeking and holding exclusive markets on the one hand, and of increasing national competing power in free markets on the other."[36] This was vital. The *Journal of Commerce and Commercial Bulletin* made almost the same claim, referring to China. "No political qualms about the dangers of territorial expansion" could save the country from possibly having to defend with violence its rights and its opportunities on, say, the Chinese market. And in his analysis of America's foreign trade in the spring of 1898, Frederic Emory stated that isolationism must be left to the past. The United States had to accept the consequences of having become "a competitor in the world-wide struggle for trade."

38

Starting from such premises, the step to a policy of expansion with annexation of new territory to achieve control of markets, was naturally not long. Prior to the peace negotiations in Paris in 1898, the Chicago newspaper *Inter-Ocean* declared that annexation of the Philippines would enable the United States to become the foremost trading nation in the world, not excepting Great Britain.[37] And Beveridge, as always less inhibited and more inclined to speak out than other expansionists, explained what in his opinion the consequences would be in terms of politics. "The power that rules the Pacific," the young Senator from Indiana said in 1900, "is the power that rules the world. And, with the Philippines, that power is and will forever be with the American Republic." Mahan, the advocate of navalism and mentor of Roosevelt and Lodge, summed up his view of the question in a couple of sentences in January 1900: Sea power, as a national interest, commercial and military, rests not upon fleets only, but also upon local territorial bases in distant commercial regions. "It rests upon them, most securely when they are extensive, and when they have a numerous population bound to the sovereign country by those ties of interest which rest upon the beneficience of the ruler; of which beneficience power to protect is not the least factor."[38]

Another source from which the intellectual side of expansionism drew support was the theories of the historian Frederick Jackson Turner and the economist Brooks Adams. When developing his frontier thesis, Turner emphasized that America was standing on the threshold of a new era, now that the last frontier had disappeared and there was no more free land. This did not mean, he pointed out, that "these energies of expansion" had disappeared, only that they had to seek new outlets: "The demands for a vigorous foreign policy, for an interoceanic canal, for a revival of our power upon the seas, and for the extention of American influence to outlying islands and adjoining countries, are indications that the movement will continue."[39] The eccentric Brooks Adams, brother of Henry Adams, also influenced the expansionists, not least his friends Roosevelt and Lodge. In his book, *The Law of Civilization and Decay*, which attracted a great deal of attention, he developed the theory that only by absolute economic supremacy could America save itself from disintegration and decay. In Adams' vision this meant American control of Asia.[40]

In a letter to his friend Henry Cabot Lodge, written during the summer of 1900, Adams declared that he was fully convinced that America was fighting a great battle "for our national supremacy, which means our national existence" ... "... we must now be masters or we must break down ... It is fate, it is destiny."[41] He developed his ideas in more detail in a book published at that time, *The Economic Supremacy of America.* Henry Cabot Lodge sent it to President McKinley, warmly recommending it and describing it as "one of the most brilliant and interesting discussions of present economic conditions and of the policy of expansion" that he had seen.[42]

The same idea, that there were only two alternatives: expansion or decay, turned up elsewhere also, as in, for example, James C. Fernald's expansionist propaganda paper, *The Imperial Republic.* In this he stated that the United States had either to go on to be a world power or to shut the door of glorious opportunities, pause in the path of natural advance and from that moment retreat towards Chinese immobility and decay. Fernald was an enthusiastic globalist and saw a future for the United States with "as wide a chain of dependencies as Great Britain."[43]

This theme, equating expansion with life and vitality and rejection of expansion with stagnation and decay, was of great importance to the leading expansionists. Thus Beveridge pronounced in one of his speeches during the presidential election campaign of 1900 that "all declining nations" had started on the downward path by abandoning their policy of colonization, while the vital, progressive nations backed expansion.[44] The Indianapolis *Journal* saw America as being forced to choose between proving that she was "a live and growing power" or voluntarily becoming one of the decadent nations. And the decisive factor was to be whether she retained or relinquished the territories she had won.[45] And Richard Olney continued on the same theme, when he declared that the absence of instinct in the line of national growth and expansion would be a sure symptom of the national deterioration of the United States.[46]

In all this the navy loomed large. Mahan, Lodge, Roosevelt, Brooks Adams and their sympathizers, such as Senators William E. Chandler of New Hampshire and William P. Frye of Maine, saw the development of commercial and military—above all naval—power as facets of the same plan of action.[47] Mahan had for years preached the necessity of a strong navy to protect interests in the Caribbean and Pacific, not least for the support and protection of trading interests, and this implied territorial expansion, mainly in the form of naval bases and coaling stations, occasionally on a greater scale, all to ensure positions and markets.[48] A canal joining the Atlantic with the Pacific had long been considered vital for commercial expansion. Annexation of Hawaii, Samoa, Puerto Rico, Cuba, was sometimes described as being necessary for protection of the projected canal.

40

For expansionists of this type it was self-evident that the United States must leave the old isolationist policy and claim a rightful place among the other actors on the stage of world politics. *Power* and *prestige* were the key words. America was a great power and must act as one. It had to be clear that the USA was "a nation that knows its rights and dare maintain them—a nation that has come to stay, with an empire of its own in the China Sea," wrote Reid in 1900. There was no way back, for "our Continental Republic has stretched its wings over the West Indies and the East. It is a fact and not a theory."[49]

America's new position brought new responsibilities, which could not be shirked. Olney, admittedly critical of some aspects of McKinley's policy, claimed that the American people were gradually realizing that earlier foreign policy had been "suitable to our infancy", but was unworthy of a nation which had reached maturity and strength and which had become "one of the foremost Powers of the earth and should play a commensurate part in its affairs."[50] The same note was struck in many quarters. Charles Emory Smith, Postmaster General and onetime minister to Russia, said in a speech of October 1898 that "We have a new position in the great family of nations. We have stepped out upon the great stage of the world's action, and have become one of the great powers. We have advanced from continental domain to world-wide influence. We have risen to a new conception of our natural possibilities and our national greatness."[51] The same ideas resounded in a speech made by the Catholic Archbishop of St. Paul, John Ireland, on the same occasion, the Peace Jubilee in Chicago: "The consciousness of what she is and what she might be has come to America. She knows that she is a great nation ... To take its proper place among the nations of the earth a nation must be known, as she is by those nations ... The world, today as never before, knows and confesses the greatness and power of America ... The young giant of the West ... is now moving as becomes his stature."[52] And Senator Platt, a convinced imperialist, declared when arguing in favor of annexation of Hawaii: "A policy of isolation did well enough when we were an embryo nation, but today things are different ... We are sixty-five million people, the most advanced and powerful on earth, and regard to our future welfare demands an abandonment of the doctrines of isolation."[53] America had become one of the great powers of the world and must conduct herself as such. This meant precisely an expansionist foreign policy, since at that time a great power was assessed in terms of its inclination and ability to build an empire, with Great Britain as the shining example. Clinging to the old policy would be acting like a man who "would reject the railway and travel by the stage-coach," as Henry Watterson, editor of the Louisville *Courier-Journal*, put it in an interview.[54]

This feeling for America's new strength, of her having come of age as a great power, was often combined with an awareness of the deep and revolutionary changes, taking place in the international power game. As early as 1895, Lodge had preached that the password of the age was consolidation, not only with regard to capital and labor but on an international level. The day of the small nation was gone, the great powers were extending their rule over an increasingly large proportion of the peoples and countries of the world. Ever greater sections of the earth were being shared out in order to insure the future development of the great powers. One of the biggest changes was the shifting of the focal point from the Atlantic to the Pacific and increasing importance of Asian markets. Watterson predicted in a homely but pointed figure of speech that the time would come when "the Pacific, and not the Atlantic, may become the washbasin of the universe." S. Wells Williams of Yale University outlined a possible development along the lines of consolidation and centralization, terminating in a world controlled by a superpower, but controlled by methods more elastic and complex than the current ones, by superior resources and economic domination. These changes, all interpreted in different ways, were used to back up demands that the United States should not let opportunities slip through their fingers but gather strength and safeguard interests while there was time. In an essay entitled *"The United States as a World Power,"* Conant claimed that the emergence of America as a great power was the result of a natural process. The interests of the nation had to be protected. It was essential to "obey the motive of enlightened self-interest ... even by exercise, if necessary, of paramount military force."

3

Motives lying behind expansionism related to commercial opportunities, power and prestige can all be placed in one category under the rubric of National Interest. Of those that fall outside this category, the most important might be described as idealistic. Robert E. Osgood has distinguished motives and ends in a similar way, under the headings of national self-interest and national ideals, in a penetrating analysis of the entire history of American foreign policy.[55] But some important points must be made here.

Firstly, it is not possible to draw a clear distinction between the two types. There are motives which, though formulated in idealistic terms, come within the sphere of self-interest. As Mr. Dooley put it: "We're a great civilizin' agent, Hinnissy, and as Father Kelly says, so is the steam roller. And bein' a quiet man, I'd rather be behind than in front when the street has to be improved."[56]

Secondly, professed and "real" motives might not be identical. The situation has been brilliantly described by Thomas A. Bailey:

"An ingenious statesman, if he wishes, can usually find a moral cloak for selfish deeds. Misled by the mirage of imperialism in 1898—1899, we found that we had a moral obligation to take up the White Man's Burden in the Philippines and civilize and Christianize and uplift these "backward" peoples. At the same time we could exploit their natural resources and induce them to buy American calico for their naked loins. Morality tends to fly out of the window when profits come knocking at the door."[57]

Thirdly the complex of motives that lie outside the National interest sphere comprises not only idealistic arguments but also the type of motive which refers to a development following laws that cannot be influenced or hindered. Such arguments usually refer to "the logic of events," "events, evolutionary or providential," "the march of events,"[58] "destiny"[59] and such like.[60]

As Charles Kendall Adams, President of the University of Wisconsin, asserted in an article in *Forum* in the spring of 1899: "... it is in the course of nature that the most prominent power in its (the Pacific) waters should be the United States."[61] This point of view was worded even better by Franklin H. Giddings. He claimed that territorial expansion was at this particular stage in the development of the United States as certain as the advent of spring after winter and that opposition to it was probably as futile as opposition to the tradewind or the storm.[62] And the enthusiastic expansionist Chicago *Tribune* described the annexations of the new territories as "the logic of events."[63]

The New York *Sun* had said in the early 1890's, when President Cleveland halted the annexation of Hawaii: "The policy of annexation is the policy of destiny; and destiny always arrives."[64] Shortly after the battle of Manila, McKinley said to his secretary: "We need Hawaii just as much and a great deal more than we did California. It is manifest destiny." This new "manifest destiny" was invoked by many expansionists, such as Congressman Gibson, when in June 1898 he spoke in favor of annexation of Hawaii, just before the resolution was put to the vote. "Manifest destiny says, 'Take them in', The American people say 'Take them'," he remarked. The doctrine of inevitability came to be one of the cornerstones of expansion.[65] Particularly when defending annexation of the Philippines, it took the form of what Albert Weinberg has called moral determinism: "the will of God," "responsibilities forced upon us by destiny," "Providence," "duty determined by destiny,"[66] "the finger of God."[67]

This group of ideas was characterized by a shifting between *destiny, right* and *duty*: the stronger nation has a moral duty to intervene to help the weaker. The stronger has a right to intervene, because his higher development has given him insight into what is best and what is needed to solve a problem. With the addition of contemporary racial ideas and Social-Darwinist arguments, the next contention was that not only duty and right existed but laws dictated by God or Nature which ordained the future. The key words were not *power* and *prestige*, but *duty* and *destiny*, with emphasis on duty, while the ideas of destiny colored the perception of reality. The categories into which motives fell can be used to differentiate between cultural imperialism, religious imperialism, and racial imperialism, often interlaced.

Osgood has pointed out that Mahan's arguments contained a strong idealism, stemming from conviction. This idealism was combined with a low opinion of the influence of principles and ideologies on world politics. Mahan saw American expansion as a moral duty, but was convinced that it was of no avail "to expect governments to act continuously on any other ground than national interest." For Mahan international politics meant not ideological conflicts but a struggle for power.[68]

Morally charged arguments for expansion were used by everyone, even by expansionists of Beveridge's and Roosevelt's caliber. Such arguments were hazardous since they implied that if the anti-imperialists could prove that the policy of the administration did not benefit the population of annexed territories then there was no justification. This problem was highlighted by the violent guerilla war that the people of the Philippines took up against their liberators. Roosevelt argued frankly and ruthlessly that he had little sympathy for what he called the mock humanitarianism that wanted to prevent "the great order-loving, liberty-loving nations from doing their duty in the earth's waste places because there is a need of some rough surgery at the outset."[69] Beveridge had no doubts either. "We cannot flee from our world duties," he declared. The American people had been chosen by God to lead the regeneration of the world: "... we will not

44

renounce our part in the mission of our race, trustee, under God, of the civilization of the world."[70]

The talk of America's "mission" drew a sarcastic comment from the Baltimore *Sun*: "The Anglo-Saxon cannot rid himself of the delusion that wherever gold fields are found he has a special mission of civilization to perform. The Anglo-Saxon rarely finds himself impelled to spread his civilizing influences unless there is the promise of rich reward in his self-sacrificing efforts."[71]

There was one motive which recurred more frequently than any other, and which appeared in practically all the expansionist talk, whatever the source. This was the humanitarian task said to be facing Americans in the new territories, the moral demands that lay behind the intervention against Spain and which continued to guide the policies of the United States.

These purely idealistic, moral arguments dominated the debate, often alone, but on many occasions combined with one or more other motives. J. T. Hudson was convinced that America had gone to war for "purely humanitarian principles," "in a spirit of purest altruism—without reward or hope of reward." Jacob Gould Schurman, President of Cornell University and Chairman of the Philippine Commission, also subscribed to the idealistic interpretation of American foreign policy: "We began a war to free the people of Cuba from the yoke of their oppressors; we are waging a war in the Philippine Islands to protect the people of the Philippine Islands from their Tagal oppressors. The conditions may vary, but the principle is identical."[70] The respected and widely read *Outlook* assured its readers that "what the expansionist desires to see is the United States giving protection, inspiration and assistance to communities emancipated from crushing despotism, and needing the blessings of freedom, justice, and self-government."[71] The enthusiastically expansionist Governor Wolcott in Colorado put it to the Republican Party Convention in 1900: "The spirit of justice and liberty prompts us in our determination to give the dusky races of the Philippines the blessings of good government and republican institutions." Subsequent variations were innumerable, but there was always the declaration that the policy of the United States on the territories surrendered by Spain was dictated by high moral motives, a duty to humanity that they had no right to evade. The anti-imperialists denied that this in itself praiseworthy feeling of moral responsibility necessitated converting the new territories into colonies, but many of those who claimed to be opposed to annexation also explained that they faced an imperative duty.

45

The Chicago *Times-Herald* provided a typical example of this kind of thinking: "Much as we deplore the necessity for territorial acquisition, the people now believe that the United States owes it to civilization to accept the responsibilities imposed upon it by the fortunes of war—a war which was undertaken solely in the interest of humanity and civilization."[72] The moral motive for expansion sounded in McKinley's letter of acceptance in 1900: "Every effort has been directed to their peace and prosperity, their advancement and well-being, not for our aggrandizement nor for the pride of might, nor for trade and commerce, nor for exploitation, but for humanity and civilization, and for the protection of the vast majority of the population who welcome our sovereignty against the designing minority." The *American Grocer*, showed the same touching concern when it wrote that the mission of the United States might be to break the moral and physical fetters which bound the eight or ten million natives of the Philippines, and possibly this could not be accomplished without retention of the islands.[73]

Even if many people felt these moral considerations to be genuine and convincing, it is obvious that they were based on or closely allied to ideas about different kinds of superiority, variations on the theme of the white man's burden. Sometimes ideas of cultural, religious, and racial imperialism were clearly expressed. American men of religion, mainly the Protestant churches, morally justified territorial expansion. They did not restrict themselves to idealistic alibis for annexations, but were a force within the expansionist movement, standing with navalists and businessmen. Organized Christianity had also helped rouse the warlike mood that preceded the war with Spain.[74] What is striking here is that the missionary zeal of which they spoke so much often ignored or concealed that the natives had been Christian for many a long year. They were Catholics, however, and it was no coincidence that Catholic churchmen in the United States were less responsive to expansionist enthusiasm than their Protestant colleagues.

A book by Robert E. Speer, *Mission and Modern History*, provides many examples of arguments put forward by Protestant leaders.[75] Speer was secretary of the Board of Foreign Missions of the Presbyterian Church. While the Social Darwinists considered all evolution the result of unshakeable laws, Speer preached the will of God. It was God's intention that Christian nations should subjugate the world, in order to liberate the peoples of the world. Christian states had the right to intervene in non-Christian countries, for religious and humanitarian reasons. In general, Speer equated Christian countries and civilized countries and consequently his arguments and opinions were close to those of the cultural imperialists. He claimed it to be the duty of civilized nations to maintain law and order, including the protection of investments. He hastened to add, however, that only moral reasons could justify the exercise of power by the Western world.

All sorts of clerics echoed these arguments.[76] The Reverend Dr. MacArthur of Calvary Baptist Church celebrated Dewey's victory at Manila with a sermon full of religious-humanitarian enthusiasm and quoted in the New York *Tribune*: "The Philippine Islands ... should be made the garden of the universe ... We will fill them with school houses and missionaries."[77] In an article in *The National Magazine*, Thomas Jay Hudson stated as a maxim of Christian ethics, the duty of every Christian nation to do what it could for the promotion of Christian civilization throughout the world. Nor did he have doubts regarding the means. Christ himself had seen that Christian civilization "could not be successfully engrafted upon human society by means less drastic than the sword."[78]

Less aggressive was the theory that the Americans were God's chosen people: "We imagine that God has called us to the rulership of the world. He sends us as He sent His well-beloved son, to serve the world and thus to rule the world", said the President of Ohio Wesleyan University in a speech in September 1899.[79] His colleague, John Henry Barrows, President of Oberlin College and a zealous supporter of the missions, held similar ideas. He said that the moment when Dewey gave the signal for battle outside Manila was the greatest moment in the history of America since Lincoln's proclamation of emancipation. God had made America into a world power and made the people of America aware of their mission in the world.[80]

4

The same tones were sounded by Samuel L. Parrish in an article in the *Journal of Social Science*. There he claimed that the guns of Dewey's and Sampson's fleets were but the instruments of progress in the hands of God. Parrish painted a vision of the future in which "Caesar Augustus, sole ruler of the world, will be the imperial democrats of the English-speaking race, ruling with directing mind and guiding with sympathetic outstretched hand a Christian world bound together by the iron bands of order, justice and of peace."[81]

A prime example of how missionary zeal went hand in hand with Social

Darwinism and racial imperialism is to be found also in a speech made by Bishop Charles H. Fowler in Chicago in October 1900. The bishop asserted that expansion was the destiny of the Anglo-Saxons and meant the spread of Christianity. He went on to develop his ideas with a patriotism so narrow-minded and conceited as to be outstanding even in these circles:

"The three greatest missionary events since Calvary were the conversion of Paul, the firing on Fort Sumter and the blowing up of the Maine, the last of which made the Anglo-Saxon race one."

God had given the Anglo-Saxon self-reliance and sent him about the job of subduing and saving the world. To fight expansion was, in Fowler's opinion, absolutely useless. Those who tried to do so were fighting not merely McKinley and the Rough Riders and the American people, but they were also fighting "the resistless force running through all ages of nature, the force of natural selection—and they were also fighting God's eternal purpose to elevate the races."[82]

As pointed out, the dividing line between these "religious expansionists" and those individuals who argued in terms of culture and civilization was fluid. In any event it was a task that America could not shirk. Lyman Abbot, the well-known Congregationalist and editor of *Outlook*, combined religious and humanitarian arguments. He represented a strong interventionism and saw the USA as the guardian of lower races: "We must maintain a force sufficient to preserve law and order among barbaric nations ... We must follow the maintenance of law and the establishing of order and the foundations of civilization with the vitalizing forces that make for civilization."[83] Jonathan Dolliver, congressman from West Virginia and convinced expansionist, linked territorial expansion with religious motives. He expanded upon the idea that God was using the United States as an instrument in the divine hand for enlarging civilization.[84] A magnificent specimen of this combination of religious and humanitarian idealism, of nationalism and a feeling of power, is to be found in a speech made by Senator John M. Thurston of Nebraska on May 25, 1899:

"God reigns; and in the sunshine of His guidance we go marching on—on under a flag, that symbolizes the highest aspirations of the human race. Washington made it the flag of independence; Lincoln made it the flag of liberty; McKinley has made it the flag of man's humanity for man—until today, on land and sea, the wide world round, serenely uplifted towards empyrean blue—kissed by the sun of day, wooed by the stars of night, feared by tyrants, beloved by mankind—it tranquilly floats, the unconquered flag of the greatest nation of the earth."[85]

Cultural and racial imperialism often went together. The transfer from one to the other was frequently undetectable, since the concept of race was usually vague and indistinguishable from civilization, culture, nation. Sometimes it was a question of a feeling that the Anglo-Saxon culture was superior, morally, sometimes a racial philosophy comprising a masterrace mentality.[86]

That the Anglo-Saxons were a superior race was an opinion generally held; sometimes the Teutonic race was included. This racialist thinking was most evident in relation to colored people where the idea of race combined easily with ideas on culture and civilization. Both imperialists and anti-imperialists agreed, and indeed one of the most common anti-imperialist arguments was that there was a great risk in annexation of lower, barbaric races. When the imperialist Chauncey Depew declared that there was no question of incorporating "the alien races, and civilized, semi-civilized, barbarous and savage peoples of these islands /i.e., the Philippines/ into our body politic," he was following the same line as his bitterly anti-imperialist colleague, Senator George F. Hoar from Massachusetts, although they drew totally different conclusions from this starting point. Congressman Champ Clark in a speech opposing the annexation of Hawaii in June 1898 used the existence of Chinese people in the islands as an argument against annexation:

"How can we endure our shame when a Chinese Senator from Hawaii, with his pigtail hanging down his back, with his pagan joss in his hand, shall rise from his curule chair and in pidgin English proceed to chop logic with George Frisbie Hoar or Henry Cabot Lodge? O tempora! O mores!"[87] And Congressman James M. Griggs from Georgia explained in the same way that he was opposed to the annexation of the Philippines "because of the eventual association of our people with their mongrel population."[88]

In reply to the anti-imperialist objection, *The Banker's Magazine* of New York admitted the dangers, physical and moral, of extending territory to distant parts and of absorbing semi-barbarous populations. It could mean demoralization of the dominant race, injustice, even cruelty to the inferior peoples. This risk must nevertheless be taken, since in the long run the peoples who were annexed benefitted so much.[89]

Moral reasons recur. The arguments are similar to those used by cultural imperialists. In an article in *Forum*, Conant declared that the cause of modern social progress had been committed to the Anglo-Saxons by the historical evolution of events. If this task were refused, the world would sink back into darkness and barbarism: "It is a mission of the highest altruism, in which commercial and economic forces play a part only because economic efficiency is the fruit of freedom, and the people of the highest moral ideas are those capable of doing the most in the world."[90] The same thought was expressed more brutally in the Detroit *Tribune,* that it was best for mankind when countries and territories were in the hands of those who could best rule: "and as a rule, those can best govern who are capable of conquering. That is the reason that conquest is moral enough for all practical purposes."[91] Robert E. Speer produced a slight variation on the theme when he hailed the expansion of the Western world as a noble duty, moved by the fact that it was better for all parties if civilized nations intervened and took over territories that were not being used by their owners, and developed them.[92]

Professor Theodore Marburg of Harvard defended the expansion and conquests of the Anglo-Saxon race, on the ground that the race was superior in qualities that contributed to human advance. He sought a moral justification: "Man's express duty is the uplifting of man. ... The duty to uplift and elevate himself and his fellows thus becomes an end in itself and a justification of ... life." But it is interesting to see the next stage of his argument: the nation that blocks the way of progress must expect to be pushed aside "by more powerful and vigorous blood."[93] With these words he came close to the racial ideas which often appeared in connection with American expansionism, namely, ideas on evolution based on Social Darwinism or similar theories. As early as 1885, Strong had in his well-known book applied the ideas of Social Darwinism to the coming American expansion. "The time is coming when the pressure of population on the means of subsistence will be felt here as it is now felt in Europe and Asia." There would be a decisive battle between the races, for which the Anglo-Saxon had been trained: "the mighty centrifugal tendency, inherent in this stock and strengthened in the United States, will assert itself. Then this race of unequaled energy ... having developed peculiarly aggressive traits calculated to impress its institutions upon mankind, will spread itself over the earth."[94] In the same year, John Fiske discussed similar ideas in an essay with the eloquent title, *Manifest Destiny.*[95] A few years later these ideas received political application, and at the same time the blessing of science by John W. Burgess, professor at Columbia and a pioneer in the field of political science. Burgess, whose work had a considerable influence, claimed that the rules of evolution would inexorably result in a world ruled by the Anglo-Saxon and Teutonic races, since they enjoyed superior abilities in building and governing states. This superiority also meant that

50

they had a duty to lead and rule the world.[96]

Theodore Roosevelt had studied under Burgess at Columbia, and his ideas on the superiority of the Anglo-Saxon race showed a close resemblance to those of his teacher. Both men used the term 'race' rather vaguely, equating it with nation or culture.[97] Compared to that of many of his contemporaries, Roosevelt's racism was reasonably moderate. He often expressed the opinion that inferior peoples were not permanently or inherently inferior, but had the chance of reaching a higher level of development. Together with Henry Cabot Lodge and other imperialists he nonetheless believed in the superiority of the Anglo-Saxon race and its inevitable victory over inferior or degenerate races. This outcome was described as unavoidable, but at the same time best for the defeated or annexed peoples.[98] The war against Spain was often put in this context. The great past of the Spanish people was acknowledged, but they were seen as a nation that had ceased to make progress. The Spaniards were a people on the decline, while the new age belonged to the young, virile, dynamic American nation—and the Anglo-Saxon race. Judge Grosscup in the Chicago *Tribune*, May 3, 1898, shared these ideas on race:

". . . The Latin race, tho still preeminent in many fields, is a diminishing race; the Anglo-Saxon, preeminent in all the arts and ambitions that make this age powerful, is an increasing race. It is the only race that has, since the beginning of time, correctly conceived the individual rights of men, and is, on that account, more than anything else, surviving, by fitness, the other races."[99]

These ideas were expounded with clarity by Thomas Jay Hudson in his essay on *"Evolution and the Spanish-American War."* The war was in the natural order of the development of civilization. Natural law governed: "War is just as essential a factor in the evolution of civilization as it is in organic evolution," and for the same reasons: every step taken forwards and upwards has been made possible by "the slaughter of the unfit, thus making room for the existence and development of the higher orders."[100]

Every step forward in civilization had been the result of war. Charles K. Adams, President of the University of Wisconsin, a firm believer in expansion, also regarded colonialism in terms of Social Darwinism. "Civilization is closing in upon barbarism as never before. The survival of the fittest seems to be the law of nations as well as the law of Nature," he stated.[101] Another scholar, H. H. Powers, an erstwhile professor of economics at Stanford University, saw the evolution of the world as a Darwinian struggle for power between races and nations. He considered the defeat and

51

routing of inferior, less efficient forms by more efficient, superior ones to be a law of nature, as immovable as the law of gravity: there was as little reason to moralize over the one as over the other. It was a matter of adapting as wisely as possible to conditions nobody could change.[102] "We want the earth," asserted Powers, but went on to say that it was not a consciously formulated program. Instead it was a question of an instinct, a desire too deep for consciousness, to constant and too regular ever to be questioned or thought of. In addition he predicted a future American protectorate over both Mexico and South America.[103]

Politicians also resorted to Social Darwinist arguments in order to rationalize the new expansionism. In an interview Congressman Cyrus A. Salloway (Republican, New Hampshire) made a statement: "You can call it destiny, or what you will, but this world is going to be controlled by the six great nations—Great Britain, United States, Russia, Germany, Japan and France. It is simply the survival of the fittest."[104]

In his usual way Beveridge went to the point as far as this motive was concerned. On January 9, 1900, he made a speech on the Philippines in the Senate which attracted a good deal of attention and took the form of a catalog of imperialism, an inventory of conceivable motives for expansion. His address was delivered with such brilliance that, as Mr. Dooley ironically remarked, you could almost waltz to it:

"God has not been preparing the English-speaking and Teutonic peoples for a thousand years for nothing but vain and idle self-contemplation and self-admiration. No! He has made us the master organizers of the world to establish systems where chaos reigns. He has given us the spirit of progress to overwhelm the forces of reaction throughout the earth. He has made us adepts in government that we may administer among savages and senile peoples. Were it not for such a force as this, the world would relapse into barbarism and night. And of all our race he has marked the American people as his chosen nation to finally lead in the regeneration of the world. This is the divine mission of America, and it holds for us all the profit, all the glory, all the happiness possible to men."[105]

In a letter to John Temple Graves of the Atlanta *Journal*, a former anti-imperialist who had been converted by Beveridge's big speech of January 9, Beveridge pointed out that the key-note of the speech was racial. He went on: "I consider conventional ethics and conventional morals man-made, and therefore finite as of absolutely no moment, compared to the higher and enduring ethics of our race."[106]

5

The attacks made by the anti-imperialists put the McKinley administration on the defensive. The question had become a matter of politics, imperialism "the paramount issue" of the platform adopted by the Democratic National Convention at Kansas City on the 4th of July 1900. The Republicans followed the "duty" line, humanitarian and idealistic, but with a variation: annexation of the Philippines—the central point of debate—was an inevitable consequence of the victory over Spain. This argument was skillfully chosen, since even the Democrats had been enthusiastically in favor of the war against Spain and often had gone so far as to claim that it was they who had taken the initiative in this "war for humanity". McKinley was now saying that there was an indissoluble connection between the victory, behind which the nation stood united, and its consequence, the annexations.[107] In his Letter of Acceptance 1900, McKinley put a question: "Was it not our duty to protect the lives and property of those who came within our control by the fortunes of war?"[108]

President McKinley often developed this theme with great skill: ". . . As it was the nation's war, so are its results the nation's problem . . . No phrase or catchword can conceal the sacred obligation it involves . . . No political outcry can abrogate our treaty of peace with Spain, or absolve us from its solemn engagements . . . We must choose between manly doing and base desertion." And this solemn duty was "the great task of lifting up and assisting to better conditions and large liberty those distant peoples who, through the issue of battle have become our wards."[109]

Shortly after Manila Bay another expansion doctrine appeared—that, in general, when a nation intervenes to overthrow oppression it takes upon itself responsibility for the people it liberates. This theme recurred and was used by Roosevelt who described it as partly "an axiom of international law," partly "an axiom of morals." And the application of the theory followed the customary pattern. The islands could not be returned to Spain. Nor could they be left to their own devices. That would result in chaos, barbarism, anarchy. Lyman Abbot of the *Outlook* used the same argument:

"It is, we believe, recognized as an axiom of international law that a power which destroys one government in a community is bound to see that another government is established in its place; it certainly is an axiom in morals."[110]

Mr. Dooley also found that the acquisition of the Philippines placed the Americans in a difficult situation:

"But I don't know what to do with th' Philippeens anny more thin I did las' summer, befure I heerd tell iv thim ... We canut sell thim, we can't ate thim, an' we can't throw thim into th' alley whin no wan is lookin'. An' 'twud be a disgrace f'r to lave befure we've pounded these frindless an' ongrateful people into insinsibility."[111]

Bashford of Ohio Wesleyan drew up an eloquent parable on the theme of duty to retain the Philippines. He said that the USA was like a man whose neighbor's daughter several years earlier had been kidnapped by a band of gypsies. The girl's parents searched in vain for her and died of broken hearts. Then one morning the man found the long-lost girl in his garden. He did not send her back to the gypsies, nor abandon her. It was his Christian duty to look after and care for the child.[112]

In his celebrated interview with a delegation of Methodist clergymen in 1899, President McKinley explained how, after praying to God for enlightenment and guidance, he had suddenly realized how the Philippine problem must be solved and had been shown how annexation was the only way open to him:

". . . and it came to me this way—. . . 1) That we could not give them back to Spain—that would be cowardly and dishonorable; 2) that we could not turn them over to France or Germany, our commercial rivals in the Orient—that could be bad business and discreditable; 3) that we could not leave them to themselves—they were unfit for self-government—and they would soon have anarchy and misrule over there worse than Spain's was; and 4) that there was nothing left for us to do but to take them all, and to educate the Filipinos, and uplift and Christianize them, and by God's grace do the very best we could for them, as our fellowmen for whom Christ also died."[113]

As Ernest May has pointed out, McKinley's story of how he reached his decision is a concoction, a pleasing little tale, that did not fail to impress his audience.[114] But at the same time the President gave an accurate summary of the arguments used most often by the administration to influence public opinion and ensure ratification of the treaty with Spain, and which also constituted the main defence against attacks by the anti-imperialists.

These arguments were summarized in their most idealistic form by Washington Gladden in an article in the *Outlook* while the war was still underway. Taking control of the areas that had been liberated from Spanish tyranny had nothing at all to do with any wish to exploit the territory for their own gain. On the contrary:

"It means that we shall give the people a thousand times more liberty than they ever dreamed of possessing . . . it means that we make every man's life safe, every man's house secure . . . that we fill the land with schools, and fit the people for liberty and self-government . . . We are not going anywhere with it (the flag) unless justice, honor, humanity, call us to go . . . The day will come, I trust, when every eye that beholds the starry flag shall rejoice in it, not merely as the ensign of our country's power, but as the emblem of a Nation that is brave to help and strong to suffer in the service of mankind."[115]

Expansionists of all shades used the argument that, quite apart from the question of national interest, the USA had a moral duty to remain in the Philippines. The strength of this argument was illustrated by the fact that anti-imperialists had great difficulty getting around it. Even Bryan was forced to consider a temporary American control of the islands, until "a stable form of government" could be established, and then continued American protection against external interference.

Catalysts

The verbose arguments of the expansionists have been shown to contain groups of motives. A feature of most of them was that there is no logical connection between their perception of reality and recommendation of an imperialistic foreign policy. This applied both within and outside the contention of national interest. Even the anti-imperialists were in favor of commercial expansion, could accept naval bases and coaling stations for the benefit of trade and shipping, were convinced of the superiority of American civilization and the Anglo-Saxon race. Since even the globalists often made such extensive use of moral terms and categories, one gets the impression that in many respects the two sides had common values, or at least professed to have. Still, these people with such similar beliefs had diametrically opposed, or at least varied, opinions on expansionism. This was partly because they often used the same words and phrases, even when their goals were widely separate. There are other explanations.

Walter Hines Page, the young editor of the *Atlantic Monthly* wrote on the threshold of the new century: "Of American life, as the century ends, the keynote is a note of joyful achievement; and its faith is an evangelical faith in a democracy that broadens as fast as social growth invites . . . /The Republic's/ influence has broadened the thought of the old World and is now felt in the Oldest World."[116] There were, however, also more militant, aggressive counterparts to these idealistic visions. Active, aware, enthusiastic expansionists often shared a dream of action, expressed in impatient, frustrated energy, in eager, newly awakened hopes for the future, in an intense desire to test their strength in a fight. Typical was the attitude of Roosevelt, put in words in a speech at the Republican National Convention at Philadelphia in June 1900: "Is America a weakling, to shrink from the world work that must be done by the world powers? No. The young giant of the West stands on a continent that clasps the crest of an ocean in either hand. Our nation, glorious in youth and strength, looks into the future with fearless and eager eyes and rejoices as a strong man to run a race."[117]

There can be no doubt that he was expressing "the spirit of expansionism," the emotional foundation of expansion at this time. It was newly awakened, emotionally charged, borne up by dreams of future triumph and greatness, filled with assurance of the nation's ever-growing strength, a surplus energy seeking new tasks. Roosevelt appealed not to reason but to emotion. The speech was received with a roofraising ovation. One reporter described the delivery as "sharp, intense, at times hissing with the steam of overpressure ... It carried everything before it."[118] Another member of the audience characterized it as a masterly demonstration of "spiritual, grammatical and physical virility."

The remarks made by Roosevelt before the Hungarian Club in New York, May 1900, are also illuminating. He told of a friend who had been asked why he believed in expansion and who had answered: "Because where I come from all those who are *not* women are men." And, added Roosevelt, "no nation can afford to lose the essential virtue of manliness."[119]

In this context we can also note another significant factor. While the anti-imperialistic movement was usually represented by older men—the average age of the fifty-odd vice-presidents of the Anti-Imperialist League that was formed in Boston in November 1898 was well over sixty—the leading advocates and publicists of imperialism were comparatively young men in their prime. In 1898 Theodore Roosevelt was forty, Albert Beveridge thirty-six, Henry Cabot Lodge forty-eight, Albert Shaw forty-one, Walter Hines Page forty-three etc.[120]

This desire for action sprang partly from the young America's feeling of strength. The Chicago *Times-Herald* declared in July 1898: "We also want Puerto Rico ... The spirit of national development has seized the people. We want Hawaii now. Fortunately we will not have to fight for it; we will annex it next week. We may want the Carolines, the Ladrones, the

56

Pelew, and the Mariana groups. If we do, we will take them." At the same time the Denver *News* stated that "The American people are overwhelmingly in favor of holding every foot of ground over which the flag is raised. The instinct is rooted in them, and it is a sound and good instinct."

The violently expansionist Chicago *Tribune* struck a similar note. The instinct of expansion was said to exist in America as it did in all other nations that were not in a state of decay. "We are a resistless world power solely because we have never given ear to paltry and puling sentimentality."[121]

This bellicose sentiment was summarized quite brilliantly in a leading article in the Washington *Post*:

"A new consciousness seems to have come upon us—the consciousness of strength—and with it a new appetite, the yearning to show our strength. It might be compared with the effect upon the animal creature of the taste of blood. Ambition, interest, land hunger, pride, the mere joy of fighting, whatever it may be, we are animated by a new sensation. We are face to face with a strange destiny. The taste of empire is in the mouth of the people even as the taste of blood in the jungle. It means an imperial policy, the Republic, renascent, taking her place with the armed nations."

But another important factor that lay behind this impatient longing for action was the increasing population pressure in the United States. As Richard Hofstadter has pointed out, aggressive expansionism was giving vent to a feeling of frustration.[122] The last frontier had closed, economic depression and immigration had given rise to a feeling of diminished opportunities, while the changing structure of society created unrest and uncertainty which could all too easily be transformed into aggression.

Franklin H. Giddings, a professor at Columbia, wrote in 1899 in the *Political Science Quarterly* that the American people constituted "the most stupendous reservoir of seething energy to be found on any continent ... If, by any mistaken policy, it is denied an outlet, it may discharge itself in anarchistic, socialistic, and other destructive modes that are likely to work incalculable mischief." Impatience was growing as a consequence of changes in American society, where "opportunity for adventure and daring enterprise" was rapidly disappearing. Americans were "liable to an outbreak of warlike spirit."[123]

Warlike mentality was partly the product of the development of society and of the current situation in the country. A similar idea was put forward in the *Banker's Magazine* during the autumn of 1898, suggesting that the new American foreign policy was beyond control. It was an instinctive reac-

57

tion in the growing population, hitherto used to elbow room, but which was finding that the country was getting crowded. According to Giddings, the situation in Cuba had given the American people "the first apparently decent excuse for fighting" since the Civil War. The country's move toward expansionism was perfectly natural; "at this stage in the development of the United States, territorial expansion is as certain as the advent of spring after winter."

CHAPTER II

The Constitution, the Flag, and Puerto Rico

The expansionists sheltered in their ranks many individuals and groups with widely differing standpoints. The ideas and arguments that comprised American expansionism at the turn of the century were often diffuse and contradictory. Many expansionists lacked a considered opinion, the same person often holding irreconcilable points of view, and many of them had obviously not realized the consequences of the policy they supported.[1]

A central issue was the constitutional status of the new territories, the question of their government organization.[2] For the conscious globalists it was self-evident that annexation should under no circumstances lead to the new territories automatically becoming part of the United States in the sense of the Constitution, or to their inhabitants becoming American citizens. But the doctrine that "the Constitution follows the flag" was one of the main arguments used by the anti-imperialists against the expansionist policy of the McKinley administration. Between these two poles lay many vague conceptions. Not only many continentalists and hemispherists but also ardent supporters of the acquisition of the Philippines expressed opinions that agreed with or were closely allied to the doctrine of the flag. Perhaps this was only to be expected since the expansionist propaganda consisted so overwhelmingly of idealistic and humanitarian arguments.

The question as to whether the United States could have colonies, that is to say, if a "formal empire" was possible, was answered in the affirmative by the Supreme Court in the Insular Cases in 1901. These originated from an intense political conflict during the spring of 1900, a conflict that sharpened the antagonism between the imperialists and their opponents. As early as 1899 the Insular Commission, which had been sent to Puerto Rico to make a survey and report with recommendations to Russel A. Alger, the Secretary of War, began striving energetically to bring about free trade between the island and the United States. Others, both private citizens and military and civil officials, were working to the same end. The problem was partly approached as a question of helping to remedy the extremely precarious economic conditions on Puerto Rico. It also came to be an important factor in the more complicated and controversial complex of problems concerning the government of the island and its position in relation to the United States.

The arguments used by the Commissioners and their allies were both economic and constitutional. It was easy to prove that Puerto Rico was in a difficult situation, now that its earlier free markets, Spain and Cuba, were no longer available. It was said that the consequences were above all catastrophic for the tobacco and sugar exports.[3] At the same time many people took the attitude that the Constitution of the United States required free trade in interstate commerce and that since the Treaty of Paris had made Puerto Rico a part of the United States, the same rule must apply to trade between the island and the other parts of the nation.

In some cases, those who recommended free trade did not base this on the Constitution, but assumed a decision by Congress. This was the case with General Davis, Head of the Military Government of Puerto Rico. Such individuals argued the difference between incorporated and unincorporated territories, a doctrine that was subsequently to be important in the debate. The inflamed, divided and confused debate that arose around the problem of the position of Puerto Rico and the Philippines stemmed not only from real political, ideological and naturally economic antagonisms, but also from a lack of clarity and certainty concerning the legal and constitutional problems and the consequences that various interpretations and solutions could have.

The Puerto Rican tariff bill came to be a rallying-point for the anti-imperialists in their attacks on the McKinley administration's policy on the newly acquired territories. However, in order to understand the implications of the antagonism it is important to realize that just as there were expansionists, who were for various reasons opposed to the bill, there were among its defenders those who had from the start been most inclined to oppose the annexations.[4] Among these were representatives of agrarian sectional interests devoted to domestic investment: producers of among other things tobacco, sugar beets and sugar cane.[5] Their resistance sprang from a fear of competition from similar crops produced in the new territories with the help of cheap labor. The fight for a tariff between the United States and these new colonies thus became an alternative to forgoing

60

colonies and was not in these cases in itself an expression of globalistic colonialism. It can also be mentioned that among the vice-presidents of the American Anti-Imperialist League were to be found two directors of the American Beet Sugar Co., George Foster Peabody and Robert Fulton Cutting.[6]

The lack of agreement among the legal and constitutional experts contributed to the confusion. The debate between these experts deserves to be more closely examined, for several reasons. First, the statements made by such people in professional journals and other publications functioned as an arsenal which provided politicians and others influencing public opinion with weapons for use in the conflict, and second, this debate elucidated some of the fundamental issues and makes it easier to grasp the otherwise often amorphous and abstruse "popular" contentions.

The "Experts," the Constitution, and the Flag

1

The *Harvard Law Review* of 1899 contained no less than five detailed articles on the constitutional and legal problems that followed with the new territories. Four of these essays appeared during the period January to March and during this period the author of the fifth article, A. Lawrence Lowell, also wrote on the subject in the *Atlantic Monthly*.[7]

The January issue of the *Review* had a rather long article with the title, *"Constitutional Aspects of Annexation."* The author was Carman F. Randolph.[8] His arguments favored the idea that the new territories must be given the same status as the other territories. They were in the same way covered by the provisions and limitations of the Constitution. The United States consisted of the states *and* territories. Political control of all territory of the United States outside of the States was vested absolutely in Congress. But Congress was here bound to rules laid down by the Constitution. There was no possibility of making an exception of the Philippines once they had been acquired, for they could not be acquired in a way that would differentiate them organically from other American possessions. The Constitution was "a self-extending law," and all new territories came under it automatically in the same way as the territories that were already held. Special legislation, such as special customs regulations, was impossible and contrary to the uniformity required by the Constitution.

Randolph supported the doctrine that the Constitution followed the flag.

61

He drew from this the consequence that the United States should *not* annex the Philippine Islands, but neutralize them, either as an independent nation under American protection or by handing them over to "an unobtrusive but competent state, like Holland." They could also be handed over to some other power that could be reasonably expected to "rule them wisely and humanely and open them to the world."[9]

Thus Randolph was an integrationist and placed himself firmly on the side of the anti-imperialists. An address given by another lawyer, George Wharton Pepper, Professor of Law at the University of Pennsylvania, formed an effectful contrast. Pepper was an enthusiastic expansionist of the "race" and "destiny" type: "It may well be our destiny to carry on the work of subjecting the world to the sway of Anglo-Saxon civilization," he claimed and went on to say that no constitutional obstacles to this development could be tolerated. The constitution was not an end in itself and the courts must "curb their newly developed tendency to fetter governmental action by constitutional restraint."[10]

In February 1899, the *Harvard Law Review* contained an article by Simeon E. Baldwin, expressing ideas close to those put forward by Randolph in the preceding issue. To Judge Baldwin it was also quite clear that "the Constitution is the supreme law wherever the flag of the Union floats over its soil."[11] This had consequences in the form of citizenship, trial by jury, uniformity of duties. But to apply the American Constitution and the rights it guaranteed to "the half-civilized Moros of the Philippines, or the ignorant and lawless brigands that infest Puerto Rico, or even the ordinary Filipino of Manila," would be an obstacle to maintenance there of efficient government.[12] When the Constitution was drawn up, the present situation was not foreseen. If it had been, some of the limits put on the legislative power of Congress would probably have been made less rigorous. Baldwin saw constitutional amendments as the only solution.

At about the same time as the debate started in the *Harvard Law Review*, the problem of the Constitution and the new possessions was taken up in the *Political Science Quarterly* by John W. Burgess, the renowned political scientist, earlier known as one of the prophets of expansionism.[13] It is perhaps surprising that he here clearly followed the line of the integrationists. Admittedly Burgess declared he was not one of those persons who thought that the United States ought never to have colonies or dependencies. He now felt considerably more doubtful about the new policy of expansion and suggested that considering that some of the internal problems still were unsolved, the Americans would "more nearly follow the natural order of things" if they stayed at home and devoted themselves to the domestic affairs of the country.[14] Burgess believed in hemispherism, and the acquisition of Cuba was likely to become a national necessity. He was critical towards acquisition of the Philippines and rejected what he described as "world-wide expansion." On the question of the Constitution and the new territories he decided that the limits upon the government of the United States imposed by the Constitution must apply in all places over which that government had territorial jurisdiction, that is to say, the new territories as well. This meant that the Constitution's decisions on judicial procedure must apply, such as uniformity in revenue, taxation, tariffs. In other words Burgess aligned himself with the doctrine that the Constitution followed the flag.

Burgess went on to state that this applied only in territories where civil government was instituted. As long as a territory stood under military government, the President had absolute power to make any decisions he considered necessary and to govern through any forms "that his discretion may dictate." Burgess recommended that the American government should wait before introducing civil government, to find out first whether the inhabitants of the new territories were capable of the form of self-government required. If this should not work, the Constitution should be amended "as to permit the national government to exercise absolute, or more absolute, civil authority in certain parts of our domain."

Burgess' article came at the same time as the Senate's consent to the treaty with Spain and at a point when theoretical discussion was at its height in the political journals. In September of the following year, 1900, he returned to the problem in a new article in which the most interesting feature was perhaps his powerful emphasis on the necessity for constitutional interpretation to take into consideration not only "legislative statutes and judicial decisions" but "history, natural reason and social conditions." He came to the same conclusion: Congress had no power to legislate, for example, on tariffs for the new territories in violation of the principle of uniformity.[15]

The *Political Science Quarterly* of March, 1899, also contained an article by Ernst Freund of the University of Chicago, expansionist but also a consistent integrationist, who declared that the Constitution seemed to leave no room for any territory belonging to the United States that did not form part of the United States.[16] Freund's solution was that the Americans must relinquish annexation and set up protectorates. This would give "absolute international and political control," without creating the constitutional complications that would arise from formal sovereignty. Freund's article consisted mainly of an examination of what a protectorate implied technically and legally according to international law, and he considered that the system should apply in both Puerto Rico and the Philippines. Instead of annexation the United States should assume the protection and political control of the territories.

2

The integrationists in no way dominated the debate. A long series of contributions were made at the same time which, although displaying considerable variations, were united in denying that the Constitution followed the flag. In an article published in the widely read *Monthly Review of Reviews* in January 1899, Harry Pratt Judson of the University of Chicago discussed constitutional problems relating to government of the new territories. He found the right to acquire territories to be beyond dispute. He rejected the theory of the extension of the Constitution *ex proprio vigore* to the territories acquired, and established that: "Indeed, until Congress has acted annexed territory is not a part of the United States so far as our laws are concerned."[17] The power of both the President and Congress to govern annexed territories was limited in the same way as any powers by those branches of the federal government, as in taxation and personal rights.

Judson declared that the term "the United States" in the Constitution implied states and nothing else. Paragraphs in the Constitution pertaining to uniformity in levying indirect taxes applied only throughout the states which formed the Union. The extent to which one decided to apply this uniformity with regard to the territories was discretionary with Congress. Similarly, so long as nothing was prescribed in the appropriate treaty, Congress should have the right to decide what inhabitants of annexed territory should become citizens. Judson claimed that an annexed territory could be held permanently as a colony for purposes of national defense or from economic considerations. He was a colonialist. He saw no difficulty in differentiating between incorporated and unincorporated territories, since in neither case did the constitutional statutes that referred directly to the United States apply.

The February issue of the *Harvard Law Review*, the one in which the essay by Baldwin was published, also contained an article by Christopher Columbus Langdell.[18] The writer took the view that the term "the United States" partly referred to the states that together form the Union and partly to a body politic consisting of the states in this corporate capacity. In the latter case the term "the United States" contained no reference to the extent of territory. When the term "United States" was used to denote all the territory over which the United States is sovereign, this was a purely conventional use of language with no legal or constitutional significance. Langdell reached the conclusion that in fact the Constitution did not extend "beyond the States which are United by and under it."

All legislative power over newly acquired territories resides in the Congress of the United States, just as executive power resides in the President. Langdell rejected the term "annexation" as misleading, with no constitutional or legal meaning. Since the Constitution does not *ex proprio vigore* extend over acquired territories and is only binding for the states, there are no constitutional reasons for bringing about uniformity in taxes, duties, imposts. According to Langdell, the fact that there had been such uniformity hitherto depended not on the rules of the Constitution but simply on there having been no reasons for having any differences. The situation was different with regard to the new territories and in Langdell's view Congress should be given a free hand. The revenue system of the United States should not extend to them.

Langdell's standpoint was as far from Randolph's as it possibly could be, while it was very close to that argued by Harry Pratt Judson.[19]

The next contribution to the debate appeared in the March issue of the *Harvard Law Review*. It had been written in January and was therefore not influenced by the earlier articles.[20] The author was Professor James Bradley Thayer, and his line approaches most closely that of Langdell, although his arguments are different. Thayer saw the right to acquire colonies as "incident to the function of representing the whole country in dealing with other nations and states, whether in peace or war," and the power of holding and governing them as an evident and necessary consequence. Congress or the treaty-making power had a free hand when it came to deciding the political status of new territories and their inhabitants, that is to say, whether they or their descendants were to be given the status of citizens. Like many others writing on the subject, Thayer pointed, as a comparison, to the position of the American Indians in the United States.

Like Langdell, Thayer emphasized that territories have no guarantees as regards self-government and political power. Congress was free to institute the form of government it found suitable. In Thayer's opinion there was no difference between territories and colonies.

Concerning the Constitution, Thayer categorically rejected the interpretation that the statutes about trial by jury must be interpreted universally and therefore apply in the territories. He admitted that there was a prevailing legal opinion that a citizen of a territory was a citizen of the United States and similarly that children born in the territories and subject to American legislation were citizens, and that territories were a part of the United States in the sense that taxes must be uniform there and in the States. But like Langdell he denied that it was possible to read from the Constitution that it applied outside the states, except in strictly limited circumstances. If no stipulations were laid down in the treaties by which the territories had been acquired, Thayer writes, one could well claim that the territories were subject to the absolute power of Congress.

Unlike Baldwin, Thayer was an expansionist. He rejected any suggestion of relinquishing areas that had been won. The United States must accept colonies. But like Burgess Thayer recommended that the military government should be retained for the time being. Above all, Americans should beware of promising the new areas "any place in the Union." "Never should we admit any extracontinental state into the Union; it is an intolerable suggestion." Thayer was a true colonialist.

The statements that have been discussed so far are formally independent of each other and were all made prior to ratification of the peace treaty with Spain in February 1899. The next article on the subject to be published in the *Harvard Law Review* is of special interest. It was in the November issue, but had been written in May. This essay by the respected Abbot Lawrence Lowell is worth attention because it presents a point of view that both differs from those dealt with above and in many ways predicts the decision the Supreme Court was to make later in the Insular Cases.[21]

Lowell gave his essay a subtitle, *"A Third View,"* with the idea that contributions made earlier could be said to represent two lines of thought, one that the Constitution followed the flag, that the limits imposed by the Constitution applied wherever the jurisdiction of the government extended, and the other that the term "United States" when used in a territorial sense included the states alone.

Both these points led to troublesome problems of interpretation, and were difficult to maintain, since in both cases weighty counterarguments could be made. Lowell presented a third view. He rejected the idea that the Constitution was only intended to apply within the states. From the start it was intended to apply to territories that belonged to the United States when the Union was formed. When new territory was later acquired, it had almost consistently been stipulated in the treaties that the new areas

66

were to be incorporated into the United States or that their inhabitants were to be given American citizenship or both. But there was nothing of that nature in the peace treaty with Spain. Lowell claimed that there was a distinction between incorporated territories and those not incorporated and that when no binding treaty stipulations existed the legislative or treaty-making authorities had a free hand to choose the solution they found best.

If an area was annexed so as to make it a part of the United States, all the general restrictions of the Constitution applied there, save those on organization of the judiciary. But a possession may also be so acquired as not to form part of the United States.[22] In the latter case statutes such as those requiring trial by jury or uniformity of taxation did not apply. It could also be claimed, however, that some of the general provisions of the Constitution must also be considered in force here, since it was a question of universal limitations of the governing powers. This applied to prohibition of bills of attainder, ex post facto laws, titles of nobility and a couple of other cases, all of which were of this special nature, that is to say, restrictions rather than guaranteed rights. In the main Lowell's opinion agreed with that later formulated by Justice White in the Insular Cases, the doctrine on incorporated and unincorporated territories. In the later case, however, it was stated that decisions on incorporation could only be made by Congress, not by the treaty-making power alone.[23]

3

The debate of 1899 was naturally conducted not only in professional journals but also in newspapers and magazines. Two articles published in the November and December issues of the *Forum* in 1899 provide examples of how discussion developed and of interpretations current at this time. Both writers had first-hand knowledge of the problems. The first was written by Dr. Henry K. Carroll, who had been asked by President McKinley to make a survey under supervision of the Treasury Department.[24] The recommendations that Carroll made in his report were repeated in the article in the *Forum*, called *"How shall Puerto Rico be governed?"*[25]

Carroll's view was that Puerto Rico was a territory belonging to the United States but not a part of the United States. Nor were its inhabitants American citizens. As long as the island remained under military government, the rights and privileges that the Puerto Ricans enjoyed were theirs by virtue of the power of the President, as commander-in-chief of the Army and Navy. Carroll then took up the three arguments put forward against giving Puerto Rico territorial status, namely that this would imply ultimate statehood, which would be preposterous, that it would lead to exemption from duties, which would hard hit the American sugar and tobacco producers, and finally that the population would not be capable of the self-government that territorial status would require. Carroll rejected the first argument with the contention that there was no obstacle whatsoever to holding the island permanently as a territory. Statehood presumed an act of Congress and naturally no such act would pass if the island was not considered ready for statehood. The second argument he described as selfish and shortsighted. The damage caused to some interests by duty-free competition would be insignificant and outweighed by the great advantage of economic development to the island, such as a higher standard of living and increased purchasing power. Carroll rejected the third reason by referring to his own experiences and observations on the island. His solution was that Puerto Rico should immediately be given territorial status like Oklahoma and New Mexico.[26] He followed the line of the integrationists insofar as he recommended incorporation. At the same time he saw no legal or constitutional obstacles to keeping the island outside the Constitution.

In the following issue of *Forum* there is an article by another expert on Puerto Rico, Judge H. G. Curtis of Iowa, a Republican like Carroll. Curtis was a member of the three-man Insular Commission that had visited the island during the year and investigated conditions there.[27] Curtis was probably the prime mover behind the Commission's report to the Secretary of War, and the ideas that he expounded in his article, *"The Status of Puerto Rico,"* largely followed the report.[28]

Like Carroll, Curtis started from the assumption that in the present situation Puerto Rico was to be seen as "a military possession" of the United States. He stated that civil government could be constitutionally exercised in Puerto Rico by military officers, acting under the direction of the President. But Curtis considered that from the moment that Congress started legislating for Puerto Rico, the island would become a part of the United States "on the simple, but convincing, ground that Congress cannot legislate for foreigners." Thus he did not agree that the Constitution followed the flag, but denied that Congress could legislate for unincorporated territories. In his view the President could take all necessary measures, such as reducing duties on imports from the United States, so long as the island remained under military government. The moment that Congress legislated, Puerto Rico became "an integral part" of the United States, and the stipulations in the Constitution about a uniform tariff system had to come into force. Curtis recommended with great emphasis that Puerto Rico should be retained under military government and not given territorial status until a later date, when and if Congress was convinced of the Puerto Ricans' fitness and competence to be citizens.

McKinley's Message to Congress

1

Puerto Rico's difficult economic predicament did not seriously come to the attention of the United States until August 1899, when a terrible catastrophe afflicted the island. A violent hurricane ravaged the island, destroyed plantations to an alarming extent and took the lives of almost 3000 people. Eighty per cent of the coffee crop, the island's most important source of income, was destroyed. The situation was critical. Since the island was still being administered by the military authorities, the problems had to be faced primarily by Elihu Root who had succeeded Alger as Secretary of War. Root approached McKinley and recommended free trade between Puerto Rico and the United States. It did not occur to him to base this proposal on constitutional arguments. In fact he did not even want the island to have territorial status and was against giving its inhabitants American citizenship. He was inclined to treating the island like a crown colony.[29] As far as he was concerned, free trade was a purely practical measure, to ease Puerto Rico's economic distress.

McKinley took the same view. When opening Congress on December 5, he brought up the question in his message:

"It must be borne in mind that since the cession Puerto Rico has been denied the principal markets she had long enjoyed and our tariffs have been continued against her products as when she was under Spanish sovereignty. She has therefore lost her free intercourse with Spain and Cuba without any compensating benefit in this market. Her coffee was little known and not in use by our people, and therefore there was no demand here for this, one of their chief products. *Our plain duty* is to abolish all custom tariffs between the U.S. and Puerto Rico and give her products free access to our markets."

McKinley was to have reason to regret his words on "the plain duty" many times over, during the months that followed.

Thus neither the President nor Elihu Root had imagined that free trade for Puerto Rico would be interpreted as a constitutional decision or that it could in some way be construed as a precedent for the Philippines. At first McKinley's message aroused no opposition, partly because of the strong sympathy of the American people for the stricken island and partly because for many individuals it seemed natural to equate the island with Hawaii and assume that it should be included in the American tariff system. Another point of view that was often heard was that such a policy would press Cuba to strive for annexation too, so as to avoid the growing competition on the American sugar market.[30]

Even though the reaction to McKinley's message was largely positive, there were some critical voices. One was the strongly protectionist *Gunton's Magazine*, another the New York *Press* (Rep.), which saw in the President's message the greatest victory for free trade during the last fifty years and took that as a serious threat: "In the admission to the home market of the least of the dependencies is the thin edge of the wedge which once inserted, will cleave our whole commercial market."[31] The New York *Times*, which had consistently supported expansionism, accepted McKinley's line, and other newspapers such as the New York *World* (Ind. Dem.) declared that for constitutional reasons the line taken by the President was the only one possible.[32]

2

Criticism was admittedly not particularly widespread, but it did not only come from protectionist die-hards who saw the slightest concession as a threat to the system. Economic interests saw a threat in the new policy: sugar, tobacco, fruit and coffee were Puerto Rico's most important export products. Americans who produced tobacco, cane sugar, beet sugar and fruit were uneasy and soon after McKinley's message it was hinted that strong opposition was growing in those quarters.[33] Opposition increased especially after January 19, when a bill was introduced concerning incorporation of Puerto Rico into the American customs and internal revenue system.

The most publicized effort against free trade for Puerto Rico was made by Henry G. Oxnard of Oxnard, California, who represented the American Beet Sugar Association. A manufacturer of about 400,000 tons of beet sugar with plants in California, Nebraska and Colorado, he gave testimony before the Senate committee on Pacific Islands and Puerto Rico and before the

House Ways and Means Committee. His argument was naturally the rapidly growing beet sugar production in the United States, while he admitted it was not Puerto Rico's present production that worried him, but what might follow. What he was fighting was "expansion in the beginning."[34] Puerto Rico's sugar export was insignificant, only about 58,000 tons compared to a total American import of 1,400,000 tons. Oxnard said that what he feared was free sugar from the Philippine Islands and possibly Cuba, which could be expected to try to achieve annexation if Puerto Rico had these advantages.[35]

Oxnard did not only use the argument of the threat to the domestic sugar production, but described the bill as fatal for the entire protection system. He brought up the threat to the American labor market, including some clearly racist arguments.

Similar attacks on the bill on free trade were made by Herbert Myrick, President of the Orange Judd Company and Chairman of the League of Domestic Producers. Myrick was also the foremost editor of agricultural publications in the United States.[36] H. S. Frye, President of the New England Tobacco Growers' Association, was another of those who protested. He too emphasized that he did not fear Puerto Rico's present production as much as the precedent created. The same position was taken up by the Cigarmakers' International Union.[38] Other opponents to both the bill on free trade for Puerto Rico and territorial self-government also made themselves heard. Motives and arguments varied, but Albert Shaw, editor of the *Review of Reviews*, declared that they could all be reduced to two words: "The first of these arguments is sugar, the second is tobacco."[39] Those thought primarily involved were the tobacco interests in Connecticut, cane sugar growers in Louisiana, beet sugar growers in Nebraska and the fruit interests in California. They soon started to make their influence felt.

The fear was sometimes expressed that free trade for Puerto Rico would form a precedent and drive the protectionists into the camp of the anti-expansionists. The New York *Press*, declared that free trade for Puerto Rico could result in "the shipwreck of the whole expansionist cause on the Caribbean reefs, toward which they now have it headed."[40]

It was clearly not the direct competition from Puerto Rico's products that provoked resistance. What worried them was the possibility that the Philippines and not least Cuba might follow Puerto Rico and that the combined sugar and tobacco production from these territories, freed from tariffs and with cheap labor, could provide competition for American production. These points of view were proclaimed in the Democratic New

Orleans *Picauyne*, which opposed the free-trade line on behalf of the sugar producers of Louisiana, and the Hartford *Times*, which warned about the effect on tobacco growers in Connecticut. The latter group had a spokesman in the state's respected Senator Orville Platt, who announced that he intended to propose that instead of introducing free trade for Puerto Rico, the current Dingley tariff should be reduced by 20 per cent. His argument was that this would give the Puerto Ricans the relief they needed without binding the Republican party to a free-trade line for the newly acquired territories.

It is interesting to follow the position taken by the expansionist New York *Tribune* and its editor Whitelaw Reid.[41] The *Tribune* was pronouncedly protectionist but there is reason to suppose that it was not simply consideration of the domestic producers of tobacco, sugar and fruit that was the force behind its energetic opposition to the free-trade line in Puerto Rico. The newspaper supported Platt's suggestion, mentioned above. Instead of a general customs exemption, there should be legislation that could be adapted to each individual territory. Extension of the American customs laws could lead to new, unwanted states coming to the Union.

Thus Reid and the *Tribune* did not enter the conflict around the Puerto Rico tariff because they thought the issue in itself was of importance. A letter sent by Reid to Platt after the senator had drawn up his amendment to the Puerto Rican Bill at the end of January is illuminating. According to Reid, it would be a catastrophe to do anything that could mean a step "even by implication" toward making "such outlying territories" part of the United States in the sense of the Constitution. They faced a trap set by opponents of expansionism and must avoid falling into it.

Reid made his attitude clear in a letter to the influential Senator Foraker from Ohio, chairman of the Senate Committee that was working on a proposition for a government of Puerto Rico. He wrote that the tariff was "of minor consideration," but that the principle was of the utmost importance. It would be better for the United States to be without these new territories than to give their inhabitants the rights to "citizenship and ultimate statehood."[42] In another letter to his friend John Hay, the Secretary of State, Reid also explained his reasons for resisting free trade in Puerto Rico: They boil down to a declaration that it was necessary to have a tariff to establish that the new territories did not come under the Constitution.[43]

It is not unlikely that Reid contributed to the administration's change of front. He was in McKinley's confidence—the President had appointed him a member of the peace commission to Paris in 1898. Above all he was on close terms with Hay. The *Tribune* was one of the few newspapers that supported Hay's recent proposal for a treaty with England on an Isthmian canal, the first Hay-Pauncefote Treaty, severely criticized by both Republicans and Democrats.[44]

Reid's expansionism was clear and consistent. He did not harbor the idea so frequently expressed that the annexed territories, at least Puerto Rico and Cuba, when the latter island's annexation had come, should be given territorial status, in order that they might be received into the Union as states at a later date when they had been shown to have attained a desirable level of development. In a letter to Senator Cushman K. Davis, chairman of the Senate's Committee on Foreign Relations, Reid stated that nothing must be left that might be considered a loop-hole for Puerto Rico's possible admission in the future as a state in the Union: "Our only safety lies in an absolute rigid adherence to the idea of the Continental Union ... We the people of the United States ... do ordain and establish this Constitution for the United States of *America*."[45] Cushman Davis, who was an expansionist and had, like Reid, been one of the delegates at the peace negotiations with Spain, was himself opposed to the bill, primarily because of the strong resistance to it in the Middle West.[46]

Congress and the Puerto Rican Tariff

On January 19, 1900, Congressman Payne of New York introduced a bill into the House, H R 6883, "to extend the laws relating to customs and internal revenue in Puerto Rico."[47] The bill was referred to the Ways and Means Committee, of which Payne was chairman. Ten days previously Senator Foraker had sponsored S 2264, a proposal that came to be closely linked with Payne's.

The Senate had in December 1899 set up three new permanent committees, one for Cuba, one for the Philippines, and one for the Pacific Islands and Puerto Rico. Chairman of the lastnamed was Senator Foraker, and he was responsible for drawing up the bill on Temporary Civil Government for Puerto Rico, which after it was passed on April 12 was often called the Foraker Act.[48] Since the work of the Foraker Committee also concerned financing questions and the relationship of Puerto Rico with the United States, the tariff problem came to be an important and publicized part of the committee's work.

At first the bills on free trade for Puerto Rico appeared to have a favorable reception even if, as pointed out, critical voices had been heard

73

in connection with McKinley's message. During the discussions that followed, opposition began to harden. By the end of January it was obvious that both the administration and leading Republicans within Congress were preparing to disregard both the promise made by McKinley in his message to Congress in December and the bill introduced by Payne (H R 5883).

As a matter of fact McKinley reversed his stand as soon as he became aware of the implications of free trade for Puerto Rico. And once the constitutional aspects entered into the debate his position was unequivocal. "The constitutional question then became paramount—for upon the proposition that Congress had the right to govern the Islands with a free hand, depends the success of our colonial policy—especially in the Philippines," stated Charles G. Dawes and added: "The President saw this clearly, and as a man to man he argued out in detail the whole question and the danger of the slightest weakening on the Constitutional proposition."[49]

In the Ways and Means Committee the original bill was reworked and reported to the House in a new form (H R 8245). It established that Congress had the right to legislate for the territories, in the present case Puerto Rico, that the island was not part of the United States in the sense of the Constitution, and that Congress consequently had the right to decide on a tariff between Puerto Rico and the United States. It was suggested that the tariff should be set at 25 per cent of the Dingley Tariff that applied for the United States.[50]

McKinley gave in. "I could ride a white horse in this situation and pass the original bill," the President told Henry L. Stoddard. But McKinley went on to state that the main thing was to keep as many votes as possible in Congress back of the whole program of the administration.

Three days earlier the Senate bill sponsored by Foraker (S 2264) was reported back from the Committee on Pacific Islands and Puerto Rico. It now carried an amendment. The so-called Foraker Act should only regulate the government of Puerto Rico temporarily, until the laws and ordinances in force in that island could be revised and codified and a more permanent form of government be framed.[51]

Consultations had taken place between the two committees and the result was a compromise. In the committees, however, there had been sharp differences of opinion. The Ways and Means Committee had issued no fewer than three reports. The majority report was supported by all the Republicans except McCall of Massachusetts who made a separate statement. The third report came from the Democratic and Silver Republican members of the Committee. The decisive factor was denial or assertion

74

that the Constitution followed the flag. The majority report declared expressly that by annexation Puerto Rico did not become a part of the United States in the sense of the Constitution. Opponents claimed the opposite.

The fight had been hard in the House, and constitutional, economic, moral, power political and racist arguments had been put forward, often revealing the lack of a considered view on expansionism and its consequences that was so characteristic of much of public argument at this time.[52] Arguments in favor of the bill were presented clearly by such men as Payne, who expounded the economic reasons that made necessary an income from duties in order to finance administration of the island and even the school system.[53] Grosvenor (Ohio) and above all Dalzell (Rep. Penn.) argued for the absolute power of Congress to govern Puerto Rico, not subject to the Constitution.[54] Dalzell put his finger on what he and many others feared to be the consequences of any other policy as far as concerned the Philippines: "I am not willing to see the wage-earner of the United States, the farmer of the United States, put upon a level and brought into competition with the cheap, half-slave labor, savage labor, of the Philippine archipelage."

Among those persons leading the attack on the bill was Senator J. D. Richardson (Dem. Tenn.), who left open the question of whether the Constitution *ex proprio vigore* had been extended to include the acquired territories. He claimed categorically that the minute Congress legislated for Puerto Rico, the island would become incorporated and must be treated as a part of the United States.[55] His arguments are similar to those used by Judge Curtis.[56] A group of Republicans joined in the attacks on the House bill, and altogether no less than twenty spoke against it. One of the sharpest critics was Littlefield of Maine, who attacked Payne's economic arguments. Although he also questioned the constitutionality of the tariff, he rejected it as morally reprehensible and, in addition, bad policy.[57] The constitutional line of argument was expounded most consistently by another Republican, McCall.

Thus the positions did not follow party lines. Not only did a considerable number of Republican Congressmen oppose the bill, but the tariff was supported by about ten Democrats, almost all representing sugar, tobacco, or fruit districts.

It became obvious that the bill had no chance of being passed in its original form. A compromise was reached by which the tariff was lowered from 25 per cent of the Dingley tariff to 15, and limited to two years.

Despite these modifications the vote was close, 172 for and 169 against. Six Republicans—Littlefield (Maine), McCall (Massachusetts), Crumpacker (Indiana), Lorimer (Illinois), Fletcher and Heatwole (Minnesota) —voted against the bill despite the compromise, and another two not present at the vote—Faris (Indiana) and Lane (Iowa)—were confirmed opponents. Many other Republicans, such as Tompkins of New York and Powers of Vermont, dropped their opposition and voted for the bill in its modified form. The Republican swing was a result of strong pressure not only by Republican leaders within Congress, but by McKinley. Defending themselves to their indignant constituents for having changed their minds and voted for the bill, Bromwell (Ohio), Powers (Vermont), Watson (Indiana), Sperry (Connecticut) and others said they had been persuaded to do so by the direct and persistent requests of the President.[58] Four Democrats voted for the bill: DeVries, who represented a fruit growing district in California, Davey and Meyer from the sugar districts of Louisiana and Sibley, Pennsylvania. The last-named based his action on an absolute refusal to accept the doctrine that the Constitution followed the flag. If that were the case he declared he would fight every form of American expansion. There was also another factor: Pennsylvania was tobacco-growing country and its tobacco districts were of the same kind as Puerto Rico's.

Thus there were several reasons for the Republican swing. The official motive, the necessity of collecting revenues to cover costs for the government and administration of the island, was obviously not taken seriously, even by the most eloquent advocates of the tariff, since they fell back on other, more important points. The work of the tobacco and sugar lobbyists had some influence. Their representations were given weight by the fact that they joined with those persons who saw the Puerto Rico free trade bill as in itself harmless but unacceptable because of the threat it could become to the protectionist system.

There was an even more significant factor in the dramatic swing from McKinley's message, a swing maintained despite the storm of opinion it aroused. This was the revolt of the globalists, their realization of the threat that treatment of Puerto Rico as an incorporated territory, a part of the United States in the constitutional sense, could be to expansionism. They saw a chance of stopping the doctrine that the Constitution followed the flag.

The press at first got the impression that Congress was making a decision in direct conflict with the wishes of the President. Almost unanimously the newspapers, including the Republican press, backed what they thought was McKinley's position and attacked the course taken by Congress. It was not until the end of February that McKinley came forward and declared support of the tariff between Puerto Rico and the United States, with the result that he himself became the object of attack.

General opinion was that the majority of Republicans in the House were in favor of free trade but had given way for the sake of party harmony. The bill had met opposition in the House, but this was nothing compared to the protest that blew up in the country and increased after the bill had passed the House on February 28 and gone to the Senate. To meet the charge that the United States was refusing Puerto Rico the relief that free trade would bring for egoistic and economic reasons, exploiting the plight of a people that had voluntarily turned to the United States for help and protection, McKinley recommended that Congress should grant a sum of money for immediate aid to Puerto Rico. This subvention was to be the entire amount that up to January 1, 1900 had been taken in as duties on goods from Puerto Rico to the United States, about 2 million dollars. But opposition to the Puerto Rico tariff bill nonetheless increased.

The struggle had started in the Senate as early as January 11, when two anti-imperialist senators, Vest of Missouri and Mason of Illinois, each presented a resolution concerning the status of the new territories. Vest held that the United States could not acquire and govern territories permanently as colonies, Mason that the United States would not govern a people without consent of the people.[59]

To counter these resolutions, Senator Ross (Rep. Vermont) submitted three resolves on January 18 of which the most important was that the Constitution did not, unaided by an Act of Congress, extend over Puerto Rico and the Philippine Islands.[60] Ross argued along the lines that Lowell among others had developed.[61]

One of those leading the fight against Vest's and Mason's integrationist resolutions was Foraker, who claimed that the right to acquire and govern territory was implicit in the constitutional right to declare war and make treaties. He categorically denied that the Constitution *ex proprio vigore* included the territories. A direct decision by Congress would be required.[62] He took the same stand as expounded by a succession of legal experts.

Arguing later from the floor of the Senate, Foraker took up a line of thought that lay close to what Lowell had said in his essay in the *Harvard Law Review*.[63] He described Puerto Rico as "a dependency" of the United States and "not a part in any integral sense" and stressed that the peace treaty with Spain contained no stipulation that the acquired land should be incorporated.[64]

In an article published in the April issue of the *North American Review,* Foraker argued what came to be the official line of defense for the proposed tariff.[65] He claimed that the tariff was solely intended to take in money necessary for government of the island. He rejected the arguments in other quarters that a tariff was needed to protect American interests against the competition of sugar, tobacco and fruit from Puerto Rico. He claimed, however, that Puerto Rico and the Philippines had the same relationship to the United States, being acquired in the same way. While Puerto Rico's production did not threat American interests, the situation was different for the Philippines. If the Constitution was extended *ex proprio vigore* to Puerto Rico—which Foraker categorically denied—the same must apply to the Philippines and that would present the country with competition of another magnitude and in addition be a threat to United States' "wage-workers and industrial interests" because of the possibility of introducing cheap labor.

Foraker made another point that he said was of greater importance. For the United States commercial expansion was a necessity. The nation had reached a point when productive capacity far outreached what could be consumed. Foreign markets must be found for the surplus and the incomparably largest markets were in the Far East, primarily China. Now the government had established an Open Door policy there that was intended to guarantee America a share of the enormous commerce. American ships and American goods would be admitted to China on the same conditions as other countries. Other states would demand the same policy for the Philippines. It was then that the relation of the Philippines to the United States would become clear. If the Constitution were to prevent the United States from levying duties on export to the Philippines, the logical result would be that exemption from duty on the lines of the Open Door principle must apply to ships and goods of other countries, and if the Philippines were part of the United States this would mean that goods from other countries admitted duty-free to the Philippines would have been admitted to the United States duty-free, which would be identical with the breakdown of the entire American protection and revenue system.

It is unnecessary to point out that Foraker here fabricated an argument that has several weaknesses and that gives a different picture of the motives for the Puerto Rican tariff than the usual explanation. He was a convinced globalist and for him as for Reid much more important issues were at stake than two million dollars to Puerto Rico. He was fighting a development that would make American colonial expansion impossible.[66]

After the Puerto Rican tariff bill had passed in the House, public opinion had become so violent that many people counted on the Senate to amend the bill sufficiently so as to grant the island free trade with the United States. The opposition appeared equally strong in both industrial and agricultural districts, with the exception of those producing sugar, tobacco or fruit. The storm of protest against the proposed tariff was noticeable not least in grain-producing areas, where Puerto Rico appeared as a new potential market. The bill's most decided opponents included the two Minnesota senators, Davis and Nelson, and Senator McCumber from North Dakota. McCumber offered an amendment permitting American grain to enter Puerto Rico free. Davis offered amendments for free trade entirely.

The heaviest share of the defense of the bill fell to Senator Foraker, who performed with great skill. He offered amendments that not only limited the proposed tariff to two years, but meant that if the local government could raise needed revenue by internal taxation at an earlier date, the island would be granted free trade.

Opponents included Republican anti-imperialists such as Senators Hoar (Massachusetts), Mason (Illinois) and Wellington (Maryland), who like most Democrats claimed that the Constitution followed the flag. Redfield Proctor of Vermont offered uncompromising opposition. Senator Proctor, who had been Secretary of War under Harrison, was no anti-imperialist and his opposition was hardly ideological. In a letter to Elihu Root he dismissed the talk about the revenue. His position was entirely determined by tactical considerations: ". . . we had better pay their bills for the next five years rather than have this row." In the letter he outlined a proposal for an amendment limiting the tariff to the present fiscal year. This would mean that it was terminated four days before the Democratic National Convention. It would establish the doctrine of protection, and at the same time take the question out of politics. The Democrats could get no thunder out of a law that had already expired.[67] The young Senator Beveridge from Indiana worked for a compromise that would give Puerto Rico free trade but at the same time state that the Constitution did not extend to the island. Beveridge weakened his opposition by declaring he would vote for the bill in its present form if an agreement could not be reached on an amendment granting free trade.[68]

Apart from Foraker, the most effective defense perhaps came from the senior senator from Indiana, Charles Fairbanks.[69] In the Senate as in the House, he had support from Democrats, primarily the strongly protectionist Senator McEnery from Louisiana, who was protecting Louisiana cane sugar interests.

On April 2 the modified bill passed the Senate with a majority of eleven votes, 42—31. All Republican senators voted for it except Hoar, Proctor, Wellington, Mason, Davis, Nelson and Simon. All Silver Republicans supported the bill with exception of Teller, while of the Democrats only McEnery voted for it. The bill went back to the House, where after a short debate it passed unchanged, by 161 votes to 153. On this occasion a small number of Republicans voted against.

The Press and the Puerto Rican Tariff

The Puerto Rican tariff bill received support from the press, in papers such as the New York *Tribune* and *Press*, the Philadelphia *Press*, which was Postmaster General Emory Smith's organ, and the Philadelphia *Times*, the St. Louis *Globe-Democrat*, New Orleans *Picayune*. Newspapers fighting the bill were in an overwhelming majority, however, and represented all regions. Opposition was most intense in the Middle West.

The bill was bitterly opposed in the Republican press as well. In exceptional cases constitutional arguments were put forward there too, in the Indianapolis *Journal* and *Press*, Philadelphia *Ledger*, Boston *Post*, and a few others, but in general it was presented as a moral issue.[70] The leading source of outrage was what was described as a flagrant disregard of elementary human considerations and a shocking violation of solemnly given promises. Free trade for Puerto Rico was described as a matter of honor, justice and good faith, and McKinley's words about "the plain duty" were constantly cited. Lurking behind the abandonment of the free-trade line, so the editors claimed, were the specters of "avarice and greed". The tobacco and sugar trust were often accused. The Boston *Traveler* wrote, "Sold out to sugar and tobacco" and the Philadelphia *Ledger* maintained that if "the Sugar Trust and the New England Tobacco Trust were out of the way, there would be no effort to starve the people of Puerto Rico, under the plea of *giving* them a government."[71] Indignation was certainly often genuine, but there was in the Republican press another noticeable motive, namely, fear of the political consequences.[72] Many observers viewed what had happened as "an amazing political blunder," "a dangerous error," "a grievous blunder, fraught with dire possibilities."[73]

The same reaction was reflected in the flood of letters that descended upon senators. "A catastrophe," "a suicidal policy for the Republicans" were typical expressions used in letters sent to Senator Spooner, and letter-writers claimed that if the Democrats were wise enough to drop Bryan and nominate a man like Richard Olney, McKinley would scarcely get a single electoral vote.[74]

The arguments in the campaign varied. In Democratic papers, constitutional arguments were brought out: the Constitution followed the flag, and the proposed tariff was a breach of the Constitution, "one of the greatest constitutional questions ever been brought before Congress," in the opinion of the Boston *Transcript* (Ind. Rep.). Its local colleague the *Herald* (Ind.) explained that this problem "goes down to the bedrock of our government principles."[75]

In the ever more violent campaign against the Puerto Rican bill, anti-imperialist Republican and Independent newspapers found themselves side by side with the Democratic opposition press. The most energetic opponents included Republican newspapers that had been clearly expansionist such as the New York *Sun* and *Mail* and *Express*, the Boston *Journal*, Indianapolis *Journal*, Chicago *Inter-Ocean*, Hartford *Courant*, as well as such Independent Republican papers as Philadelphia *Inquirer*, Washington *Star*, Indianapolis *News*, Chicago *Evening Post*, and Philadelphia *North-American*.[76]

In the Middle West practically the entire Republican press went against the bill. Among the Chicago newspapers it was not only the *Inter-Ocean* and *Evening Post*, but the *Times-Herald, Tribune, Record, Journal* and *Chronicle*. Apart from opinions expressed in the press, there was one remarkable example of the height to which opposition grew in the Middle West. The Iowa legislature, which had a clear Republican majority, unanimously passed a resolution that no duties be levied between Puerto Rico and the rest of the United States.

While the majority of Democratic newspapers followed the constitutional line some Republican papers fought the Puerto Rican tariff, while claiming that the Constitution did not hinder such a decision by Congress. Others took the side of the Democrats, in their view of extension of the Constitution. The positions of the newspapers on the constitutional question of principle were nevertheless often unclear.

Toward the end of the year and during the spring of 1901, the question was clarified when taken to the Supreme Court. What are known as the Insular Cases not only aroused great interest but had extremely widespread consequences. There was general agreement that a decision reached by the Court would be of utmost importance. The issue was described by the *Literary Digest* as the most important the Supreme Court had had to decide for a generation and it was said that the entire future of United States colonial policy rested on the decision. "The nation stands breathless awaiting the decision of the great tribunal which is to determine the future of the Philippines," wrote Charles Denby, former Minister to China.[77]

The constitutionality of the tariff imposed came up in the case of Downes *v.* Bidwell (182 U S 144/1901/). The result was that of nine Supreme Court judges, five held that Puerto Rico belonged to but did not form a part of the United States in the sense of the Constitution. Mr. Justice Henry Billings Brown delivered the official opinion of the Court, but it is in the concurring opinion of Mr. Justice Edward Douglas White that we find the important distinction between incorporated and unincorporated territories that was to become the Court's established doctrine. It is the same distinction made by Lawrence Lowell in his essay in the *Harvard Law Review* and by Senator Foraker in debate in Congress.[78] Incorporation did not take place by acquisition, but by decision of Congress, which had freedom of action. Congress had the same right to make decisions concerning unincorporated and incorporated territories. An incorporated territory became subject to all provisions of the Constitution, while in an unincorporated territory only certain "fundamental" provisions would apply.[79]

The decision of the Supreme Court was given, as was only to be expected, a mixed reception. The slight mysticism emanating from the doctrine caused Elihu Root to comment: "Ye-es, as near as I can make out the Constitution follows the flag—but doesn't quite catch up with it."[80] And Mr. Dooley too had his own analysis: "No matter whether th' constitution follows th' flag or not, th' supreme coort follows th'illiction returns."[81]

Examination of the reactions and opinions in the newspapers can help elucidate the conflict over the Puerto Rican tariff. In the fight over the bill the dividing line that is of most interest here, separated those who accepted a colonial system and those who supported the doctrine of the Constitution and the flag.[82] Practically all anti-imperialists were on the latter side, and all radical expansionists, the globalists, on the former. Otherwise the allegiance was diffuse. Continentalists and hemispherists— Democrats and Republicans—usually followed the flag-constitution line, but so did many of those who supported the entire policy of expansion.

82

After the Puerto Rican bill had passed, when party lines were on the whole followed, Republican newspapers that had opposed the bill abandoned their opposition. After the election, however, many earlier critics among the Republican newspapers once more proved negative. In some cases they spoke out more clearly, since it was no longer necessary to take party tactics into consideration.

In the spring of 1900 many Republican newspapers had a wavering attitude toward the constitutional question, among them the Indianapolis *Journal* (Rep.)[83] which repeatedly published editorials that declared Puerto Rico to be covered by the Constitution, which followed the flag. Under pressure the newspaper abandoned this view, but in December it returned to its stand and stated without the slightest reservation: "Looking at the matter from a constitutional point of view, and without reference to politics or the arguments of inconvenience there can be no doubt that the Constitution in its entirety extends over all territories of the United States as soon as they are annexed." That Democratic newspapers continued to reject the idea of a colonial form of government is less surprising.

A limited number of newspapers had from the start supported the Puerto Rican tariff. When the issue became current again in connection with the Insular Cases, it was consistent that they should deny that the Constitution included the new territories. It is interesting, however, that there were exceptions. The reason is easily found. Among the exceptions were the Democratic Hartford *Times* and New Orleans *Picayune*. Their support of the Puerto Rican bill had stemmed from, in the one case, the tobacco-growing interests in Connecticut, and in the other Louisiana's sugar producers. When the issue was decided they could afford to support the party-line, and they swung over to the position held by the majority of Democratic newspapers. Republican papers that had supported the tariff, such as the New York *Tribune* and *Press*, Boston *Journal*, Philadelphia *Press*, St. Louis *Globe-Democrat*, Chicago *Tribune*, Hartford *Courant*, were consistent and supported the line taken by the majority of the Supreme Court.

The New York *Times* (Ind. Dem.) provided the most marked exception from the rule that newspapers with Democratic connections followed the "flag line". The newspaper had consistently supported expansionism, and now commented on ex-President Harrison's declarations in support of the "flag-doctrine" by saying that he was suffering from "a curable nervous excitement which has been communicated to him from the excessivly sceptic literature of anti-imperialism." Other Democratic newspapers that like the New York *Times* denied extension of the Constitution *ex proprio vigore* to the newly acquired territories were the New York *Journal* and Macon *Telegraph.*

More common than this deviation from the usual pattern was one in which Republican newspapers wholeheartedly supported the doctrine that the Constitution followed the flag. This occurred, as pointed out, in the Indianapolis *Journal* and in two Chicago newspapers that had fought the tariff, the *Times-Herald* and the *Evening Post.* The same group included such papers as the Philadelphia *Ledger, Bulletin* and *North American,* the Boston *Advertiser* and *Record,* Cleveland *Leader,* and San Francisco *Chronicle.* With a typical choice of words, the Chicago *Evening Post* declared: "We want healthy, American expansion, not crown colonies or vassal territories."

Newspapers that described themselves as Independent split. As a rule those that had Democratic connections followed the line of Democratic papers: The Philadelphia *Times* and *Record,* Richmond *Times,* Baltimore *Sun,* and Cleveland *Plain Dealer.* Independent Republican newspapers usually followed the opposite line, although there were exceptions, notably the Springfield *Republican* and New York *Evening Post,* both of which belonged to the most energetic and convinced advocates of anti-imperialism.[84]

If instead of party affiliation we take the previous stand of newspapers on expansionism, it proves natural that anti-imperialist organs dominate among advocates of the flag line. However, there are examples of anti-imperialist newspapers that denied that the Constitution followed the flag. The foremost example is probably the Chicago *Journal* (Ind.), which fought the Puerto Rican tariff but then welcomed the decision of the Supreme Court. As a rule the attitude taken to the question of principle in the spring of 1901 agreed with the newspapers' earlier anti-imperialist views.

More worthwhile is examination of the attitude taken by newspapers previously in favor of expansion. If the majority followed the line adopted by the Supreme Court, there were exceptions and they deserve attention. Many Democratic press organs—usually Gold Democratic—had been in favor of expansion but went over to the doctrine that the Constitution followed the flag or expressed a point of view close to it. This applies to the Philadelphia *Record,* Washington *Times,* Louisville *Courier-Journal* and the New Orleans *Picayune.* The pattern was the same in a succession of Republican or Independent newspapers, such as the Chicago *Evening*

Post, New York *Herald,* Philadelphia *North-American,* Indianapolis *Journal* and *News* and the Boston *Advertiser.*

If we summarize the possible conclusions from these surveys of press opinion in connection with the Supreme Court's hearing of the Insular Cases, the first and most noticeable fact is that if compared to the reaction to the Puerto Rican bill in the spring of 1900, the picture is now different. The explanation is that opponents of the bill had different grounds for opposition and did not hold a common stand on the constitutional question of principle. The dividing line did not go between the parties, nor did it pass clearly between anti-imperialists and expansionists.

The struggle over the Puerto Rican tariff in the spring of 1900 is of interest for several reasons. It revealed how little the expansionists had considered the consequences of territorial expansion, how diffuse their ideas were about the legal and constitutional aspects of the problem and the complications that could arise as soon as the indefinite, vaguely idealistic and emotional expansionism came into conflict with economic interests.

Behind the change of heart shown by the McKinley administration on the tariff issue lay several well-defined interests: tobacco planters of Connecticut, cane sugar growers in Louisiana, beet sugar producers in Nebraska, fruit growers in California. In addition there was fear of the reaction of labor to competition from cheap labor from the new territories.

Another factor was the anxiety felt by the protectionists that free trade for Puerto Rico could hurt the protectionist system.

To understand the policy of the administration one must see it in a wider perspective. The issue was not Puerto Rico, but the Philippines, Cuba, and in general the foundations of American expansion. The globalists emerged from the conflict as victors, having prevented the establishment of a precedent that could lead to the fall of the entire expansionist policy.

CHAPTER III

"A Political Cyclone" or "a Tempest in a Teapot"? Indiana, Imperialism, and the Puerto Rican Tariff Bill

Problems involving the domestic environment of the American foreign policy process are usually dealt with on a national level. The Executive, State Department, Congress, leading political figures and wellknown commentators, big business and influential organizations, big newspapers and periodicals occupy the center of the stage. State politics and to an even greater extent politics at grass-root level are normally left standing in the wings. This is partly owing to practical difficulties, partly because there is a general feeling that questions and problems involving foreign policy are not important in local politics. The difficulties are obvious. At the same time it is clear that a study aiming at shedding light upon the role of foreign policy in domestic politics, as an issue in party politics, must also try to get at the possible effects on the local level.

When we try to assess the part played by foreign policy issues in the presidential election campaign of 1900, the same problems turn up as in all such investigations. The basic sources of material are naturally political statements, platforms, speeches, editorials in newspapers etc. This is the material, together with opinion polls and the actions of Congress, which is normally used as a basis for statements about changes in the attitudes of Americans to foreign policy, estimation of how strong isolationist, internationalist or similar currents are etc. A careful use of such material can produce valuable results. But too often impermissible generalizations are made on the basis of limited press material and Congressional debates. The greater part of the material available originates from politicians or newspapermen and publicists with political ties and commitments. Obviously this does not necessarily mean that their attitudes are representative for a significantly sized group.

The question is: how much did all this mean to the general public, to the man in the street? There is no difficulty involved in establishing which line was followed on foreign policy by the Republican, Democratic or independent press respectively, with sectional and individual variations. Nor is it difficult to see in this material fluctuations over time in the interest in foreign policy. But was this a debate which engaged the interest of ordinary people, which led to their deciding to support one side or the other? Or was it more of an academic discussion, conducted over the heads of the people and with no significance for the majority of voters? William Jennings Bryan and the Democrats tried desperately to make imperialism the paramount issue in the election campaign. Was there any reason to believe they might succeed? And last but not least: what part was played by foreign policy at state level and below? It is also a question of the relevance of foreign policy in the context of domestic politics.

One way of illuminating these problems is to make an intensive study of a single state on a controversial question. The fight over the Puerto Rican tariff bill in Indiana, which coincided with the pre-convention campaign of 1900, provides an excellent focal point for a study of this kind. Indiana was a state of medium size. Only four states had more electoral votes.[1] The state's fifteen electors made Indiana a factor to be reckoned with in a close election. In addition, the state had an unusually interesting political structure. In almost every single election during the 1880's and 1890's the outcome was decided by a majority of a few thousand votes and in many counties the balance between the Republicans and the Democrats was so fine that a few dozen votes were decisive. The situation was unstable in the extreme and everyone was aware of this fact, not only within the state but at the top national party level, and every little sign that might indicate the trend was assiduously noted. In 1892, Cleveland won with a majority of over 7000 and in 1896 the Republicans had won with a majority of 18,000 and received 50.9 % of the votes. On that occasion they had the additional support of the Gold Democrats in the state. But since in 1900 the silver question was no longer so topical there was no guarantee that the Republicans could count on getting this bonus in the coming election.

As a matter of curiosity it may be pointed out that after Indiana became a state in 1816, on only three occasions was a president elected in the United States who had not won in Indiana. The state was considered by both parties to be pivotal and both concentrated on the campaign there. Both parties in 1900 had a man from Indiana on the Executive Committee of their respective National Committees: Harry S. New, Republican and editor of the Indianapolis *Journal*, leading Republican newspaper in

Indiana, and Thomas Taggart, Democratic mayor of Indianapolis. In addition, the Secretary of the Republican National Committee was Perry S. Heath of Indiana, former first assistant Postmaster General. It was no coincidence that Bryan on August 8 made his speech of acceptance in Indianapolis.[2]

There are other reasons which make Indiana suitable for a closer examination of this problem. It was not a onesidedly agrarian state, since it also had a sizable working-class population. Leading industries were lumber with 14,467 wage-earners, glass 13,239, clothing 11,813, railroad cars 11,418 and foundry and machine-shop products 10,868.[3] Indiana was balanced from the point of view of religious and ethnic groups. Hoosiers of foreign birth in 1900 reached a total of about 150,000 of whom nearly half were Germans. The Irish came second, with about 16,000.[4] Nor was the state dominated by a metropolis. The largest city, Indianapolis, had a population of about 170,000 and was about three times as large as the second largest.[5]

The Census Bureau in 1900 determined Columbus, Indiana, as the center of population in the United States. This fact is little more than a curiosity, but it is interesting that Indiana was, both then and later, regarded as "the average state," and "the Hoosiers" as average Americans par préférence.[6] Mark Sullivan asserted in "Our Times" that "a fair case might be made out to the effect that the typical American of 1900 had possibly more points of identity with the typical inhabitants of an Indiana community than with most other persons in other backgrounds ... In politics, the representativeness, so to speak, of the citizen of Indiana and Ohio was universally recognized, and won for him something close to omnipotence; for his ideas, his prejudices, his economic interests, were universally considered and generally deferred to."[7] These circumstances make Indiana an object of very special interest.

Indiana has another advantage as a case study. The two Indiana senators in 1900 were unusually important men. The senior senator was Charles Warren Fairbanks, who was considered to have close links with President McKinley and the administration,[8] and who was sometimes named as a possible candidate for the vice presidency. He became Taft's running mate in 1908. The junior senator was a man of special interest, the young Albert Beveridge, who was at this time emerging as one of the most eloquent and enthusiastic advocates of radical expansionism.[9] Both senators have left behind considerable collections of recorded material, of great importance in the investigation which follows.[10]

Indiana and the Issue of Imperialism at the Beginning of 1900

1

One way of establishing whether expansion was an issue in Indiana at the beginning of the year 1900 is to study the local press. The frequency of articles and editorials on a question and the intensity of feeling expressed should provide evidence as to the significance accorded the question on the local level and the interest it was expected to hold for the readers.

Many of the numerous local newspapers, dailies, semi-weeklies and weeklies, had no editorials and often devoted only a small amount of space to issues on the national level. When the issues reached a certain magnitude, and political—not least party-political—importance, even many newspapers which were usually reserved, with no regular editorials or similar comments, took sides.

Daniel T. Pierce, editor of the *Public Opinion*, made an interesting point in an essay titled "Does the Press Reflect Public Opinion?" According to Pierce, a large majority of the newspapers could not afford not to represent the opinions of their readers. This did not apply to the same degree to all newspapers, however, and Pierce divides them into different groups, according to the number of inhabitants in the town where they were published, and concludes that he is convinced that the newspapers of the rural communities—"the despised 'country newspaper'—" are the truest reflectors of public opinion. He makes out a good case for his position.[11]

The problem is not a simple one. However, quite apart from the complicated and controversial question of the role of the newspaper in reflecting or forming opinion, it is obvious that politicians—rightly or wrongly—considered the press to be a gauge of public opinion. Very often press opinion was equated with public opinion. That congressmen and senators and other politicians, for whom it was important to keep their ears close to the ground, shared this belief is demonstrated by the extensive collections of newspaper clippings—mostly editorials—they have left behind. And a large proportion of the cuttings are from the local press of their home states.

Now of more than 600 Indiana dailies, semi-weeklies and weeklies, the vast majority belongs in the "country paper" category.

All newspapers of any importance that have been preserved in Indiana have been studied for the period in question. Of about 250 newspapers studied, approximately 55 % have been found to have taken a stand on the issue. These newspapers represented about three-quarters of the counties in Indiana and were spread fairly evenly over the thirteen Congressional districts, with exception of the first, which was underrepresented. A little over half the newspapers studied were described as Republican or Independent Republican, a smaller group was Independent or Local, and about forty per cent Democratic.

At the beginning of 1900 expansionism generally followed party lines in the Indiana press. Practically all newspapers which clearly approved of the expansionist policy were Republican. There were Democratic papers which agreed with many of the Republican ones. For party-political reasons, however—great advances had already been made in producing party standpoints that would be of use in the coming campaign—they safeguarded themselves by claiming that they were admittedly for expansion but against imperialism. They did not always explain what they meant by this latter term, nor is it always easy to deduce which form of expansion—and with which consequences—the pro-expansionist newspapers represented.

The current arguments were produced, but seldom consistently. It is nevertheless possible to discern some differences between the two camps. The leading Republican organ in the State, the Indianapolis *Journal*, stressed the economic motive. "We want the Philippines for their trade and for the advantage their position would give us in the world's commerce," as it states at the beginning of January with a typical choice of words.[12] The "duty" line dominated in the Indianapolis *Press* (Ind. Republican). Otherwise the usual arguments cropped up. A great many of the Republican newspapers ignored the issue.

Anti-imperialist arguments appeared frequently in the Democratic newspapers, but not many devoted attention to the question or conducted any campaign. The main organ, the Indianapolis *Sentinel*, adopted a critical attitude, as did several other Democratic papers, following, for example, Senator Beveridge's major imperialistic speech to the Senate on January 9.[13] The usual arguments were brought out, but the impression given at this point is that the question was not considered by the Democratic press to have any real potential in the election.

The study of the Indiana press for January 1900 indicates that foreign policy at this time played no prominent part as a controversial issue. The Democrats were on the defensive politically, partly because of the clear split within the party between the Bryanites and a more conservative wing, which though it had supported the party in 1896 now considered the time right to drop the 16 : 1 demand. In addition there was the question of whether it would be possible to win back the gold-standard Democrats who had bolted in 1896, but of whom many now indicated that they would be willing to return on condition that the monetary question was pushed into the background.

Among more conservative individuals were Mayor Taggart of Indianapolis and S. E. Morss, publisher of the Indianapolis *Sentinel*. Papers which followed the same line as the *Sentinel* were the South Bend *Times*, New Albany *Press*, LaPorte *Argus-Bulletin*, Winchester *Democrat*, Rockville *Tribune*, Bloomington *Star*. These newspapers urged that the demand for free silverminting at the ratio of 16 : 1 should be dropped and numerous Democratic papers chose to ignore the question, which in fact indicated the same point of view.

There were other newspapers which backed Bryan in his demand that 16 : 1 should be retained without compromise. They included the Vincennes *Daily Sun*, the Shelby *Democrat*, the Greencastle *Star-Press*, the Lafayette *Weekly Journal*, and Jasper *Weekly Courier*. Thus the Democrats of Indiana were divided on the issue which had dominated the election of 1896. The problem was that for 1900 they had no powerful substitute which could both unite the party and attract the voters. There was always the trust question, but prosperity had taken some of the wind from the sails of this issue. The same applied to the tariff question, which some made rather feeble attempts to launch as the main issue of the election.

The Republicans exuded an air of solid confidence about the election. Their arguments were dominated by the "prosperity line," and the trade boom was brought constantly to the fore. Expansionism was only taken up on rare occasions. Republican foreign policy was naturally praised, however, and there were newspapers which used expansionist jargon.

This was particularly noticeable in the editorial comments on the widely-reported speech, mentioned above, delivered by Albert Beveridge, Indiana's junior senator, to the Senate on January 9.[14] Even newspapers in Indiana which did not normally concern themselves with foreign policy seized the chance of backing up the McKinley administration. But in general, comments on foreign policy in the Republican press were couched in defensive terms. They defended themselves and party from charges of imperialism and tried to draw a line between expansionism, which they were for, and imperialism, which they claimed to be merely an electioneering fantasy of the Democrats.

Of the newspapers studied, over sixty—nearly all Republican—expressed plainly expansionist views, but only a fairly small group was globalist, actively committed to and enthusiastic about the new policy. Moreover, in remarkably many cases they seem to be extremely vague about what it was they were recommending. Often they were doing no more than dutifully supporting the party line.

Many Democratic newspapers in Indiana were staunch adherents of Bryan's anti-imperialism. A good forty of the newspapers studied contain anti-imperialist statements. These were not common at the beginning of the year, however, and above all they seem a matter of routine, in much the same way as the expansionist declarations of the Republicans.

The Republicans returned constantly to the split within the Democratic ranks on this question. The Indianapolis *Journal* repeatedly printed accounts of the strong pro-expansionist feelings among Democrats in the South. The Winimac *Republican* in the thirteenth Congressional district, one of the organs which was enthusiastically in favor of expansionism, had items about Democrats who had abandoned their party because they could not swallow anti-imperialism. The same applies to the South Bend *Tribune* and other papers.

It is obvious that the newspapers are not wholly adequate as gauges of public opinion at grassroot level. Sometimes, as pointed out, the papers lacked editorials, in other cases they used the material distributed by the party and that limits their value in this study. There are, however, other means of getting closer to the impact on local opinion of the controversy over expansion, to what people really thought.

2

The picture which has emerged from the previous investigation can be illuminated by examples from press-notices about the county and district conventions held by the two main parties. Many of the resolutions passed have been reported and provide pointers.

Also in this context the Democrats give a heterogeneous impression both on the monetary question and on foreign policy. In the first congressional district a resolution was passed which reaffirmed 16 : 1, endorsed Bryan and denounced imperialism and trusts. The wording makes it clear that the monetary question still had priority.[15] The second district excluded 16 : 1 and placed the antitrust plank in the center.[16] As in most other local platforms, there was a plank endorsing Bryan, but there are also several other cases where it has obviously been decided not to go into the currency question. Thus the eleventh district had a confirmation of the Chicago platform of 1896 and placed the trust question before imperialism.[17] As early as May 1899 S. E. Morss, editor of the Indianapolis *Sentinel*, stated in a letter to Bryan that he did not believe that the silver issue ought to be paramount in the campaign of 1900.[18] Throughout 1899, Morss strove to tone down the currency issue and remove it from the current debate.

The situation was similar in the eighth district. The convention there was held on January 10 and was attended by over four hundred people from Adam and Wells counties. Since representatives from the other five counties of the district were present, there must have been many hundreds of Democrats, giving the convention a distinct grass-roots flavor. The resolutions adopted were headed by a plank reaffirming "our faith in the wisdom and justice of the principles laid down in the national democratic platform of 1896." So there was no reiteration of the 16 : 1 demand. It was followed by a plank endorsing Bryan. "The financial bill now pending before congress" was attacked and the exploiting financial interests, "the Money Kings of Wall Street," were castigated. The next plank concerned imperialism and established "that it is inconsistent with, and inimical to our republican form of government to exercise monarchial authority over foreign colonial dependencies." The resolution also contained a statement expressing sympathy with the Boers.[19]

The ninth district devoted its first plank to trusts and monopolies, the second to endorsing Bryan, and the third to expressing sympathy with the Boers—something most of the Democratic resolutions contained at this time—but did not mention the monetary question.[20] The sixth district went further, not only excluding 16 : 1 but omitting to endorse Bryan.[21]

Anti-imperialist planks were common in Indiana's Democratic district party platforms, but they did not usually occupy a dominant position. There was no question of it being a "paramount issue."

The information which can be gleaned from the press about resolutions passed at country conventions confirms this picture. They sometimes contained, however, detailed and aggressive anti-imperialist planks, which went much further than resolutions later adopted at the district conventions.[22]

There is no mistaking the doubt in people's minds about how far imperialism as an issue could be used in the coming campaign as a substitute for the silver question. This feeling of uncertainty was increased by reports in the press of Democrats in favor of expansionism. Thus in January the chairman of the Democratic committee in Benton County left his post in protest against Bryan's anti-imperialist agitation. He stated: "I believe that where ever one drop of an American soldier's blood has been shed, over that spot the stars and stripes should float for ever."[23]

Captain W. R. Myers from Anderson created much more of a stir. He had once been the Democratic Secretary of State in Indiana. At a conference for Democratic newspaper editors held in Indianapolis on February 1, Myers made a speech enthusiastically in favor of the new expansionist ideas. He claimed that the Democrats had always been "a party of expansion." "Our flag is in Cuba and is there to stay. It waves over Porto Rico and there it will float forever. Dewey planted it on the Philippine islands and there it will remain." Myers spoke powerfully in support of expansion on other occasions, and he was not alone in his views among the Democrats of Indiana.[24] From Grant county in the eleventh district came reports that one of the leading Democrats had changed party because he was an expansionist.[25]

There could hardly be a question of resolutions from Republican county and district conventions doing anything but expressing support for the foreign policy of the McKinley administration, in view of intimations that the Democrats would be making this one of the issues in the coming election. All the Republican district conventions included statements along these lines, although they were usually of a routine nature. The same applies to resolutions traced from Republican county conventions.

Three different expansionist motives dominate: what has previously been described as the "duty-line," commercial and economic advantages, and great power and national prestige. A typical example is a plank in a resolution passed at the fourth district's convention in North Vernon at the end of January, which combined these three aspects: "We glory in the extension of the Flag of our Fathers over the islands of the sea, introducing the blessings of freedom and civilization; making America's sphere of influence as wide as the World, and ushering in a new era of Commerce and markets for our products hitherto untouched." The Vevay *Reveille* declared this to be "sound Republican Doctrine." The theme recurred in a resolution adopted at a Republican "mass convention" in Lawrence county in the second district: "The Republican party is not afraid of expansion, but welcomes that destiny that carries our flag to the islands of the sea, not only bringing their people relief from oppression but gives them good government, and to us new fields for our growing trade, though it causes us to take our place among the nations of the earth."[26] The "duty line" was the most frequent, often combined with economic arguments. Above all the county convention resolutions which have been recorded show that the idea of national prestige also played a prominent role. An example is Elkhart in the thirteenth district which declared support of the McKinley administration's "policy of territorial expansion so as to place the United States on an equality with the Great Powers of the earth."[27]

As with the Democrats, resolutions from Republican county conventions give the impression of being more extreme than the district party platforms, probably because tactics and necessary compromises between different points of view modified the resolutions at the higher level.

It must once more be emphasized that foreign policy does not even dominate those resolutions which most fervently came down on the side of expansionism. The main motive here, as in the Republican press, was and remained the "prosperity" theme, often combined with panegyrics on sound money.

3

A recurring problem, in the absence of opinion polls, is how to get behind what was written in newspapers and political declarations and plumb attitudes and opinion at the grass-roots level. In the Charles Warren Fairbanks Collection in the Lilly Library in Bloomington there is material which is of considerable interest in this context.

The Republican congressmen of Indiana kept in touch with their constituents, but four of the districts were held by Democrats and it was there that they could expect to get the clearest indications about what their opponents had in mind. Here it was possible for Senator Fairbanks to carry out an investigation at the real grass-roots level. After his election Fairbanks had become the sole dispenser in Indiana of the offices being abandoned by outgoing Democrats.[28] He used this opportunity to build up a powerful organization.[29] Now, through local postmasters, many of whom stood directly in debt to him for their appointments, Fairbanks had access to observers and reporters who were perfectly placed. Fairbanks sent almost identical letters to over a hundred people, mainly postmasters, in southern and northeastern Indiana, plus a few other places—in other words, to the Democratic strongholds. He asked in the letters for immediate information as to how the person in question assessed the political situation in his district, which questions the people were discussing among themselves, what the general attitude was to the administration's policy on expansion, the currency and other questions, and what local people thought of the political prospects. In brief, Fairbanks wanted a concise political analysis, an account of the situation at the lowest level. About a hundred replies to

Fairbanks' letter are extant and they provide what was for this period a relatively unique example of the opinions of the people on a given occasion.

Roughly two-thirds of the answers came from counties which had a Democratic majority in the election of 1896. The value of the information that can be culled from these reports is increased by the fact that in several cases more than one person reported from the same county. Some counties provided up to six different reports, which can be compared.[30]

The replies sent to Fairbanks vary greatly in both quantity and quality, ranging from long, detailed accounts, which sometimes developed into discussions of current political questions, to short and sometimes relatively meaningless letters. They agreed in seeing the local political situation in an optimistic light and they referred consistently to the same reason for this: the prosperous times.

"Over the country politics is very quiet. The farmer has pocket money. His boy buys a buggy and his daughter takes piano lessons. Never since the high prices at the close and after the civil war has he felt as light of step and as optimistic. Merchants have closed a most prosperous year and factories are overloaded with orders."

Thus wrote Albert Shaw from Osgood, chairman of the Republican county committee in Knox county.[31] In 1896 the county had been won by the Democrats with a clear majority,[32] but according to Shaw the situation had since changed completely. He gave an uncommonly elegant summary of the important change which had taken place during the past three years in the economic situation in the United States, and which had brought about a radical change in the political situation. As the depression let up and the price of grain rose it was obvious that the Populists were bound to lose ground. But the Democrats were also making heavy weather of it and for the Republican administration the boom was invaluable.

Another correspondent from Knox county, A. G. Nicholson i Wheatland, pursued the same theme: "prosperous times, general satisfaction in all lines of business . . . nothing but fair sailing ahead with plenty of Republican enthusiasm."[33] The Democrats kept quiet and made little complaint, he continued. The good times had robbed their criticism of its sting. A third reporter from the same county, the postmaster in Freelandville, A. L. Osterhage, expressed the same opinion: "We can hardly find a Democrat here any more. They all has (!) confessed they never seen better times than this."[34] This theme recurred with only slight variations in many reports. It was often combined with some statement on the silver question.

According to the reports many Democrats in Indiana considered it

96

futile to enter the new campaign with a demand for free silver minting. The Democrats were pessimistic over "the prospect of a platform of 16 to 1," wrote Albert Shaw. Other reports from Knox,[35] Orange,[36] Decatur,[37] Sullivan,[38] Daviess,[39] Lagrange,[40] Martin,[41] Greene,[42] Jennings,[43] and Jackson[44] counties stated that the Democrats were no longer talking of free silver. It is claimed in the reports from Sullivan,[45] Greene,[46] Lagrange,[47] Daviess,[48] and Monroe[49] that the Silver-Republicans were expected to return to the Republican party. H. I. Dickinson from Epsom in Daviess county wrote: "I believe that the Demopops and the Silver-Republicans are in the transitional state and the majority of each will drift back to the old parties."[50] And from Steuben at the other end of the state came assurances from David M. Leard, Ray: "many strong advocates of 16 to 1 are swearing by McKinley and good times."[51]

The pictures given by reports of the situation in those Congressional districts of Indiana in which Republicans could expect to meet the hardest resistance is that prosperity had spiked the guns of the Democratic opposition. The silver question was considered obsolete and the administration could count on a large portion of good will, thanks to the good times. What then about the question which Bryan and the other opposition leaders were trying to make into the decisive factor in the coming campaign, "imperialism"? This issue is naturally mentioned in the reports, but a large proportion of them are silent on the subject. Other stated that the issue had not aroused much interest or created any opposition to speak of: "On expansion they say nothing,"[52] wrote C. N. Simmons from Schnellville in the strongly Democratic Dubois county, which he himself described as "the very Gibraltar of Democracy."[53]

Dubois county had a very considerable German population and Simmon's report is of interest in view of the fact that the German-language press in the United States was as a rule clearly anti-imperialistic.[54] German voters were expected to play a key role in the coming election campaign in Indiana.[55] They were far and away the most numerous immigrant group in the state, nearly five times as great as the Irish, who came second.[56]

A generally positive attitude to the Government's line was reported from Knox,[57] Crawford,[58]—both these counties had Democratic majorities in 1896[59]—Greene,[60] and Steuben.[61]

The Republicans supported McKinley's foreign policy regarding the newly acquired territories, according to many reporters, who sometimes also expressed enthusiastic approval of the new imperialism.[62] Of greater interest is that according to some reports the local Democrats were plainly in favor of expansionism. This applied to the strongly Democratic Sullivan county;[63] Martin county,[64] also Democratic in 1896 and Jennings county.[65]

In other districts the Democrats were said to be divided on the issue, for example in Democratic Allen county[66] and Orange county.[67]

In conclusion it can be said that none of Fairbanks' many reporters considered imperialism an issue of any real significance in the approaching election campaign. In many cases it was ignored and when it was discussed it was not thought to constitute any political risk. The Democrats were reported to be either indifferent, divided, or positive. There was nowhere any report of a united opposition to the policy of expansion pursued by the Government. On the contrary, in some cases expansion was seen as an asset for the election campaign. In general was it, however, considered of secondary interest. Insofar as they were expecting a battle on any issue, it was over the trusts and several of Fairbanks' scouts recommended a strong anti-trust plank in the coming party platform.[68] The prevailing optimism was based primarily on the belief that the Democrats had no issue for the campaign and imperialism was considered the least likely issue to fill the gap.

The Republicans seemed fully justified in their optimism over the election—the Democrats were divided and lacked a unifying issue. The reports sent to Fairbanks radiated confidence, seemingly well founded. And yet after no more than a few weeks the situation appeared fundamentally changed.

Gathering Storm

1

A study of the local press leaves no doubt that the Puerto Rican tariff bill provoked a strong reaction in Indiana. Newspapers that almost never discussed national issues leaped into the fight and took sides.

It has been pointed out that of the 250 local newspapers studied just over half made on some occasion a statement dealing with the policy of expansion. Most of these newspapers also took up the question of the tariff bill. The division along party lines has some interesting features.

Seventy-five of the newspapers concerned were Republican or Independent-Republican. Sixty of these had declared that they were in favor of expansionism in the form pursued by the McKinley administration. Indiana had a noticeable lack of Republican anti-imperialistic newspapers.

Those that were most strikingly pro-expansionist were minor newspapers, such as the Winimac *Republican*, English *News*, Tipton *Advocate*, Marion *Morning News*, Marion *Daily Chronicle*, Fairmount *News*, Vincennes *Commercial*, Vevay *Reveille*, Worthington *Times*, Madison *Courier*, Kokomo *Tribune*.

Remarkable is that of these sixty pro-expansionist newspapers nineteen declared themselves in favor of the Puerto Rican tariff bill, fifteen against it, and twenty-six did not decide one way on the other. The third alternative was naturally also a form of criticism. Party loyalty forbade them to join the critics, but they did not defend McKinley against their attacks. This means that only onethird of these pro-expansionist newspapers backed the administration and the party line.

Considering the violent storm that is reflected in the letters available from the period and that for a time shook the entire Republican party,[69] it may seem surprising that there were in fact so few Republican newspapers in Indiana that openly opposed the administration. The figure is misleading, however, since this group included many of the largest and most influential newspapers in the state, including the entire press of Indianapolis, which had an extraordinarily large circulation.

Among those responsible for the loudest opposition were also some of the provincial papers named above: the two Marion newspapers, and the Worthington *Times*, and others such as the Richmond *Evening Item*, Huntington *Herald*, and Hamilton *County Ledger*, to name just a few.

Of the pro-expansionist provincial newspapers listed above, the Madison *Courier*, Vincennes *Commercial*, English *News* and Kokomo *Tribune* came out in favor of the tariff bill, while the others chose to remain silent on the subject.

Most of the nineteen newspapers that supported the Puerto Rican tariff, moreover, were noticeably on the defensive. Only in a few cases was any enthusiasm expressed. In addition most of the declarations of support for the bill followed the speech made by Senator Fairbanks, which had considerable effect in reinforcing the party line and toning down the critics.[70]

It is worth noting that half a dozen Republican newspapers that had not taken sides on the question of foreign policy and expansionism now stood up in defense of the tariff bill. They have obviously been called up as supporting troops, closing the ranks in face of attacks which could have serious consequences in the coming election. The newspapers involved here included the Muncie *Morning Star*, La Porte *Herald*, Columbia *City Mail* and Huntingburg *Argus*.

Fifteen newspapers which had kept out of the fight between expansionists and anti-imperialists now joined the critics. Their earlier failure to commit themselves was naturally the result of lack of interest in these questions, but when the dispute now flared up and became so heated, forcing them to decide where they stood, they came down on the side of the critics. Newspapers such as Terre Haute *Tribune,* Clinton *Republican,* Muncie *Times* and the Anderson *Bulletin* fell into this group. To some extent the Indianapolis *Sun* can be included here, since it had been uncommitted on the subject of the policy of expansion but now joined the other Indianapolis papers in criticizing the Puerto Rican tariff.

The situation is simpler as far as the Democratic press is concerned. Forty-two of the fifty-five newspapers that had on some occasion during the period made some statement about expansionism or the Puerto Rican bill or both, followed a definite anti-imperialist line. This usually meant that they used the Democrats' standard arguments against McKinley. Active anti-imperialist agitation only occurred in a few cases, as in Indiana's leading Democratic newspaper, the Indianapolis *Sentinel.* The other more active anti-imperialist papers included the Columbia *City-Post,* Michigan *City-Dispatch,* Fountain-Warren *Democrat* (Attica), Winchester *Democrat,* New Albany *Public Press,* Terre Haute *Evening Gazette,* Columbus *Herald* and Tell City *News.* Most of the Democratic newspapers only brought out the usual arguments as a matter of routine and some papers showed clear pro-expansionist tendencies. As party tactics made the question inflamed, they were driven to attack something stamped as imperialism, at the same time as they declared themselves in favor of expansion. The pattern is easily recognizable. Among these newspapers that were really pro-expansionist, but which dutifully reported anti-imperialist criticism pro forma, were the Fort Wayne *Sentinel,* LaFayette *Weekly Journal* and a few others. Moreover, only about half of the Democratic newspapers studied took up an active anti-imperialist position.

Of the forty-two Democratic papers that showed some form of anti-imperialism during the period studied, thirty-two protested the Puerto Rican tariff, while ten made no comment. These ten were for the most part small newspapers that only mentioned national issues sporadically. The newspapers that conducted an active anti-imperialist line all leaped into the fight over the tariff bill.

It is hardly surprising that ten Democratic newspapers that had not previously taken any particular standpoint on imperialism now joined those attacking the administration.

In summarizing the results of the investigation, no direct visible connection exists between the Republican newspapers' views on expansionism and their attitude in the fight over the Puerto Rican tariff. Even strongly pro-expansionist publications were now among the most active opponents. The most common form of protest was passivity, failure to go to the defense of the Republican administration. It was only to be expected that the majority of the Democratic press-organs would join in the attack on the tariff bill. A number of the newspapers taking part in the debate, both Republican and Democrat, had not earlier during the period studied declared on expansionism, but now usually joined with the critics, although in a few cases they defended the line taken by the administration.

Concerning the regional structure of opinions expressed in the press, the material should not be pushed too hard. It is self-evident that the number of newspapers with a certain standpoint in no way gives a picture of the opinion situation. Also they vary greatly in size of circulation, frequency of publication, and interest for non-local questions. Certain traits can be noted. In the second, third, fourth and twelfth districts, the Republican press' criticism of the Puerto Rican tariff bill was of little significance, even taking into consideration the fact that above all in the southern districts the newspapers in question were few and small. The opposition was strongest in the sixth, seventh, eighth, ninth, eleventh and thirteenth districts. It was most noticeable in the ninth district, where the Indianapolis press naturally dominated the scene. The sixth district was second and there are many accounts of how intense and protracted the indignation of the Republicans was, above all in Richmond. Both the Richmond *Palladium* and the *Item* were bitter opponents to the tariff bill. The latter newspaper had an editor, J. Bennet Gordon, who was an ex-pansionist and who tried repeatedly to persuade the two Indiana Senators to try to stop the bill. In his opinion passage would mean defeat for the Republicans in Indiana.[71]

Support for the tariff from Republican newspapers was proportionately most powerful in the out-and-out Republican districts. Since the Democratic press, when it touched national issues, largely made use of the situation to attack the Republicans, the distribution of their standpoints has no features of any special interest.

2

The Indianapolis press deserves closer attention because of the size of its circulation, its geographical range, and its political importance. The Puerto Rican tariff bill was violently attacked from the very first in the *Sentinel,* the main Democratic journal in the state. The tone of criticism in the Indianapolis *News, Press* and *Journal* was hardly more restrained. The *Journal* took the lead in the fight against the Puerto Rican tariff and was considered by many to be responsible for the intensity of the opposition to the bill in Indiana. The attitude taken by the paper was decided by its editor, Harry S. New, and during March fruitless attempts were made to get him to give up his opposition.

The Indianapolis *Journal* was the most influential newspaper in the state and certainly helped form the attitudes of many local Republican publications. New was a prominent figure in the Republican party, appointed in May 1900 not only as Indiana's representative on the Republican National Committee but also to its Executive Committee. We have the opportunity of getting behind the standpoint taken by the newspaper, because Harry New discussed these problems in considerable detail in a correspondence with Senator Fairbanks, with whom he closely associated.

The Indianapolis *Journal* was decidedly pro-expansionist and was utterly negative to the propaganda of the anti-imperialists.

The *Journal* differed from many other Republican newspapers in being negative to the Boer question and opposed the idea that Congress should express sympathy for the Boer cause.[72] The paper was pro-British, as is shown by its support of the Hay-Pauncefote treaty, so strongly criticized in many quarters. It urged that the United States and Britain should "stand together and work together for the interests of the English-speaking race and Anglo-Saxon civilization."[73]

The *Journal* was in favor of retaining the Philippines, not only for the usual idealist-humanitarian reasons but for reasons of national interest.[74] The Open Door policy in China was praised and the newspaper insinuated that the anti-expansionism displayed in New England could stem from narrow-minded egotistical considerations. The enormous opportunities for commercial and economic expansion that would follow in the wake of expansion would primarily benefit the West and South in the United States, and be of lesser advantage to the Northeast region and so the anti-expansionism in New England is explained as fear of a change in the balance between the states.[75]

The anti-imperialistic Senators Hoar and Hale were dismissed as being un-American, stupid, senile and the big speech made on January 9 in the Senate by Senator Beveridge was reported with approval. Two points worth noting, however, are firstly, that the *Journal's* praise of the young senator from Indiana was amazingly moderate and balanced compared to that in many other newspapers, and secondly, that during the days following the speech the newspaper to a surprising extent reported not only the many declarations of assent and acclaim but also critical comments. There is a marked difference when a comparison is made with the Indianapolis *News*. The explanation is probably a matter of personal relations. Harry New was close to Fairbanks, while Hilton U. Brown of the Indianapolis *News* stood on good terms with Beveridge. A rivalry between the young, ambitious Beveridge and the senior senator was making itself felt here.

Immediately after McKinley's address in December the Indianapolis press, like most newspapers in the Middle West, came down on the side of free trade between Puerto Rico and the United States. When information started trickling out that the Ways and Means Committee was inclined to favor retaining some form of tariff, the *Journal* did not mince words. If the Committee defied the President's address, then it should be defeated. They should not, out of consideration for the Sugar and Tobacco trusts, turn aside from "plain duty."[76] What was right must weigh more heavily than the interests of the sugar and tobacco growers.[77]

At this point the *Journal* did not argue on the basis of any clearly formulated principles. An editorial published in the middle of January, however, did give the impression that the newspaper was of the opinion that a tariff would be unconstitutional. It stated that nobody claiming to have any acquaintance with logic could assert that a part of "United States territory is not part of the United States."[78] The line of argument is not quite clear and on other occasions it is simply said that wisdom, if nothing else, enjoined them to abolish the tariff,[79] and that consideration for the difficult situation of the Puerto Ricans should be reason enough.[80]

When the bill was presented in the House of Representatives, attempts were made to reach a compromise among the Republicans by making the tariff temporary. This compromise was firmly rejected by the *Journal*.[81]

Thus, like the *News*, and the *Press*, the Indianapolis *Journal* was unbending in its refusal to accept the tariff. On the whole no attempt was made to deny that Congress had the formal right to impose a tariff— although they were not clear on this point and were later to alter their standpoint—but they rejected a tariff as being unwise and inhuman and scented the interests of the trusts behind the changed bill.

The general line was the same as that of Republican newspapers such as the Minneapolis *Tribune,* Chicago *Inter-Ocean, Times-Herald, Record* and Milwaukee *Sentinel,* in other words many of the most important organs of the press in the Middle West.[52] When the bill was passed in the House of Representatives, a storm really broke. The entire Indianapolis press was united in condemnation. And during the weeks that followed, a campaign was conducted that was surprisingly heated. Senator Davis' suggested amendment, which would have repealed the part of the bill that imposed a tariff between Puerto Rico and the United States, was supported by the Journal.[53] The newspaper declared all the arguments that had been put forward to be untenable because they did not go to the root of the problem, "which is the demand for Justice, consistency and fair play."[54]

The compromise that had been concocted to make it possible for the Republican senators to agree, under which imports to Puerto Rico from the United States would be duty-free while a tariff of up to 15 % of the Dingley tariff would be imposed on exports, did nothing to change the attitude of the Journal.[55] The "plain duty" argument was stubbornly repeated and defined as "a moral as well as a political duty." If anything the *Journal* became more severe in its condemnation towards the end of the month, and started arguing along constitutional lines, in much the same way as the *Sentinel* and the other Democratic opponents of the Puerto Rican bill.[56] In an editorial published on April 2, that is, at a point when there was no longer any doubt that the bill would be passed, the *Journal* took up the constitutional question and achieved a compromise solution, which was not followed to its logical conclusions. It was stated that the Constitution followed the flag in the sense that when the flag was raised over new territory the inhabitants there came under the protection of the Constitution, while at the same time Congress acquired the right to institute laws and regulations for the area. The Constitution was a higher authority than Congress. This did not mean that "a territory is entitled to ultimate statehood," nor that its inhabitants became full citizens of the United States.[57]

The *Journal* had rather vague ideas about the constitutional side of the matter. When Beveridge made a speech on March 30, the *Journal* published an editorial expressing full agreement with Beveridge's "ethical" and moral arguments, but also stating that it could not accept his view that Congress had "unlimited power over new possessions irrespective of the Constitution."

There were other Republican newspapers with more decided opinions

104

on this aspect of the question. And the Democratic newspapers went straight to the point. "Suppressing the Constitution" was the heading given to an editorial in the Indianapolis *Sentinel* on February 3. A week later the heading was "Overthrowing the Constitution" and this line was maintained. In the opinion of the *Sentinel*, Congress had accepted the principle of imperialism.

At a very early stage the *Journal* had decreed that the legal and constitutional reasons against free trade for Puerto Rico were not relevant and mere pretexts: behind them lay the interests of the tobacco growers. In an editorial mentioned earlier that was published on January 31 under the heading *"Self-Interest and Anti-Expansionism,"* the newspaper claimed that opposition to free trade for Puerto Rico had the same root as anti-expansionism in New England, namely, "sectional and selfish considerations."[88]

The charge that the Puerto Rican tariff was the work of the sugar and tobacco trusts—sometimes the fruit trust were included—was a popular theme in the Democratic press, which often called the tariff "the sugar and tobacco trust tariff."

3

An even stronger impression of the violent reaction, not least among the Republicans in Indiana, when the Puerto Rican tariff bill was passed in the House at the end of February, can be obtained from the flood of letters that poured in to the two senators, Fairbanks and Beveridge. In one way this material is more interesting than the newspapers, since it reflects in quite a different fashion the currents of feeling both at the top and at different levels in the Republican party within the state. Moreover, the letters were not in the same way influenced by the necessary tactical considerations that often colored the leading editorials in the press. The stream of reports and letters reveals quite clearly that this was not just a question of feelings of irritation and indignation, but a state of panic.

Fairbanks and Beveridge received hundreds of letters from Republicans all over Indiana who predicted a catastrophic defeat if the Puerto Rican bill was not stopped in the Senate. The intensity and violence of the opposition is amazing. "I have never known in my thirty years' experience within the Republican organization as much disgust felt, and so generally felt," wrote the Auditor of State, W. H. Hart, to Fairbanks.[89] "The whole affair has spread like a wildfire of the prairie until it has reached the workingman, the precinct committeeman, and all classes ... In the barber shop, on the streetcars, at the clubs, in short in every public place, it is the one topic of conversation," claimed Harry S. New. Robert A. Brown, clerk at the Indiana Supreme Court, compared the opposition to "a political cyclone."[90] The mood of the Republicans in Indiana was approaching "open and positive revolt," wrote New, who claimed that 95 % of "leading and conservative" Republicans in the state were sworn opponents of the bill.[91]

Persons with prominent posts within the party and the state administration largely agreed with these opinions. Charles Wilson, Governor Mount's secretary, said that he was convinced that unless the bill was stopped, it would lead to defeat for the Republicans in the coming election. Many other letters expressed the same opinion. One of Fairbanks' closest associates was R. O. Hawkins. He had belonged to the Harrison group within the party,[92] but when Fairbanks continued to retain a firm hold on the party machine, Hawkins moved closer to the senior senator. Hawkins had visited Fairbanks in Washington at the end of February, and after returning to Indiana he wrote to the senator, giving a careful report of the mood in Indiana. He stated that he had found not only Indianapolis but the entire state in a perfect uproar over the Puerto Rican bill. He had never seen anything in politics to compare with it. Hawkins had tried to explain and to defend the bill, but without success. Even the leading Republicans were furious: "... Republicans seem to be absolutely stampeded ... Everybody declared that the party was gone, and this state would go democratic, and in the present condition of affairs, I believe they are right." County conventions had been held in a number of counties, including Marion county (Indianapolis) and it was only with the greatest difficulty that they had succeeded in preventing resolutions condemning the Puerto Rico tariff.[93]

Jesse Overstreet, the Republican congressman from the seventh district, had met the county chairman in his district and according to Hawkins was "thoroughly frightened." The county chairman had condemned the whole way in which the bill had been handled and even said they would be unable to appoint delegates for the National Convention who were for McKinley. Hawkins was worried. Personally he supported the bill, but like many others in Indiana he could see the whole affair turning into a political disaster. Instead of being sure of a simple victory the Republicans were forced to go on the defensive "and a defensive campaign is almost always disastrous."

The anger also encompassed McKinley, who was considered to have

106

broken the promise given in his annual address. That the President "had given evidence of weakness in a crucial moment," was a sentiment shared by many,[94] and there were people who predicted that he would suffer a bad defeat as a result of the Puerto Rican bill.[95]

It is worth noting that many of the Republicans, who claimed to be ardent expansionists, rejected the Puerto Rican tariff not mainly because of its catastrophic consequences for the Republicans' election prospects in Indiana, but because they considered it objectionable on principle. They made the same distinction as many Democrats at this time: "Expansion is one thing, and true imperialism is quite another. The people favor the former, in my opinion, but not the latter," wrote Martin Hugg, a close friend and supporter of Fairbanks of many years' standing.[96] Another letter-writer expressed the matter in a similar fashion: "While a large majority of the people of this country are unquestionably in favor of expansion, there are a great many who fear imperialism."[97] "No grander issue was ever presented in a campaign than that of expansionism ... I think we could easily sweep the state of Indiana with it, so long as we could appeal to the altruism of the people, to their nobility, to their willingness and desire to benefit other peoples."[98]

The impression that these critics had of the tariff was that it was a cold-blooded attempt to exploit a small, defenseless people, an act of imperialism in the very worst sense. "It certainly means imperialism with a vengeance,"[99] one letter from Indianapolis stated and similar notes were struck in other quarters: "The measure is vicious in principle and cannot possibly be defended in the campaign,"[100] "we can be charged with Imperialism in place of expansion. We Republicans have contended that the Democrats used the word imperialism for what is in fact Expansion,"[101] wrote someone else, and added that the new law could prove their opponents right.

The question of the trusts figured largely in many of the protesting letters that both Indiana senators received from their Republican voters. McKinley was accused of having capitulated to the sugar and tobacco trusts: "It looks to me as if the Sugar and Tobacco trusts have complete control of our President," wrote Beveridge's loyal supporter Frank Littleton to him.[102] In the same way rumors were circulating about the activity among the sugar and tobacco lobbyists in Washington.

As already pointed out the editor of the Indianapolis *Journal*, Harry S. New, was on good terms with Fairbanks. New's father, John C. New, had been a Harrison man, but his son, like several others in this situation, had gradually approached Fairbanks as he consolidated his position. New's violent opposition to the Puerto Rican bill, where he and Fairbanks were on different sides of the fence, did not appear to affect in any way the good relationship between the two men. It was largely thanks to Fairbanks' backing that New won the fight for the place as Indiana's representative on the Republican National Committee.[103] Fairbanks attempted, partly personally and partly through R. O. Hawkins, to convince New that he was wrong in his view of the tariff, or at least to temper his opposition.[104] New, for his part, did everything possible to influence Fairbanks and Beveridge, to persuade them to fight the bill, and he was fully convinced that he had the overwhelming share of the Republicans in Indiana behind him. He did not believe that the senators in Washington realized the depth of the indignation in their home state and tried by every means to drive home to them that passing the bill could mean a crushing defeat for the Republicans in Indiana: "and you cannot even now comprehend the intensity of feeling that exists on this subject. To me it is a revelation. It extends from General Harrison at one end, to the scraper in Kingan's pork house at the other and the entire gauntlet almost without exception."[105] New predicted that if the bill went through, the Republicans would not stand a chance of winning in a single Congressional district in Indiana, except in the tenth, Crumpacker's, the only one of the Indiana congressmen who voted against the bill.

New was naturally no stranger to tactical considerations, but he appears to have been convinced that the bill was inhuman, despicable and in addition dubious from a constitutional point of view. His letters reveal yet another important factor and something which should in fact be the key to the almost incomprehensible bitterness and vehemence with which he and many other Republican newspapermen fought the Administration's line. Charles Hernley, chairman of the Republican State Committee in Indiana, had opposed the bill from the start. When it got through in the House he succumbed to Fairbanks and the administration and changed his opinion. Not so New. The explanation is to be found in a letter to Fairbanks at the beginning of March:

"The trouble is that ever since the President said in December that it was our plain duty to establish free-trade relations with the people of Puerto Rico, the Republican press acting largely upon his advice has been manufacturing sentiment and shaping public opinion to that end. No man has ever had a party more solidly or more unitedly at his back than had Mr. McKinley, and they have accepted his position on this question

108

and talked it for three months. The Indianapolis *Journal* in common with other Republican papers of the country, has argued the pro's of this question until it loses all its influence when it takes up the cons to the abandonment of all that which it has been asserting as a principle enforced by sentiment. Had the President stated with frankness that he had changed his mind on the proposition before the bill of the Ways and Means Committee was reported, instead of permitting the Republican press to proceed for days upon the theory that the Committee was disregarding the wish of the Executive, and later permitting it to appear that his change of front was the result rather than the cause of this measure, matters might not have been quite so bad. In other words, the public mind should have been prepared in advance for this change of front, instead of being brought face to face with the passed bill—the fact accomplished."[106]

It also was clear that many of the protesting Republicans—including many of the most aggressive—were not reacting against the Puerto Rican bill because they considered it unconstitutional, imperialistic, immoral or the work of trust interests. Their rage stemmed from fear. They saw the run of events as an unforgivable political stupidity, because of the effect it could have on the coming election campaign, not only on the national level, but above all locally. Indiana was, as pointed out, a state in which the balance in many counties between Republicans and the Democrats was extremely sensitive and a swing of a few dozen voters could be decisive. In over twelve counties the margin had been less than a hundred votes in 1896 and in some cases it was no more than a dozen or two.

At the beginning of the year the prospects of the Republicans had appeared extremely good. The Democrats lacked an issue which could attract voters. This deficiency had now been made good and the Republicans had been forced on the defensive. Charles W. Moore wired from Indianapolis to Fairbanks after the bill had passed in the House: "Republicans overwhelmingly against Puerto Rico tariff. It offers Democrats their only positive issue and puts Republicans on defense in an utterly untenable position."[107] Variations on the theme by other correspondents were: "The Republicans are giving one more club to the Democrats,"[108] "they are putting a club into the hands of the Democrats to break our skulls with,"[109] "it will give a club of imperialism to the Democrats to break over our necks in the coming campaign. Without this wretched bill the Democrats would be left without an issue."[110]

A comparison of the many protests sent to the two Indiana senators and the arguments put forward in the Republican press reveals a marked and in itself quite natural difference. The newspaper editorials naturally did not give way to the same panic-stricken reactions, the same categorical predictions of a Democratic victory in the state in the event of the bill being passed. Nor did they express as openly what was obviously for many of those writing the letters the dominating reason for their condemnation of the tariff, namely, the fear of its effect on the coming election campaign in the state. The trust arguments dominated, together with those referring to humanity and principle.

It is naturally not always easy to decide how much of the opposition sprang from tactical considerations and how much was indignation over the content of the bill, but the hundreds of letters that both Republican senators received came largely from Republicans working in local politics, right down to precinct level, and in a considerable number of cases it is clear that it was fear of the political effect in Indiana and not discontent with the bill that was behind the opposition. This meant that as soon as it became plain that the effect in Indiana was only temporary or that fears had been exaggerated, the storm against the Puerto Rico tariff should subside.

The Senators, the Bill and Republican Intra-party Politics in Indiana

1

From 1882 to 1894 the Democrats had control of the Indiana legislature. Indiana was represented in the Senate by two stalwart Democrats, David Turpie and Daniel W. Vorhees. The depression and the crisis which had befallen the Democratic party during the Cleveland administration put an end to the dominance of the Democrats in Indiana, and it had in any case never been overwhelming. McKinley's victory over Bryan in 1896 had confirmed the defeat of the Democrats and the Republicans now began what was to be a long period of control of the legislature of Indiana, though with only small majorities in the beginning. In 1897 Vorhees' term in the Senate came to an end and the legislature that was now dominated by the Republicans appointed Charles Warren Fairbanks, a successful, wealthy young attorney who had spent the previous years building up his Republican machine in Indiana in defiance of the supporters of ex-President Harrison.[111]

Turpie's term as senator expired in 1899. Thus his successor was to be appointed by the legislature elected in November 1898. The Republicans had even greater success in this election.[112] There was no doubt that a

Republican would be appointed. That Beveridge should win, however, was something of a sensation.

Beveridge was young, only thirty-six. He had the handicap of coming from Indianapolis, which already had one senator. Without being a Harrison man, he was not on the best of terms with Fairbanks. His greatest asset was his popularity, acquired through his brilliant public speaking, demonstrated during the years as he travelled all over the state and outside it, speaking tirelessly for the Republicans. Irrepressible energy, unlimited self-confidence, burning ambition, and an immovable conviction that he was called to play an important part in the new era that had started were the hallmarks of his political image and he had been noticed at an early stage, in connection with the Spanish-American War, as being one of the most enthusiastic and eloquent of the imperialists. He had an unmistakable appeal, above all for younger voters. Beveridge gained a not unimportant power base in Indiana when in 1898 his friends were elected into the legislature: Frederick Joss in the Senate, Mr. Noel, Alfred M. Glossbrenner, and Lars A. Whitcomb in the House, while Frank Littleton became Speaker.[113]

Beveridge's election to senator in 1899 was not simply or even primarily a result of his political assets or his and his friends' purposeful and skillful campaign. He was accepted as a compromise candidate in the struggle between factions of the Republican party in Indiana: on the one side stood the Fairbanks machine that had as its candidate Frank Hanly, former congressman and later governor, and on the other the Harrison group that was more divided but that backed Judge Robert S. Taylor of Fort Wayne.[114]

When it became obvious during the ballot in the Republican caucus that the only way of preventing the election of Hanly was to back Beveridge, all those opposed to Hanly and Fairbanks cast their votes for him, the scales tipped and Beveridge received the votes of all the Republicans. This was a decided defeat for Fairbanks and it created an atmosphere of distrust which persisted long after the election. It was also rumored that President McKinley had done his best to prevent Beveridge's election, in Fairbanks' interest.[115]

2

The storm of protest in Indiana was directed with particular violence against the Republican congressmen who had voted for the tariff bill. The only one who voted against it was Crumpacker, who was consequently praised to the skies in the press. Watson of the seventh district, where the Republicans were especially savage, was bitterly attacked and forced in the end to obtain permission from the President to inform his constituents that he had voted for the bill in response to the urgent and very insistent request of the President.[116]

The final decision would come in the Senate, and severe pressure was brought to bear upon the two Indiana senators to persuade them to take up the fight against the administration's line. The situation was extremely serious. Both the McKinley administration and the Republican establishment in Congress had staked their prestige on a line that was now not only being fought by the Democrats but seemed to have aroused a violent storm in all political camps and that penetrated deep into the most reliable Republican ranks. The storm centered on the Middle West, not least Indiana, and since in this state the balance between the two main political parties was so precarious, there was a risk that the election might bring substantial changes.

Both senators were aware of the pressure. There was an additional complication, since it was no secret that relations between the senior and the junior senators were such that an open fight for power might develop within the party. Fairbanks controlled the party machine, but Beveridge was ambitious. An earlier close acquaintance and colleague of Beveridge's described him as "bold—conceives himself a prophet and speaks out and believes that he is the reincarnation of Hamilton."[117] His sensational debut in the Senate, the renown he had so quickly acquired on the national level, encouraged him and his supporters to dream ambitious dreams for the future, realization of which would involve a threat to the aspirations of Fairbanks.

The two senators and rivals reacted to the challenge in ways that reflected not only their different experience and temperament, but illuminated the problem that we are primarily interested in here, that is to say, the role of foreign policy in the political life of the individual states and the converse problem, the possibility of political circumstances on the micro-level shaping national policy on foreign affairs.

Beveridge had from the start taken foreign policy as his speciality, in particular the policy of expansion and its problems. In January not only the Senate but the entire nation had listened attentively to what he had to say. Now a struggle developed that concerned nothing less than the foundations of the new policy. It was naturally tempting for Beveridge to throw himself into the fight. Most important from his point of view was to prevent a decision which could be interpreted as acceptance of the doctrine that the Constitution followed the flag. At the same time he saw the storm of public opinion as a threat to the policy of expansion as a whole. The natural way out was a compromise and that was what Beveridge tried to accomplish.

Before taking any action he tested his idea for a compromise by submitting it to several political experts for their opinion. These were partly political friends in Indiana, partly newspapermen such as Paul Dana, editor of the New York *Sun*, H. H. Kohlsaat, editor of the Chicago *Times-Herald*, Albert Shaw of the *Review of Reviews*, J. C. Shaffer and Harry S. New of the Indianapolis *Journal*, John H. Holiday, Indianapolis *Sun*, and Hilton Brown of the Indianapolis *News*. He sent them all a confidential letter in which he sketched the outlines for a compromise, by which an amendment to the bill would make all imports to Puerto Rico from the United States duty-free, while exports from the island would be subject to a duty charge up to 25 % of the Dingley tariff. The argument he gave in his letter was not original, and it had become the standard answer of those defending the tariff: "The exports from that country to this country are sugar, tobacco and coffee, and these are exported by the great land-owners of the Island, nearly all of whom are Spaniards living in Spain. Every dollar of the revenues thus produced would come out of alien pockets, and be used exclusively for the welfare of the Island."[118]

The circular is dated March 7. Beveridge rejected the idea that the Constitution should also encompass the newly acquired territories. He declared it to be nonsense and like Whitelaw Reid asserted that if annexation made them into a part of the United States then it would be best to release them immediately: "Puerto Rican, Philipino and Hawaiian Senators and Congressmen are not a refreshing prospect."[119]

The answers that Beveridge received to his outlined compromise were not encouraging. He had, however, the wholehearted support of, for example, Albert Shaw, who considered Beveridge's standpoint to be absolutely right and justified.[120] New and Brown emphatically dismissed the suggestion. They were not prepared to accept any kind of tariff. They claimed it was a question of justice and principle and Brown tried to convince Beveridge that his great opportunity here was to go against the bill, which would gain him popularity.[121] Another letter sent at the beginning of March said that the young senator had "the political chance of his lifetime."[122]

Another of Beveridge's close friends and confidants in Indianapolis, Lars A. Whitcomb, a member of the Indiana House of Representatives, was one of those who had worked most energetically to get Beveridge elected as senator and he was dubious of the junior senator's proposed amendment. He wrote that the people would see it as a concession to the sugar trusts. Some thought the President's change of mind was the result of pressure from the tobacco trust and Whitcomb said that he had never heard "such a general out-cry against a proposed law" as that which he had experienced in Indiana since the Puerto Rico bill had got through in the House. The congressmen who had returned to Indiana to be nominated had had a difficult time. In some cases their situation was "almost pitiable." Whitcomb was in favor of duty-free trade between Puerto Rico and the United States, not only for reasons of political tactics, but because he did not believe that Puerto Rico should be treated differently from other "states and territories of the Union."[123]

Frank Littleton, Speaker of the Indiana House of Representatives, and a friend to whom Beveridge was always prepared to listen, energetically backed up the young senator in opposition to the tariff. Littleton suggested to Beveridge that if he did not go against the Puerto Rican tariff he would lose everything that he had gained by his "Philippines speech."[124] In answer to Beveridge's circular he said that he shared Beveridge's view that there was no constitutional objection that could prevent Congress from doing what it liked with Puerto Rico. When he gave the reasons for his opinion, he like so many others did not argue consistently and his arguments against the tariff included some that were unmistakably constitutional. Littleton warned Beveridge against taking up a position contrary to what he had said earlier in his famous speeches, "The March of the Flag" and "The Philippines." Littleton claimed that if anything opposition to the bill had grown in Indiana and quoted several examples. He was against Beveridge's suggested compromise, not so much because of principles of the matter, but from a political point of view: the worst thing about the whole situation was not so much the Puerto Rican tariff but the fact that the Democrats opposed expansion and "could argue with telling effect that if little Puerto Rico has raised so much trouble as one of our foreign possessions what end of trouble may we not expect when we get into the Philippine question and Cuba?"[125]

Frederick A. Joss, another of Beveridge's lawyer friends,[126] was if possible even more negative both to the bill and Beveridge's suggestion for a compromise. In his opinion there was from the point of political tactics only one answer. Only one thing could save the Republicans from a catastrophic defeat, namely, absolute defeat of the administration measure in the Senate, and establishment of a territorial form of government in Puerto Rico. He considered that the introduction of a tariff between the island and the United States was, if not formally unconstitutional, nevertheless unjust and objectionable:

"In the people's mind Puerto Rico is a part of the United States as much as Arizona ... Any effort to create a new class of territory belonging to the United States, which has not the rights heretofore given to American citizens, will be imperialism, which the people of all classes are unalterably against. The people believe in expansionism: they believe in our mission to extend the blessing of our government to all lands over which our flag has waved, and they mean such a form of government as we have adopted towards the territories possessed by us during the last thirty years, and the people are right."

Joss was close to being an integrationist and for him as many others the dividing line between expansion and imperialism followed the boundary between incorporation and integration on the one side and colonialism on the other. He did not go so far as to claim that the Constitution follows the flag.

Like Littleton and many other critics of the Puerto Rican bill, Joss puts his finger on the sore point. At this time the Democrats had the trusts as their main target of attack. The Republicans had the confidence of the voters, but below the surface there was distrust of "centralization of power," "accumulation of power in the hands of centralized capital." And all these fears had now been awakened by the Puerto Rico bill. The people saw the hand of the trusts behind the President's change of course, "evidence of the power of concentrated capital and an evidence of the purpose of concentrated capital to centralize power and break up the territorial system which has existed for thirty years in territories of the United States not one wit less hard to control and govern than Puerto Rico."[127]

Many letters struck the same note. E. H. Hart, the state auditor, insistently urged Beveridge to go against the bill.[128] Newton W. Gilbert from Angola, shortly to become Republican candidate for Lieutenant Governor,[129] was one of the many who did the same. Angola and Steuben county were centers of criticism of the Puerto Rico bill.[130]

Harry S. New, editor of the Indianapolis *Journal* and Hilton U. Brown, editor of the Indianapolis *News*, wanted an uncompromising fight, as did Frank Payne, owner of both the *News* and the *Press*.[131]

115

Morris Ross of the Indianapolis *News* was one of Beveridge's friends among the newspapermen of Indianapolis and he condemned the Puerto Rico bill as emphatically as Harry New. As early as February 28, Ross declared that passage of the Puerto Rican tariff would mean loss of Indiana for McKinley, whom he described as being a weak opportunist: "His submission in the Puerto Rican tariff bill, eating his own words, swallowing his own position, will endow him with the contempt of many people." Ross saw it all as the work of the trusts.[132] The editor of the Indianapolis *Sun*, Fred L. Pussley, was equally caustic, considering what had happened to be the result of McKinley's cowardice.[133]

Beveridge listened to the many appeals made to him to fight the bill and he participated in discussions with the Republican members of the Senate, who tried to find ways of compromising. His negative attitude was noted, but Beveridge was realistic enough to hesitate before committing himself to rejection as urged by the Indianapolis press and many of his Republican friends. The proposed compromise that he sent around for comment had not met with much approval and it seems as if this encouraged the young senator to sharpen his attitude. Beveridge was hard pressed, however, and he vacillated backwards and forwards. His wife was dying and he felt strong pressures being brought to bear on him from a number of different quarters. Charles G. Dawes had been deeply impressed after Beveridge's speech on January 9 by the young senator's "wonderful intellect" and wrote in his diary: "His views of broad questions are correct always. He makes no mistakes from the public's point of view." Dawes went so far in his admiration as to admit to Beveridge "the right of genius like his to exact recognition from some rules of conduct which govern those of us less gifted."[134] But now Dawes was greatly worried, perhaps not so much over Beveridge's opinions, as over his behavior and he deplored his young friend's "indecision at such a time of individual crisis."[135]

On March 19 Beveridge presented a suggestion for a compromise to members of the Republican harmony committee in the Senate. His proposal included abolition of all tariffs between Puerto Rico and the United States and thereby satisfied the critics. At the same time it contained a categorical statement of support for the principles upon which the McKinley administration was acting and of rejection of the argument of their opponents: "this act shall not be construed as extending the Constitution of the United States, or any part thereof, over Puerto Rico."

Members of the committee were largely positive to the proposed compromise and it was said that the President, who had been informed, was well-disposed. Beveridge seemed to hold the solution of the crisis in his hand. But then he proceeded to make a fatal mistake. Instead of letting the older Republican senators take over his suggestion and present it as their own, he presented it himself in the Senate in his own name. This was almost unforgivable of a young debutant in the Senate. The matter worsened when it became known that Beveridge intended to make a speech when presenting the proposal. In his biography of Beveridge, Claude G. Bowers explains Beveridge's behavior as the result of "inexperience and his ignorance of the traditional attitude towards new members."[136] There might be something in this. But the attitude of senators towards newcomers was no secret but a rooted, wellknown custom. The more probable explanation is that the exceptionable success of Beveridge's big speech at the beginning of the year had caused him to overestimate his position. He was ambitious and filled with a feeling that he had been called to speak for a new era and new problems, and he now saw a chance of taking the center of the stage in a question occupying the thoughts of the whole nation and where he had already made a name for himself.

Even if the great majority of the letters Beveridge received from Indiana condemned the Puerto Rico bill, they also concluded warning voices, particularly toward the end of March. These emanated partly from some of Beveridge's friends, who anxiously saw what he was going to do and were afraid that it would be a threat to his political future. Beveridge's young friend and great admirer, Leo Rotschild, urged him to take care: "I was surprised that you were going to make a speech. It strikes me as a very dangerous thing to do."[137] Whatever standpoint Beveridge advocated, he was bound to get a large group of Republicans in Indiana against him. Rotschild also warned him of the reaction that could be expected from the congressmen from Indiana, all of whom, with exception of Crumpacker from the tenth district, had voted for the bill.[138]

Beveridge's friends were not the only ones who were beginning to get worried. At first the storm against the Puerto Rican tariff had swept with it most of the leading Republicans in Indiana. When it became clear that McKinley had no intention of giving way, and that the Senate was prepared to bring about a compromise that would mean a limited tariff, the state party organization started to get wary. With the election so close they could not afford to be on bad terms with the administration. Instead they decided that the best way out would be to tone down the opposition and remove the question from the agenda as quickly as possible. When politicians in Indiana then heard that Beveridge intended to speak against the bill and thus go against the administration, they were extremely uneasy.

On March 28 a meeting was held in Indianapolis of the Republican State Central Committee, at which chairmen of the party committees of the congressional districts reported. The treasurer of the committee, Beveridge's friend Henry W. Bennet, was then asked to report to Beveridge, in an obvious attempt to persuade him to be moderate. According to Bennet's letter, the storm among the Republicans against the Puerto Rican tariff had subsided in most places. There was discontent in the *second, fourth, seventh, tenth, eleventh,* and *twelfth* districts, but it was considerably less than before. Elmer Crocket from South Bend, chairman of the thirteenth district's party committee, described the entire Puerto Rico agitation as "a tempest in a tea-pot" and several others had expressed similar opinions.

Bennet's letter was biased. The committee declared that it would be best if a quick compromise could be achieved in the Senate. The Republicans in Indiana would be sure to accept this once it was accomplished and support the decision. If the conflict were to be prolonged, and the decision postponed, the consequences could be serious, leading to a breach within the party that would be hard to heal. They advised against opposing a compromise on the question.[139]

Beveridge's maiden speech had been a striking success for the young Hoosier politician, an overwhelming triumph.[140] It is perhaps not so strange that this success should cause him to overrate the position he had attained, to overlook the risk of suffering a setback. He could not say that he was not warned. Among others, his friend Lars Whitcomb wrote an anxious letter from Indiana, reminding him of "the value of silence." But Beveridge was not prepared to take the warning.[141]

The junior senator was really to speak on March 30, but Senator Proctor agreed to change with him so that he could speak on the 29th and then travel home to his wife. Several days before Beveridge was to make his speech, rumors started that "the graybeards" intended to make use of the occasion "to clip his wings". As early as March 21, Charles G. Dawes had warned his friend of what was brewing and had tried to hold him back.[142] The rumors were true. When Beveridge started to speak the Senate Chamber was full. But he had not had time to say more than a few words before almost all the senators left the room, and several of the few who remained demonstrated their lack of interest in what the speaker had to say by carrying on whispered conversations or rustling their papers. The contrast to the reception Beveridge's big speech on the Philippines had received on January 9 could not have been greater. The senators achieved the effect they had desired: Beveridge was heartbroken. The cruelty with which the senators had humbled the young senator from Indiana was, however, in many cases strongly criticized in the press.

The content of Beveridge's speech was in no way sensational. He spoke against the Puerto Rican tariff, but combined this criticism both with a categorical statement that the island was not covered by the Constitution and with a declaration that if a compromise could not be reached giving free trade to Puerto Rico, he intended to support the original bill. The weakening of Beveridge's stand was partly due to a last minute effort by Dawes and another friend, George Perkins, who on the evening of March 28 came over and urged the Hoosier to fall into line.[143] As a result he placed himself between chairs. His mistake was not only that he challenged the Republican establishment within the Senate, but that he misjudged the political situation that arose from the fight over the Puerto Rican tariff.

3

Fairbanks had far more political experience than Beveridge. The senior senator was more rooted in Indiana and controlled the Republican machine in the state. Charles Hernley and Warren Bigler, chairman and vice-chairman of the State Central Committee, were his men and he had links with many of the district and county chairmen and other politicians on the local level. The information he could glean was more valuable than that which Beveridge could get from his friends. Beveridge's popularity was more spectacular and his eloquence as a public speaker far superior. It was only a superficial popularity, however, without corresponding political power. The senior senator was much more cautious and showed better judgement.

Like Beveridge, Fairbanks received large numbers of letters during the first week in March, all attacking the bill passed by the House. But while the junior senator listened more to those who spoke of "a chance of a lifetime" than to those who warned of "a very dangerous thing" and soon declared opposition to the tariff, Fairbanks bided his time and tried to quieten the opposition. Both senators sought information about the mood of Republican voters. But while Beveridge wrote early in March to his friends in Indianapolis and to several newspapermen, who were often already in the fight, to get their reaction to his proposed compromise,

Fairbanks waited until the middle of the month. And it is significant that he then turned to the men holding key positions in the party organization in the state, politically experienced and strategically placed observers. Fairbanks asked for a report from each of the Republican district committee chairmen in Indiana. He had received some reports which suggested that the talk of a stampede among the Republicans of Indiana was not correct. As early as March 4, D. R. Lane, secretary of the Senate in Indiana, had written a reassurring report in which he placed most of the blame for the storm of opinion on the Chicago newspapers.[144] More important was a letter sent on March 8 from Elmer Crocket of South Bend, editor of the South Bend *Tribune* and chairman of the Republican District Committee in the thirteenth district. According to Crocket opinion was beginning to swing the other way and he did not think it would be long before "all good Republicans will acknowledge that the President is right."[145] At the same time G. W. Farrell reported a similar view among the farmers of the district.[146] From Miami county which belonged to the eleventh district but bordered on to the thirteenth, came further soothing assurances: "In thirty days, my prediction is, there will be no further talk on the whole subject."[147]

During the days that followed, several letters with similar content arrived, but the majority was still critical of the bill and bore witness to the panic that had gripped Republicans. This applied particularly to the reports from Indianapolis and Marion county, where New and others still predicted a catastrophe for the Republicans in Indiana if the Puerto Rican bill was passed.

Fairbanks took no rash action. At the same time as he tried to further the bill's chances in the Senate and diminish opposition from the Republican senators, he was careful not to do anything that might threaten the Republican position in Indiana. Thus on March 15 he wired all the Republican district chairmen and asked for reports on what was happening in the districts. During the next few days he received their answers and it is probable that it was what they had to say that decided Fairbanks as to which line he would take.

Fairbanks had started to work for a compromise, but he made no secret that he stood on the side of the party and the administration. "I always try to hold myself in such a position as to support the party faithfully whenever it decides upon a policy," he wrote to New.[148]

The different ways in which Fairbanks and Beveridge approached the problem of sounding out how the ground lay before taking any action over the Puerto Rican bill provide an excellent illustration of their differing outlooks. Fairbanks turned to the chairmen of the Republican committees in the congressional districts, that is to say, people who not only had opportunities of judging the mood among the rank and file Republicans in their districts, but also were key people in the Republican party machine of Indiana.

The answers Fairbanks received gave the following picture. It was reported from the *tenth district*, which comprised the counties farthest to the northwest, nearest Chicago, that the majority of the Republicans were still against the Puerto Rican tariff.[149] In the *twelfth*, which had a Democratic majority, there was opposition.[150] Reports from the *eleventh* and *thirteenth* districts spoke of a swing in opinion, despite continued agitation by the Chicago press. Crocket reported "a decided change favorable to Puerto Rican bill,"[151] and Warren Bigler declared that the situation had improved considerably during the past ten days.[152] The *ninth* district struck nothing but notes of optimism: "Sentiment overwhelmingly with President."[153] The same applied to the *first, third* and *fifth* districts,[154] and the *fourth* was also said to be out of danger, even though there still was some discontent over the bill.[155] There is no answer from the *eighth* district on record, but a week or so later one reporter wrote that the Republicans of the district gave their loyal backing to the policies of the administration.[156] The *second* and *seventh* districts were still dominated by the opposition in Indianapolis, but Charles Hernley, chairman of the Republican State Central Committee, wired that the situation had improved during the past few weeks.[157] Hernley added that although the Indianapolis press was frantically fighting the bill, large sections of the provincial press were "with the President on the proposition and uphold the action of the House," a statement which was plainly an exaggeration. And in a letter of March 23, Hernley claimed the storm over the Puerto Rican bill was now limited to Indianapolis and Richmond.

Fairbanks kept in touch with Hernley and during the most critical weeks in March they exchanged a long series of letters and telegrams. Fairbanks made his position clear. "It is my purpose to stand by the administration. It has stood by me and I shall not desert it."[158]

At the beginning Hernley, as mentioned, had been as opposed to the Puerto Rican tariff as New, but he returned converted from a visit to Washington during the first days of March and thereafter devoted all his energy to quietening the opposition.[159]

For the senior senator the whole problem was not too complicated. For him unity of the party was of paramount interest. "Free trade or a tariff for Puerto Rico is of insignificant consequence compared with the solidarity of the Republican party."[160] In a letter Hernley expressed the great satisfaction that both he and the entire state committee felt over the attitude taken by Fairbanks: At the same time he hinted that members of the committee were dissatisfied with and anxious about Beveridge's activities. It was also at this point that the Central Committee approached Beveridge through the agency of Henry W. Bennet, in an attempt to restrain the junior senator.[161]

It is perfectly obvious that Fairbanks had far more comprehensive and discerning information about the situation in Indiana and the reaction among Republicans in different quarters than Beveridge, and he could base his decision on a much more realistic view of the affair.

On March 31, Fairbanks spoke in the Senate on the pending Foraker bill. He reviewed and defended in detail the administration's point of view and arguments, and the speech was afterwards printed and widely distributed in an effort to tone down the criticism. He stated that the conflict involved two questions: "One is a question of Congressional power and the other a question of national policy."

Fairbanks then went on to say that the controversial question of whether the Constitution automatically applied to acquired territory could only be decided by the Supreme Court and until such a decision had been reached Congress should retain the greatest possible freedom of action. Thus Fairbanks' line was that as long as the Supreme Court had not expressly established that the Constitution should be extended to newly acquired territory *ex proprio vigore*, Congress should act as if that were not the case. He also advised against any immediate decision on the incorporation of Puerto Rico, since the Puerto Ricans were not mature enough for all this would imply, such as the right to trial by jury.

Fairbanks repeated Foraker's arguments:[162] The annual cost of governing and administrating Puerto Rico was about 2 million dollars. There was no possibility of covering this expense by direct taxation. There was no question of arranging a loan before some form of government had been organized on the island. Customs receipts were a question of a tariff for revenue and not a protective tariff. It involved only 15 % of the Dingley tariff and it would apply only to exports from Puerto Rico to the United States.

Fairbanks spoke at length in refuting accusations that the tariff had been imposed to favor interests of the trusts. He claimed that as Puerto Rico exported raw sugar and the sugar trust was primarily occupied with the refinement of sugar and used raw sugar for the purpose, the Sugar trust could not benefit from this tariff.

The situation was similar for the Tobacco trust. Here again raw tobacco was used and that was what Puerto Rico exported. Opposition to imports from Puerto Rico could well come from tobacco farmers, but hardly from the trust. Fairbanks was naturally simplifying the problem here. Above all he ignored the fact that really the fight did not at all concern Puerto Rico's relatively insignificant production of both sugar and tobacco.[163]

4

At the end of March, the Indianapolis *News* (Ind. Rep.) undertook an interesting survey of public opinion in Indiana.[164] The survey investigated political attitudes and reactions to the coming election and covered eight cities: Evansville, Richmond, LaFayette, New Albany, South Bend, Terre Haute, Anderson and Muncie. The target population was men who in 1896 had voted for either Bryan or McKinley. They were asked how they would vote in the 1900 election if the same candidates were nominated. If they had changed horses they should state their reasons, and they were asked what they felt about current political questions. In all, the group consulted included 342 Democrats and 373 Republicans.

The result was as follows:

	Voted for Bryan in 1896	Will vote for Bryan this year	Will vote for McKinley this year	Doubtful this year
Democrats				
Evansville	56	53	1	2
Richmond	31	25	2	4
LaFayette	42	41	0	0
New Albany	36	36	0	0
South Bend	63	55	2	6
Terre Haute	39	37	2	..
Anderson	50	47	0	3
Muncie	35	30	2	3

	Voted for McKinley in 1896	Will vote for McKinley this year	Will vote for Bryan this year	Doubtful this year
Republicans[165]				
Evansville	56	26	1	29
Richmond	52	41	2	9
LaFayette	48	48	0	0
New Albany	36	36	0	0
South Bend	63	45	9	9
Terre Haute	43	40	3	..
Anderson	50	50	0	0
Muncie	25	23	0	2
Totals	373	309	15	49

The Democrats are strikingly stable. In no case are there more than a couple of former Bryan supporters who have decided to vote for McKinley, and the doubtful column also has low figures. This poll was taken at a point when the party had not committed itself to a reiteration of 16 : 1. This cannot have had any great significance for the Democrats asked here, however, since all of them had supported that issue in 1896.

The Republican table is by far the more interesting and it reveals a noticeably lesser degree of stability. While more than 8 % of the 1896 Bryanites asked were doubtful or had decided to desert their party, the corresponding figure for Republicans is over 17 per cent, more than double. In South Bend the figure is almost 30 per cent and in Evansville the situation was critical, with over half coming in the doubtful column. These are exceptions. Corresponding figures are low for the other cities, apart from Richmond which is over 20 %.

But Evansville, South Bend and Richmond were responsible for almost all the defections. There was an additional factor, which obviously largely contributed to the high number of defectors or doubtfuls, namely, that the material included a number of Gold Democrats, who had voted for McKinley in 1896. This applied in particular to South Bend where all the defectors came in this category.[166]

A point of interest is naturally the motives given for the swings in the cities in question. Discontent with the McKinley administration was reported from Evansville. The primary reason was said to be the Puerto Rican tariff question. The secondly motive mentioned was "McKinley's attitude towards trusts and friendship for England." According to the report, "many frankly confessed that they could not conscientiously indorse the administration's present policy in these affairs, and unless a change occurred between now and election day, they would vote against McKinley." South Bend reported discontent among the Republicans for the same reasons, although in the opposite order: McKinley's "seeming favoritism on trusts, and his shifting attitude on the Puerto Rican tariff measure." In fact these two issues are linked, since agitation against the Puerto Rican tariff bill had as its main argument that it was a measure dictated by the trusts. Richmond, the third city which was problematic for the Republicans, gave exactly the same picture. All those reported as being doubtful referred to McKinley's policy on the tariff bill.

Reports from several of the other cities mentioned the Puerto Rican question. From LaFayette it was said that the question had given rise to a heated debate, but that the storm was beginning to die down and most of the former critics now considered McKinley's attitude justifiable since the issue had come to center on the right of Congress to legislate for the islands. On this issue no Republican losses were expected. The Puerto Rican problem was of no importance in New Albany or Terre Haute and no change was expected among Republicans. There was still some discontent over the Puerto Rican tariff in Anderson, but not so much that any of the Republicans hesitated to back McKinley. Finally, according to the report, Muncie had a floating vote in the factory districts. The workers in the gas belt were sensitive on the question of the trusts, and although the Republicans usually retained the majority, not much was needed to disturb the balance. The Republicans would have to do something to show they were prepared to tackle the trusts. No mention of Puerto Rico was made.

Information about the Gold Democrats is of interest, although reports from South Bend and Anderson were the only ones to have such information. Other reports spoke only of Republicans who voted for McKinley in 1896, which suggests that the selection was made on different principles.[167] All Gold Democrats questioned in Anderson who had voted for McKinley in 1896 stated that they did not intend to vote for the Republicans this time. Most said they would vote for Bryan and gave as their reason the fact that the currency question would be of no importance. In one case the person asked said he was returning to the Democratic party because of McKinley's attitude to "the new possessions of the United States." Another of those returning to the Democratic fold was Captain W. R. Myers, former Secretary of State in Indiana, who was an ardent expansionist.[168]

South Bend provided the most detailed information. No less than twenty-eight of the persons included in the poll were Gold Democrats who had voted for McKinley in 1896. Eleven now said they were going to vote for McKinley, nine for Bryan, six were doubtful, one did not intend voting for anyone. Those who were hesitant said their final decision would depend on the currency plank adopted by the Democrats, and at the same time they often expressed hope that a man such as Olney would be nominated instead of Bryan.

Obviously, the Gold Democrats were not being driven back to their party by the new issue of imperialism. Those who returned did so simply because they were convinced that the silver question, which had made them leave the party in 1896, was now obsolete.

This material should not be stretched too far, but some conclusions can be drawn from it. Firstly, the survey had been made at a point when the worst of the storm over the Puerto Rican tariff had died down, a factor which was emphasized in some of the reports. The question was important, since interviewers gave it as the reason for the resentment against the Republican administration felt by rank-and-file Republicans in some cities. As far as Richmond was concerned, the result of the survey could have been influenced by the violent agitation against the Puerto Rican bill carried on not only by the Democratic *Sun Telegram* and *Dispatch* but by the Richmond *Palladium* (Republican) and *Evening Item* (Indepedent Republican), while in South Bend the *Times* (Dem.) and the *Courier* (Ind.) had been backed in their campaign against the Puerto Rican bill by the Chicago newspapers, also read in the city.

The *News* survey showed that the fight over the Puerto Rican tariff had had a negative effect for the Republicans, but that this effect was showing signs of diminishing. At the same time the different reports confirmed that the Democrats in Indiana did not see the silver question as a decisive issue in the election and many Gold Democrats were prepared to return if 16 : 1 was pushed into the background and another issue given the central position.

This was the state of opinion in Indiana at the end of March, according to the survey, and the picture agrees with the flood of letters and reports being received by both senators at this time, and with the development of public opinion that was registered in the many local newspapers. It is obvious that the storm had passed its climax when Beveridge and Fairbanks spoke in the Senate on March 29 and 31 respectively.

The treatment Beveridge had received from the Senate was a hard blow for the ambitious young senator. But it was plain that his speech had been a serious mistake also in other respects. There was not a trace of the enormous response with which he had been met in the press and in public opinion after his sensational speech at the beginning of the year.

Beveridge had not only offended the administration and the establishment within the Senate, but the party politicians in Indiana. Opinions had started to swing there and Beveridge was speaking for a lost cause. Moreover he did it in such a way as to increase the difficulties on the local level and give new life to the lingering opposition to the President and the Republican party leaders. He earned the enmity of the Republican congressmen from Indiana, all of whom, with the exception of Crumpacker (and Faris, who was absent), had voted for the bill and who after weeks of violent criticism from their districts finally glimpsed a chance of pacifying their constituents.

But Beveridge made things even more difficult for himself by antagonizing many influential Republicans and ending up voting for the bill, thus losing the support of those who like himself opposed the tariff. Several newspapers, mainly Democratic, did not miss the chance of sarcastically noting that Beveridge had taken the right standpoint on the bill but had promised to vote wrongly if necessary.[169] Several Republican newspapers that had continued to be hostile to the tariff reacted negatively.[170] And one of Beveridge's most faithful supporters among Republican politicians in the state, J. M. McIntosh, went so far as to describe the effect of Beveridge's speech in Indiana as "disastrous" and to wish that it had never been made.[171] Beveridge's friend Rotschild advised him against having his Puerto Rico speech distributed. It would cause ill will not only among those who accepted the tariff but among the Republicans opposed to the tariff, who could not forgive Beveridge for having concluded his attack on the bill by announcing that he would vote for it.[172]

The senior senator received confirmation that he, unlike Beveridge, had judged the situation correctly, in the form of congratulatory letters and telegrams from people who, only a few weeks before, had strongly criticized the bill and feared its effects.[173]

The Indianapolis *Journal* had like New, moderated its attitude, but it was nevertheless closer to Beveridge's point of view.[174] The *News* had swung earlier, while the *Press* took longer. Their common owner, Frank Payne, was still negative.[175] So were on the whole both the *Sun*—and, of course, the *Sentinel*.[176] Most Republican newspapers outside Indianapolis reacted positively to Fairbanks' speech. Some negative voices were heard. Not unexpectedly, these were to be found in papers such as the Richmond *Item,* New Albany *Tribune,* Anderson *Bulletin* and Columbus *Republican,* which had been among the most vehement critics of the Puerto Rican tariff.[177] The Republican party politicians were on the whole satisfied,[178] and Fairbanks' speech was distributed in offprint throughout the state and felt to be a splendid argument against any criticism that might remain.[179] McKinley's open satisfaction with the speech added to its value.[180] Indeed the Republicans used it not only in Indiana but circulated it in other states, to counteract opposition to the bill.[181]

The Republican State Convention

The rivalry between Fairbanks and Beveridge penetrated right down to county level. It was most noticeable when the time came to nominate candidates to the state Senate. These elections were important because they could have direct consequences for the two U.S. senators, both of whom were appointed by the Indiana Senate. Although Fairbanks had four years left of his term there were speculations about threats to his renomination and he left nothing to chance. He demanded reports from supporters in the counties, often postmasters, and intervened where necessary.

In his usual way Fairbanks remained in the background and let his lieutenants do what had to be done. This became the task of Joseph Kealing, vice chairman of the Republican State Committee and Fairbanks' most influential machine operator. Kealing was involved in the nomination of James M. Barlow for joint senator of Boone and Hendricks county,[182] and in the same way nominations were manipulated in La Grange and Noble counties,[183] and in Carroll and Clinton counties.[184] Another example is the fight that developed in Vanderburg county.

Andrew J. Clark of Evansville was an enthusiastic supporter of Beveridge and tried with the help of the junior senator's friends to be nominated for the state Senate. Clark was not accepted by Fairbanks, who felt Beveridge's efforts to build a machine to be a serious threat, Kealing intervened, contacted the Evansville people,[185] and Fairbanks' machine produced a rival candidate, Samuel Crumpacker, "a red hot Fairbanks man."[186] As was only to be expected Fairbanks proved so strong that Beveridge's men did not have a chance. The senior senator's control of patronage was, as in so many other cases, decisive. On May 5 the county convention was held and an account in the Indianapolis *Sentinel* stated dramatically that Clark, who was described as "a pronounced Beveridge man," "was knifed un-

128

mercifully by Postmaster Parvin and George Cunningham, who are rank Fairbanks men."[187]

Several of the Republican District Conventions held during the weeks when the fight over the Puerto Rican bill was raging had been stormy and it was only by the narrowest margin that resolutions against the bill had been prevented. The sitting Republican congressmen were renominated, but with a marked lack of enthusiasm. The exception was in the tenth district where Crumpacker, who was the only who had voted against the bill, was hailed as a hero.[188]

Although many of those reporting to the Indiana senators assured them that opposition to the bill was fierce over the state and encompassed practically every Republican, it is possible to establish that especially after the storm to some extent had died down the opposition centered on certain districts. These included the seventh congressional district, above all Indianapolis and Marion county, and the sixth district, where Richmond and Wayne, Henry and Rush counties were the centers of resistance.

Jesse Overstreet and James Watson, congressmen from the seventh and sixth districts respectively, were subjected to violent criticism from their constituents, criticism that shook them and took them by surprise. Watson tried to pacify his antagonists by getting President McKinley's permission to declare that he had voted for the bill by direct request of the President,[189] but this did not seem to have any effect. What the Republican politicians feared above all was that excited delegates at the county and district conventions would pass resolutions condemning the Puerto Rican bill, which would be fatal before the coming election. They managed to avoid this but only by organized efforts.

The Republicans in Marion county had held their convention in Indianapolis on March 3, just when the storm had broken. One of the delegates proposed a resolution against the Puerto Rican bill. The party officials were prepared and the county committee had arranged to have men sitting in different parts of the hall who demanded that all suggested resolutions should be referred to the committee without debate, and the chairman of the convention had been instructed to use all means to prevent any such resolution being passed. All those standing close enough to hear the resolution proposed by the delegate were enthusiastic and if countermeasures had not been arranged in advance, the resolution would have been adopted almost unanimously. This is according to the account given by Harry New.[190]

Events were similar in Richmond, where Charles Hernley, chairman of the Republican State Committee, managed with help of some stalwart Republicans to keep opposition in the sixth districts in check. According to one of New's informants, this was accomplished with help of "not only the party whip, but by that of a large green hickory-elm club."[191]

In the northern part of the state, resistance was extremely strong in the tenth district, which backed Crumpacker unhesitatingly.[192] The mood was the same in the twelfth district. Opposition remained in these districts later, when it had started to diminish in most other places. The indignation had also been great in the thirteenth district, but according to the chairman of its district committee, the editor of the South Bend *Tribune,* Elmer Crocket, opinion was swinging by the middle of March and by the end of the month he described the entire affair as "a tempest in a teapot."

In the fifth, eighth, ninth and eleventh districts there was only insignificant opposition among Republicans and they remained loyal to the administration. There had been some opposition in the ninth district, but it had been subdued.

The bill had caused little discussion in the first and third districts. The Republicans in the second district were negative to the tariff, but towards the end of the month the resistance petered out, as it did in most other places. The same applied to the fourth district.

Thus the Republican opposition to the Puerto Rican tariff was mainly in the eastern part of central Indiana—the seventh and sixth districts— and in the north of the state, above all in the northeast and northwest corners, that is, the tenth and twelfth districts.

Prior to the state convention, which was due to be held on April 25—26, the mood of the Republicans was restless. They feared that opposition to the Puerto Rican bill would lead to some action that would split the ranks, or at least embarrass the administration, and they were afraid that the rivalry between the two senators would become notorious.

The first problem that had to be settled was the chairmanship at the convention. Beveridge had hoped to be chosen, but after his catastrophic misjudgement and the impossible situation he had landed in even his warmest admirers realized that this was out of the question.[193] Fairbanks could have arranged to be appointed chairman, but let it be known that he did not want to be considered. He realized that he was no spellbinder, and his aim was to tone down the antagonisms and prevent bitterness. Charles Hernley had visited Washington at the beginning of April to discuss the problem with Fairbanks and Mark Hanna.[194] They agreed that J. Frank Hanly of LaFayette should be chairman at the convention. And the platform that was on the same occasion settled on all essential points—most of it probably written by Fairbanks—ignored the Puerto Rican question.

The Independent Indianapolis *Press* reported that in some quarters the reaction to Hernly's visit to Washington was very negative. Local Republican politicians felt insulted at the idea that decisions concerning the state party's platform should be dictated from Washington. The greatest indignation had been aroused by reports that Hanna had helped to decide the content of the platform. The *News* insinuated that this demonstrated the power of the bosses within the Republican party.[196] Similar notes were struck in other newspapers. The LaFayette *Times* spoke of Hanna as "the party boss" and Fairbanks as "the state boss."[197]

Like many other newspapers in Indiana,[198] the Indianapolis *Journal* had reduced its criticism of the Puerto Rican tariff once the final decision had been made, and now backed Fairbanks' line of closing the ranks and healing the wounds. The tone was quite different now. The Puerto Rican question should be kept outside the convention. The matter had been settled and now they should let bygones be bygones.[199] There was a special reason why the *Journal* changed its tune and went over to the side of the administration. New was extremely anxious to be appointed member of the Republican National Committee. His only chance of achieving this was to gain the support of Fairbanks and blot out the impression that he was opposed to the administration.[200] His efforts met with success. Fairbanks agreed to back him and New achieved his aim. He also became a member of the Executive Committee of the National Committee.

The *Journal* would have preferred to see Governor James A. Mount as chairman. He appeared a natural candidate, identified with neither Fairbanks nor the Beveridge camp. Mount was rejected because he had gone against the administration on the Puerto Rican question.[201]

Frank Hanly held a strong position in the party. He was young, but had considerable experience, and was a brilliant speaker, even considered by some to be superior to Beveridge. Hanly had been Beveridge's rival in the close senatorial election of 1899 and had only been defeated when all state senators backing other candidates joined forces and voted for Beveridge when it became clear that their own candidate could not win.[202] Hanly appeared to have Fairbanks' support, even though the senior senator did not intervene energetically enough to secure Hanly's victory. After Beveridge's victory Hanly had in any event moved even closer to Fairbanks.[203] There can be little doubt that Hanly was Fairbanks' man at the convention.

Other features of the convention made plain that the Fairbanks machine was in charge. Congressman Landis from the ninth district had been bitterly attacked in connection with his renomination at the district convention, because he had voted for the Puerto Rican tariff bill. He now made a speech which, according to reports in the press, was greeted with tumultuous applause. Together with James E. Watson, Charles L. Henry and James Hemenway, Landis belonged to what was known as Fairbanks' "congressional clique."[204]

Fairbanks himself was called up to the platform, where he made what was claimed to be an improvised speech which, despite the fact that he had difficulties with his voice, was said by the *Journal* to have been received with great enthusiasm.[205] The speech turned into a skillful and energetic defense of the Foraker Act, and in particular its controversial tariff provisions. Frank Hanly, chairman of the convention, made this the keynote of his speech.[206]

Apart from adoption of a platform the item which attracted the greatest interest was nomination of the Republican candidate for governor. No less than six candidates sought the nomination, each with his backers: Frank B. Posey (Evansville), John L. Griffith (Indianapolis), E. G. Hogate (Danville), W. S. Haggard (LaFayette), Winfield T. Durbin (Anderson) and J. S. Dodge (Elkhart). The frontrunners were Griffiths and Durbin, of whom the former had long been in the lead.

Griffiths was backed by the Beveridge group and several others who opposed Fairbanks. Although the senior senator would have preferred to remain in the background it was essential for him politically to make sure that Griffiths was defeated. The rival candidate in whose favor he mobilized his machine was Colonel Durbin, a veteran and wealthy banker from Anderson. Durbin had successfully led the Republican campaign in 1896. He was on good terms with Mark Hanna, and with Fairbanks and his men.[207] As usual, Fairbanks stayed on the sidelines and let others make his moves. One of the key figures here was again Joseph Kealing, but the others included New, who had been forced not only to give up his resistance to the Puerto Rican tariff to appease Fairbanks and the administration, but to work for defeat of Griffiths at the convention.[208]

Durbin won on the seventh ballot and Fairbanks' influence was demonstrated by the fact that the delegates who now cast the decisive votes all came from counties with influential federal offices. Many of the delegates at the convention were postmasters, revenue officers and other federal appointees. They were controlled by Fairbanks and it was they who gave his machine its strength.[209]

132

Beveridge was not present at the convention. He had a legitimate excuse, as his wife was mortally ill. At the same time he had strong political reason to keep away. Fairbanks and his supporters were in control. It can be estimated that since the beginning of the year Fairbanks had held nine of the thirteen members of the Republican State Executive Committee in his hand,[210] and even though they had for a time panicked when the storm of opinion had been at its height, Fairbanks' hold had never been seriously threatened. It had been consolidated when it became obvious that his line on the Puerto Rico question was going to win.

Charles Hernley, chairman of the Republican State Committee, was also chairman of the platform committee at the convention. As mentioned he had during a visit to Washington discussed the content of the platform with Fairbanks and Hanna. There were problems that concerned them— above all that of the Puerto Rican bill, where they decided to keep the entire question not only out of the platform, but outside the convention. The other question was the controversial ship subsidy bill. Apparently Hanna wanted a plank endorsing the bill, but the opposition against it was strong in Indiana and it suffered the same fate as the Puerto Rican tariff. When the platform was adopted at the convention on April 26, omission of both the Puerto Rican issue and the ship subsidy bill attracted more attention than the issues included.

The theme in the platform was an appreciative review of what the Republican administration had achieved, with prosperity as the refrain. The economic expansion was praised: ". . . additional markets opened to our surplus products of every kind, taxing production to its utmost capacity to meet consumption and demand." The Open Door Policy was included in the general introduction, as was the war against Spain, whereby "Spanish cruelty and oppression forever has been banished from this hemisphere and the Philippine island."

Eight of the platform's eighteen planks were devoted to national issues. There were the usual endorsements of the Republican financial, monetary and tariff legislation, one plank favoring legislation for control of trusts and monopolies, one recommending liberal pensions for veterans. Fairbanks had been chairman of the Senate Committee on Immigration, so it is natural to find a plank favoring the enactment and enforcement of "laws restricting and preventing the importation of such undesirable foreign population as is prejudicial to free American labor." Another of the standard items is a plank recommending that the Nicaraguan canal should be built with all possible speed, under the immediate direction and exclusive control of the United States government.

Two planks dealt with the new foreign policy and the annexations. The first followed the idealistic line, humanitarian duty and the responsibility of the victor. The war was begun and carried on from humane and disinterested motives. When victory had been won, it was not possible for America to refuse its responsibilities. The principle was said to be to promote the highest welfare for the people of these islands with the largest possible freedom of control in their own affairs. This is the usual phraseology, presented in a reasonably modest way.[211]

Thus the Puerto Rican tariff was not explicitly mentioned. This sensitive question did in fact appear, though well disguised, in plank number three, which shows the extent to which the opposition had been quietened, or rather brought under control:

"We unhesitatingly approve and indorse the policy and course of the administration and the legislation by Congress in respect to our newly acquired possessions and express full confidence in the wisdom, integrity and ability of the administration supported by a republican Congress, to deal wisely and justly with the questions concerning the same, as they may arise."[212]

The Republican state convention in Indiana was a veritable display of party discipline. The sarcastic comments that the Washington *Post* permitted itself are worth quoting:

"Not a word or hint of dissatisfaction appears in any part of the platform. All is as serene as if sweet peace and blissful serenity had never been interrupted. Has the tornado left no debris, no mark of devastation to show that it ever came? Are there no sulkers who will be too busy on election day to go to the polls; no malcontents whose resentment will take them over to the enemy? We cannot answer those questions, but we are bound to declare that the Indiana indorsement of the Porto Rico tariff "legislation by Congress" is an exhibition of party discipline so superb that in the estimation of practical politicians it must seem almost sublime."[213]

Otherwise the platform consisted only of endorsement of "the clean and able administration of Governor James A. Mount" and Republican achievements in state affairs, together with a few conventional, noncontroversial pledges of further reforms.

The party machine had kept a tight hold on the proceedings. The entire convention was dominated and steered by the desire of the party officials to avoid conflict, prevent opposition, smooth over antagonisms as far as possible and get the party to close its ranks before the coming campaign. They succeeded beyond all expectation and if one were to believe the press reports of the enthusiasm that greeted Fairbanks, Landis, Hanly and Durbin when they praised the McKinley administration, then the storm had not only blown over, but every trace of it had been so thoroughly erased that one might seriously wonder whether it had ever existed.

It was not so simple. The opposition had greatly diminished once the bill had passed and after the party had brought severe pressure not only on the politicians but also on the Republican press to make them rally to support the administration. In many cases they only did so with the greatest reluctance and there was still open criticism in many Republican newspapers. However, the tone even in the papers that had attacked the Puerto Rican tariff most vehemently was more muted, and there was a swing to the party line as the election drew closer.

This question involved in the fight over the Puerto Rican tariff bill was fundamental to the whole policy of expansion. The struggle did have some effects at state level, although these were nothing like what the Democrats had hoped for when the storm was at its height. It had at least been decisive in the matter of who was to be chairman at the state convention, had weakened Beveridge's position and strengthened Fairbanks' and possibly affected the nomination—and thereby the election—of the Republican gubernatorial candidate.

The revolt in Indiana can be seen as a clash between the two motives usually given for expansion: national self-interest and ideals. The expansionists had exploited the humanitarian and idealistic arguments to the full in their propaganda and consequently many reacted when the administration went in for a line which they felt was incompatible with their idealistic declarations and which at the same time proved the Democrats and anti-imperialists right in their accusations of hypocrisy.

The Indiana Democrats and the Puerto Rican Tariff

The mood in the Democratic camp at the beginning of the year had been depressed, to say the least.[214] There appeared to be no weak points in the Republican position, while the Democrats were divided, above all over the silver question. Nor did imperialism seem to present an issue which might appeal to the voters, since it was too abstract ideologically and was felt by the ordinary voter to be of little importance. The violent storm of

135

opposition that blew up around the Puerto Rican tariff changed the situation at a stroke.

The Democratic politicians and newspapers welcomed this so unexpected opportunity with open arms. As criticism within the Republican party became more bitter at the end of February and throughout March, the confidence of the Democrats grew. The tone changed, defeatism disappeared, and they abandoned their defensive attitude for attacks on their opponents. The great majority of the Democratic newspapers, even those that had not earlier declared any standpoint on expansionism, or that had even been positive to the idea, attacked the bill as a flagrant example of imperialism, driven through and decided by the trusts. The arguments were usually on constitutional lines and with a few exceptions the doctrine flourished that the Constitution followed the flag.

The Democrats were naturally greatly benefited in their campaign by the storm of opinion that was raging in the Republican press. As the Laporte *Argus* sardonically stated: "The best matter to be found at present in Democratic papers is reprint from Republican papers."[215]

At the end of March the Democratic optimism had reached its zenith. The Indiana Democrats allowed their enthusiasm to convince them that they would elect both the state and national ticket.[216] Even at the beginning of April they still thought that a lot of the Republican congressmen who had voted for the Puerto Rican tariff bill would be defeated: Hemenway, Landis, Brick and Cromer, probably Watson too and possibly even Overstreet.[217] Since they naturally also counted on retaining the mandates they had, they looked forward to getting a safe Democratic majority among the thirteen congressmen that Indiana was to send to the House.

To some extent the hopes of a Democratic victory were reinforced by Democratic successes in the city elections held late in April and early in May. Brazil was now controlled for the first time by the Democrats, who appointed three of the five councilors. The former large Republican majority in Elkhart shrank to almost nothing. What attracted most attention was that in Anderson, the home town of the Republican gubernatorial candidate Durbin, the former Republican majority of 600 votes disappeared and the Democrats won.[218] But by this time even most Democrats realized that the Republicans had ridden out the storm, that the possibility of a Democratic victory in the coming election was almost illusory or slight. Republicans had recovered from their divisions and tribulations and had consolidated the standing of the party. But what had been absolutely decisive was the elimination of the Puerto Rican issue as a topical, concrete, controversial question. The Democrats were thrown back upon the more abstract, anaemic issue of imperialism and they had few illusions about its usefulness, particularly in the state elections. At the same time they were left with the unsolved problem of what to do about the currency issue.

There were newspapers and naturally politicians too who were diehard silverites, who would not accept anything less than a reiteration of the magic 16 : 1, but they were in a clear minority.

The strong men within the Democratic party organization in Indiana, Taggart, mayor of Indianapolis, and Samuel Morss, proprietor and editor-in-chief of the *Sentinel*, both belonged to the conservative wing of the party, like Menzies, Dougherty and Murdoch. Taggart and Morss were both aware that the party's chances of winning in Indiana with a 16 : 1 platform were practically nonexistent. They made a canvass of leading Democrats in the state and found strong support in favor of dropping the silver plank. This was considered essential if they were to win the German voters.[219] They approached Bryan, but he rejected any suggestion that it might be wise to relinquish the demand for free silver coinage at the 16 : 1 ratio.[220]

Bryan was generally thought to be the obvious choice as the Democratic standardbearer in the coming election, but for some conservative Gold Democrats he was so unacceptable that even a retreat in the currency question would have had no effect. (James) Maurice Thompson, Indiana's most widely read writer—after Lew (Ben Hur) Wallace—was a typical example. In the very year 1900, Thompson published his most successful book, "Alice of Old Vincennes." He was interested in politics and a regular contributor to *The Independent*. He was a Democrat, but violently anti-Bryan. He had voted for McKinley in 1896 and intended to do so again. Thompson's view of Bryan was such that nothing the Democratic leader could do would have affected Thompson's attitude in the slightest. Just as Bryan aroused in some of his supporters a devotion and adoration that was almost fanatical, many conservative Democrats reacted passionately against him. "Bryan is a terror. He stands for all that is bad and evil in our social, moral and political life."[221] "...he is as unscrupulous in politics as any gambler at cards. He has everything that is bad in his crowd of supporters. Traitors, aliens, populists, anarchists, socialists of all shades, disgruntled office-holders, repudiators—whatever is vile is for him from Maine to Texas."[222]

With Bryan as candidate it was inconceivable that Democrats of this type could ever be won back. Thompson considered Bryan so dangerous that

137

issues paled into insignificance in contrast and what was most important was to avoid anything that might weaken the position of the Republicans. It is an interesting point that Thompson was sceptical to the storm of opinion against the Puerto Rican tariff bill. He gave assurances of his sympathy "for all suffering people," but said he could "smell a negro in the woodpile" here "in all this tremendous spurt of sentiment from certain politicians whom I know to be absolute demagogues." Thompson could not see how the proposed tariff could harm the Puerto Ricans, since all revenues collected were returned to their relief by the American government. He queried whether there was any reason to be sentimental about Puerto Rico at the expense of the people of Connecticut, Florida and Louisiana. And in any case "a slight temporary injury" to Puerto Rico was not so important that it should be allowed to threaten the greater, more important goal, defeating Bryan at any price in the coming election, which in Thompson's opinion was the most important since Lincoln's.

Thompson was a convinced expansionist. He defined himself as "not only a gold Democrat," and anti-populist, "but also a thoroughgoing expansionist." His arguments on the Puerto Rican tariff were no concidence: the motives that he stressed came into the area of national interest and he reacted against what he saw as false humanitarian and idealistic jargon, used to decide foreign policy: "The only thing in McKinley's attitude that I don't like," he wrote in the middle of March 1900, "is the flabby pretense that we are going to give Cuba absolute independence." If the United States was to build the Nicaraguan canal, a point on which everyone agreed, Cuba would have to be American: "Happiness and safety to the greatest number demands it." No consideration for the tobacco or sugar trusts should be allowed to stand in the way with their "false cry of our obligation to keep the promise of Congress to Cuba."[223]

The task facing Democratic party tacticians was difficult to say the least. To have any chance of winning, it was imperative that they should win back the voters lost as a result of the silver demand in 1896 and also gain a foothold among the traditionally independent voters. Their only chance lay in relinquishing the currency plank, or at least playing it down and backing anti-imperialism which met with a good response from some independents. But voters such as Thompson, who were both for gold and expansion were hopeless cases.

Democratic leaders in Indiana decided on trying to win back Democrats who had bolted in 1896. The party machine was led by conservative men and the same men were in complete control of the State Convention, held on June 6.[224] The chairman was Samuel M. Ralston, who in his keynote speech kept the currency question in the background and attacked the Republican policy on the trusts and the McKinley administration's imperialistic foreign policy. The machine's gubernatorial candidate, John W. Kern, was elected on the first ballot. The gloomy prospects had made it difficult to find anyone prepared to stand. The strongest candidate was thought to be Benjamin F. Shively, who had been nominated in 1896.[225] He refused, and in any case lacked Taggart's backing.

The strength of the conservative element at the convention is illustrated by the fact that all those elected as delegates at large to the Democratic National convention in Kansas City opposed a reiteration of the 16 : 1 demand. Three of them, G. V. Menzies (Mount Vernon), James Murdoch (LaFayette) and Hugh Dougherty (Bluffton) can be described as sound money supporters.[226] The fourth, Samuel E. Morss, had from the beginning been a silverite but now, like many others, considered the question both obsolete and politically impossible. In fact the entire twenty-two-man Indiana delegation to the National convention proved, with one exception, to be opposed to the insertion of 16 : 1 in the National platform.[227]

The state party platform written by Morss and adopted by the convention showed clearly that this pivotal state was not silver country.[228] It devoted a large space to abstract reaffirmations of allegiance to "the principles of the Declaration of Independence," "the principles of the constitution of the United States," and in this context "the principles of the Chicago platform of 1896." It is important that they did not even have a special reaffirmation of the money plank of 1896, far less a reiteration.

One detailed plank denounced trusts and monopolies and a few others were devoted to state politics.[229]

At the Kansas City convention a month later Bryan forced the party to go to the election with a platform which had a plank containing an explicit demand for free silver coinage at 16 : 1, demolishing all the efforts in connection with Indiana's state convention to smooth the way for the defectors of 1896.[230] Not altogether, however, for Kern and other Democrats conducted their campaign with imperialism, trusts and the tariff as the issues, avoiding the silver question, and in the election Kern ran ahead of the national ticket.

139

CHAPTER IV

The Issue of Expansion in the Pre-Convention Campaign

The State Party Platforms

Once the Democrats and Republicans had held their national conventions, nominated their candidates, adopted their platforms, most people concerned more or less adjusted to the positions that had thereby been settled. This applied both to the press and active politicians on both sides, who were naturally anxious to tone down any possible dissent, and to the rank and file. Adoption of the election programs and the consequent locking of the parties' policy positions had a strong effect on public opinion. Many people, especially those who were undecided or badly informed, made up their minds by identifying with the party rather than being convinced by its arguments.[1]

For this reason it is important to be aware of the process by which the parties reached the positions expressed in the national platforms. There can be a difference between ideas circulating within parties during the pre-convention campaign and those which became normal after the national conventions. This aspect should be of interest primarily in the Democratic party, since the Republicans can be assumed to have been bound by loyalty to the McKinley administration.

The material to be treated here consists of the state party platforms adopted at conventions which Republicans and Democrats held during the months prior to the national conventions. This material, not previously used for such a purpose, can spotlight both individual and regional variations within the parties and differences between the standpoints of the parties.

The material has its limitations. The foreign policy planks were often brief and stereotyped. In some cases the influence of party leaders is easily discernible. It was common for planks to be lifted word for word from platforms adopted by other states. A systematic analysis of foreign policy planks nevertheless can provide interesting information about which standpoints were accepted in the states. Since the question of expansion and annexation was so controversial and likely to play a part in the election campaign, variations in standpoint are significant.[2]

Republican State Party Platforms

1

The Republican state party conventions were generally held between the beginning of April and the middle of May. All the platforms adopted by Republicans in the Northeast region, in New England and the Middle Atlantic states, contained a plank on foreign policy, expressing approval of McKinley's line, particularly with regard to the newly-acquired territories. Since the attacks by the opposition on McKinley's foreign policy were increasingly severe, any state omitting such a plank from its platform would in effect have been demonstrating against the policy of the previous years.

The sections of the platforms devoted to foreign policy vary, however, in many respects. Within New England and the Middle Atlantic region, the *New York* platform had by far the most detailed presentation of the foreign policy issue.[3] It was verbose but vague. An analysis shows that it contained extremely few concrete statements. It referred to the war and subsequent events that had created the current situation and brought in the "responsibility" motive. There had been no alternative: "It was impossible to destroy sovereignty without creating another sovereignty to take its place." Only Cuba was ready for self-government. In all the other cases it would have been "a coward's part to remove Spanish authority without ourselves assuming responsibility for the preservation of public order." The closely related "humanitarian duty" motive followed. The only purpose of the government's measures in the new territories had been "to render life and property secure, to preserve individual liberty and freedom of thought and action, and to prepare a way for local government, administered through local agencies, in which strength and stability should be guaranteed in the popular respect for law and order." It was a markedly defensive plank, without even an unconditional demand that the Philippines should be kept as a colony and with no real expansionist arguments or statements.

The majority of platforms in New England took up a similar position on the acquisition of the Philippines, even though there were variations.

141

Massachusetts laid emphasis on the responsibility of the victor. It argued on the basis of the Treaty of Paris, which settled that the Philippines and Puerto Rico were to go to the USA, a tactically well-chosen argument, in view of the fact that Bryan had pressed for ratification of this treaty. To now "abandon /the Philippines/ to local anarchy or to the lust of the invader would be cowardly and dishonorable and a betrayal of its trust impossible to be contemplated by a great free and enlightened nation."[4] As in New York's platform and those of *Maine, Vermont* and *Connecticut,* retention of the Philippines under American protection was presented as a duty, dictated by idealistic and humanitarian considerations. "Liberty, law and order" were to replace "anarchy and barbarism."

All the platforms were dominated by civilizing and humanitarian motives. Massachusetts had an additional one, even if it was not allowed to occupy so prominent a position, namely commercial expansion: "material interests ... of the nation whose trade and commerce are competing for the markets of the world."

The same motive turned up in Connecticut's platform, with an additional factor in the sphere of national interest. The victory over Spain had given the United States "absolute title to distant islands of great *strategic* and commercial value." In contrast to New York, the majority of other platforms in New England and the Middle Atlantic states had a clearly formulated demand for the retention of the Philippines.

Some platforms, especially Connecticut's in which nationalistic elo-quence was allowed to blossom, displayed a note of triumph and delight over the new world which seemed to be opening for the United States as a result of the victory: "The flag of the union has been raised above all other flags in the respect and admiration of the world, the great republic has become the greatest of nations."[5]

On the whole planks in this region dealing with foreign policy and the territorial acquisitions were restrained, in some cases almost defensive. The only platform in New England and the Middle Atlantic region which openly discussed problems of government organization in the new areas is Vermont's which stated:

"Whether or not the constitution follows the flag, we believe that the good faith of the American people must stand unquestioned wherever the stars and stripes are seen and that we are bound by justice and humanity to deal with the question arising out of our own new possessions in the spirit of the American constitution and civilization."

Compared with the Eastern states, the interest in foreign policy shown in Republican platforms of the North Central States was limited and in some cases almost nonexistent. The latter applied to *Wisconsin* and *Michigan,* both of which had similar planks, simply expressing approval of measures taken by the McKinley administration.[6]

The platform of *Indiana* must also be described as restrained. The Republicans in Indiana held their convention while the waves of discussion were still breaking high over the Puerto Rican bill, which had caused such a storm that it had threatened to split the state party.[7] The leading Republican newspaper had appealed for exclusion of the delicate issue from the state party platform in the interests of unity.[8] The platform did turn out moderate in tone, under the strong influence of Senator Fairbanks, who was later to participate in drawing up the Republican National party platform as chairman of the Committee on Resolutions.[9]

The Republican party in *Illinois* held its convention on May 8—9, two weeks after Indiana's. Its platform was drawn up by the influential Charles G. Dawes, Comptroller of the Currency and member of the Republican National Committee.[10] The platform displayed great similarity with that of Indiana, which Dawes had probably used as a model. Like the author of Indiana's platform, Charles Warren Fairbanks, Dawes was one of those closest to McKinley. The platform's foreign policy plank concentrated on one motive but this motive was developed more fully than in any other platform. The motive was a variation on the theme of "the responsibility of the victor." The treaty with Spain had been approved by the Senate with a two-thirds majority and Congress almost unanimously had voted 20 million dollars, which under terms of the treaty was to be paid to Spain. "The sovereignty thus deliberately assumed by the conjoint action of the great treaty-making and law-making powers of the United States it was the duty of the executive to maintain ... That sovereignty must not be repudiated."

With undeniable skill the whole issue was here put in quite a different light: acquisition of the Philippines was in no way the work of McKinley or the Republicans but an enterprise in which the entire Congress was involved. Responsibility rested not only with the President, nor with him and the Senate, whose two-thirds majority could never have been attained without Democratic help, but with Congress, which by granting the appropriation had placed itself behind the administration's policy.[11]

The Republican state convention in *Ohio* was held at the end of April and not unexpectedly was dominated by Mark Hanna.[12] There is probably little risk in assuming that this shrewd political tactician was directly responsible for the plank on annexation of the Philippine Islands.

All platforms from the West North Central States were with rare exceptions, extremely brief and usually consisted of nothing more than general endorsement of policies of the McKinley administration. The foreign policy plank of the *South Dakota* platform was made up of the final lines of the plank in the platform adopted by Indiana a month earlier.

Iowa's plank—taken word for word a week later by *Missouri, Montana* and *Minnesota*—was nondescript in both content and wording.[13] The platform of *Kansas* was purely negative, consisting of an attack on the Democrats. It had two themes, both of which frequently recurred during the election campaign. One was the accusation that the Aguinaldo uprising was holding out in hope of a Democratic victory, encouraged by "the false cry of imperialism." The other point of attack, also used during the campaign, not least by Theodore Roosevelt, was the accusation against the Democrats of "hypocrisy." They were said to pretend to feel deeply for "the governmental welfare" of the inhabitants of Puerto Rico and the Philippines, while at the same time ruthlessly denying the franchise to thousands of American citizens in the Southern states because of the color of their skin.

North Dakota's Republican state platform declared clearly and categorically that "we favor the retention by the United States of every foot of territory of which the stars and stripes now float." The brief plank also contained an unusually concrete and energetic demand for commercial expansion. Market expansion was felt to be essential, not only by industry and the business world, but by farmers.[14]

"We favor extension of our commerce into China and the Far East, to further the introduction and establishment of a market for our surplus grain, cattle and other products."

The plank with the most detailed and comprehensive motives is to be found in *Nebraska's* platform, Bryan's homestate. The convention took place on May 3 and the platform can be seen as a reply to the Democrats which had been adopted previously, containing a comprehensive and aggressively anti-imperialist plank. The method used by the Republicans was not to draw up an aggressively expansionist program but to try to

144

take the wind out of the Democratic sails by appearing to follow the same line.

The opening words set the tone: "We are unalterably opposed to imperialism and militarism as practised by European nations." The plank rejected the idea of a large standing army in time of peace. In antithesis to these assurances stood declarations that implied acceptance of the policy of the McKinley administration. The Nebraska Republicans differentiated between European imperialism and America's acquisition of new territories and declared: "We are willing to accept all the legitimate results of honorable warfare and to assume the burden of governing and holding acquired territory." While claiming to be against a large standing army when at peace, they recommended "increasing our navy to such strength and power as will make us secure from foreign aggression, and the maintenance of such an army as may be necessary to quell insurrection, establish peace and maintain good order in our islands in the sea and to protect the flag from insult at home or abroad." Commercial expansion appeared in the demand for enlargement of the American merchant navy and expansion of America's foreign markets. The Open Door policy in China, which was to give American merchants free access to trade with the Chinese empire, was praised and described as one of the greatest achievements of diplomacy, a theme found in many other Republican platforms.

3

As far as the South Atlantic states were concerned, *Maryland's* platform contained a plank on the newly acquired territories which was taken almost word for word from platforms adopted by the Republican party in Indiana and Massachusetts about two weeks previously.[15] The *Delaware* platform asserted that the Paris peace treaty had made Puerto Rico and the Philippines the "legal and rightful possessions" of the United States. *West Virginia's* platform was brief and uncommitted, with the exception of a strong element of commercial expansionism.

In the southern part of the region only two states adopted a Republican platform in 1900, *South Carolina* and *Georgia*. The platform of the latter was constructed in the same way as those of New York and the New England states. More interesting is South Carolina's, which contained a short plank praising what the administration had done to break the Spanish yoke and liberate the oppressed, "instituting American authority in our newly acquired territory." So far the plank was conventional, but the concluding sentence is worth noting: ". . . till the people of these possessions are able to establish and maintain stable governments of their own." It is not clear how this temporal clause was to be interpreted, but it showed great similarity to what we are going to find in several Democratic platforms[16] and in the Democratic National platform.[17]

Kentucky had the only Republican platform in the East South Central States lacking a plank dealing directly with foreign or colonial policy. Two of the remaining states, *Alabama* and *Mississippi*, both devoted a great deal of space to the Puerto Rican tariff, which was praised to the skies.

The position of the new territories did not cause the *Tennessee* platform any difficulty. They were "ours to deal with as we may see fit." The platform achieved a high degree of expansionist enthusiasm: "We are proud of the magnificent results of the war with Spain and of the brilliant foreign policy of the present administration, which together have made possible an "open door" to the trade of China and the *Far East*, laid the groundwork for the building of the Nicaragua canal and given to the United States high rank as a world power." It is surpassed, however, by the brilliant, almost comic, rhetoric of the *Mississippi* platform: ". . . our armies and our navies have been unexcelled in the record of achievement since the world began." The enthusiasm for expansion cannot be mistaken: ". . . we have enlarged the borders of the United States till they almost equal the circuit of the sun." But in this platform too it was the idealistic motives that dominated, and the author of the platform soared to the heights of oratory:

". . . the islands of the sea have become our possessions and their people shall have the benefit of our laws, they shall be trained in our factories and farms: they shall be educated in our schools; they shall be taught in our churches the doctrines of the cross; their burdens shall be lightened, their hearts shall be gladdened, their homes shall be brightened, their children shall be dedicated to a wider, purer and deeper civilization; our hands and our heads shall help them to labor and to think."

Within the West South Central region, the only planks dealing with colonial or foreign policy came from *Arkansas* and *Texas*. The Arkansas platform was brief but explicit: "We favor the expansion policy of the administration. We favor the annexation of the Philippines as the most beneficient thing that could happen to the Philippines, and as giving us command of the vast trade of the orient not otherwise possible." The "humanitarian motive" was naturally present but was not gone into in more detail.

There were in Texas at this time two factions within the Republican party. The state convention was held at Waco on March 6 and 7. The

146

convention split and as a result we have two different platforms, one adopted by the "regular" Republicans and the other by the McDonald faction.[18] Both contained a plank in which the policy of the McKinley administration on the newly acquired territories was praised in positive terms, witnessing to "broad," "wide" statemanship and "eminent patriotism."[19]

4

Within the Mountain region we find as a rule platforms containing a formal plank in support of the administration's colonial policy. This applies to *Colorado, Idaho* and *Montana,* the plank of the latter, like Missouri's, being taken from the platform adopted a week earlier in Iowa.[20] Idealistic motives were stressed. The Montana platform was one of those that touched the question of government organization and spoke in favor of "the extension of self-government to all people that have lately come under the protection of this country as rapidly as they demonstrate their capacity to exercise it."[21]

The *Utah* platform had taken over the plank adopted in New Hampshire three weeks earlier. *Wyoming,* has copied the Ohio platform.

Most of the planks named above were worded with great restraint. The *Nevada* platform had a more energetically expansionist spirit. The commercial motive appeared in commending the Open Door policy, but otherwise, there as in so many other cases, it was the humanitarian and civilizing arguments that dominated. The plank declared that McKinley's achievement in driving the Spanish flag from the western hemisphere was only surpassed by Abraham Lincoln's abolition of slavery.

Republican conventions in the Pacific region clearly asserted their belief in expansion in their platforms. "We oppose any backward step on the subject of expansion," stated the *Washington* platform and when expressing their full support of the Republican administration's foreign policy, the Washington Republicans spoke particularly warmly of the acquisition of the Philippines. In addition to the usual idealistic motive, there was an economic-commercial one here. The *Oregon* platform commended the Open Door policy.

Republican state platforms in the West demanded that the Philippines be retained, but tried to guard themselves against accusations of imperialism. One of their methods was the usual emphasis on the blessings which would descend upon the Filipinos. The Washington platform was of particular interest, however, in that it plainly stated that it favored home rule for the new territories.

Democratic State Party Platforms

1

All the Democratic state platforms in New England and the Middle Atlantic region contained a plank attacking what was described as imperialism. Some did this in considerable detail. In the *Massachusetts* platform the war with Spain was explained to be "rightly waged." Far from trying to escape from responsibility, the Democrats counted it a merit. The war was "forced upon an unwilling Republican administration by the insistence of Democrats in House and Senate." But, the platform went on, this rightful war had been followed by a war on the Philippines, a war of "criminal aggression." It was unconstitutional not only because it had been started without congressional action, but because it implied a denial of the right of self-government, one of the bulwarks of the constitution. A demand was made for independence for the Philippines. This should be combined with a guarantee of American protection against attack from other powers. Lurking behind imperialism was "the less spectacular but more terrifying form of militarism," a deadly threat to American society. Imperialism and militarism were in fact a means of maintaining the domination of trusts and monopolies, "a menace to every man who holds his liberties dear." These were some of the standard anti-imperialist arguments. The *New York* platform concentrated on constitutional arguments. A colonial system was contrary to the Declaration of Independence and the Constitution. "There is no place for subject colonies under the American flag", stated the New York Democrats, "We maintain that the constitution follows the flag... A republican congress has no more right to establish or govern a territorial or colonial system outside the constitution than it has to create a king." The Puerto Rican tariff should be immediately removed.[22]

Similar planks were to be found in the platforms of *New Hampshire* and *New Jersey*. Immediate freedom and independence was demanded for Cuba, as promised and for the Philippines as soon as possible. The argument against the Puerto Rican Tariff was the usual one: "taxation without representation is tyranny" (*New Jersey, Rhode Island*). "No people should be annexed against their will, and however willing to come, no people should be admitted except to equal rights" (*Rhode Island*).

148

The demand for freedom for the Philippines was not formulated so clearly and categorically in all the Democratic platforms. The *New York* platform attacked as mentioned McKinley's imperialistic policy. There was no direct demand that the Philippines should be set free, only a statement that "every part of our possessions shall be governed according to American precedents and American principles." No objective was named, a feature that was common.

Massachusetts demanded an immediate declaration of independence for the islands.[23] *New Hampshire* demanded independence "as soon as they are capable of self-government." This reservation was fundamental.

The corresponding sections of the Democratic platforms of *Vermont* and *Pennsylvania* are of interest. Pennsylvania's came first, in the middle of April. "We favor granting at once to the people thereof (the Filipinos) home rule and the right to govern themselves under the protection of the United States." Following the same line Vermont declared two months later: "We therefore favor Home rule for the Filipino people under the protection of the United States." These statements imply American supremacy, even if at the same time they opposed keeping "the Filipinos as a subject people and the Philippine Islands as an imperial colony."

Several of these planks on foreign policy contained anti-British statements, mainly sympathy for the Boers in their fight against English imperialism (Pennsylvania, New Jersey, Massachusetts, Vermont). There was criticism of Britain on other grounds, not least the Hay-Pauncefote treaty. The most detailed and severest condemnation was in the Pennsylvania platform:

"We deplore the subservience of the present administration to the behests of England and English statesmen, whether the same be intentional or caused by the ignorance of our officials in the State Department. We denounce the Hay-Pauncefote treaty as a complete abandonment of the claims of our statesmen of our right to construct and control an interoceanic canal and as un-American and a base surrender of our inherent right of self-defence."[24]

2

All the Democratic state platforms in the East North Central States contained a detailed plank on colonial and foreign policy. They were similar and had features different from those of the Eastern states. They all contained a harsh attack on the "imperialism" of the McKinley administration, but the Philippines were scarcely explicitly mentioned in their arguments. The islands were not even mentioned in the planks of *Michigan, Ohio* and *Wisconsin*, the *Illinois* platform only included them in a list together with Cuba and Puerto Rico and that of *Indiana* in a subordinate clause. Arguments dealt with principles of government and concentrated on Puerto Rico. All platforms condemned the Puerto Rican Tariff and asserted that "the Constitution follows the flag." A typical example was the platform of Ohio:

"We enter our protest against the doctrine that the President or Congress can govern acquired territory outside and independently of the constitution of the United States as a doctrine utterly subversive of every foundation principle of our government. The declaration of independence, the flag and the constitution must everywhere stand together as emblems of human liberty and equal rights for all, and where one goes all go."

This argument turned up with slight variations in all platforms together with an explicit rejection of the Puerto Rico Tariff. Many platforms expressed sympathy with the Boers and condemned militarism.

It is remarkable that in this entire region there was not a single demand that the Philippines be granted independence. The placing of Puerto Rico in the spotlight is natural since it was in these states that the introduction of the Puerto Rican tariff bill had met the strongest opposition.[25] The only platform that specifically mentioned the Philippines in connection with organization of the new territories, *Illinois*, did so in a strange way:

"We invoke public condemnation of the administration policy which denies to Cuba, Puerto Rico and the Philippine Islands the principle of home rule and self-government and seeks the subjugation of a free and enlightened people for the glory of an imperial policy, revolting to our traditions and a defiance to the principles of our federal constitution."

What this statement implies is not altogether clear, but its construction is surprising. It prescribes the same treatment for Cuba, which had been promised independence by Congress; for Puerto Rico, the annexation of which was accepted by the Democrats; and for the Philippines—and the wording "home rule and self-government" does not indicate independence.[26]

Among the Democratic state platforms of the West North Central states, that of *Nebraska* is naturally of special interest. It reflected Bryan's standpoints and was of importance not only to other Democratic state platforms but to the National Democratic platform.[27] Its plank on foreign and colonial policy was comprehensive and contained many of the motives in the anti-

150

imperialistic planks discussed earlier: primarily rejection of a colonial system as unconstitutional, and declaration that the Constitution follows the flag. Contrary to most platforms in the Middle West, there was a clear demand for independence for the Philippines: ". . . we favor an immediate declaration of the nation's purpose to give to the Filipinos, first, a stable form of government; second, independence, and third, protection from outside interference." An anti-militarist statement was included, together with a declaration of support for the Boers. Nor was the usual condemnation of the Puerto Rican tariff absent.

Quite naturally the press devoted a great deal of attention to the Nebraska platform. A number of Democratic newspapers were, however, critical of a reiteration of the demand for silver coinage at a ratio of 16 : 1.[28] On the other hand they, like the anti-imperialistic independent and Republican papers, were well satisfied with the platform's foreign policy plank. But there were exceptions. Democratic newspapers that favored expansion were naturally unenthusiastic. More interesting is that attacks were also made from the opposition quarter, with accusations of a lack of anti-imperialist consistency. Later in the campaign the same criticism was to be aimed at, for example, the Kansas City platform and at Bryan's speech of acceptance. This criticism was expressed with a typical turn of phrase by the Indianapolis *Sentinel*,[29] the main Democratic organ in Indiana, which asserted in an editorial that the Nebraska platform's declaration as to the Philippines was "contradictory and unsatisfactory." If lawful authority could not be exercised outside the Constitution, as stated in the plank, and the Constitution was not to encompass the Philippines, "what business have we to undertake to give to the Philippines 'a stable form of government'?"

Opposition to the Puerto Rican tariff had been violent in the East North Central states, and occurred throughout the Middle West, even though it weakened further west. As has been pointed out, opposition was remarkably strong in *Iowa*, where the state's House of Representatives passed a resolution denouncing the tariff.[30] This attitude was commended in the Iowa Democrats' platform which, like the Democratic platforms of *North* and *South Dakota* briefly and dutifully criticized McKinley's policy in the Philippines, without specifying any aspect of it.

The *Minnesota* platform had the usual condemnation of imperialism and its fellow-traveler, militarism, with the customary constitutional motive and declaration that the Constitution follows the flag. There was no demand for the release of the Philippines, nor any such demand in the platforms

151

of *Missouri* or *Kansas*. All platforms save that of North Dakota contained a pro-Boer statement.

There is one feature of the *Missouri* platform worth noting. The Democrats of Missouri opposed McKinley's colonial acquisitions but at the same time favored hemispherism, "expansion of contiguous American territory" and annexation of Cuba whenever its people of their own volition should determine that they wished their country to become a part of the United States.

3

The Democratic party platforms in the South Atlantic states all contained a plank condemning imperialism and the colonial system, giving the usual constitutional reasons. They all either declared directly—which is most common—or implied that the Constitution followed the flag. They all had a statement denouncing militarism.

When it came to recommendations, the planks of *Virginia, South Carolina* and *Florida* demanded immediate fulfillment of the promise of independence for Cuba. Attacks on the Puerto Rican tariff that were so common in the Middle West turned up again in *Maryland, North* and *South Carolina, Georgia* and *Florida*. The Philippines figured much more prominently here than in platforms of the Middle West. The fight to subdue the Aguinaldo uprising was sometimes attacked as "an act of criminal aggression and a wicked exercise of despotic power" (*West Virginia*), "a greedy and bloody use of power" (*Delaware*), "the benevolence of murder and assimilation of Robbery" (South Carolina).

As in the other regions no clear picture emerges of what action the Democrats recommended for the Philippines. The Florida platform urged the same freedom for the islands as promised to Cuba, i.e. independence. The Virginia platform demanded that the islands be handed over to their inhabitants "as soon as is practicable." The system of holding colonies outside the Constitution was denounced and the plank stated that it was impossible to "raise the level of American citizenship by pouring into it a horde of Asiatics," an argument not unexpected from the South and which recurred in Georgia's platform. Working from these two premises, the alternative was complete Philippine independence. The same demand was implicit in the West Virginia platform.

North Carolina adopted no position on the question. The Delaware platform asserted: "Whereever our flag flies we desire it to mean liberty

152

and homerule for the people beneath its folds and maintain that the constitution must follow the flag." The colonial system was rejected, but since the American flag also flew over the Philippines and no demand was made for independence of the islands, this would imply that the Philippines should be given the same status as Puerto Rico, and both territories incorporated into the United States. Delegates in Delaware, however, had not worked out this logical consequence, any more than other Democrats had. There is another example of expediency. Anti-imperialism was exploited to attack the McKinley administration and policies, but nobody dared to go so far as to demand openly a retreat from the Philippines, acquired as the result of a very popular war.

Finally the platform of South Carolina, which made a sharp attack on the war on the Philippines, demanded that inhabitants of the Philippines should be helped "in the establishment of a free government of their own choice under a protectorate by the United States." There was an unmistakable ring to these words, reminiscent of the resolutions of Vermont and Pennsylvania.[31]

The majority of platfoms (Maryland, West Virginia, South Carolina, Georgia and Florida) had anti-British feeling, usually declarations of sympathy for the Boers.

There was no lack of enthusiasm for commercial expansion in the South Atlantic States. But while Georgia denied that "acquisition and domination of lands in distant hemispheres" was necessary for this end, or would even promote it, Maryland made one exception: "except as coaling or naval stations."

All four Democratic state platforms in the East South Central region denounced the Puerto Rican tariff. *Mississippi* alone had a demand for release of the Philippines and recognition of the islands' independence. *Kentucky* and *Tennessee* condemned the system of colonies as unconstitutional and imperialistic. The Kentucky Democrats did not mention the Philippines, but the problem of the islands appeared in the Tennessee platform, in a surprising way. The American government was said to have a double duty: to the new territories, which must be helped to establish and maintain liberty and self-government: and to the United States, which must be guaranteed all such rights, privileges and control "as may be necessary for its welfare, security and interest ... including all things that may be necessary for military or naval purposes." American direction and control of the foreign and commercial relations of the new territories was necessary in so far as they affected the United States. This

153

applied as long as the United States was in any way responsible for their conduct and welfare. The interesting point is that the plank passed over the status of the Philippines: "Whether in the solution of this problem there be in the result total separation from the United States or otherwise, yet in any event free government and the protection thereunder granted to them must be accompanied by proper safeguards to the United States."

The difference between the policy objectives hinted at in this plank and those in many Republican ones is so slight as to be almost nonexistent.

The three Democratic state platforms within the West South Central region have several common features. They all demanded the rapid fulfillment of the promise of independence made to Cuba and similar treatment for the Philippines. The reasons given were the customary constitutional ones.

It is worth noting that no mention was made of the Puerto Rican tariff, particularly noticeable in the *Louisiana* platform which with this exception followed the Nebraska platform closely.[32]

This is connected with the fact, discussed in other contexts that Louisiana was one of the few states that actively supported the Puerto Rican tariff bill. Two congressmen from the state went so far as to defy the party line in the decisive vote and the New Orleans *Picayune* also proclaimed squarely in favor of the bill. The background to their support was the interests of the sugarcane planters in the state.[33]

At the *Texas* Democrats' convention a minority group of delegates tried to push through a corollary to the demand that the promise to Cuba should be kept, explaining that they were in favor of the annexation of Cuba if the Cuban people, having gained their independence, desired to join the United States.[34] This was the same line as that followed in the Missouri platform.[35]

4

The Democratic state platforms in the Mountain region were similar. The *Montana, Wyoming, Colorado* and *Utah* platforms condemned the colonial system practiced by the McKinley administration, with the usual arguments and references to the Constitution and the Declaration of Independence. But it is striking how all these platforms, with exception of Wyoming, which was brief, contained an emphatic declaration in favor of expansionism of the continentalist type: "expansion as practised by Jefferson," (Montana), "contiguous territorial expansion" (Colorado), "the kind of expansion which Jefferson advocated" (Utah). What they were denouncing was "criminal war of aggression and conquest."

What all these Democratic platforms were asserting was that the Constitution followed the flag and that the Republican administration should be condemned for the imperialistic way in which it treated the acquired territory "as colonies or conquered provinces and their people as slaves" (Colorado).

The Montana platform presented two anti-imperialist arguments which are less common. One is a warning for the serious consequences for the American workman from the labor of "millions of half civilized people," the other a denial that the simple wants of these people could ever create a market for American products.

None of the Democratic platforms in the Mountain states contained a clear demand that the Philippines should be relinquished and their independence recognized. Utah came closest, demanding that Congress should make an immediate declaration "by such measures as may be deemed most expedient, to secure the blessings of liberty and free government to the peoples of the Philippines." As in parallel cases the implication of this statement is not clear.

The majority of the platforms denounced militarism in the usual way and the Colorado platform contained in addition an expression of sympathy with the cause of the Boers. No mention was made of the Puerto Rican Tariff.

Among the Pacific states, we find that the *Oregon* platform had a plank on colonial and foreign policy which, apart from details, was taken from the Nebraska platform, like many others. The same applies to some extent to the *California* platform. The platforms denounced the Puerto Rican tariff, declared that the Constitution follows the flag, and opposed wars of conquest and colonial possessions. What was omitted is the entire section on the Philippines. As in many other cases, the platforms were asserting a principle without stating its consequences, speechifying while avoiding policy.

The *Washington* platform devoted the foreign policy plank to the Puerto Rican tariff, which it condemned. All three platforms declared sympathy with the Boers.

Regional Variations

1

In summarizing the Republican platforms adopted in the *Northeast* region, it can be said that they supported the expansionistic foreign policy of the McKinley administration, but usually expressed their support with restraint and in some cases almost apologetically. Idealistic humanitarianism dominated the motives. In second place there are some commercial points of view followed by occasional arguments dealing with strategy. Active "great power" expansionism was not absent, but had only a small part.

As far as the status of the new territories was concerned, Republicans usually urged retention of the Philippines, even if only indirectly. The question of government organization of the territories was left open in one case, but otherwise it was usually implied that these territories were not covered by the Constitution, but should be governed in accordance with its principles, following "the Spirit of the Constitution," with "every measure of local self-government for which they may show themselves fitted" (New Hampshire), assuring them of "a just government and a progressive civilization" (Maine).

The Massachusetts platform held a clause which appeared to abolish the distinction between new expansionism and the old "continentalism." It illustrated the lack of clarity and precision that so often afflicted the platform-writers as soon as they touched problems involving territorial expansion. The Democrats constantly stressed the difference between old-style continentalism and the new imperialism. On one hand territories were incorporated into the union, covered by the Constitution, and prepared for ultimate statehood, on the other territories were acquired which were not incorporated but governed outside the Constitution, not considered a part of the United States, excluded from ultimate statehood. The declaration in the Massachusetts Republican platform, that "the same policy which governed our fathers in dealing with the acquisitions of territory made in their time should be pursued with respect to these new possessions" should mean integration of new territories and acceptance of the doctrine that the Constitution follows the flag. The delegates at the convention which adopted this platform can hardly have realized what the logical conclusion of their declaration was.

In the *North Central* region there was a more markedly defensive aspect to the foreign policy planks of the platforms than in the Eastern states. Remarkably little space was devoted to foreign policy and related issues.

156

This applied in particular to the West North Central region. Striking is the almost total absence of declarations concerning the status of the new territories.

The longest plank on foreign policy was in the Nebraska platform, but even this was mainly defensive, answering attacks of the Democrats. Motives given here for a policy of expansion were mainly commercial. This tendency was particularly noticeable in the North Dakota platform, which refrained from any of the usual idealistic, humanitarian arguments and demanded retention of the annexed territories for purely economic and commercial reasons.

Platforms of the *South Atlantic* region were reminiscent of those in the North-Eastern states, but devoted less space to foreign policy. The "duty" line, idealistic-humanitarian arguments for retaining the new possessions, dominated. The point of self-government was emphasized: there was little difference between these planks and several Democratic ones as far as recommendations were concerned.[36]

The *South Central* region showed more enthusiasm for expansion than any of the regions previously discussed. Commercial expansionism was accented while defensive statements about self-government to be granted to the Philippines, so common in the Eastern states were absent. They had been replaced by attacks on the anti-imperialists.

In the *West*, platforms in the *Mountain States* in no way showed stronger expansionist feelings than others. In many cases the planks had been taken from platforms in the Middle West or Eastern states.

The picture that emerged from platforms of the *Pacific Coast* states was different. The Washington and Oregon platforms contained direct demands for retention of the newly acquired territories—something implied in most other Republican platforms. Secondly the economic reasons for retaining the Philippines were stated more emphatically.

The *Outlook* claimed in an editorial in the Christmas number for 1898 that there were three popular arguments for a colonial policy, each of which was associated with a region: "the Eastern conscience, the Western enthusiasm and the Pacific self-interest". West of the Rocky Mountains, commercial expansion, i.e. the hope of extensive trade in the Far East, was the motive. The Middle West was fired by conviction that the spread of American civilization was the duty of the United States and a blessing for the rest of the world. And on the East coast the strongest argument was that as a consequence of the victory over Spain it was the unavoidable duty of America to look after, protect and educate inhabitants of the Philippines

157

in particular.[37] Commercial expansion, humanitarian duty, and responsibilities of the victor, these three themes within expansionism were supposed
to have regional links. Investigation of the state platforms from the spring
of 1900 only partly confirms this theory. It is true that humanitarian arguments, above all those asserting the responsibilities of the victor, dominated
on the East coast, not only in the Northeast, but in the South Atlantic states.
Similarly, commercial motives were strong in the Pacific states. This applied
even more in the South Central states. Perhaps the most significant
modification of *Outlook's* theory is that "the spirit of enthusiastic Ameri-
canism," which the leading article ascribed to the Middle West, did not
appear in Republican platforms of the region, where the tendency rather
was to play down the issue.

2

Democratic planks adopted in the *Northeast* region all contained a plank
condemning the imperialistic policy of the McKinley administration. Arguments were constitutional and idealistic. Colonial rule was a crime against
the Declaration of Independence and the American Constitution and
represented a deadly threat to the foundations of freedom in the United
States. It is remarkable, however, that unqualified demands for independence for the Philippines were the exception rather than rule. Demands
usually referred to independence at some later point, or "home rule" and
"self-government" under American protection.

The Philippines attracted far less attention in the *North Central* region
than in the Eastern states, and instead Puerto Rico occupied a central
position and in particular the Puerto Rican tariff. Even here the arguments
were constitutional, working from the principle that the Constitution follows
the flag. It was only the Nebraska platform, the closely associated Kansas
platform, and the platform in Iowa that clearly demanded independence
for the Philippines. This can be said to be implied in many of the other
platforms, but considering that the issue was so controversial and that
many of those who asserted that the Constitution followed the flag recommended that the islands should be under American sovereignty in one way
or another, this failure to demand independence for the Philippines explicitly must be deemed significant and important.

Also worth noting are elements of expansionism in the platforms of
North Dakota and Missouri, which favored not only commercial expansion,
but territorial expansion of the continentalist or hemispherist type.

158

The *South Atlantic* states had platforms with the customary declarations of anti-imperialism. But as soon as one gets down to hard facts, the picture is, as usual, less clear-cut. Virginia and Florida demanded independence for the Philippines, while South Carolina and Delaware spoke of "a free government of their own choice under the protectorate of the United States," and "home rule" respectively. Commercial expansion appeared and Maryland, like Missouri and several other states in the West region, declared in favor of expansion of the continentalist type. Forcible annexation was accepted when necessary for securing coaling or naval stations. The northern part of the region was similar to New England and the Middle Atlantic area in that the Philippines dominated while Puerto Rico played a minor part and was not mentioned at all in Delaware, West Virginia or Virginia.

The Democratic platforms in the *East South Central* region had conventional anti-imperialistic platforms, but only one, Mississippi demanded independence for the Philippines. The picture from the *West South Central* region differed from that of the other region in that the Puerto Rican tariff was passed over. This was striking in the case of Louisiana, which had taken over the plank from Nebraska but omitted this section. The reason was that the tariff was supported by the sugar interests in Louisiana. It is worth noting that all the platforms in this region demanded independence for the Philippines, partly for the same reason.

Finally, what is most noticeable in the *West* region is that the *Mountain States* combined rejection of what was described as the McKinley administration's imperialism with acceptance of expansion of the continentalist type. The *Pacific coast* states had the usual planks on colonial policy, but only one, Oregon, followed the Nebraska platform and demanded independence for the Philippines, while California and Washington did not even mention the islands. The Puerto Rican tariff was conspicuously absent from the platform of the Mountain States, and was also missing from the Oregon platform.

Party Differences on Foreign Policy

This study of the foreign policy planks in the state party platforms of the Republicans and Democrats in the spring of 1900 shows that there were regional variations within each party. The general impression is that there also was a clear difference in the positions of the parties.

How essential was this difference? The nature of the material can easily

159

lead to an overrating of the disparities. Routine endorsements and denouncements reveal little when expressed in general terms. In many cases the Democrats used phrases and formulations from the standard anti-imperialist arsenal to attack the Republican administration, but failed to state any policy or round off their arguments with clear recommendations.

Nor can we expect to get all that much information from the planks about the objectives of the Republicans. What we have are endorsements of the administration's policy. These could be interpreted differently, and the terms in which they are couched do not tell much about the delegates' attitudes to expansionism. Not even on the subject of government organization of the annexed territories do planks provide unequivocal information, even if it is usually possible to distinguish a rejection of the doctrine that the Constitution follows the flag.

In the case of the Democrats, practically all the platforms contained a routine anti-imperialist plank, and often an explicit declaration that no territory might be ruled outside the Constitution, which followed the flag. In some cases the Democratic planks accepted the continentalist type of expansion—sometimes even hemispherism, and annexation of naval and coaling stations.

Three motives dominated the Republican platforms. Commercial expansion was often the only motive given in the category of national interest. But the dominating motives were moral and idealistic: humanitarian duty and responsibility of the victor. The anti-imperialist arguments of the Democrats centered on the constitutional and humanitarian aspects.

Not least because of the vagueness of these political platforms, intended to satisfy as many people as possible, it is difficult to get a grasp of the disparities between the parties when working with the terms "policy objectives and motives" as used here. A better approach is to take these planks as forms of policy positions and concentrate first on their recommendations and then on arguments used to back these.

We can use the term "standpoint" to denote argument plus subsequent recommendation. "Recommendation" is sometimes the final phase of a policy argument, but here the term "argument" is used to denote reasoning which leads to a recommendation. An argument then comprises both a statement of facts, analysis, and a judgement. 'Argument' is closely allied to 'motive' in the structure analysis in the first chapter, but this term is less limited. If we define a recommendation as "a statement suggesting that some action be taken by some individual or corporate actor whom the maker of the statement believes capable of taking that action,"[38] here also

160

the maintenance of the *status quo* in a controversial issue, e.g., retention of the Philippines as an American possession, can be regarded as an action.

STANDPOINTS

Recommendations

Republican

1. The Philippine Islands should be retained as an American /colonial/ possession

2. The Philippine Islands should be given every measure of self-government for which they show themselves fitted

3. The Philippine Islands should be given self-government under American protection /home-rule/

Democratic

1. The Philippine Islands should be given independence

2. The Philippine Islands should be given Independence under American protection

3. The Philippine Islands should be given self-government under American protection /home-rule/

It must be emphasized that in assessing the difference between party platforms, direct recommendations naturally have the greatest value, while general expansionistic or anti-imperialistic phrases specifying no action are routine tactics which give little to work on. Nor is the problem eliminated when we have recommendations, since they can be difficult to define. When these factors have been taken into consideration, it is possible to see that the clear difference between the two parties which later appeared in their national platforms and in speeches made at the national conventions and acceptance ceremonies does not to the same degree exist in this material.[39]

Almost a third of the Republican state party platforms went out of their way to advocate some sort of self-government for the Filipinos. They usually used the more cautious wording of the second recommendation above: "the largest share of self-rule that future condition may seem to warrant" (Delaware), "every measure of self-government for which they may show themselves fitted" (Utah). In several cases home-rule or self-government was without reservation.

The third recommendation or its counterpart was advocated in more than ten of the Democratic platforms. This is remarkable in view of the fact that the demand for independence for the islands was central in what the party later declared in its national platform to be "the paramount issue" in the campaign.[40] In fact, less than a third of the Democratic state party platforms directly demanded independence for the Philippines and about half of those which did so have some reservation or qualification. They spoke of "independence under American protection"—the second recommendation above—or introduced a time element: first "a stable form of government", sometimes "as soon as they are capable of self-government." Bryan's Nebraska platform and the planks modelled on it recommended both establishment of a stable government and continued American protection.[41]

Arguments: Analyses

Republican

1. The new possessions belong legally and rightfully to the United States through the fortunes of war and by the terms of the treaty with Spain

2. The material interest of the United States in the competition for the markets of the world requires the United States to take the Philippine Islands. These islands are giving the United States a command of the vast trade of the orient not otherwise possible

3. The Philippine Islands have great strategic value. The victory over Spain and the acquisition of the new possessions have given the United States high rank as a world power. No backward step is possible

4. Wherever the American flag has gone, there the liberty, the humanity and the civilization which that flag embodies and represents must remain and abide forever

5. The Philippine Islands cannot be

Democratic

1. Independence for the Philippines would advance American trade by creating a market among people grateful for their independence

2. Inhabitants of the colonies, these "millions of half-civilized people," must come into competition with the American workman

3. Colonial conquests will lead to militarism at home

4. Imperialism and militarism will become instruments for trusts and monopolies

5. Imperial policy will lead to heavy tax burdens

6. The Filipinos cannot be American citizens without endangering American civilization or subjects without endangering the American form of government

7. A colonial system is a violation of the principles laid down in the Declaration of Independence and the Constitution and will destroy the American system of government which is based on the belief

turned back to Spain. They cannot be left unarmed for defense and untried in statecraft to the horrors of domestic strife or to partition among European powers. To abandon the islands to their fate would be "cowardly and pusillanimous"

that a just government derives its power from the consent of the governed

8. Colonial rule will lead to corruption

These Republican arguments represent the most common motives on the expansionist side, while the Democratic ones provide an inventory of anti-imperialistic motives. Arguments that appear most frequently and at the greatest length are the fifth Republican one above, and the seventh Democratic.

Arguments: Values

The expansionists and anti-imperialists had many common premises. Their perception of reality differed in some respects, as shown in the analyses above, but partly this was due to a fundamental difference in values:

Republican

The United States has become a World Power and must accept the political, strategic and economic consequences of its new position

Democratic

Under no circumstances must the United States accept a policy which might be dangerous to or inconsistent with the traditional American system of government based on the Declaration of Independence and the Constitution

Other Republican Statements

Recommendations

1. The inhabitants of the Philippine Islands should be given civilization, individual liberty and free institutions according to the spirit of the American Constitution

Arguments

No greater trust than the uplifting and educating of these defenseless people has been imposed upon the United States. It is the high and solemn duty of the nation to accept this trust, to give this people the blessings of liberty, peace and happiness

2. The commercial relations of the new possessions and the rest of the country should be regulated in a way that substantial justice may be rendered to all concerned	The Congress and President may lawfully control and govern the new possessions as they deem best. They are bound by justice and humanity to deal with these questions in the spirit of the American Constitution and civilization
3. Foreign markets for American products should be expanded	It is necessary to extend American commerce into China and the Far East, to further a market for the United States' surplus grain, cattle and other products

Other Democratic Statements

Recommendations	*Arguments*
1. Annexation of naval and coaling stations	No forcible annexation of foreign territory, except as coaling or naval stations. The United States must retain all such rights, privileges and control in the Philippines as may be necessary for its own welfare, security and interest, including all things that may be necessary for military or naval purpose
2. Expansion in the form of annexation of contiguous territory	Consistent with the American tradition and with the views of Jefferson and the Democratic party is expansion in the form of acquisition of contiguous or neighboring territory that can be erected into states of the union and whose people can become American citizens

3. Free trade for Puerto Rico. All American territories must be incorporated	The Puerto Rican tariff is erected in disregard to distinct pledges given and of their constitutional rights.
	    An executive or a congress, created and limited by the Constitution, cannot exercise lawful authority beyond that Constitution or in violation of it.
	    The Constitution follows the flag

164

4. Commercial expansion by peaceful means	The expansion of trade should be promoted by every peaceful means, but trade secured and held by force is not worth the price that must be paid for it

The table shows differences, which we can trace to the judgements listed above. The Democrats were no strangers to expansion. The term "commercial expansion" occurs nearly as frequently in their statements as in those of the Republicans. Five Democratic platforms favored the traditional form of territorial expansion, two recommended annexation of Cuba, and the annexation of naval and coaling stations was considered. Statements demanding that the United States should build a canal in Nicaragua linking the Atlantic and Pacific Oceans, a goal closely associated with the demands for "commercial expansion" were more often made by the Democrats than by Republicans. It is not surprising that the canal was often mentioned in the Southern states.[42]

In Search of a Paramount Issue: A Democratic Dilemma

Throughout the spring of 1900, right up to—and even during—the national convention in Kansas City at the beginning of July, the Democratic party was discussing which issues should have priority in the campaign. Opinions differed widely and Bryan was under strong pressures.[43] All the Democratic preconvention state party platforms, above all those from the months from March to May, contained declarations warning against trusts and monopolies, and these planks were often detailed and harshly critical. The traditional tariff question is mentioned in over half of the platforms, but has not the same topical interest.

It was evident that the party's national platform would have to pay attention to these issues. But as times were getting prosperous, it became obvious that such questions were nor vital enough from the voter's point of view to enable the Democrats to make the necessary breach in the Republican stronghold. Nor was the trust question an ideal issue, since it was not clear-cut on a party basis. The majority of Republican platforms contained anti-trust planks.

These issues were not controversial within the Democratic party, unlike the old currency question. A heated debate emerged among leaders of the party as to whether the national platform should reiterate the demand from 1896 for free silver coinage at a ratio of 16 : 1 or be content with reaffirmation of the Chicago platform. Both those who were convinced opponents to free silver coinage and those silverites who wanted to push the question into the background for tactical reasons, applied all their energy and influence to making imperialism the paramount issue.

Did the platforms from the various states provide any pointers to help the Democratic leaders decide? Trusts and monopolies were dealt with in practically every platform. The same applies to imperialism but, as shown above, the anti-imperialist planks had a strong tendency to stop at words.

What then was the case with the silver question? The first important point is that disagreement did not concern bimetallism, but whether the magical figures 16 : 1 should be repeated. Even a reaffirmation of the Chicago platform would appear a backing-down if 16 : 1 was not explicitly named. Few of the currency planks adopted by the Democrats before the National convention included 16 : 1. Only seven did so, and only two from regions east of the Mississippi (Massachusetts and Florida). The remainder demanded bimetallism, attacked the Republican's gold standard legislation, or contented themselves with support for the Chicago platform without further comment. The majority of platforms follow the third course. Support for 16 : 1 came mainly from states with little political significance, such as Montana, Utah and Colorado, naturally anxious to protect local silver production, from Nebraska where Bryan dictated the platform, and from Missouri. The line that Bryan forced the party to accept Kansas City, had little support from the state party organizations.

CHAPTER V

The Appearance of the Paramount Issue

One reason for American "territorial" imperialism being so shortlived is to be found in the increasingly hostile opinion developing within America during the crucial years around the turn of the century. Other reasons gradually emerged—realization among politicians that colonies often cost more than they were worth and that the system was already obsolete; among businessmen that territorial occupation with all its resultant complications was by no means a requisite for economic exploitation. Even when expansionist enthusiasm was at its height during the years immediately following the victory over Spain, the anti-imperialist sentiments, ranging from doubt to pure negativity, expressed by a broad and above all articulate opinion, was a major restraining influence. A very important factor in this development was that one of the major parties clearly and categorically took an anti-imperialistic stand and thereby—despite electoral defeat—came to influence the attitudes of a large section of American voters.

Although the Democrats showed a growing interest in anti-imperialism during 1899, and some polarization of public opinion along party-political lines could be observed, the Democrats were in no way unanimous. The mood at the beginning of the year 1900 was not such that it seemed only natural and expected to make the foreign policy of the McKinley administration the issue of the coming campaign. How then did the "paramount issue" arise?

One factor influenced the party tacticians, namely, the storm of opinion aroused by the Puerto Rican tariff bill, primarily in the Middle West, which seemed to provide the Democrats with what they had lacked, a weapon in the approaching campaign. Although the storm largely died down after the bill was passed, despite persistent efforts by the Democrats to keep the issue alive, the incident had shown that, regionally at least, imperialism was controversial enough to engage the interest of voters.

In attempting to establish how it came about that the Democrats entered the election campaign with a program dominated by anti-imperialism, there is good reason to start with the activities of William Jennings Bryan. Since his candidacy was never seriously questioned, the party's platform could be expected to be in agreement with his intentions, or at least acceptable to him.

The Anti-Imperialists and Bryan

The ambivalent attitude of the organized anti-imperialists towards Bryan and the Democratic Party is not surprising. The Commoner's resolute fight against imperialism had many roots. He had rapidly realized its potential as a unifying campaign issue, a factor that was undoubtedly decisive in determining the action he took in connection with the ratification of the peace treaty with Spain. He was also fully aware that sugar from the Philippines would compete with the product of the Colorado beet growers and the Louisiana cane planters, thus weakening his agrarian allies. Immigration of cheap labor from the newly acquired territories could have the same effect on the standard of living of American workers.[1] But first and foremost Bryan's opposition was based on moral and ideological grounds. The reason why the anti-imperialists found it so difficult to back him was that the majority of them were violently opposed to the Peerless Leader in other respects.

At least six of the seven acting vice-presidents of the National Anti-Imperialist League were actively supporting sound money. The majority of the organized anti-imperialists were mugwumps, independent Republicans or Gold Democrats and silverites were a minority.[2] In addition, the passage of the treaty with Spain in February 1899 had been a major defeat for the anti-imperialists and a major victory for their opponents. Many anti-imperialists could not forgive Bryan for his support of the treaty.[3] As the election approached, the anti-imperialistic agitation increased and at the same time the internal antagonisms among the anti-imperialists became more pronounced. The decisive question was naturally whether they should support Bryan and in this way try to defeat McKinley and crush imperialism, or whether they should introduce a third ticket.[4]

Spasmodic attempts had been made in conservative and anti-imperialist quarters during 1899 to launch candidates who could become the Demo-

168

cratic standard-bearer in 1900 instead of Bryan. The greatest hopes had been centered on Senator Gorman, who soon proved to be impossible, however. The efforts of a number of easterners to push Judge Augustus Van Wyck of New York for the presidency were equally unsuccessful. The conservatives were forced to admit that Bryan's position was far too strong.[5]

Among those who were most sceptical of Bryan was Andrew Carnegie.[6] He alone covered a large proportion of the American Anti-Imperialist League's expenses. For long periods he was responsible for half or more of all contributions.[7] In addition he gave generous support to both local branches of the League and to anti-imperialist newspapers.[8]

A meeting was held at the Plaza Hotel in New York on January 6, 1900. Among those present were Carl Schurz, Gamaliel Bradford, ex-Senator J. B. Henderson, Andrew Carnegie, Edwin Burrit Smith, Senator Pettigrew, Franklin H. Giddings, Herbert Welsh, John Jay Chapman, Erving Winslow and William A. Croffut. The main question was tactics for the presidential election that year. According to the account Pettigrew, the Silver Republican from North Dakota, gives in his memoirs, Carnegie strongly urged a new party, since neither of the two existing parties was acceptable. He was backed by Schurz and Henderson, among others, and it was decided that the work of organizing a third party should be started forthwith.[9]

Pettigrew's memoirs are extremely unreliable, and his account of this occasion is clearly misleading. He was right in so far as many of those present, not least those named above, greatly disliked Bryan. But no formal decision was taken. In fact the debate about which line should be followed continued right up to the Democratic National Convention on July 4 and resumed afterwards.

At the meeting in New York it was decided to follow a course which implied party-political neutrality. It was a compromise between those who wanted to go in for a third ticket and those who wanted to back Bryan. There was a third group not yet represented within the organization, consisting of those, who despite anti-imperialist convictions, had decided to remain with the Republican Party. The line was laid down, however, in a circular letter on March 22, from Erving Winslow, Secretary of the New England Anti-Imperialist League, which stated that they should continue "for the present the strictest nonpartisan action." In this way they kept open the possibility of backing the most suitable candidate.[10] This course was supported by the former Republican senator from Maryland, Henderson, ex-Governor Boutwell, president of the organization, and others.[11]

Carl Schurz was among those who at this point advocated a third party. Early in March he tried to gather support from such leading anti-imperialists as Moorfield Storey and Edwin Burrit Smith. In the eyes of Schurz, Bryan was a thoroughly repugnant alternative. He preferred a third ticket headed by an "old Republican" who would appeal to the voters. The best man would be Henderson, but other names were conceivable, such as Rufus Smith. This would attract all those who were "thoroughly disgusted with McKinley but repelled by the idea of voting for Bryan."[12] Schurz argued that while the German press opposed imperialism, it was negative to "Bryanism."[13] Among those who seconded Schurz were Samuel Bowles, publisher of the Springfield *Republican*, one of the leading anti-imperialist organs,[14] and somewhat more uncertainly Storey.[15] Charles Francis Adams was another of those who were negative to Bryan.[16]

Neither George Boutwell, Erving Winslow, Edwin Burrit Smith, David G. Haskins nor the many others with whom Schurz discussed the matter were convinced that the solution he was recommending was the correct one. Smith rejected the idea outright as indefensible in view of the fact that one party held "entirely sound" views on the main issue, imperialism.[17] Winslow was of roughly the same opinion and Haskins described a third party as "suicidal folly."[18]

The opposition to Bryan and the Democrats from Independent and Republican anti-imperialists was widespread; men such as Winslow and Burrit Smith were no admirers but they regarded the Commoner as a lesser evil than McKinley. The great stumbling-block was the silver question. As early as December 1898 the problem was formulated thus by Dana Estes: "If Bryan and his crowd can be induced to drop silverism and present a policy of this kind as the principal issue before the country, we may still have a party for which a man may be able to vote without blushing."[19] And Carl Schurz declared that the expansionist policy would certainly be defeated if the Democratic party could get rid of "the silver nonsense."[20] Throughout the spring of 1900 great efforts were made by anti-imperialists to persuade Bryan to go in wholeheartedly for anti-imperialism and drop the silver plank from 1896. The attempts to make Bryan relinquish the Chicago platform's silver plank had been started much earlier. Such efforts were made, for example, by Louis R. Ehrich of Colorado Springs, member of the Executive Committee of the National Sound Money League. When Ehrich had spoken to Bryan in July 1899, he had come to the conclusion that Bryan would not recede from the Chicago platform simply because he feared the alienation of many followers. Ehrich had got the impression that at bottom Bryan was very much lukewarm on the silver question. However, Bryan had pointed out that 6 1/2 millions had voted for him on that basis in 1896 and he did not like to take chances with such a following. At the same time, however, he had declared that if any movement towards Free Silver "would have the effect which we foretell, he would at once recede from such a position. I still cannot but entertain the hope and the feeling that if a sufficiently large demonstration should be made by men who would express their opposition to 'Free Silver' and their readiness to follow Bryan on 'Anti-Imperialism' he might be led to put aside the Financial Question in the coming campaign."[21]

One of those who tried to persuade Bryan of the wisdom of this course was David Starr Jordan. Jordan was president of Stanford University, a Republican, one of the vice-presidents of the American Anti-Imperialist League, and among its more noted members. He was also one of the very first to engage in anti-imperialist agitation. The day after news of Dewey's historic victory in Manila Bay reached San Francisco, Jordan made a widely publicized speech on the dangers of victory and the curse of imperialism. The speech was published during the summer of 1898 under the title, *"Lest we forget."* The printing was financed by John J. Valentine of San Francisco, a convinced anti-imperialist. The following year the speech was re-printed, together with other anti-imperialist speeches and articles by Jordan, in a book called *Imperial Democracy*. This is one of the most interesting contributions to the abundant literature on the subject and was regarded in some circles as the best summary of the anti-imperialist arguments that existed.[22] In his attempt to influence Bryan in the spring of 1900, Jordan was acting in agreement with Edwin Burrit Smith, chairman of the Executive Committee of the American Anti-Imperialist League,[23] and Schurz was also initiated into the plan. In his first letter to Bryan, dated February 7, Jordan described himself as "an American citizen, who is not much of a politician, but who is deeply interested in the realities of which politics is the play." He defined the overpowering threat which he saw in imperialism: "the adoption of a system of colonies in which inferior races are ruled unwillingly for their own good and for the good of their captors. Imperialism begins with the permanent seizure of regions of which the inhabitants are not or cannot be made citizens of the United States with all the rights and privileges held by you and me." Twice Bryan had failed in the duty of every citizen who professed to believe in the democracy of Lincoln and Washington. The first occasion was when he defended the war against Spain and the second when he voted in favor of ratification of the peace treaty. The new choice which faced him was infinitely more important.

Jordan sought to force Bryan to choose between anti-imperialism and the silver issue. The latter issue was dead, he claimed. When times were hard and debts burdensome it might interest people, but not even under these conditions would it suffice to win a victory. And now it was out of the question. A matter of far greater importance was at stake and in a decisive battle there could be only one issue, not two or three: "If imperialism is an issue, it is the sole issue possible." If Bryan could not bring himself to follow this line, it was his duty to step aside for someone who could.[24]

In his answer, which he emphasized was not for publication, Bryan commented on Jordan's insistence that the demand for free silver should be dropped in order that everyone might unite in a struggle against imperialism. Bryan was clear on this point and stated it with remarkable acerbity. Six and a half million voters had supported the Democrats in 1896, he pointed out. If only five per cent of those who voted for McKinley then could be won over to the Democrats, victory was assured. Those who voted for Bryan in 1896 voted for silver. What reason was there to believe that it would be easier to persuade nineteen silver men to follow a gold-standard program than one gold man to join the nineteen who supported silver, he asked somewhat sophistically. Jordan had naturally never proposed that Bryan should back the gold standard.

Bryan stated his dilemma clearly. He received many letters with advice, but the advice differed: "some advising me to drop everything else and make the fight against imperialism, some advise me to drop everything else and make the fight against the gold standard, some advise me to drop everything else and make the fight against trusts." He would follow his own judgement and what he thought his conscience told him. And it was obvious that he would not drop the silver demand from the Chicago platform in order to win support of Gold Democrats and Gold Republicans: "I am doing my duty as I see it, whether I shall be classed as a patriot or as an opportunist is not for me or for you to say. The future will determine that and neither of us is gifted with prophesy."[25]

Jordan was not convinced. In a second letter he stressed that in his opinion the silver issue was dead and pursuance of it in the campaign would guarantee victory for McKinley. He again made clear his attitude: when the foundation of democracy were threatened, issues such as silver or trusts had to take second place. "Either this is vitally important to every

172

citizen or else it is a mere bugaboo conjured up to carry elections." Imperialism was no "bugaboo." It was "the most dangerous usurpation since the slave power seized the machinery of our government to build itself up by the conquest of Mexico."[26]

When Jordan replied to Bryan's letter on March 7, he was on a visit to the Eastern states. On March 17 a letter from him to the editor was published in the Boston *Evening Transcript*, one of the papers which supported expansionism. It took the form of a pacifist protest against those who looked upon war as good for a nation. The interesting point here is the arguments. Many of the most enthusiastic expansionists took their ideas from Social Darwinism. Jordan got his arguments *against* martial self-assertion from the same source. He worked from the theory that "the nature of a race is determined by the qualitites of those of its numbers who leave offspring." The only way in which a race could be ennobled was by its protecting its best individuals and ridding itself of those who were inferior. Democracy was the form of society that best encouraged this process, since it gave everyone an equal chance and the qualities of the individual decided whether he made his way or went under. Race degeneration could only occur through the arch-enemies of democracy: slavery, aristocracy, militarism, imperialism. These tyrannical forces, which accompanied each other, destroyed the best individuals and left the worst to propagate the race. Jordan recalled the French Revolution: "The strongest, wisest, fairest" were the victims of the terror and "the blood of France has been poorer, her men less manly and her women less fair since the day of her great slaughter." The bloody wars during the nineteenth century completed the destruction. "Thus it has always been in history. The war-like nation of today is the decadent nation of tomorrow. It has ever been so and in the nature of things must ever be." Such is the fate of every empire. Worse than the loss of all the men who perish on the battlefield and in the camps is the loss of all the "fair women and brave men" who could have been their descendants but who were never born.[27]

Jordan was a biologist, which explains the slant to his arguments. Since getting caught up in anti-imperialism, he had spent time studying the effects of war on mankind. He worked from what had been discovered by Spencer, and above all Darwin. In *The Descent of Man*, published in 1871, there is the following passage: "In every country in which a standing army is kept up, the fairest young men are taken to the conscription camp and there enlisted. They are thus exposed to early death during war and are often tempted into vice and are prevented from marrying during the prime of life. On the other hand, the shorter and feebler men with poor constitutions are left at home and consequently have a better chance of marrying and propagating their kind."[28] The similarity to the letter to the Boston *Transcript* is conspicuous. Jordan later expanded upon these ideas in different works: *The Blood of the Nation* (1902), *The Human Harvest* (1906), and *War and the Breed* (1915).

One of those individuals who worked persistently to win for Bryan the support of the organized anti-imperialists was Elwood S. Corser, a banker from Minneapolis, a vice-president of both the American Anti-Imperialist League and the National Association of Anti-Imperialist Clubs. He was closely acquainted with Edwin Burrit Smith in Chicago, chairman of the organization's Executive Committee. Corser was a Silver Republican, but considered the currency question no longer of immediate interest. Imperialism was now the important issue. He tried to convert the Silver Republicans to "Lincoln Republicans" with anti-imperialism as one of the main points of the program.[29] During the spring of 1900 he acted as a go-between for Bryan and the anti-imperialists.

In the many letters he sent to anti-imperialists during the spring of 1900, Corser argued powerfully in favor of support for Bryan. "Mr Bryan stands to-day the one man who has unified the public sentiment against imperialism. To-day he commands a personal following greater than any other living man in the United States."[30]

Corser had also been appointed by Charles A. Towne, Chairman of the Silver Republican National Committee, to function as an intermediary during the campaign of 1900 between the Silver Republican National Committee and the National Committees of the Democratic Party, of the People's Party, and also of the Anti-Imperialist and Anti-Trust organizations.[31]

Despite the fact that he did not agree with Bryan—or Corser—on the monetary question, Edwin Burrit Smith too believed that the anti-imperialists must go for Bryan in the coming campaign, and consequently put Corser in touch with Carl Schurz.[32] Corser tried to influence Schurz, both when meeting him and by letter, but he had little success.[33] As a result of his discussions with Edwin Burrit Smith, Schurz and even George Mercer, the leader of the anti-imperialist organization in Philadelphia, however, Corser tried to win the support of the anti-imperialists for Bryan by broadening the base. When it came to the monetary question, the most he could hope for was moderation on the part of the Bryan Democrats, so that the platform was not too repugnant to the groups which formed the

174

core of the anti-imperialist organization. Corser sought support from these groups, by working for a plank in the Democratic platform on a matter which was dear to many leading reform men among the anti-imperialists, namely, the civil service.[34] He seems to have got the idea from Smith.[35]

Among Schurz's most important reform efforts were those concerning the civil service. Since 1892 he had been president of both the National Civil Service Reform League, which he had helped found in 1881, and the Civil Service Reform Association of New York, and was a tireless champion of "good government." Few things were more likely to conquer Schurz's deep-rooted scepticism of Bryan than a plank dealing with civil service reform.

Schurz was not the only one of the leading anti-imperialists involved in the Civil Service Reform organization. Several vice-presidents in the anti-imperialist organizations headed the reform movement, e.g., Moorfield Storey, Charles Francis Adams, Edward Atkinson, Gamaliel Bradford, Edward M. Shephard, William Potts, Horace White, Chester Bowles, Herbert Welsh and others.[36] There were influential newspapermen such as Pretorius, Godkin and Oswald Ottendorfer, anti-imperialists but also sceptical of Bryan. There were good reasons for choosing the civil service as the way to closer relations between Bryan Democrats and mugwumps and independent anti-imperialists.

Smith and Corser had met on the occasion of the congress held in February by the American Anti-Imperialist League in Philadelphia, and a week later Smith wrote a long letter in which he suggested a way of assuring Bryan of support from the anti-imperialists. The best way to win these voters was by going for a strong civil service plank. The one included in the Chicago plank was unsatisfactory to all those in favor of the "merit system," and the resultant distrust affected Bryan. What Smith suggested was an action not only to wipe out this distrust but guarantee Bryan enthusiastic support from the reformists.

"It will be worth much and will secure many voters if Mr. Bryan takes some early opportunity, in his own way, to arraign Mr. McKinley for his betrayal of the cause of civil service reform and for his violation of his own and his party's solemn pledge to enforce it and extend its operation. It will be especially effective if it is coupled with the charge that the controlling motive for the acquisition of the Spanish islands is spoils ...

It can also be made the basis for a strong affirmative position in the Democratic platform. Independent support of the Democratic nominees and platform will largely depend on whether this open door of opportunity is frankly entered."[37]

Corser approached Senator James K. Jones, chairman of the Democratic National Committee. He referred to talks in Philadelphia with leading anti-imperialists and informed the senator that these men were planning a large National Convention to be held after the Democrats' convention. If the Democrats adopted a clear anti-imperialist plank, and the Republicans in turn declared for "the so-called imperial policy," it would be safe to assume that the anti-imperialists would decide to back the Democratic candidate. There was one way of improving these chances; he had been urged by men very high in the councils of the anti-imperialists, to press upon leading Democrats the fitness and political expediency, as well as the righteousness, of a declaration of the principles of the civil service reform. Corser said that he favored this idea and believed it would be well received by both Silver Republicans and Populists.[38]

Corser made a direct approach to Bryan.[39] He gave him a copy of the letter to Senator Jones and expanded on his opinions. He emphasized that Schurz and Smith were the keymen among the anti-imperialists and both were strenuous civil service reformers.[40] He urged Bryan to follow the suggested course and claimed that this would assure him of support from the mugwumps and guarantee a decision by the convention to be held by the anti-imperialists in Indianapolis at the beginning of August, to support Bryan in the campaign.

Bryan was not unsympathetic, but Jones was more positive and continued the discussion of the matter with Smith. According to Smith, Jones' attitude was very satisfactory to those in charge of the National Civil Service Reform League,[41] and it was from those quarters that proposals for a civil service plank for the Kansas City platform were drawn. Two suggestions were forwarded by Smith to Bryan and Jones, prior to the Democratic convention in Kansas City, one long and one short plank.[42] Smith claimed that the former had been written by Carl Schurz when the leading anti-imperialists had met at the Plaza in New York. The long version was the work of McAneny, secretary of the National Civil Service Reform League, and Charles J. Bonaparte of Baltimore, a prominent mugwump lawyer and one of the most active members of the same organization's executive committee.[43]

A civil service plank was also brought to Kansas City by another reformer, Edward Osgood Brown of Chicago. It was approved by Senator Jones, was incorporated into the Silver Republican platform, but was left out of the Democratic platform. This plank too was originally written by Carl Schurz.[44]

Smith's letter reached Bryan just when leading forces within the Democratic National Committee were making a final effort to persuade him to abandon the silver issue. The effort failed. Smith's attempt to get through a civil service plank met with the same fate.

Bryan and the Eastern Democrats

It was not only convinced anti-imperialists who put pressure on Bryan to abandon the silver issue, which many found so obnoxious. Many of the gold-standard Democrats, who had left the party in 1896, believed that the issue was dead. Rising prosperity and an increase in the supply of gold had made the question at least moribund and they wanted to return to their party. Of even greater importance were the many Democrats who had remained within the party and supported Bryan, but lacked his fanatical belief in the currency issue and who considered that there were no grounds for attempting to win an election by reiteration of the controversial 16 : 1 demand.

The efforts of the eastern Democrats, above all in New York, to get Bryan to change course were strenuous. Bryan's stubborn determination to retain the silver demand was frustrating for these Democrats, since voters in their part of the country were clearly gold-minded. If the attempt to make Bryan keep quiet on the currency question failed, they wanted at least to persuade him to show enough judgement and tactical flair to adapt his message on a regional basis. The opinion expressed by the influential Pulitzer was typical. He claimed that the election could be won by the Democrats if Bryan could be induced "to keep silent on silver east of the Blue Ridge Mountains, and leave us in the East to fight the battle on the balance of the platform, and as we deem expedient." Bryan could talk silver in the West, but not in the East. Pulitzer promised the backing of the New York *World* if Bryan would follow this course.[45]

Hearst also tried to influence Bryan. He was not a gold-standard Democrat and energetically supported Bryan, but had great doubts about how far it was wise to push silver. Hearst was ambivalent not only on the money issue but on the question of expansion.

In a letter to Bryan in the summer of 1899 Hearst stated that he believed that expansion was "good Democratic doctrine" and refused to come out for Philippine independence. In his opinion the Philippine Islands would be of great advantage to the United States.[46] At the beginning of the year

Hearst still seemed uncertain whether to support Bryan. He declared, through Arthur Brisbane of the New York *Journal*, that the Philippines should not be given up and that the attitude taken by the Democrats on expansion was a threat to the chances of the party in the coming election. "Americans are not of the give up kind," Brisbane wrote, and expressed the hope that, after a Democratic victory, which was possible, they would abandon their "policy of retrogression" and once more become faithful adherents of American expansion as they had been under Jefferson.[47]

Hearst wanted the party to battle the trusts. There was widespread discontent in the country and Bryan should draw up a reform program for all those who were oppressed, measures that would help them as much as McKinley helped the trusts and the millionaires. It might then be possible to win their votes: "I don't think that interest in Aguinaldo or any metallic ratio will move them."

In a telegram to Bryan on May 20, Hearst said he had received unanimous reports from the entire continent that the mood of the voters was not in favor of free silver: "I have become convinced that people don't want free silver and that we can't make them want free silver and that if we try we will lose the opportunity to do great good in other directions."[48] Even after the Kansas City convention had adopted a platform containing a plank reiterating 16 : 1, Hearst gave Bryan continued support, which made Theodore Roosevelt call him "the most infamous scoundrel in America today."[49]

George Gray, the Democratic senator from Delaware who was one of the commissioners who had concluded the peace treaty in Paris and its most convinced anti-imperialist, also made plain that he would not lend support to a platform concentrating exclusively on silver.

Another newspaperman from New York who made his point even more clearly than Pulitzer and Hearst was James Creelman, editor of the New York *Journal*. Creelman was clearly pro-Bryan, although he had not backed him in 1896. He did not consider the silver issue essential, however. Creelman tried to keep Bryan informed of the situation, above all the mood of the New York Democrats, and did everything in his power to influence him: "The more I enquire the more I am convinced that the Kansas City Convention will make a simple reaffirmation of the Chicago platform and will not specificly mention "16 : 1" unless the convention is put under the pressure of threat from you that you will not be the candidate, as I know you well enough to believe that you will leave the delegates free on that point, after having offered your individual opinion."[50] Creelman saw

Bryan's stubborn refusal to turn aside from the 16 : 1 silver currency as a political blunder of the first order, a disastrous misjudgment, which could result in nothing other than defeat. "We cannot, cannot, cannot, and will not, will not take up '16 to 1' in the East. ... I want to say that I have seen most of the leaders east, west, north and south and they are all abhorred to any specific mention of free silver in the platform." Creelman and all other discerning Democrats agreed that the Chicago platform should just be briefly confirmed, and all the rest of the time be devoted to the new issues. It was not a question of *abandoning* the Chicago platform: "It is simply a question of reaffirmation or reiteration or, as I should say, 'reirritation'." New York was essential for a Democratic victory. Such a victory was possible, but not if the platform contained 16 : 1.[51]

With its thirty-six electoral votes, New York was a key state in the election. The Democratic leaders were the arch-enemies Richard Croker, "The Tammany Tiger," and David Bennet Hill, ex-governor and ex-senator. The latter, one of "the reorganizers," had gained his position from control of the party machine in the state, its state committee and executive committee, while Croker was the undisputed boss of Tammany.

Croker had suffered a severe loss of prestige when his protégé, Robert Van Wyck, was defeated by Theodore Roosevelt in the gubernatorial election of 1898.[52] He left New York and paid a long visit to Europe, but did not relax his hold on politics. The schism among New York Democrats widened when Croker announced in August 1899 that he was backing free silver, and thus aligned himself with the Bryan faction, a course which was unacceptable to Hill.[53] Willis Abbot, Bryan's faithful supporter, relates that Croker asked him to inform Bryan that if he dropped the silver demand, Tammany would carry New York State for him. The Commoner's answer could not have been more definite. It was clothed in Biblical words, a form of speech which certainly suited Bryan more than Croker: "Please say to Mr Croker that I say to the Chicago platform, to every plank in it, including the silver plank, as Ruth said to Naomi: 'And Ruth said, Intreat me not to leave thee, or to return from following after thee, for whither thou goest, I will go; and where thou lodgest, I will lodge; thy people shall be my people, and thy God my God'." When Croker heard Bryan's answer he said disgustedly: "I didn't think Bryan was that kind of a feller. You can tell him from me that I am through."[54] Croker eventually returned, however. In reality the Tammany Tiger felt little interest in either the silver issue or foreign policy. He assessed these issues primarily in the light of their usefulness in the political game. He decided to back Bryan and silver because in that way he gained a weapon against Hill and other enemies. "The Tammany Tiger will come to K. C. tamed and chained and ready to do your bidding both before and after the convention," wrote one of the initiated to Bryan a few weeks before the National Convention opened,[55] and Croker did in fact come to play an important part there.[56]

Hill saw opposition to imperialism as a chance to bring together the Democrats of New York and at the same time as an issue which could attract Independents. His dislike of the silver heresy remained, but intensive pressure was brought to bear upon him to induce him to accept a compromise which would make it possible to avoid an open fight over the currency question at the Kansas City convention. Creelman tried to persuade him to accept a national platform containing a brief affirmation of the Chicago platform of 1896. If the silverites refrained from a repetition of the demand for 16 : 1, Hill would undertake not to try to force through a different moneyplank. At the end of April, Creelman thought the chances of such a solution good.[57]

Senator James K. Jones, chairman of the National Democratic Committee, also spoke to Hill in an attempt to reach an agreement which would avert a fight at Kansas City. Democrats ought to "reaffirm the Chicago platform and declare against Imperialism, militarism and trusts."[58]

When Hill was making preparations for the New York state convention to be held on June 5, a month before the National Convention, he was aware that there was nothing to be done as far as concerned the nomination of Bryan. At first he sought to prevent the New York convention from reaffirming the Chicago platform with its free-silver plank, and wished it to back anti-imperialism. He did not wholly succeed. The Bryanites, strengthened by a telegram from Croker who was still in England, threatened to call a convention of their own on June 6 and appoint a rival delegation to Kansas City. At this point an important part was played in the opposition to Hill by Norman E. Mack, owner and editor of the Buffalo *Times* and a member of the State Committee.[59]

Another of Hill's opponents was Congressman William Sulzer, a Silver Democrat and Bryan supporter, who was one of those aspiring to be Bryan's running mate. He shared these ambitions with John H. Girdner, who also considered that the vice-presidential candidate had to come from New York if a Democratic victory was to be secured. "You and the right man from this state on a platform which reaffirms in a few lines the platform of 96, and then comes out strongly on the newer issues, especially anti-imperialism, and anti-trust and anti-constitution breaking, can beyond

180

question carry this state by a handsome majority," Bryan was assured by Girdner, who thus like Sulzer saw himself as "the right man." From what he said, he was in favor of following the more cautious line on the delicate silver issue. Sulzer had no reservations when it came to reiteration. Both warned Bryan against Hill and kept him informed of developments in New York. Girdner was attempting something of a balancing act: he stated that Hill had suggested that the delegation from New York State to the National Convention should be instructed to vote not only for Bryan as the presidential candidate, but for Girdner as vice-presidential candidate, although Girdner said that he had for the time being turned down the suggestion. Girdner also cooperated with Hill in drawing up New York's Democratic state party platform.[60]

Although Girdner at the start held roughly the same views as James K. Jones on the role of the silver issue in the approaching campaign, he turned right about when it became obvious that Bryan refused a platform which did not contain an explicit reiteration of the 16 : 1 demand. The dream of becoming vice president drove Girdner to write a long letter to Bryan, presenting himself as an uncompromising, hundred percent silver man, who refused to budge an inch despite pressure: "We would not deserve to win if we weakened in the slightest from what we know is God's eternal truth and justice. But it is political wisdom not to compromise, and the louder the clamor for a modification of the money plank in the K. C. platform, the more necessary it is for us to stand firm."[61] Girdner now joined those who supported Bryan in his refusal to back down on the silver issue, such as the unwavering silver man George Fred Williams from Massachusetts, at the time another hopeful for the place as Bryan's running mate.

The Bryanites' threat to send a rival delegation to Kansas City forced Hill to give way. He tried a compromise, that the New York state convention should not make any decision but should wait and endorse the national platform from Kansas City at the convention in September. A bitter struggle took place and it was only by threatening to reveal to the convention's plenary assembly the connections between some of his opponents, such as Robert Van Wyck, the Mayor of New York, and Tammany's notoriously corrupt Ice Trust, that Hill could retain control and drive through a platform which did not contain any acceptance of the Chicago platform from 1896. The platform endorsed Bryan's nomination, demanded parity of gold and silver as currency, denounced trusts, and devoted a lot of space to imperialism.[62] Hill, Croker, Edward Murphy Jr., and Van Wyck were appointed delegates-at-large to the National Convention. Hill's success in preventing endorsement of the Chicago platform was a serious warning to the Democratic leaders.

Hill belonged to the group of conservative Democrats prepared to accept Bryan, since his nomination could not be avoided. There were many, however, who had left the party in 1896 and who were still not prepared to vote for Bryan, including the circle around the former president, Grover Cleveland. They tried to persuade Bryan to retire in favor of someone else who would be more generally acceptable. Thus in January one of the former members of Cleveland's Cabinet, John S. Seymour, appealed to Bryan along these lines, suggesting that Bryan was far too closely identified with the demand for free coinage of silver.[63]

The gold-standard Democrats were hampered by the fact that they had no popular name to offer as a candidate for the presidency. At one point they thought that Admiral Dewey, the celebrated victor of Manila Bay, would fit the bill. A boom was started for him and efforts were made to get Bryan to step back in favor of the naval hero.[64] The campaign for Dewey collapsed at an early stage. Dewey's popularity proved far too frail a craft to be trusted to carry them to success and also the Admiral quickly demonstrated a quite amazing lack of political judgement. The backing of Dewey was a desperate attempt to avoid Bryan and the silver issue of 1896.

It was not only New York and the other Eastern states which were anxious to push the currency issue as far into the background as possible.[65] In Wisconsin, Louis G. Bohmerich, an active silver man in 1896, claimed his state would go Democratic in the election in November, if the money plank were modified. Bohmerich of German birth was considering seeking nomination as the Democratic candidate for the governorship, and said that he had received representations from every quarter to do all he could to bring about such a modification.[66]

The anxiety felt over Bryan's continued faith in the silver question was also expressed in Washington, D.C., where a group of Democratic senators, including John Morgan of Alabama, Arthur Pue Gorman of Maryland, and Francis Cockrell of Missouri tried to persuade their colleague, James K. Jones, chairman of the National Committee, to use his influence to avoid a reiteration of 16 : 1 in the party's coming platform.[67]

Faced with all these attempts to make him relinquish silver and go for a purely anti-imperialist program, Bryan brought out all the arguments he had used to Jordan in February. Although on several crucial occasions, such as in the fight for ratification of the peace treaty, he had shown little skill in political tactics, Bryan was no stranger to tactical considerations.

However, in this case, he was apparently not prepared to place expediency before conviction. His refusal to push the currency question into the background was on the other hand undoubtedly also based on the fact that in his opinion it was still a vital issue. He was apparently convinced that a reiteration of the Chicago platform's 16 : 1 demand was also correct from a political point of view. His standpoint is well expressed in a letter to Merril at the end of April.

Opinions differ, Bryan wrote, as to the significance of "the money question, the trust question and imperialism." Personally he considered them all equally important and had no desire to give any of them first place at the expense of others. It seemed to him that the world ought to be able to see the folly of his taking sides in the dispute. Why should he disappoint those who opposed the gold standard and the trusts, to satisfy those who saw imperialism as the dominant question, why antagonize the anti-imperialists by giving the trust question the central position or them and the trust opponents by putting up the money question as the only one of importance? Others might lay the emphasis on any of these questions, Bryan wrote, but he intended to back them all.[68]

"Why alienate nine in order to please one?" the Commoner asked, in almost the same words as he had used to Jordan. The weak point in Bryan's argument was naturally whether it was possible to satisfy the Populists and silver Republicans on the currency issue and at the same time achieve with the help of the anti-imperialists the breach in the ranks of the Independents, the gold-standard Democrats and Republicans which was the requisite for victory. Many doubted it. Arguing in much the same way as Jordan, Sam Busbur Martin, editor of the *Cosmopolitan Magazine*, declared that, while there were many questions which had supporters within the Democratic Party, "Imperialism, trust rule, militarism and all mean but one thing—all represent but one issue; and upon this issue every Lincoln Republican and every Jefferson Democrat may unite." For there was no room in the campaign for the money question—however important. If it was taken up, the more essential issue would be endangered.[69]

Bryan had many who agreed with him and he received many letters urging him not to yield. One of them was Geo Fred Williams of Massachusetts, member of the Executive Committee of the Democratic National Committee. Williams was a staunch silverite and one of Bryan's most loyal and reliable supporters in New England. He made a point which illuminates the sometimes bewildering problem of "the silver-craze." It was true, he wrote, that the great increase in monetary supply and the resulting rise in prices, had belittled the immediate necessity of the free coinage of silver. However, "the people who withstood the pressure of 1896 have taken to heart the silver issue ... It is the love of the mother for her first-born." Williams warned against "any inclination to neglect or slight the issue upon which the new party came into existence."[70]

There was after all no unity at all within the Democratic party when it came to expansionism, as has been made plain earlier. Antagonisms were deep and powerful. The Democratic Party organization in the state of Washington was threatened by divisions and paralysis through lack of agreement on expansionism.[71] And in New York some observers advised against too extreme an attitude in the platform concerning the Philippines. The result would only be that the Democrats would lose votes. "A few people are making a noise greatly disproportionate to their number about imperialism," stated Judge Gaynor of the State Supreme Court, and he hoped Bryan would not listen to them.[72]

Drafting the Platform

Pressure was not only being put on Bryan by those who wanted for various reasons to push the silver question to one side. It was balanced to some extent by pressure from those who, either from conviction or for tactical reasons, wanted to base the campaign on the silver question again. In the Western states, with their strong representation of Populists and Silver Republicans, many people considered that abandoning the Chicago platform on the currency question could be disastrous. In Colorado there was the influential Silver Republican, Senator Teller. Relations between Silver Republicans, the Democrats led by Governor Charles Thomas, and the Populists were strained and silver was the common interest on which they based their hopes.[73] A similar situation was to be found in Idaho and many other states, such as North Dakota, where the Silver Republican Pettigrew awaited difficulties since he had incurred the intense enmity of Mark Hanna, the man expected to be leader of the Republican campaign.[74] Other influential Silver Republicans and supporters of Bryan were Charles A. Towne and Corser of Minnesota. But Corser at least no longer considered the silver question to be of first importance.[75] Many others embraced bimetallism almost as a religious creed.

The internal conflict within the Democratic party concerning the monetary plank in the platform can be expressed briefly: "Reaffirm or reiterate?" The position of anti-imperialists and Democratic reorganizers was clear

184

and they received support from leading silver men, who considered it necessary for tactical reasons to place the silver question in the background and go for anti-imperialism as "the paramount issue." It was a question of getting Bryan to accept "reaffirmation" instead of "reiteration."

The fight was conducted with perseverance and continued right up to the time of the convention in Kansas City. It can be followed as a study of the making of the Democratic national platform of 1900.[76]

Those who were primarily responsible for the content of the platform which was presented to the Committee on Resolutions at the convention were—besides Bryan—Senator James Jones, chairman of both the Democratic National Committee and its Executive Committee; J. G. Johnson, vice-chairman of the Executive Committee, the Governor of Missouri, William J. Stone, vice-chairman of the National Committee, and Colonel Charles H. Jones, editor of St. Louis *Post Dispatch*, who drew up both the celebrated Chicago platform of 1896 and the 1892 Democratic platform. At the beginning of May, James Jones wrote to Johnson and suggested it was time to start writing the platform. The Senator emphasized the delicate nature of the task and stressed the need of exercising as much restraint as possible, in order to make it easier for those who had deserted the party in 1896 to return. "I also believe, that we should avoid the appearance of receding from any position we held in 1896, but that while standing firmly by our whole position we should make the way as smooth as we can for those who wish or seem to wish to come back to us." Jones still thought Bryan could be persuaded to accept reaffirmation of the Chicago platform without reiteration of its moneyplank.[77] Jones had approached Colonel Charles H. Jones who had agreed to work out a draft on these lines, on condition that the part played by him was kept secret.[78]

Charles Jones later told Bryan that he first made one draft for the platform. When this was ready he received the Nebraska State party platform.[79] Since he knew that this not only reflected Bryan's views on a whole series of questions, but as far as he could tell from the style had been written in part by Bryan, he had chosen when revising his draft to follow this Nebraska platform closely on vital points.[80]

Charles Jones sent his draft for the platform to Senator Jones and he, Johnson, and Bryan made changes. Charles Jones' draft, together with the alterations made by Senator Jones, Johnson, and Bryan were then sent on to Governor Stone and also back to Charles Jones.[81] On June 25, Stone gave his opinion to James Jones. He sent a copy of both his letter and suggested alterations to Bryan. Stone's proposals are of interest. Two of the six suggestions for changes and additions proposed by Stone were of importance for the final shape of the platform. One concerned the plank dealing with trusts, where he added a paragraph "especially denouncing the open and flagrant interference of trusts and other corporations in political and public affairs."[82] The second concerned a plank on the Monroe Doctrine, included in the draft he had received.[83] More interesting than these are additions and changes made by Stone which were not accepted. He proposed an addition to the section on Puerto Rico which he found much too negative. Apart from rejection of "the Puerto Rican law" and Republican policy on Puerto Rico, he wanted a positive statement "in form of an affirmative proposal." Stone's draft has not been preserved, which might make it seem uncertain what he intended, but apparently he wanted a declaration on incorporation of Puerto Rico.

When it came to Cuba, Stone wished to go further than mere criticism of the McKinley administration's policies. As far as he could see, peaceful annexation of Cuba, "done with the consent of the people," had been urged by the Democrats ever since the days of Jefferson. He wanted a plank which recommended annexation as soon as the population voluntarily wished it. A statement should be placed alongside an assurance that the promise of independence for Cuba would be kept. It is not surprising that Stone's suggestions appeared as planks in the party platform of his home state, Missouri.[84] Neither his addition concerning Cuba, nor the one on Puerto Rico, was included in the Kansas City platform.

The same fate was suffered by another suggestion from Stone, which he earnestly recommended and which he said was a subject dear to him. It concerned a paragraph "relating to our merchant marine and navy." He believed that a large merchant fleet was a blessing and wanted the Democrats to take up the demand for "reviving and rehabilitating our maritime interests" and make it into a leading issue. It would appeal to the patriotic feelings of the voters, while attracting "the commercial instincts and aspirations of our people."

Interesting here is that the unaccepted additional suggestions by Stone reappeared in the program of the expansionists. Both points were unassailable, since they involved nothing but expansion and the extension of power by peaceful means, and Stone did in fact make the usual distinction between imperialism and expansionism. Both the proposal for Cuba and the one concerning the merchant navy and the marine appealed to sentiments not far removed from the expansionists, and the Democratic leaders were possibly afraid of offending the anti-imperialists.

186

Nearly half of Stone's letter is on another subject: the money plank. Stone described himself as "a positive believer and ardent advocate of bi-metallic coinage at the ratio stated." Despite this he put forward a detailed argument in favor of reaffirmation rather than reiteration. A repetition of 16 : 1 could reduce the chances of victory, particularly in view of the wishes of the Democrats in New York, Indiana, and Illinois, who considered that repeating 16 : 1 could be disastrous; Republican newspapers were anxious for the Democratic platform to repeat the silver demand of 1896. They should not play into their hands by doing so.[85]

Stone joined the ranks of those who were trying to persuade Bryan to go to the election without burdening himself with the silver plank of 1896. His letter shows that, although he belonged to the inner circle of Democrats, he did not accept that the question had been settled, despite Bryan's declarations.

At the same time as he returned the draft for the platform to James Jones with his proposed alterations, Stone sent a copy of the letter and revised draft to Bryan. In the accompanying letter he took up another question which had come up and which he thought that they should consider including in the platform, namely, developments in China. Stone said he was convinced the European powers intended dividing China. He opposed this, just as he opposed the idea of acquiring Chinese territory. If the Chinese question was to be touched, it should be "in favor of maintaining the integrity of the empire."[86]

Senator Jones had also returned to Charles Jones the draft he had drawn up, together with alterations by the senator, Bryan and Johnson. Colonel Jones revised the draft, taking into account not only changes but the platform now published by the Republicans. He sent the new version to both James Jones and Bryan. He said he was satisfied with the result: "If the Platform can be adopted as it stands, I think we shall have the best declaration of principles ever put forward by a national convention." He compared it triumphantly to the Republican platform, "a botched piece of patchwork in style," "which devotes 3000 words to dead issues of the past and 200 to living issues of the present," while on the other hand "we give 2000 words to the vital issue of the present and less than 100 to anything that could justly be described as past issues."

Colonel Jones did not count the silver question among the dead issues. He assessed the situation the same way as Bryan. Excluding the silver demand "would lose us a hundred votes at one end of the line for every one it gained for us at the other end." Jones urged Bryan to get the platform accepted as it stood, without alterations.[87] It should be noted that, when making his final version of the platform, Charles Jones did not have access to the suggestions for changes and additions by Stone described above, which Stone had sent to James Jones the previous day.

Bryan now received Charles Jones' final draft for the platform and Stone's proposed alterations for an earlier version. In a letter to Stone on June 30, just a few days before the convention at Kansas City, he went through all the alterations he had proposed and gave his opinion on each.[88] Bryan explained that he had omitted Stone's additional paragraph on Puerto Rico. If the Committee on Resolutions wanted a paragraph to this effect he would not raise objections, since the Puerto Ricans obviously accepted the idea of annexation. The matter had never been formally submitted to them, and in view of its significance as a precedent—the Philippines—Bryan would prefer to have their formal acceptance. The Republicans had defended their policy toward Puerto Rico by speaking of the danger that Puerto Rican labor might compete with American workers and so a direct demand for incorporation might arouse opposition. Bryan had rejected the extra paragraph on Cuba suggested by Stone. The question had not been taken up by the Republicans and the Democrats ought not to take the initiative. A declaration in favor of future annexation, even on these conditions, could raise doubts about how serious was the promise of independence for Cuba and cause opposition at the convention, while it could encourage the Republicans to ignore the promise of Cuban independence. It should be noted that Bryan did not in fact declare against a voluntary association of Cuba with the United States.

Stone's suggestion for a plank on the Monroe Doctrine was accepted enthusiastically by Bryan, as was the addition on trusts. He was wary of the question of the merchant fleet and the navy: "I fear that the plank on the navy might be misconstrued into support of the imperialistic idea that our navy must be as large as any navy in the world. If we pursue a policy of justice and fair dealing, we do not need as big a navy as a landgrabbing nation."

Stone's idea of a plank on China appealed to Bryan and he drafted a proposed form for the Committee on Resolutions:

"While we believe that it is the duty of government to protect the lives, the property and the commercial interest of its citizens in China, yet we protest against the use of present disturbances in China, as a pretext for the seizing of territory or as an excuse for joining with European nations in the dismemberment of the ancient empire."

188

However, a plank on China was not included in the final platform. When going through Stone's suggested changes and additions to the draft, Bryan came to the money issue and there he was inexorable. The arguments were the usual ones.

After receiving Stone's suggestions and Charles Jones' final revised version, Bryan had made the changes described in the letter to Stone. He said he had consulted not only James Jones and Johnson, both present at earlier discussions on the platform, but R. L. Metcalf who was to represent Nebraska on the Committee on Resolutions. Metcalf and James Jones had received Bryan's final draft for the platform, together with a copy of Bryan's letter to Stone, and Stone could talk freely with both men.

Thus Bryan had refused to listen to representations to relinquish 16 : 1 and had sent such a plank to Senator Jones in Kansas City. Members of the Executive Committee gathered in Kansas City a few days before the convention. After discussing the situation, five of them—the chairman James K. Jones, the vice chairman John G. Johnson, W. M. Stone, who apart from being vice chairman of the National Committee was also a member of its Executive Committee, Daniel J. Campau from Detroit, and James M. Guffey from Pennsylvania—decided to combine in a last-minute attempt to make Bryan give in. They composed a statement which they all signed.[89]

The old contention over reiteration or reaffirmation now entered its final phase. The five committee members claimed that a large majority of the delegates who had arrived at Kansas City were of the opinion that it would be enough with a "general declaration of reaffirmation." They were convinced that "nine out of ten of the most thoughtful and conservative men of the party now here" considered that was the line to follow. The five declared that "severally and collectively they strongly concurred in this sentiment as we conceive it to exist." The only thing that could hinder such a platform was the rumor that Bryan would refuse to stand as candidate if the 16 : 1 demand was not in the platform. The five laid out a series of detailed and sharply worded arguments to convince Bryan that it was necessary for him to reconsider his position and agree to exclude 16 : 1. They had not changed their views on the subject, but for practical reasons an alteration in the platform was inescapable. They suggested a formula to replace the demand for free silver in the ratio 16 : 1.

"We re-affirm and endorse, in whole and in part, in letter and in spirit, the platform adopted by the Democratic National Convention held in Chicago in 1896."

189

The issues of 1900 as seen by cartoonists Nelan (1), Opper (2; 3; 5), Bart (4), Davenport (6), and Rogers (7)

"Troubles which may follow an Imperical policy." A Representative from the Philippines arguing with Thomas Reed, Speaker of the House.

1

2

"What are you crying about now, Willie?" "Little Johnny Hay and I are playing imperialism, and Billy Bryan, next door, is squirting water on us."

190

3

"Yes, Willie, we'll have a rehearsal of Imperialism for your children's masquerade party. You'll be His Majesty, Nursie will be the Queen Regent, Teddy will be the Master of the Horse, Johnny Hay will be the Chief Flunkey-in-Waiting, little Chauncey will be the Court Jester, and I'll be the Executioner."

4

The dilemma of Bryan and the Democrats. "Miss Democracy's crazy quilt."

"Yes, Willie, we are going to rehearse our Republican Campaign Play. Nursie will be the Good Fairy with he Magic Wand, I'll be the Nice Old Gentleman who gives away Full Dinner Pails, Teddy will be the Fearless Knight, and—let's see, Willie, you can be one of the trees in the background."

5

6

McKinley and Hanna taking a walk with the trusts. Davenport always dressed Hanna in a suit with dollar signs.

"If you are just foolin', Uncle Sam, don't you think you'd better quit?"

In practice this would mean the same as a reiteration, but the very mention of 16 : 1 had been given a magical content, had become charged with emotion, was like a red rag to large groups of voters. Jones and colleagues emphasized that the feelings of the Eastern states had to be taken into consideration. Large numbers of Democrats, especially in New York and Maryland, had stated that reaffirmation instead of reiteration "would make a very material and important difference with them." The silver question was impossible there: "If we win in New York or any Eastern state, we must win upon the Trust Issue, and Imperialism and not upon the coinage of gold and silver at the ratio of 'sixteen to one'." The New York Democrats had said they were optimistic about winning, but only if they received the help that abstention from reiteration of the silver plank of 1896 would mean.

The Democrats of the Eastern states were not the only section of the electorate whose wishes had to be considered. A Democratic victory also depended on whether German and Scandinavian voters would, as was hoped, vote Democratic because of the issue of imperialism and militarism. At the same time these groups were staunch opponents of silver and nothing should be done to place a stumbling-block in their path as they moved into the Democratic camp. Democratic leaders from Iowa, Wisconsin, Michigan and other states containing many German voters agreed on the necessity of being content with reaffirmation. The story was the same among many Democrats representing the South and West, anxious to ease the return of the gold-standard Democrats who had left the party in 1896. In the event of Bryan's insisting on 16 : 1 in the platform, he would succeed. He would not achieve it without a struggle and it was far preferable to have an unanimously adopted platform.

Such an appeal from five members of the executive committee, including its chairman and vice chairman, carried weight. But its effect on Bryan was negligible. The Commoner was in Lincoln, Nebraska, when he received the letter and he replied immediately to Jones. He said he had pondered the question for months. He admitted that Jones and colleagues were older and more experienced in politics, "and being a democrat I must accept the doctrine that the presumption of rights is with you five as against me and in a still greater measure would be with the convention as against me." Nor did he want to deny that a Democrat with such a platform and with views wholly in harmony with it ought to win. He refused to change his decision. He did not wish to avoid the money question and would not stand on a platform not containing a plank demanding free coinage of silver,

16 : 1. The convention was naturally free to choose the other alternative, but in that case they should not count on Bryan as their candidate.[90]

The combined efforts of the five members of the Executive Committee had as little effect as other attempts made to coerce or persuade Bryan into changing his mind. All the months spent by anti-imperialists, gold-standard Democrats, moderate silver men and party tacticians had no result. Conflict was inevitable. The draft for the platform which would be presented to the Committee on Resolutions would contain a silver plank reiterating 16 : 1 and it could not pass without a fight.

CHAPTER VI

The National Conventions

The Case for Expansion: Philadelphia, June 19—21

1

The unanimous nomination of McKinley as Republican candidate for the Presidency was inevitable, but prior to the National Convention in Philadelphia between June 19—21 it was in no way self-evident that Roosevelt would be nominated as his running mate. He would have preferred to be reelected as Governor of New York and was aiming at being nominated as the Republican presidential candidate in 1904. Roosevelt feared that the post of vice-president would shelve him, forcing him into an inactivity that would spoil his chances for the nomination in 1904. Mark Hanna, chairman of the Republican National Committee, had quite different reasons for not wanting Roosevelt nominated and McKinley was also negative to his candidacy even if he did nothing to stop it.[1] Tom Platt, the powerful Republican boss in New York, however, wanted to get rid of Roosevelt, who was in his opinion far too independent and so he supported the nomination, as did the controversial Pennsylvania boss, ex-Senator Quay.[2] Roosevelt's friend, Senator Henry Cabot Lodge from Massachusetts, permanent chairman of the Convention, also supported the nomination, believing unlike Roosevelt that the post of vice-president was important and could be used as a spring-board to the Presidency.[3] Roosevelt's enormous popularity, not least in the Western states, and the absence of strong opponents led to an unanimous nomination, however. The only vote that Roosevelt did not get was his own.

It has been said that in the election of 1900 the Republicans avoided speaking of foreign policy, that they tried to avoid at any price "expansionism" or "imperialism" as issues in the campaign.[4] This is a misleading generalization, however. Foreign policy in no way held a back seat at the Convention in Philadelphia. The Convention's key-note speech was made by Senator Edward O. Wolcott from Colorado, Temporary Chairman of the Convention, and a convinced expansionist. The speech developed into a grandiose account of the past four years of Republican rule. In addition to the usual comparison between then and now, on the theme of poverty and prosperity, Wolcott devoted considerable space to the question of foreign policy.

He declared that "the spirit of justice and liberty" had always been cornerstones of Republican policy. "It compelled our ears to listen to the cry of suffering across the shallow waters of the Gulf two years ago." "It / the spirit of justice and liberty / prompts us in our determination to give to the dusky races of the Philippines the blessings of good government and republican institutions."

The first section of the speech is couched in general terms and it is typical that both Wolcott and the Democrats referred to traditional values as a basis for the party's actions and standpoints. The motives of duty and humanity run through the entire speech.[5]

When dealing with the Spanish-American War, Wolcott stressed emphatically both the President's desire for peace and the fact that only "lofty and unselfish motives," "the noblest purposes" drove America to intervene. A bloody sacrifice was made for "the freedom of another race." On the delicate subject of the Philippines, Wolcott became even more verbose. The cruelties that had been inflicted upon the Cubans were nothing compared to what had afflicted the Filipinos and if the Americans had returned the islands to Spain, they would have been abandoning the people to a fate worse than slavery, worse than barbarism. "We had our hand to the plough, and every instinct of honor and humanity forbade us to turn back." "A universal demand arose from all over the country that we should retain our hold upon these islands, afford their people the protection of our laws, lift them out of their unfortunate condition, and fit them if possible, for self-government."

Time after time Wolcott emphasized the noble motives that had alone directed the American policy: "No civilized nation in the world, no Christian nation, could have turned these people back to Spain." "We are told that the islands are rich in all the products of the tropics, in mineral wealth, and in the possibilities of their future development. So much the better. But if they were as barren as the Libyan desert, we would have taken them just the same."

The Achilles heel of the Republican presentation of their policy was naturally the revolt led by Aguinaldo. Wolcott dealt with this in the only way possible. Aguinaldo was said to be supported only by the Tagal tribe,

198

a small part of the population, the greater part of which gratefully welcomed American government. But Wolcott also placed the responsibility for Aguinaldo's revolt on the American Democrats, claiming that the chief inspiration and encouragement of the Tagal insurrection come from the Democratic headquarters in the United States.[6]

Wolcott also placed the American expansion in a wider context; America's discovery of the world around her, of her own strength, her greatness and her duty:

"The American people are neither poltroons nor pessimists, and they will not signalize the dawn of the new century by the surrender of either convictions or territory ... Our way is new but it is not dark. In the readjustments of world conditions, where we must take our place with the great nations of the earth, we shall move with caution, but not with fear."[7]

On the second day of the Convention, Wolcott handed over the chair to the Permanent Chairman, Henry Cabot Lodge. He proceeded to make a speech similar to that made by Wolcott the previous day. Lodge also embroidered further on the theme of prosperity, of course, but he also devoted a considerable part of his speech to foreign policy. Not surprisingly, he expressed himself in bolder terms than Wolcott and above all he brought in arguments that Wolcott had avoided. Like the senator from Colorado, he attacked the idea put forward by the Democrats that the Constitution followed the flag and he also used what became above all Theodore Roosevelt's favorite method later in the campaign of accusing the Democrats of hypocrisy, since they repressed the freedom and rights of the negroes in their own country and then noisily denounced the government for violating the Filipinos.

Cabot Lodge described Aguinaldo as a "self-seeking adventurer and usurper," "a highwayman," "a Chinese half-breed." And like Wolcott he accused the Democrats of supporting the insurrection. Again like Wolcott, Lodge conjured up a picture of some form of self-government in the future, but he expressed himself more clearly than Wolcott had done:

"We make no hypocritical pretence of being interested in the Philippines solely on account of the others. While we regard the welfare of these people as a sacred trust, we regard the welfare of the American people first ... We believe in trade expansion ... Greatest of all markets is China. Our trade there is growing in leaps and bounds. Manila, the prize of war, gives us inestimable advantages in developing that trade." "Manila is the cornerstone of our Eastern policy."[8]

199

Lodge went on to explain that the entire American Open Door policy in China that had been so successful depended on American control of the Philippines. Here we find the self-interest motive, commercial expansion, and are suddenly far from the strictly humanitarian line of argument that Wolcott and many others put in first place.

As was only to be expected, the speeches of Wolcott and Lodge offended the anti-imperialists. The Indianapolis *Sentinel* (Dem.) described their performances as "An appeal to the Boys" and compared them to a young college student who suggests to his friends that they should put the Dean's cow on the roof: "An appeal to the thoughtless people, the hurrah-people."[9]

The same day the party's platform for the coming election was presented to the Convention and was unanimously accepted.[10] The chairman of the Committee on Resolutions was Charles Warren Fairbanks and he had had no difficulty in obtaining agreement on the party's program.[11]

The nomination of candidates took place on the third day of the Convention. The nomination of McKinley was purely a matter of form, but even Roosevelt's nomination was by this time completely clear. Hanna had resisted right to the end, but when McKinley refused to express his views openly, the matter was decided.[12]

The honor of nominating McKinley had been given to Senator Foraker from Ohio, Chairman of the Committee on Puerto Rico and the Pacific Islands.[13] In his complimentary speech to the President, Foraker naturally also touched upon the events in foreign policy of the past years and as in Wolcott and Lodge, there is a note of triumph, self-awareness, pride and a somewhat dazed eagerness to accomplish great deeds that resounds through his words which are at the same time characteristic of one side of the newly-awakened expansionism:

"It is no exaggeration to say, that in all American history there is no chapter more brilliant than that which chronicles, with him as our commander-in-chief, our victories on land and sea. In one hundred days we drove Spain from the Western Hemisphere, girdled the earth with our acquisition and filled the world with the splendour of our power. In consequence the American name has a greater significance now. Our flag has a new glory."[14]

After Foraker, it was Roosevelt's turn and he too took up the question of the Philippines. He claimed that the bloody revolt continued there because the Democrats had given the insurgents the senseless idea that a Democratic victory in the election would lead to America's leaving the islands. Roosevelt's words were as strong as Lodge's when describing the insurgents:

". . . savages, who would scramble for the bloody plunder."[15] But Roosevelt also introduced an argument that had not been heard previously at the convention but that otherwise belonged to the standard accessories of the expansionist movement: If America failed in her obligations, "some other strong civilized nation" would intervene.

Roosevelt's speech ended like a fanfare, an exposition fired with strength and enthusiasm for the new tasks that awaited them, the new horizons that had opened up for the strong, young, expansive America:

"We stand on the threshold of a new century big with the fate of mighty nations. It rests with us now to decide, whether in the opening years of that century we shall march forward to fresh triumphs or whether at the outset we shall cripple ourselves for the contest. Is America a weakling, to shrink from the world-work of the great world-powers? No. The young giant of the West stands on a continent and clasps the crest of an ocean in either hand. Our nation, glorious in youth and strength, looks into the future with eager eyes and rejoices as a strong man to run the race. We do not stand in craven mood asking to be spared the task, cringing as we look at the contest. No. We challenge the proud priviledge of doing the work that Providence allots us, and we face the coming years high in heart and resolute of faith that to our people is given the right to win such honor and renown, as has never yet been vouchsafed to the nations of mankind."[16]

Roosevelt's speech made a very strong impression on the convention. The Governor of New York had an unerring instinct for what was effectful, an inclination towards the theatrical, that exactly fitted the mood of the era. He received the ovations of the audience "straight as an arrow, with head thrown back and shoulders squared as if on dress parade, the hero of San Juan." Throughout the convention, Roosevelt insisted on wearing the wide-brimmed hat that he had used as commander of the legendary Rough Riders during the war. He made a conscious effort to personify the new age, the heroic action, the new development of strength, the pioneer prepared for the great tasks that awaited "The Giant of the West."[17]

Among the more noteworthy of the expansionist speeches made in support of McKinley's nomination was that of George A. Knight, chairman of the delegation from California. The interesting feature in it is that he completely abandoned the entire complex of "responsibility," "sacrifice," "struggle of freedom for the oppressed" etc. The Philippines were not a burden, a place that the Americans must retain in order to protect its inhabitants from anarchy, to carry out an act of humanity, to create order, law and freedom etc. Knight's testimony breathed an unbending expansionism, totally centered on National self-interest: "We are tired of history; we want to teach our children geography, and the textbooks of two years ago cannot guide the young mind of today on account of the advancement and work of the Republican party of this nation. We have changed the map and the flag floats now under skies that never knew it before."[18] "No grander achievement has ever been chronicled in the history of our country than the acquisition of the islands of the Pacific."[19]

More strongly than any of the previous speakers at the Convention, Knight stressed the economic and commercial implications of the annexations: "The King of Commerce has tapped us on the shoulder and said: 'I am coming to the fair Pacific to make her my sea-side home'." America needed the Philippines both commercially and politically. Knight too placed the acquisition of the islands in a wider political context in the Far East, the fight for China. "We need those islands as a great depot in the Pacific for the distribution of the output of our inventive genius and industrial hand."

Of all the nomination speeches made for Roosevelt, the most interesting was that of the New York Senator Chauncey M. Depew. Depew was a well-known campaign speaker and his contribution was received with ovations. It came to be described as one of the highlights of the Convention, "the spiciest, most eloquent" of the speeches made.[20] Depew's address lacked Wolcott's well-reasoned arrangement, but was more immediately appealing. He attacked the Democrats and in particular their silver platform with burlesque satire and bitter sarcasm. Bryan was described as being "a bodysnatcher, carrying a corpse in a coffin, the dead silver issue."[21]

Depew naturally also dwelt on the prosperity line and the most interesting feature of his speech was his linking of America's economy, her future opportunities for maintaining and increasing her prosperity and the new foreign policy. We see here the millionaire and financier, the economic expansionist.[22]

2

If the platform that was accepted unanimously on June 20 is compared to the speeches made during the three days the convention lasted, one point immediately becomes apparent. While almost all the speakers devoted considerable attention to the foreign policy of recent years and the problems that were to be found in this area, these questions played remarkably little part in the platform.

The war against Spain and the annexations were dealt with in the platform exclusively along the lines of idealism and humanitarianism. The victory is said to have been won in a war fought for "liberty and human rights." "No thought of national aggrandizement tarnished the high purpose with which American standards were unfurled." The consequences of the victory: "To ten millions of the human race there was given a new birth of freedom, and to the American people a new and noble responsibility."[23] It is evident that the sensibilities of those representing this attitude were troubled by the fact that on the Philippines a bloody conflict raged, in which a not inconsiderable number of these "ten millions of the human race" fought for their lives in opposition to "the new birth of freedom."

The last section of the platform consisted of planks concerning foreign policy. From the point of view of the amount of space occupied, however, foreign policy filled no more than 15—20 % of the entire platform. After having expressed its approval of McKinley's policy in Samoa and Hawaii, a number of brief points followed, agreeing with measures taken by the President in his foreign policy: participation in the peace conference in The Hague, the offer of the USA's bona officia in the war between England and South Africa, whereby it is at the same time declared that America maintained her belief in the Monroe Doctrine and a policy of non-intervention in European controversies. The subject of the peace treaty with Spain and its consequences was then taken up. This plank reads as follows:

"In accepting by the treaty of Paris the just responsibility of our victories in the Spanish war, the President and the Senate won the undoubted approval of the American people. No other course was possible than to destroy Spain's sovereignity throughout the West Indies and in the Philippine Islands. That course created our responsibility before the world and with the unorganized population whom our intervention has freed from Spain, to provide for the maintenance of law and order, and for the establishment of good government and for the performance of international obligations. Our authority could not be less than our responsibility; and wherever sovereign rights were intended it became the high duty of the Government to maintain its authority, to put down armed insurrection and to confer the blessings of liberty and civilization upon the rescued peoples.

The largest measure of self-government consistent with their welfare and our duties shall be secured to them by law.

To Cuba independence and self-government were assured in the same voice by which war was declared, and to the letter this pledge shall be performed."

It is immediately noticeable that this plank was of a defensive nature, lacking the positive drive to be found in the majority of the speeches described above that were made on these issues during the convention. In fact it could be said that the plank consisted of an extremely moderate minimum program, evidently intended to provide as small a target for attack as possible. At the same time, however, it meant that for the Republicans foreign policy could hardly, with this platform, become a central issue. No votes could be won on these formulations, although possibly a few could be saved.

The Republican platform was not given a particularly enthusiastic reception. It was natural that the opposing side should be negative. The pugnacious John Peter Altgeld described it as "hypocritical cant, pompous posing and strenuous strutting."[24] Even in Republican quarters it was admitted that its style was dull and its content nebulous. "Inane and tedious" the document was called by the Republican Philadelphia *Press*,[25] "a humdrum and commonplace production" by the Portland *Oregonian* (Ind. Rep.), while the New York *Journal of Commerce* described the platform as being completely empty of content.[26]

The platform's main problem, apart from its stylistic deficiencies, was naturally that, as is usually the case with such programs, it was a compromise, intended to satisfy as many people as possible and irritate the smallest possible number of voters. As was only to be expected, the result was that in the controversial question of the new colonial policy the platform was attacked by both convinced expansionists and radical anti-imperialists.

The strongly expansionist New York *Sun* was among those that expressed astonishment and disgust over the Philippine plank. The newspaper on the other hand praised the speeches made by Wolcott and Lodge and would have liked to see a platform showing the same spirit. The debate on the platform took an interesting turn when it was revealed that important planks that had been included in an original version, approved by President McKinley, had been omitted. One of these concerned the point on which the silence of the platform was most noticeable, namely the status of the newly acquired territories, that is to say, the controversial question of the Constitution and the flag. Postmaster General Charles Emory Smith had taken with him to Philadelphia one of the drafts for the platform that had been approved by McKinley. In addition to Smith, Congressman Grosvenor and Senator Foraker had been among those involved in the preliminary work on the platform. The final editing naturally took place in the Committee on Resolutions, of which Senator Fairbanks from Indiana was chairman, and in one of its subcommittees. The style of Charles Emory Smith's draft was over-heavy and it was subjected to a thorough revision. The changes concerned not only the style, however, but also the contents. Thus one plank that had been approved by the President and that was of central importance was omitted. It was later published by Smith, who had his entire original draft printed.

"We reassert the principle, which was the watchword of the Republican party on its first great battle, of which Abraham Lincoln was the illustrious champion, and on which he was elected president, that congress has full legislative power over territory belonging to the United States, subject only to the fundamental safeguards of liberty, justice and personal rights."

The successful opposition to the proposed plank appears to have been led by Lemuel E. Quigg from New York, who managed to get a majority of the committee on his side. He was later attacked bitterly from various quarters, by among others the firmly expansionist Congressman Grosvenor from Ohio, who claimed to have been the one who originally formulated the point.[27] Quigg had been secretary in the sub-committee that was responsible for the final editing of the platform. But it is possible that even more influential anti-imperialists had been actively involved.[28]

Naturally, the disclosure of the omitted plank produced varying reactions. The New York *Tribune*, not surprisingly directed a biting attack on Quigg and those who had backed him in eliminating this point on the program. The *Tribune* declared adamantly that the Republican party must accept responsibility for the policy it had pursued and "educate people to understand the tremendous importance, while doing our duty to the lands committed by the fortunes of war to our care, of maintaining our own civilization and institutions undiluted by partnership of barbarian races in the conducts of our government." The Philadelphia *Press* (Rep.) also considered that it was a serious error to remove the plank and expressed the hope that President McKinley would repair the damage in his letter of acceptance, and this did in fact happen. On the other hand, the Washington *Post* (Ind.), together with anti-imperialist organs such as the Springfield *Republican* (Ind.) saw what had happened as an expression of "sagacity," not least considering the fact that the question had been referred to the Supreme Court.[29]

Another omitted plank concerned the delicate question of the civil service. It was said to have been drawn up as a result of promptings from

205

both President McKinley and Senator Fairbanks by Nicholas Butler, a professor at Columbia University. Its omission can have been connected with the fact that it also took up conditions on Cuba, Puerto Rico and the Philippines.[30]

Of the other changes from the final platform, one severely modified a declaration that in the original version came down very heavily in favor of ship subsidies. The same line was followed here: reduce the target area for attack, lie low in all controversial questions.

KANSAS CITY

1

The convention in Kansas City aroused no excitement over the nomination of the presidential candidate, since Bryan was all too obvious a choice. The question of who was to be his running mate was open. However, interest concentrated on another problem, namely what the platform was to say on the silver question. From the start attention centered on the New York delegation. Without New York, Bryan had little chance of winning and the delegation itself was divided. Opponents of silver were led by David B. Hill, the conservative, influential former governor and ex-senator.

Bryan was fully aware that Hill had to be reckoned with. He wanted an agreement in advance, to avoid an open fight at the convention. He wrote to Hill, therefore, and invited him to break his journey to Kansas City at Lincoln. Hill refused, on the ground that the Commoner's letter had arrived so late that time would not allow him to visit Lincoln.[31] He changed his mind after arriving at Kansas City[32] and left on July 1 for Lincoln, the same day as Jones and colleagues sent Bryan the letter discussed previously.[33] Since Hill was working on the same line as that expressed in this letter, namely to keep the money question outside the campaign, Bryan was subjected to intense pressure during these days immediately prior to the convention.

Hill had an additional reason for wanting to exclude 16 : 1 from the platform. There was a feeling that the vice-presidential candidate should come from the Eastern states, if possible from New York, and Hill had many backers, above all among conservative Democrats. There was no question of him being chosen if the platform contained a silver plank. There were even those who suspected that Hill was trying for first place on the ticket in the event of an exclusion of 16 : 1 leading to Bryan's refusal to stand.[34]

In his attempt to dislodge the Peerless Leader from his position, Hill met with as little success as the others and he returned empty-handed to Kansas City. Neither he nor Bryan issued any statement about their conference. Since Bryan refused at this stage to say anything about whom he would like to see as vice-presidential candidate, speculation about Hill's candidacy continued. A rumor was going round that Hill and Bryan had come to an agreement and that Bryan wished to have Hill as his running mate, something which was as far from the truth as anything could be. It was only after getting into telephone contact with Bryan that some Californian delegates could be persuaded to give up their plans for Hill.[35]

The way things were turning out, a battle was to be expected in the Committee on Resolutions. Each state was allowed one representative on the Committe. When affairs were so uncertain, it was a matter of importance for the Bryanites to prevent Hill from being placed there. Bryan could naturally not intervene personally. He remained at Lincoln and although in constant touch with colleagues at Kansas City he took no active part in the convention. He made clear in statements to the press where he stood on the silver question.

The Commoner's spokesman at the convention was Richard L. Metcalf, the delegate for Nebraska and editor of the Omaha *World-Herald*, a member of the Committee on Resolutions. One of Bryan's most reliable supporters, Norman E. Mack, editor of the Buffalo *Times* and one of the delegates from New York, has given an account of the maneuvres which resulted in New York, to everyone's surprise, not placing Hill on the Committee on Resolutions.[36]

At the outset the leader of the New York delegation, Croker, "the Tammany Tiger," together with ex-Senator Murphy, Shevlin, and others, shared the feeling that Hill should be on the Committee on Resolutions. As it became plain that the conservative ex-senator was becoming a rallying point for the anti-Bryan phalanx at the convention, and as Metcalf and other delegates close to Bryan set to work to persuade them not to give Hill a committee position, opinion started to swing the other way.

There were already quite a sufficient number of delegates at the convention opposed not only to 16 : 1 but to Bryan. It was necessary to call a halt, and the New York delegation had to decide either for Bryan or his opponents, a decision which could influence the entire convention. Mack wrote to Bryan, "It's but fair to say that the big New York fellows were

207

with you conscientiously and honestly."[37] Croker succeeded in getting a reliable Tammany man, Judge Van Wyck, on the Committee on Resolutions.[38] He defeated Hill within the New York delegation by 40 votes to 26, most of the Van Wyck votes being cast by delegates under Croker's control.[39]

Croker's enthusiasm for the Peerless Leader was by no means unqualified, but was dictated by how far he judged him useful to the political ends of Tammany. A photographer covering the convention, Robert Lee Dunn, has given an amusing illustration of this point. Bryan's nomination was greeted by "the most tumultuous sort of hullabaloo, and the people were jumping to their feet, tossing their hats, and shouting." At that moment Dunn took a photograph. Immediately afterwards he was approached by a man sent by Croker and requested to take another picture and not publish the one he had taken. The reason became obvious when the first photograph was developed. Croker was sitting alone motionless, indifferent in the midst of the shouting assembly.[40]

After a whole day's intensive negotiations in the Committee on Resolutions, Bryan's line finally won. It was a narrow victory. There was only a two-vote majority and it was not until Bryan had stated that he refused to stand if they restricted themselves to mere reaffirmation that even this was reached. If one takes into account that among the delegates who voted for 16 : 1 were those for Hawaii and Alaska and that Bryan had no chance of winning the election with the sole backing of states which now supported his line, the significance of the decision emerges. In a letter to Bryan a member of the Hawaiian delegation to the convention claimed that he, knowing that Hawaii's vote might be an important one, in caucus secured a definite instruction to their member of the committee to vote in favor of reiterating 16 : 1. At the same time he stated that the delegates from Hawaii with the exception of himself and one other "had but faint idea of the importance of this question."[41]

Observers later claimed that three-quarters of the delegates had been against reiteration of the silver demand and this does not seem exaggerated considering that only a few Democratic state party platforms had included a 16 : 1 plank.[42] And it is true, that the minority on the committee voting against the reiteration of 16 : 1 represented 3/5 of the delegates of the convention.[43]

In his memoirs Bryan has related that he had no intention of giving up the fight for 16 : 1 in the platform, even if the plank had lost in the Committee on Resolutions. If that had happened he would have gone to

Kansas City and made a fight in the convention for the adoption of the plank. If he had then not succeeded, he would have refused to be candidate."[44]

Those whose line had been defeated in the Committee on Resolutions discussed drawing up a minority report which, considering the mood of the delegates at the convention, should have stood a good chance of winning at the plenary session. Once again the New York delegation played a decisive role. Van Wyck had voted against 16 : 1, following the line decided on by the State Convention.[45] Norman Mack, in cooperation with Croker, managed to get the New York delegation to support the majority report.[46] Opposition to the Committee on Resolutions' proposed platform collapsed.

2

While the Committee on Resolutions was occupied with the long-drawn-out struggle over the platform, the same tug-of-war was apparent in the speeches to which the plenary assembly was listening. In his long keynote speech Charles S. Thomas, the Governor of Colorado, who was Temporary Chairman, argued vigorously for retention of silver as the leading issue, while he paid due attention to trusts and imperialism. He kindled great enthusiasm by combining the two latter questions with a scathing attack on the Republican administration:

"The Bill of Rights has become a bill of platitudes ... the Republican party now maintains the right to govern subject peoples by the sword ... There was a time when it put its trust in the people. Since then it put the people in its trusts. There was a time when its standards were lofty and enobling. Its only standard now is Standard Oil ... Its battle cry years ago was, 'Freedom and the Union'. If due credit is given to one of its modern leaders, its motto for 1900 is 'Gold and Glory'."[47]

Even more caustic was the well-known Governor of Illinois, Altgeld, who joined Thomas in demanding loyalty to the Chicago Platform's money plank.[48] The former Governor of Texas, J. S. Hogg, expressed the same opinion.[49] But a long line of speakers presented the opposite point of view: Joshua W. Miles from Maryland, J. R. Williams from Illinois, J. A. McCollough from Indiana, David S. Rose from Wisconsin. They all voiced the earlier misgivings and attempted to tone down the silver question.

Joshua Miles spoke on behalf of the Eastern states. Maryland and New

Jersey had attracted interest since their delegates were the only ones not under instruction to support Bryan.[50] Miles stated that many Maryland Democrats had left the party in 1896 because of the money question, and were anxious to return. In his appeal for moderation he referred to men such as John W. Daniel, Virginia, and Carter H. Harrison, Illinois, and addressed himself to "such doubtful states as New York, New Jersey and Indiana, and such rock-ribbed Gibraltars of Democracy as Virginia, Louisiana, Florida, North Carolina and Texas."[51] Senator Daniel had been Permanent Chairman at the convention of 1896, but now joined those who wanted to push the silver question into the background.

One of the most interesting speeches was that of the newly elected mayor of Milwaukee, David S. Rose, who energetically urged the importance of support from the states east of the Mississippi and north of Ohio. His appeal must have expressed what most delegates at the convention were thinking. "Let us reaffirm that platform (1896) in letter and spirit, but it seems to me that reaffirmation means reaffirmation, and that it is not necessary for us to travel over the thorny, broken paths that led us to defeat in 1896."[52] Rose emphasized the need to take new groups into consideration. Thirty-eight per cent of the population in Wisconsin was of German origin.

The next speaker, J. A. McCollough from Indiana, also stressed that German voters would play a key role in the election. Every tendency to division among the Democrats must be smothered. He mentioned imperialism, the trusts and the tariff but not the money question.

J. R. Williams from Illinois repeated both the warning and recommendation. He thought the Democrats could best be united in a fight against imperialism and McKinleyism.

"When we submit to the liberty loving people a platform and candidates in favor of a Republic as against an Empire they will surely haul down McKinley; they will snatch from his imperial brow his glittering crown, bought with the blood of his countrymen, and enthrone in his place of power that fearless champion of human rights, that brave defender of human freedom, and crown him with the Declaration of Independence and the Constitution of the Republic."

A. M. Dockery from Missouri continued the theme of unity. What makes his short speech interesting, however, is the fact that he expressed the expansionist ideas shared by many Democrats although, largely for tactical reasons, he obscured them with anti-imperialist phrases. Dockery included

210

a dutiful reference to Jefferson and the lofty ideas under which the Democrats were to fight. But he spoke mainly of opportunities for commercial expansion. Ahead of America lay "a contest for commercial expansion that will bring prosperity to the farms, the mines, the manufacturers, and the labor of the United States." The Nicaraguan Canal came in:

"one of the great means to bring prosperity to the people, and especially to the South half of this Republic, is to shorten the line of ocean transportation to the Orient, because in the East, almost within gunshot of where Dewey won his glorious victory on the 1st of May, 1898, live one-third of the human race. Now, that market we can get under the policy of the Democratic party as administered by William J. Bryan. Therefore, I want to dig that canal."[53]

Only a short time before, Henry Cabot Lodge, Chauncey Depew, and others had spoken along much the same lines at the Republican Convention.[54] The aims and hopes were similar, although opinions differed somewhat on the means.

3

Bryan could not win without compromise. He was forced to give in on two points. One concerned the platform, the other the choice of his running mate.

The platform was read out by Senator Ben Tillman from South Carolina and received with overwhelming enthusiasm, above all in the anti-imperialistic passages. When the speaker reached the words: "But the burning issue of imperialism, growing out of the Spanish war, involves the very existence of the Republic, and the destruction of our free institutions. We regard it as the paramount issue of this campaign," a storm of jubilation and applause arose in the huge hall. American flags blossomed from the hand of every delegate and appeared in the galleries, waved by enthusiastic spectators. The standards of the different state delegations were carried to the platform; and just over the Chairman's stand an immense American flag was let down, which completely hid the speaker's table. Across the flag were printed in large letters: 'Governments derive their just powers from the consent of the governed', 'The Constitution and the Flag, one and inseparable, now and forever', 'Flag of the Republic forever and the Empire never', 'A Republic can have no colonies'. The demonstration lasted for eighteen minutes, and it was with great difficulty that the Chair was able to secure order so that Senator Tillman could proceed with the reading of the platform.[55]

The man behind this striking flag ceremony received with such enthusiasm was Governor Stone who, prior to the Republican convention in Philadelphia, had suggested it when he had heard that the Republicans planned to make the campaign that year into a flag campaign. In a letter to Bryan Stone wrote that the Republicans intended to try to monopolize the flag. "The cry of the party would be 'Where the flag goes up it shall remain'. This they intend to supplement with a great scheme of commercial expansion, looking to the construction of the Nicaragua Canal and the control of the commerce of the Orient."[56] Stone's idea of having an enormous flag with suitable slogans, was one way of getting the better of the Republicans.[57]

An interesting detail is that the original intent was for this flag ceremony to be performed at the culminating point of the convention, at the moment Bryan was nominated. The change in plans, which led to it all taking place when the platform's anti-imperialist plank was read, was no coincidence. It was a means of counteracting the negative effect of the fight over the money plank and establishing in the most striking manner possible what the platform's "burning issue" really was.

The timing of the flag ceremony, which judging by all the newspaper accounts was felt by everybody to be the climax of the convention, showed the efforts made following defeat in the silver question to use all means to mark imperialism as the central and decisive issue. The position occupied by foreign policy in the Kansas City platform of 1900 was the more conspicuous in view of the fact that the 1896 platform had hardly said a word about foreign policy.[58] Over half the new platform was devoted to one aspect or another of the "burning issue," imperialism, or other questions connected with foreign policy.

The platform began by invoking and declaring loyalty to the Declaration of Independence, and continued,

"We declare again that all governments instituted among men derive their just powers from the consent of the governed; that any government not based upon the consent of the governed is tyranny; and to impose upon any people a government of force is to substitute the methods of imperialism for those of a republic. We hold that the Constitution follows the flag, and denounce the doctrine that an Executive or Congress deriving their existence and their powers from the Constitution can exercise lawful authority beyond it or in violation of it. We assert that no nation can long

212

endure half republic and half empire, and we warn the American people that imperialism abroad will lead quickly and inevitably to despotism at home."[59]

This declaration of principles, the ideological foundation of anti-imperialism, preceded an application of the principles. First came rejection of the Puerto Rico law, "government without their /the Puerto Rican people/ consent and taxation without their representation." Then followed a demand for independence to Cuba. The Philippines naturally received attention. This plank was mainly a copy of the Nebraska platform.[60]

"Filipinos cannot be citizens without endangering our civilization; they cannot be subjects without imperiling our form of government; and as we are not willing to surrender our civilization nor to convert the Republic into an empire, we favor an immediate declaration of the nation's purpose to give the Filipinos, first, a stable form of government; second, independence; and third, protection from outside interference."[61]

Thus the solution does not suppose an immediate, unqualified withdrawal from the Philippines. The difference between this and the Republican platform is not excessive. Both platforms were modifications, and the wording of the Democratic platform showed how difficult it was to draw up a plain program.

This modification of the demand for independence for the Philippines provoked criticism from some radical anti-imperialists. *The Nation* was delighted with the plank on Imperialism, which it said was "extremely well written" and showed "the hand of a master," but protested the sentence which spoke of first establishing a stable government. This, *The Nation* wrote, left the government of the United States the sole judge of what constituted a stable form, and of the time within which independence should be granted. The platform should have made a statement that the Filipinos would be given independence *"as soon as they establish a government of their own . . .* Anything less than this comes short of our ideals."[62]

A special plank was devoted to the Monroe Doctrine. The policy pursued by the Republicans was said to be directly contrary to the spirit of the Monroe Doctrine. It was incompatible "to acquire and hold sovereignty over large areas of territory and large numbers of people in the Eastern Hemisphere." According to this interpretation, European nonintervention in the affairs of the Western hemisphere implied reciprocity: that America refrained from extending power outside the hemisphere.[63]

213

A detailed plank took up militarism. It conjured up a specter which was real for many immigrants, especially those from Germany, but which otherwise made little impression. The method of presenting militarism as a corollary of imperialism had been a favorite of many Democratic state party platforms.[64]

This long introductory section, devoted entirely to imperialism, was followed by planks concerning trusts and the tariff and, not least, the controversial silver plank with reiteration of 16 : 1. After the economic and financial questions the platform returned to foreign policy. One plank discussed the Nicaraguan Canal, partly condemning the Hay-Pauncefote treaty as a surrender of American rights and interests, partly pledging support of "the immediate construction, ownership and control of the Nicaraguan canal by the United States," following in both points the usual wording of state party platforms.[65] The corresponding plank in the Republican platform was declared to be "insincere" and a shaft was also sent in England's direction. Jefferson's words, "Peace, commerce and honest friendship with all nations; entangling alliance with none," were quoted and an attack made on "the ill-concealed Republican alliance with England." And when the Boer War came up, the anti-British tone became sharp indeed. The platform expressed indignation over "the purpose of England to overwhelm with force the South African Republics", and proclaimed sympathy for "the heroic burghers in their unequal struggle to maintain their liberty and independence."[66]

4

The nomination of the party's presidential candidate was devoid of excitement, but some of the nomination speeches were not without interest. William Oldham from Nebraska was granted the honor of nominating the state's great son. By diligent use of antithesis he managed in his speech to attack McKinley at the same time as he paid tribute to Bryan:

"Your candidate must be able to distinguish between Democratic expansion and Republican imperialism, the first a natural growth by addition of contiguous American territory, into every foot of which is carried the Constitution, the flag and the decalogue; where over the shoulders of every inhabitant of the added territory is thrown a purple robe of sovereign citizenship.

How different from the bandit policy of Republican imperialism, with its standing army and bayonet rule of conquered provinces; its government

214

against their will of sullen subjects by force and fraud, its denial to them of the protection of the Constitution or the command which says: 'Thou shalt not steal'. This is a policy which would send our Uncle Sam off his American range with a Cowboy hat, a rope, and a branding iron, to rustle and brand over all the loose islands of the Orient while hypocritically chanting the long-meter doxology."[67]

Attention naturally centered on the speech by "that sterling Democrat," David Bennet Hill who urged the party to form a front, and although he spoke warmly of Bryan his dissatisfaction with the platform was apparent:

"The platform although not meeting my approval in some respects, is, as a whole, worthy of the vote of every man who claims to be a Democrat in this country. Those who do not entirely approve some portions can speak well of others."[68]

Only one of the other nomination speeches was of any special interest, namely that by Louis Bomerich from Wisconsin, a German-American. Earlier during the convention[69] McCollough had stressed the importance of German voters. Mayor Rose of Milwaukee had spoken likewise.[70] Now Bomerich claimed that as far as German voters were concerned, anti-imperialism and hostility to England would carry the day, even among those who could not subscribe to the Democrats' view of the money question as laid down in the platform.

Bryan received every vote, totalling 936.

5

Imperialism as the paramount issue in the Democratic platform of 1900 was not the work of Bryan. There is no question of his not being a convinced anti-imperialist, but he did not feel this question to be the dominant one in the approaching clash. He stubbornly refused to make the concessions which would secure him unreserved support of the anti-imperialists: toning down the silver question and including a civil service plank in the platform. There were for him three issues: money, trusts and imperialism. If any one was to have priority it would not be imperialism but silver, which had so dramatically swept him to the head of the Democratic party in 1896 and with which he was totally identified.

Immediately prior to the convention Bryan had published an interesting article in the *North American Review* called "The Issue in the Presidential Campaign."[71] In publishing what can only be called a "personal platform" just before the party held its national convention, he was bringing strong pressure to bear on the delegates in their task of drawing up the party platform. Exclusion of any of the points laid down in his article would undoubtedly appear to be a repudiation, even in the unlikely event of his accepting nomination in such circumstances.

In itself Bryan's article contains no surprises. The opening lines established the tone, which was consistent with Bryan's repeatedly stated views:

"The issue presented in the campaign of 1900 is the issue between plutocracy and democracy. All the questions under discussion will, in their last analysis, disclose the conflict between the dollar and the man—a conflict as old as the human race, and one which will continue as long as the human race endures."[72]

Bryan then specified the essential issues of controversy: "... today three questions contest for primacy—the money question, the trust question, and imperialism." It is worthwhile to note the order in which he placed these questions: silver, then the trust question, finally imperialism. That is also the order in which he discussed them in his article, and it is equally worth noting that the greater part of the article concerned strictly economic aspects, the tyranny of plutocracy and methods of oppression. The last part, less than a third of the length, was devoted to imperialism, and not at all in such a way as to give the impression that this was the dominant issue.

The placing of imperialism in the center of the Democratic platform and its being proclaimed "the burning issue" and "the paramount issue" was a concession on Bryan's part, compensating for the fact that he forced the convention to accept his silver plank, seen by many Democrats as a dead weight and by others as a specter, maybe not dangerous but liable to frighten many people.

6

Election of the vice-presidential candidate was awaited with considerable excitement. The fight lay mainly between Adlai E. Stevenson of Illinois, David B. Hill of New York, and Charles A. Towne of Minnesota. Stevenson had been vice-president during Cleveland's second term. He was getting on in years (born 1835), respected, but with no clear profile. Hill was one of the most prominent figures within the party. He had been a senator between 1891 and 1897. Towne had originally been a Republican. Together with Senator Teller he had left the party at the 1896 convention because

216

of the goldstandard plank, and since then had become one of the leading Silver Republicans. The Fusionist faction of the Populist Party had nominated him as their vice presidential candidate at their convention at Sioux Falls and there was a strong current of opinion among the Silver Republicans, who were holding their convention in Kansas City at the same time as the Democrats, in favor of making him their vice-presidential candidate too.[73]

The strongest argument in favor of Towne was his power of attracting Populists and Silver Republicans. This was at the same time a drawback: association with the Populists did little to make him attractive to the conservative Democrats. The point was also made that it would be unwise to choose both the presidential and vice-presidential candidates from west of the Mississippi.[74] The election could not be won without a breach in the Eastern states and there Towne would be of no help, so supporters of Stevenson and Hill argued. Hill's connection with the Eastern states strengthened his candidacy, but his name carried little weight among the silverites. Stevenson's strong point was that he covered the whole field: he was conservative enough not to cause ill feelings in the South, but had a sufficiently satisfactory record on the money question to be acceptable to Fusionists and Silver Republicans. "He is a man that belongs to no wing or faction of his party and if nominated he will be candidate for the entire people. He is a conservative man, and always speaks and defends the platform enunciated by his party." So one of his supporters from the Southern states expressed it.

Towne was a candidate to the taste of the left wing of the Democratic party, but even Democrats who were on the whole inclined toward him considered his candidacy tactically unsuitable.[75] Those backing Hill were building on sand, since Hill no sooner had been proposed by Senator Grade of New York than he declined nomination in such a way as to make plain that it was not a question of tactics but that he did not intend to accept nomination.

On the first ballot Stevenson received 588.5 votes, Towne 89 1/2, Hill 207.[76] After Towne's candidacy had been withdrawn and the delegations had replaced their votes, Stevenson was elected unanimously.

The choice of Stevenson as Bryan's running mate aroused no enthusiasm. The Fusionists had nominated Towne, and not only the Silver Republicans but the Bryanites among the Democrats would have preferred him. It is equally clear that there were elements who would gladly have seen the nomination of a conservative like Hill, as was obvious by the tumultuous ovations which greeted his name during the nomination. Stevenson was a compromise. The result was also criticized, however, in Independent circles. Feeling there was in many cases negative to the platform, partly because of reiteration of the 16 : 1 plank, partly because of absence of civil service planks.[77] This latter point was especially associated with Stevenson, since he had an extremely bad record in this respect during the period he was in Cleveland's Cabinet ("when he was in the Postmaster-General's office he didn't leave a Republican standing.")[78]

Bryan's favorite was undoubtedly Towne.[79] The nomination of Stevenson was yet another concession on Bryan's part, and was to all appearance forced upon him by James Jones, Stone, Johnson, and other members of the Executive Committee who had tried unsuccessfully to make Bryan give up the silver plank.[80]

CHAPTER VII

The Paramount Issue and the Campaign

Mending the Fences: Republican Notification Ceremonies and Letters of Acceptance

On July 12 the Republican delegation arrived at Canton, Ohio, to give President McKinley official notification of the nomination. Chairman of the delegation was Henry Cabot Lodge and the delegation was accompanied by Mark Hanna, chairman of the Republican National Committee.

When the Democrats declared in Kansas City that imperialism was "the paramount issue," the inadequacy of the Republican platform on the question of foreign policy was seen to be an obvious blunder. The speeches that were exchanged in Canton on July 12 between the chairman of the Republican delegation and the President were clearly intended to repair the damage as far as possible. Thus while a bare 20 % of the platform was devoted to questions related to foreign policy, McKinley divided his speech almost equally between domestic and foreign affairs.

"The Philadelphia Convention had adopted your policy, both in the Antilles and the Philippines, and has made it their own and that of the Republican Party," Lodge declared in his speech. But the presentation of this policy given by the Senator from Massachusetts was much more in line with his own speech at the Convention than with the platform accepted there. "This great new policy had made us at once masters of the Antilles and a great Eastern power, holding firmly our possessions on both sides of the Pacific . . ."[1]

More important than Cabot Lodge's speech was naturally that made by McKinley. The President expanded upon the Republican platform, but without really adding much in the way of information.[2]

One of the points that had been missing there, however, was a plank on the power of Congress over acquired territories, the intricate question of the Constitution and the flag. This omission was now made good by McKinley:

"We reassert the early principle of the Republican party, sustained by unbroken judicial precedents, that the representatives of the people in Congress assembled have full legislative power over territory belonging to the United States, subject to the fundamental safeguards of liberty, justice and personal rights, and are vested with ample authority to act for the highest interests of our nation and the people entrusted to its care."

In fact this statement was largely in complete verbal agreement with the plank that had been omitted from the platform. So the views pressed by the hawks were ultimately accepted.[3]

McKinley had chosen his words very cautiously. There was little trace of the panorama conjured up by Theodore Roosevelt and his supporters of the endless opportunities, the great adventure, the leading role in the global theatre that awaited America in the new century. It is not the opportunities, the power and the glory that are emphasized by McKinley: ... "our steps have been guided by honor and duty. There will be no turning aside, no wavering, no retreat. No blow has been struck except for liberty and humanity, and none will be." And McKinley compared the liberation of 4,000,000 negro slaves in the South by the Republican Party with its new achievement, "the liberation of 10,000,000 of the human family from the yoke of imperialism."[4] It is immediately apparent that McKinley, like the Republican platform, was on the defensive when presenting foreign policy, and in particular expansionism.

The delegation that on the same day, July 12, officially notified Theodore Roosevelt of his nomination as vice-presidential candidate, was led by Edward Wolcott, senator from Colorado. Roosevelt received the delegation at his country house, Sagamore, near Oyster Bay.

Wolcott's speech was brief, with no remarkable features. Roosevelt's reply was even shorter. It was formulated in very general terms, but there was a slight hint of the line that was the hallmark of his speech at the Convention and that portended his later letter of acceptance.

This emerged even more clearly in a speech made by Roosevelt in St. Paul a few days after the notification ceremonies. In what was described by the newspapers as being "the key-note of the campaign," Theodore Roosevelt then went to the attack on the sensitive issue of foreign policy. The speech was received with violent indignation by the anti-imperialists. "... It makes imperialism and colonialism the supreme question. It is thick and thin with the brutality and savagery of an Asian despot." (Pittsburgh *Post*) and "He has much the martial spirit of the warlike emperor of Germany, and longs for new fields for his country to conquer" (Philadelphia

Ledger). This was the voice of anti-imperialist papers, while others noted above all Roosevelt's skill in exploiting the demands of the Kansas City platform for the establishment of "a stable form of government" in the Philippine Islands. The main impression was, however, that Roosevelt was fully prepared to take up the paramount issue chosen by the Democrats.

McKinley's letter of acceptance of September 8 and Roosevelt's of September 15 both appeared at a point when the campaign was in full swing, when it was obvious which issues would dominate and when the tactics to be adopted by the Democrats were clear. McKinley's letter is very detailed, about six times as long as the Republican platform. An examination of the letter reveals the tactics that the Republicans intended to use during the campaign.

McKinley expressed his approval of the platform accepted by the Convention and then proceeded immediately to the question of the currency. He referred to the way in which this question had dominated the previous election campaign in 1896 and explained that although the Republican Party was reluctant to take up this issue again, the Democrats were forcing them to continue the fight on the same lines as before. In fact the Republicans wished for nothing more than to repeat the conflict from 1896. If the question of free silver coinage versus the gold standard could be made the paramount issue, the result was a matter of course. The introductory section of McKinley's letter had as its theme the gold standard, tariffs and prosperity. The powerful expansion of America's foreign trade was described and the President promised that every effort would be made to increase the size of the United State's merchant marine. In this context, he also touched on the question of a canal: "The construction of a maritime canal is now more than ever indispensible to that intimate and ready communication between our eastern and western seaports demanded by the annexation of the Hawaiian Islands and the expansion of our influence and trade in the Pacific."[5]

It is hardly a coincidence that McKinley here named only Hawaii and not the Philippines. He insisted that their acquisition had nothing at all to do with material interests.

No less than two-thirds of McKinley's letter of acceptance was devoted to the territories gained by the United States during his administration and considerably more than half the letter concerned the acquisition of the Philippines and the position of the islands. A comparison with the platform of the Republican Party clearly shows that so far the tactics of the Democrats had been successful. The Democrats' platform and even more Bryan's speech of acceptance forced McKinley to produce detailed arguments, intended to neutralize the Democratic attacks.

To the delicate question of the Philippines, McKinley allowed between two and three times as much space as the entire Republican platform. McKinley's presentation of the issue consisted mainly of excerpts from instructions, letters and reports of various kinds with connecting text.[6] His intention was to demonstrate how American policy had consistently been to fulfill the interests of the Philippine people, to introduce law and order, protect lives and property, safeguard freedom.

McKinley summarized his long review thus:

"This shows to my countrymen what has been and what is being done to bring the benefits of liberty and good government to these wards of the nation. Every effort has been directed to their peace and prosperity, their advancement and well-being, not for our aggrandizement nor for pride and might, not for trade or commerce, not for exploitation, but for humanity and civilization; and for the protection of the vast majority of the population who welcome our sovereignty against the designing minority, whose first demand after the surrender of Manila by the Spanish army was to enter the city that they might loot it and destroy those not in sympathy with their selfish and treacherous designs."[7]

At the end of his letter, McKinley left the defensive and counterattacked the Democrats, trying to get them against the wall. He said that there was no antagonism between the government and those who supported first the war against Spain and then the ratification of the peace. "Upon these two great essential steps there can be no issue, and out of these came all our responsibilities. If others would shirk the obligations imposed by the war and the treaty, we must decline to act further with them, and here the issue is made." As in so many other contexts, it was Bryan's support of the ratification of the peace treaty that provided his opponents with their ammunition. McKinley asked: "Are our opponents against the treaty"?, only to point out immediately that the ratification could not have been carried through without their support. The President continued to put questions: "Would our opponents surrender to the insurgents, abandon our sovereignty, or cede it to them"? McKinley demanded that if this were not the case, it should be made clear immediately, since the bloody war in the Philippines was prolonged by the hope of the insurgents that a Democratic victory in November would lead to the Americans withdrawing their troops. The argument was not an original one and had been used during the Convention by both Wolcott[8] an Roosevelt.[9] Another familiar argument was also brought out: The insurgents were said to represent only a small minority on the islands. America was now being asked to remove its protection from the great majority and hand over the power to this small minority, these murderers of American soldiers, these cruel bands of guerillas who threatened the rest of the population. "The issue is clear," claimed McKinley:

"Empire has been expelled from Puerto Rico and the Philippines by American freedom. The flag of the Republic now floats over the islands as an emblem of rightful sovereignty. Will the republic stay and dispense to their inhabitants the blessings of liberty, education and free institutions, or steal away, leaving them to anarchy or imperialism? The American question is between duty and desertion, for the republic against both anarchy and imperialism."[10]

The presentation of arguments was undeniably clever, and McKinley exploited to the utmost the ambiguity of the position adopted by Bryan and the Democrats, particularly the active support given by the Democratic candidate to the ratification of the peace treaty with Spain. The President's attempt to present the American annexation of the Philippines as a blow *against* imperialism was characteristic of him. The distinction he made between American annexation policy and that represented by the European powers was in complete agreement with the idealistic interpretation he pursued in his arguments.

McKinley's letter of acceptance was on the whole given a good press. Both supporters and opponents were in general agreed that the President had produced the best arguments for his cause so far. The Republican press praised the document and the typical reaction was expressed in the Boston *Journal*, to take one example: "It is hard to believe that an intelligent and patriotic man can read the record and yet prate about imperialism." The same point of view is to be found in the Brooklyn *Eagle* (Ind. Dem.): "Not only should the letter destroy the bugaboo of imperialism, but it should cover with shame those who have deliberately falsified the case and fill with satisfaction those whose sincere misconceptions of the case the letter should remove."[11]

In one respect McKinley's letter had meant a retreat from his acceptance speech on the disputed question of the Constitution and the flag, upon which he now, like the Republican platform, refrained from commenting. This fact naturally made it easier for Republican newspapers such as the Cleveland *Leader*, Omaha *Bee*, St. Paul *Pioneer Press*, Boston *Transcript* and others to accept the letter and greet it with enthusiasm.

223

All Republican newspapers were not satisfied, however. The anti-imperialist Philadelphia *Ledger* still rejected McKinley's policy of "beneficient paternalism" as destructive of American principles of government. As far as the independent press was concerned, the leading anti-imperialist organs such as the Springfield *Republican* and New York *Evening Post* maintained their negative attitudes still, while others expressed their appreciation and in some cases clearly softened their earlier criticism. This applied on the whole to newspapers with obvious Republican leanings.

It is noticeable that many Democratic newspapers had difficulty in expressing their criticism of McKinley's letter. This was a result of the cautious, conciliatory line chosen by the President, as well as of the Democratic platform's reservation concerning "a stable form of government" as a prerequisite for American withdrawal from the Philippines. In fact, the difference was not all that great, as both the New York *Tribune* and the *Nation* pointed out, though from different angles.[12]

Democratic newspapers that had previously represented an anti-imperialistic line quite naturally took a negative view of McKinley's declarations. It is worth noting, however, that a number of formerly pro-expansionist Democratic organs departed from their previous line as a result of the question being brought into party politics in the election campaign and also attacked the policy of the Administration. Among those whose opinions swung was not least the New York *Journal*. It had earlier been clearly pro-expansionist, but had during its campaign for Bryan adjusted its views on foreign policy to agree with the Democratic party line. The change had come gradually, as soon as William Randolph Hearst had decided to give Bryan his wholehearted support.[13] Hearst proved to be a great asset for the Democrats. He demonstrated his splendid talents as organizer and businessman by the feat of starting in the summer of 1900 at almost incredible short notice the Chicago *American*, thus creating with his enormous resources what the Democrats had hitherto lacked, an effective mouthpiece in Chicago. In gratitude, James K. Jones arranged for Hearst to be appointed President of the National Association of Democratic Clubs. In this capacity he worked with an energy that was later duly commended by Bryan at the great Democratic rally at Madison Square Garden at the end of the campaign.[14] The New York *Journal* now described McKinley's letter as ressembling "a folding bed with a piano front. When you look at it first you think it is a financial argument, but when you let it down you find that it is an apology for imperialism."[15]

Democratic newspapers that were wholly in line with McKinley included as was to be expected expansionist anti-Bryan papers, such as the New York *Times*, Brooklyn *Eagle* and Philadelphia *Record*. The New York *Times*, greeted with enthusiasm the fact that McKinley had accepted the challenge of the Democrats to make imperialism the paramount issue of the campaign and declared that McKinley's account was so convincing that the Democrats would come to be "sick to death of the very name of imperialism and sorry that they ever made it a paramount issue."[16]

Among other newspapers that supported McKinley's viewpoint were the expansionist Birmingham *News* (Ala) and somewhat more surprisingly the Nashville *American*, which had previously followed what was on the whole a moderate anti-imperialist line.

Roosevelt's letter of acceptance was much less verbose than McKinley's. From the very start Roosevelt made his point clear. There were two issues in the coming campaign. The Republicans stood for the prosperity of the country and for the honor and renown of the American flag. A Democratic victory would mean "disaster, reaction, disorder at home, and dishonor of the flag."

But Roosevelt's letter too was marked by the developments after the Democratic Convention at Kansas City, with its heavy stress on making imperialism "the paramount issue." Replying directly to the Democratic platform on the monetary question, Roosevelt declared: "No issue can be paramount to the issue they thus made, for the paramountcy of such an issue is to be determined not by the dictum of any man or body of men, but the fact that it vitally affects the well-being of every home in the lands." Thus we have here a direct counterattack, a categorical declaration that free silver and not imperialism was the paramount issue.

Despite this insistence, however, Roosevelt devoted more than two-thirds of his letter to foreign policy, more precisely to the question of annexation. He introduced his theme thus: "The history of the nation is in large part the history of the nation's expansion." He dwelt with particular detail on the Louisiana purchase, which he described as being a direct parallel to the acquisition of the Philippines. He established that the doctrine "the consent of the governed" was never for a moment considered by Jefferson or anyone else to apply to the inhabitants of the enormous Louisiana area, whether they be whites, negroes or Indians. Jefferson had sent troops to Louisiana for exactly the same reasons as McKinley sent troops to the Philippines. The doctrine "the Constitution follows the flag" had not occurred to him for a second. It was a much later creation, constructed in connection with internal political controversies, for the purpose of making it possible to extend slavery to the territories.

Roosevelt developed his review further: the acquisition of Florida, Texas, the gains in the Mexican war, Alaska, Hawaii. It was in exactly this context that the acquisition of the Philippines should be placed. It had nothing to do with either imperialism or militarism. It was simply a continuation of the expansion that had been a fundamental feature of the history of the United States from the very birth of the Union. It was not a question of imperialism, it was instead a great victory in the fight *against* imperialism:

"We made a great anti-imperialistic stride when we drove the Spaniards from Puerto Rico and the Philippines ... The reasoning which justifies our having made war against Sitting Bull also justifies our having checked the outbreaks of Aguinaldo and his followers, directed as they were, against Filipino and American alike."

The distinction Roosevelt made between expansionism and imperialism provides a good illustration of his own views. There is little here about the Philippines being an idealistic responsibility, a duty, that the Americans could not shirk. For Roosevelt it was truly a question of expansion.

"Properly speaking, the question is now not whether we shall expand —for we have already expanded—but whether we shall contract. The Philippines are now part of American territory. To surrender them would be to surrender American territory."[17]

Roosevelt naturally considered that he had to include the expressions that had completely dominated McKinley's approach to the subject, namely that the islands must be governed "primarily in the interests of their citizens." But he also went on to explain that this need not at all mean that they should be governed just as the inhabitants wished at the moment. To give Aguinaldo self-government would be like giving an Apache chief self-government in some Indian reservation. And Roosevelt here fell back upon the description he had used during the Convention of Aguinaldo and his supporters: "a syndicate of Chinese halfbreeds."[18]

From Kansas City to Indianapolis

1

"If President McKinley proves that imperialism is not an issue and Mr. Bryan demonstrates that 16 : 1 is not an issue, the campaign will be wonderfully clarified." This was the ironic comment of the Detroit *Free*

226

Press. The New York *World* printed a cartoon in which McKinley is pointing at an enormous inscription on Bryan's shirtfront with the next "16 to 1", while Bryan in turn is pointing to the imperial crown which ornaments the President's head. One of the essential features of the 1900 campaign was the debate over whether there was a paramount issue, and if so, whether it was silver or imperialism.

The reactions among Bryan's supporters varied. John Peter Altgeld spoke enthusiastically of the Commoner's "heroic stand," which not only saved the cause but made him the "grandest figure in the civilized world." Altgeld also predicted a victory in the coming election: "Providence is guiding and the fates are smiling."[19] William A. Croffut, on the other hand, hoped that the votes lost on the silver plank would not exceed 100,000, but considered that New York and Connecticut were being given away.[20] The same reaction is to be found in Fred Feigel, editor of the *Tammany Times*, who declared that the East must take care of itself. After the reiteration in the Kansas City's platform of the 1896 silver plank, it was in his opinion meaningless to waste resources in the Eastern states.[21]

Uncertainty was plainly reflected in the press reaction to the Kansas City platform. Reiteration of the demand for free silver, minting at a ratio of 16 to 1, was praised by such loyal silver newspapers as the Denver *News*, Memphis *Commercial Appeal*, and Louisville *Dispatch*, but editorials in most Democratic newspapers emphasized that imperialism and trusts were the issues and sometimes openly declared the silver question of lesser interest.[22]

The Republicans on the other hand regarded with satisfaction Bryan's success in getting 16 : 1 reiterated. As Thomas B. Reed commented maliciously, Bryan "had rather be wrong than President."[23]

The reaction of the independent press was important. The reiteration of 16 : 1 indisputably cost the Peerless Leader the support of many gold-standard Democratic and Independent newspapers and magazines, which otherwise would have been prepared to back him. Democratic and Independent Democratic newspapers which had turned against him in 1896 and which now once more refused to lend him their support, e.g. the St. Paul *Globe*, Manchester *Union*, New Haven *Register*, Nashville *Banner*, Chattanooga *Times*, Richmond *Times*, Hartford *Times*, New York *Times*, Philadelphia *Record*, Detroit *Free Press* and Brooklyn *Eagle*, turned to the currency question, and sometimes combined it with a denial that imperialism was the dominant issue. Several of these newspapers were decidedly anti-imperialist but could not bring themselves to back Bryan.

227

The same applied to many Independent and Independent Republican newspapers, including some of the leading anti-imperialist publications.

On the whole, newspapers which had opposed Bryan in 1896 refused to support him in 1900, even if in favor of an anti-imperialist line. There were exceptions. The Louisville *Courier-Journal*, whose owner, W. B. Haldeman, was a member of the gold-standard Democrats' National convention, had bitterly opposed Bryan in 1896, but now backed him on the ground that the silver question had become less significant in comparison to "the paramount issue." Papers such as the Cleveland *Plain Dealer*, Boston *Post*, Charleston *News and Courier*, Nashville *American*, Chicago *Cronicle* and Montgomery *Advertiser* reasoned the same way. Independent newspapers like the Springfield *Republican*, Boston *Traveller*, Philadephia *Times* and Philadelphia *Record* declared they would not support McKinley because of his imperialist policy. But not all of them went so far as to state plainly that they would back Bryan.[24] They also joined many Democrats, especially in the Eastern states, who declared that "free silver is not an issue in this fight," "free silver is not in politics."

In some cases the opposite happened, so that newspapers which had supported Bryan in 1896 now went over to McKinley. Two of the most striking examples were in the West: the Denver *Republican* (Rep.) and the Salt Lake *Tribune* (Ind.). Paradoxically, the reason why they were now prepared to back McKinley was that they accepted the line that made it possible for other newspapers that had formerly opposed Bryan to support him, i.e. the silver question was no longer topical and imperialism had become decisive. Both newspapers had lost their reason for supporting Bryan, the silver interest, and being pro-expansionist had a clear motive for going against him.

A closer look at one of the most important targets for the election propaganda the German-Americans, shows developments after the parties had held their national conventions.

At the turn of the century there were about three million German-born Americans and perhaps twice as many of German origin. In the Middle-West they formed a large proportion of the population and in states such as Minnesota, Michigan, Illinois, Indiana and Ohio, any swing in their loyalty would have had an immediate effect. Traditionally the Germans voted Republican and it was commonly thought they had secured McKinley's victory in 1896. Bryan was estimated to have received less than a third of the German-American votes, and the Germans were generally thought to oppose the soft-money line. It has already been pointed out that Democrats in states with numbers of German voters had made frantic efforts to tone down the silver question and bring up imperialism.[25] The anti-imperialist agitation was considered a better vote-getter among the German voters than from any other group of the electorate.

The German-Americans found themselves in the dilemma of being forced to choose between silver and imperialism. We can study the problem in leading German newspapermen such as Oswald Ottendorfer in New York *Staats-Zeitung* and Dr. E. Pretorius in *Westliche Post* (St. Louis). These two papers were among the largest and most respected of German-language publications. Both had conducted an intensive campaign against Bryan in 1896 and were sworn opponents of bimetallism. When the new issue of imperialism turned up, both newspapers took a radical anti-imperialist position. This applied not least to the *Westliche Post*, and Dr. Pretorius stated in an interview that he had even been contacted personally by both McKinley and Hitchcock, Secretary of the Interior, in an attempt to get the paper to soften criticism of the administration's foreign policy.[26]

Ottendorfer's antipathy to Bryan was notorious, but at the same time, possibly due to the influence of Carl Schurz, his disgust with the new expansionism and the line followed by the Republican administration increased. Shortly before the Democrats' National Convention in Kansas City, Ottendorfer was interviewed in the New York *Herald*. He described the dilemma of German voters: McKinley's imperialism which they despised, or Bryan's currency policy which they found unacceptable. "In their dilemma they will accept that which they fear the least, and as a body they will cast their votes, I believe, for Bryan," he concluded, with a remark which attracted a good deal of attention.

This interview coincided with another expression of opinion which received great publicity. At a congress of the North American Turner-bund in Philadelphia at the end of June, a strongly anti-imperialistic resolution passed, which described the current expansionist policy as "an act of brute force" based upon "hypocrisy and greed for gain."[27]

The anti-imperialist press took this as evidence of the attitude of German-American voters and a warning to Republicans as they prepared their campaign. Another result was a series of attacks on German-Americans, with a strong quality of nativism; examples appeared in the New York *Times*, Boston *Transcript*, Cincinnati *Times-Star* and also in *Harper's Weekly*.[28] Theodore Roosevelt put forward similar views in a letter in which he admitted that the Republicans were in difficulties over the German vote in the West. The reason he gave was that the local German leaders in the press and elsewhere tried to turn the Germans against the administration, and that the ultimate cause of this was that "these particular Germans are still Germans and are not Americans and are against those in America."[29] Accusations of alienism in the press were laced with insinuations about un-American loyalties. Other publications responded by pointing out that German-American voters always had shown little tendency to blockvoting. As the Washington *Post* put it, there was no more reason for believing that this group "will hang together, either for Bryan or McKinley, than there is for the supposition that all the redheaded or round-shouldred or snub-nosed men will vote as a body."[30]

As an indication of how the German voters would vote in their dilemma between imperialism and free silver, the St. Louis *Globe-Democrat* (Rep.) cited recent elections in Oregon where "militarism" and imperialism had played a prominent part in the campaign. There the Republicans had great success and the many German-American voters were thought to have voted Republican almost to a man.[31]

In interviews published in the middle of July, many prominent Germans declared that the German voters would support McKinley in the coming election. In several cases the Democrats' silver plank was described as "an irreparable mistake."[32]

Although many observers shared the opinion expressed by the Washington *Post*, speculations over how the German-Americans would vote continued, both in the press and in discussions of party tacticians.

At the beginning of August the Brooklyn *Eagle* (Ind. Dem.) carried out a survey which gives an insight to how the German-language press stood and how their editors assessed the situation. It deserves close attention. The *Eagle* directed its questions to the foremost German newspapers in states which the Democrats considered doubtful. Answers came from 24 papers, with a total circulation of over 325,000. 19 of the 24 were from the Middle West, the area which was most interesting. Of the others, one each from Texas, Colorado, Delaware, New Jersey and New York, we shall only mention the most respected of all the German-American newspapers, the New York *Staats-Zeitung*, which with a circulation of over 50,000 also was the largest.

The editor of the Staats-Zeitung, Oswald Ottendorfer, had stated a month or so previously that he believed Bryan would gain the majority of German votes in the election. In its reply to the *Eagle*, however, the newspaper expressed itself more cautiously. The majority of the German voters, it said, were equally opposed to imperialism and free silver. It was impossible to say how they would vote; it would depend on which of the two evils they felt most dangerous, and this would depend on how the parties conducted their campaigns. There was no doubt that in comparison with 1896, McKinley would now receive fewer German votes and it was doubtful whether he would even get the majority.

Questions put by the *Eagle* to German-American newspapers were as follows:

1. Which candidate will, in your opinion, get the majority of the German-American vote?
2. Will this be a change from the election of 1896? If so, how?
3. Do the German-American voters regard the issue of imperialism as a real and vital issue?
4. Do the German-American voters regard the money question as a real and vital issue?
5. Is Imperialism or is the money question regarded by the German voters as the paramount issue?
6. What are the chief causes that you think will influence the German-Americans in casting their votes?

They are questions directly aimed at the debate which was being conducted both in the press and not least within the Democratic party and which had stirred up such controversy.

Of the nineteen newspapers from the North Central area, no less than eleven said in answer to the first question that Bryan would receive the majority of German votes. Five thought McKinley would get them, and three left the question open. All the newspapers described as Democratic or Independent Democratic believed in Bryan, while the Republican side put their faith in McKinley. The division of opinion here clearly demonstrates wishful thinking, the victory of the candidate one supports. Of the eleven newspapers designated independent, six gave Bryan as the likely winner, one McKinley and three considered it immpossible to say. The most decidedly anti-imperialist newspapers believed that Bryan would win the support of the majority of German voters.

It is significant that all newspapers which predicted victory for McKinley among German voters denied that the Germans saw imperialism as a real issue, while all others declared, with varying certainty, that they did. On silver, the picture is more divided. All those who believed in McKinley, i.e., primarily those with a Republican or Independent Republican label, claimed the issue was "real and vital," while this was denied by all those for Bryan. Typically, all three newspapers that considered it impossible to

231

predict the outcome stated that both silver and imperialism were "real and vital issues" for German voters. The same applied to another two newspapers, *Abendpost* in Chicago and *Westliche Post* in St. Louis, although the former believed that imperialism and the second that silver was the most serious.

Answers to questions five and six follow the same pattern as above. Those who believed in a victory for Bryan saw imperialism as the paramount issue. The same applies to newspapers with Democratic leanings. These sometimes included trusts in their answers. Those who put their faith in McKinley named the silver question in the same way, sometimes with the addition of prosperity.

It is obvious, and sometimes directly stated in the answers, that newspaper editors concentrated on the situation within their own areas, or at least within their states. The material is much too limited, however, to allow any conclusions about regional differences. The large number of newspapers believing in a majority for Bryan should be weighed against circulation statistics. The situation then becomes reversed, so that newspapers which think a McKinley majority probable represented a greater circulation than those believing in Bryan. Of the larger publications only *Freie Presse* in Chicago had faith in Bryan, while *Republikaner* and *Abendpost*, both of Chicago, *Westliche Blätter*, Cincinnati, and *Westliche Post*, St. Louis, gave McKinley as the probable victor.

The Westliche Post is of special interest. It was described as Independent in the *Eagle's* presentation, but had on other occasions been given the more fitting label of Republican. The newspaper had been an ardent supporter of McKinley in 1896, and its editor, Dr. Pretorius, was a sworn enemy of Bryan and soft money. But the newspaper had reacted just as fervently against expansion, and in its answer to the *Eagle*, which took the form of an interview with Pretorius, both imperialism and silver were declared real and vital issues. At the same time Pretorius declared that *Westliche Post* would back the Republicans and McKinley and stated that he was convinced that the majority of German voters would do likewise. "Expansion is comparatively an academic question; free silver a practical ... The Germans are above all opposed to a fifty cent dollar, and while they may hold the same ideas on expansion as I do, they will set the importance of protecting the laborer through the maintenance of a sound financial system above everything else." Thus *Westliche Post* refused to support Bryan and believed that most German-Americans would react the same way, and the reason for this supposition was silver. Even though party loyalty was obviously an extremely important factor, it can hardly be denied that Bryan's insistence on free silver was a serious hindrance to the Democrats in their attempts to attract German-American voters and Independents in general. The silver banner created a psychological barrier for people considering changing party and benefitted the Republicans.

It is obvious that anti-imperialism expressed in the German-American press was taken seriously and considered to have a strong influence on the German-American electorate.[33] It provided leaders of the Republican campaign with a pointer to their best tactics: revive the silver question, emphasize the prosperity line, tone down expansionist propaganda.

As was to be expected, Bryan insisted that the platform that had been accepted was the best possible one from a tactical point of view too. In his opinion, it was impossible to find 100,000 voters who would have voted for him on a platform simply reaffirming the silver plank and who would now vote against him on a platform restating it. According to what he wrote in a letter to one of his supporters, he was convinced that he would instead have lost many more votes if he had consented to run on a platform which he would have had to explain or apologize for.[34]

2

During the convention in Kansas City, and increasingly as the campaign got up steam, the dynamic, colorful Republican vice-presidential candidate, Roosevelt, rather than the President, came to act as Bryan's chief opponent. In his notification speech at the ceremonies in Indianapolis on August 8, James D. Richardson[35] spoke of the scandalous attacks on Bryan and his supporters who were called "dishonest and lawless at home, and . . . cowards abroad." This was a quotation from a speech by Roosevelt and Richardson said he was convinced such attacks would be made "only by someone whose coarse manners before the public are equaled by the roughness of his riding habit."[36]

Roosevelt, "the Rough Rider," was perhaps the American politician most closely identified with the new policy of expansion. And it was above all this policy that Bryan castigated in his speech of acceptance. He wasted few words on other issues. The speech is of value because, together with the Democratic platform, it is the clearest formulation of the anti-imperialist standpoint, which had become the official position of the Democrats and on which they based their campaign.

This overwhelming emphasis on imperialism as the "paramount issue" in the speech of acceptance was not wholly Bryan's idea. In general the organized anti-imperialists had no complaint about the way their cause had been treated in the Kansas City platform.[37] But they had other reasons for discontent. On August 14 the anti-imperialists were to hold their important "Liberty Congress" at Indianapolis, where they would decide whom to back in the election. To ensure that they did not nominate a third ticket instead of supporting Bryan, the secretary of the Anti-Imperialist League, Erving Winslow suggested Bryan should devote almost the entire speech to imperialism. Bryan followed his advice and so wholeheartedly that when he published his speeches he gave this one the title, "Imperialism."[38]

Before Bryan started on the burning issue he spoke a few words about domestic policy. He repeated what he had said on various occasions, when he had made the dominant question "a contest between Democracy on the one hand and plutocracy on the other." The Democrats had no intention, however, of fighting "the honest acquisition of wealth," only unjust exploitation.

Bryan quickly entered into the Philippine question and started by dealing with the delicate matter of the part he took in ratification of the treaty with Spain. He gave the explanation he was so often forced to repeat: He thought it safer to trust the American people to give independence to the Filipinos than to trust the accomplishment of that purpose to diplomacy. He stated that he believed that "we are now in a better position to wage a successful contest against imperialism than we would have been had the treaty been rejected. With the treaty ratified a clean-cut issue is presented between a government by consent and a government by force."[39]

He also brought in the Bacon resolution in his apology. This was to assure the Filipinos of independence on the same terms as the Cubans, Bryan supported this resolution, defeated by the deciding vote of the Republican Vice President.

"If the Bacon resolution had been adopted by the Senate and carried out by the President, either at the time of the ratification of the treaty or at any time afterwards, it would have taken the question of imperialism out of politics and left the American people free to deal with their domestic problems."[40]

Bryan clearly did not know which leg to stand on. He had supported the ratification to get a "clean-cut issue," but he supported the Bacon resolution which "would have taken the question of imperialism out of politics."

234

Despite the fact that Bryan's actions in connection with the ratification of the treaty had led to violent accusations and had undermined his credibility with many anti-imperialist, he insisted that he had acted correctly. He maintained the same line in his memoirs, denying not only that he regretted the standpoint he had adopted then but even declaring emphatically that he had "never showed more statemanship than then."[41]

Bryan took up the accusations made by the Republicans, that Philippine insurgents had been encouraged by Democrats in the United States. His answer was that the Filipinos did not need encouragement from any living American. The whole history of the United States was an encouragement to all people fighting for freedom, for the right to independence. He cited Patrick Henry, Jefferson, Washington and Lincoln. He pointed out that anyone wanting to set the United States on the path to imperialism must contemplate not only the effect this would have on the Filipinos but consequences for the people of America. Imperialism corrupts those practising it. Imperialists had not mentioned, by so much as a word, the Boers fighting for freedom in South Africa.

Bryan made the usual distinction between expansionism and imperialism which has cropped up in so many ways.

"The forcible annexation of territory to be governed by arbitrary power differs as much from the acquisition of territory to be built into states as monarchy differs from a democracy. The Democratic party does not oppose expansion when expansion enlarges the area of the Republic and incorporates land which can be settled by American citizens, or adds to our population people who are willing to become citizens and are capable of discharging their duties as such."[42]

In Bryan's opinion none of these conditions applied to the Filipinos. The islands had a large population. Even if uninhabited, no Americans would have wanted to move there, since the islands lay too close to the equator.

Bryan then conjured up the specter of militarism. An imperialistic policy necessitated a large standing army. This was not only a heavy burden for taxpayers, but "a menace to a Republican form of government." In dealing with the future of the Filipinos, their status as subjects, non-citizens, Bryan followed the usual anti-imperialistic pattern. Since these eight to ten million Filipinos, "so different from us in race and history," could not be citizens of the United States, the only course was to make them subjects.

But neither the platform nor candidate would accept the second solution: "A Republic can have no subjects. A subject is possible only in a

235

government resting upon force; he is unknown in a government deriving its just power from the consent of the governed."[43]

In his speech Bryan compared, not unskillfully, the attitude of the Republicans to the Filipinos with the attitude taken by the English to the American colonies. The statement in the Republican platform, that the Filipinos would get "the largest measure of self-government consistent with their welfare and our duties," corresponded exactly to the view of the American colonies taken by the English government. But "The whole difference between a Monarchy and a Republic may be summoned up in one sentence. In a Monarchy the king gives to the people what he believes to be a good government; in a Republic the people secure for themselves what they believe to be a good government." He concluded: "I submit that history furnishes no example of turpitude baser than ours if we now substitute our yoke for the Spanish yoke."

Bryan discussed the arguments in support of annexation of the Philippine Islands. He rejected all talk of a duty for America. A duty could only derive from generally accepted principles and Bryan claimed categorically that the same moral rules applied for a nation as for an individual. And when it came to rights, no boundary could be drawn between the rights of the Cubans and the right of the Filipinos to freedom and independence.

Bryan rejected all arguments that America had assumed obligations that made it necessary for her to retain the islands under American rule, on the ground that the first duty of a nation is to be true to itself and its ideas. Nor did the argument so persistently repeated by Republicans, that the Filipinos were incapable of self-government, make any impression on him. He refuted it, partly by referring to a report by Admiral Dewey often quoted by the anti-imperialists, partly in religious-ideological terms: no people can be created without the capacity for self-government.

There were four arguments for imperialism, Bryan said:

"First—that we must improve the present opportunity to become a world power and enter into international politics.
Second—that our commercial interests in the Philippine Islands and in the Orient make it necessary for us to hold the islands permanently.
Third—that the spread of the Christian religion will be facilitated by a colonial policy.
Fourth—that there is no honorable retreat from the position which the nation has taken."

On the first point, Bryan declared that America had been a world power for over a hundred years, not only a world power but "it has done more

236

to affect the policies of the human race than all the other nations of the world combined."

He illustrated the second argument, said to be aimed at the nation's pocketbook, by quoting from the speech by Henry Cabot Lodge at the Republican convention. He rejected the idea "that it is profitable to purchase trade by force and violence," and referred to Franklin for support in fighting "the sordid doctrine of those who would put a price upon the head of an American soldier and justify a war of conquest upon the ground that it will pay."

But the Commoner also claimed that a war of conquest was not only wrong but foolish. All that the United States needed, commercially and militarily, was a habor and coaling station in the Philippines and Americans could get that whenever they wanted. There was no reason whatsoever "to own people in order to trade with them." Trade with China, Japan, Central and South America was steadily increasing, without their owning these countries. Bryan continued with words that were closely reminiscent of those of the Democratic platform:

"When trade is secured by force the cost of securing it and retaining it must be taken out of the profits, and the profits are never large enough to cover the expense." Profits would go to army contractors, shipowners, civil servants with American salaries and Philippine living costs. But for "the farmer, the laboring man and to the vast majority of those engaged in other occupation it would bring expenditure without return and risk without reward."

Bryan followed this appeal to the working man by yet another argument which was by no means new but which was thought to give a good response. The worker would be hurt if laborers from the Orient made their way to America, or if American capital was invested in the Philippines in order to get, with the help of Philippine labor, products for trade with China. Labor would be the first to be affected by the world regime of militarism.

The religious argument inspiring an imperialist policy by its effect on mission activity, was categorically dismissed: "If true Christianity consists in carrying out in our daily lives the teachings of Christ, who will say that we are commanded to civilize with dynamite and proselyte with the sword." "Imperialism finds no warrant in the Bible." "Let it be known that our missionairies are seeking souls instead of sovereignty."

He refused to accept the argument that although it was regrettable that America had become involved in Philippine affairs, the naval victory at Manila had necessitated annexation. Annexation was in no way an unavoidable consequence. The navy had also won a victory at Santiago, but Cuba had been granted freedom.

So far Bryan had restricted himself to sweeping criticism of what were said to be the Republicans' arguments in favor of imperialism. He did not rest at this, but concluded by declaring what in his opinion should be done in the Philippine question and what steps he would take if he became President of the United States:

"If elected I will convene Congress in extraordinary session as soon as inaugurated and recommend an immediate declaration of the nation's purpose, first to establish a stable form of government in the Philippine Islands, just as we are now establishing a stable form of government in Cuba;[44] second, to give independence to the Filipinos; third to protect the Filipinos from outside interference while they work out their destiny, just as we have protected the republics of Central and South America, and are, by the Monroe Doctrine, pledged to protect Cuba."

This program demonstrates, as did the Democratic platform, how difficult it was to launch a practicable alternative to the Republican policy in the Philippines. The platform had promised a stable form of government in the islands and to give them full independence. One of the arguments against retaining the islands was the Monroe doctrine, said to assume American non-interference outside the Western hemisphere.[45] But both the platform and Bryan's speech of acceptance promised protection against outside interference. And Bryan directly compared this protection to what the United States was obliged to give Cuba according to the Monroe Doctrine. There is an inescapable contradiction. In one case the Monroe Doctrine is interpreted as an obstacle to commitments in the Philippines, in the other the Filipinos are promised the same protection as the Monroe Doctrine afforded Cuba.

Bryan devoted the concluding phrases of his long showdown with imperialism and its standardbearers to castigating those individuals who saw the new imperialism as the destiny of the American people. "Destiny is the subterfuge of the invertebrate, who, lacking the courage to oppose error, seeks some plausible excuse for supporting it."[46]

The speech made by the vice-presidential candidate, Adlai Stevenson, had no notable features. In contrast to the Republicans, the Democrats combined the ceremonies of notification for the two candidates, which helped put the already rather insignificant Stevenson even more in the shade. The fact that he was a compromise candidate had undoubtedly left

238

its mark on his attitude. But Stevenson gave Bryan full support in the attempt to make imperialism the paramount issue.[47]

3

Bryan's refusal to relinquish silver was taken by opponents among the anti-imperialists as confirmation that they had been right. Thus Donelson Caffery, the gold-standard Democratic senator from Louisiana, wrote to Edward Atkinson in the middle of May, "it looks to me as if there is no hope in Bryan for the success of our cause."[48] Erving Winslow maintained his earlier opinion, that silver was dead and should not prevent anyone from supporting Bryan: "The great body of Anti-Imperialists is content with the fact that circumstances have made the Chicago plank a dead issue and are willing to condone the perfunctory repetition of it, accepting such votes as it will bring to the Anti-Imperialist Candidate ... all of us who believe in the paramount importance of the right solution of the question, Republic or Empire, must I think support the Anti-Imperialist candidate and party, whatever else we have to swallow, with all our might."[49]

At the beginning of the year the anti-imperialists had made plans for a large anti-imperialist congress after the Kansas City convention, at which the decision would be made as to which candidate they should back.[50] On June 25 the executive committee of the Anti-Imperialist League again met at the Plaza in New York, to decide upon convening the congress. Leading anti-imperialists were present: Boutwell, Schurz, John B. Henderson, Sterling Morton, Horace Boies, Moorfield Storey, Senators Wellington and Bacon, W. A. Croffut.[51] Edwin Burrit Smith put the matter in a nutshell when he said the crucial problem was how they should unite all Independent voters and settle the election.[52] Among those at the meeting there was a clear tendency to support Bryan, but this feeling was by no means unanimous. "I must say that for myself the spectacle of a lot of well-meaning and estimable men, such as those gathered together last Monday, going pell mell for Bryan under the circumstances was saddening," wrote Thomas Osborne to Edward Atkinson, who was of the same opinion.[53] Osborne strongly opposed Bryan and later was one of those who made the greatest effort to launch a third ticket.[54] In the meantime it was decided to call the Liberty Congress in Indianapolis on August 14.

The Kansas City convention did little to solve the problem of how the anti-imperialists outside the silver parties were to react to Bryan's candidacy. The old conflict of loyalties remained. As often emphasized, the majority of anti-imperialists were anti-silver and the necessity of choosing between Bryan and McKinley, between silver and imperialism, put many of them in a great dilemma. Anti-imperialists such as Edwin Burrit Smith, Louis R. Erich, Sterling Morton and Foster Peabody were at the same time members of the Executive Committee of the National Sound Money League, and among its vice-presidents was also Edward Atkinson. As expected, the anti-imperialists found different ways out of the dilemma, and the development of events in this respect during the autumn of 1900 illuminates the problem of the part played by foreign policy issues in domestic politics. There were naturally three ways of solving the anti-imperialists' quandary, each of which produced its variations: vote for McKinley, vote for Bryan, or vote for neither.

4

Party loyalties and internal political attitudes that appeared in connection with the election and the election campaign put a great strain on anti-imperialist organizations and gave rise to tensions so severe that they threatened to split the movement. The anti-imperialists included Populists, Bryan Democrats, Gold Democrats, Mugwumps, other reformists with Republican links, and conservative Republicans. The issue of imperialism set up a new front line, which crossed many others.

Senator George F. Hoar of Massachusetts, one of the most active and respected opponents of the foreign policy of the McKinley administration, stood apart from his own state's anti-imperialist organization, led by Mugwumps and reform Republicans and thus politically wholly foreign to the conservative Hoar. He kept in contact with the organization and the anti-imperialist speeches he made to the Senate were among the most widely appreciated contributions to the great flood of pamphlets and campaign literature released by the Anti-Imperialist League.

Hoar had never been able to forgive Bryan for his part in ratification of the peace treaty with Spain, and refused to accept the explanations given repeatedly by Bryan both publicly and in letters to Hoar.[55] Personal bitterness was obviously involved. It emerges in a letter by Hoar to Edward Atkinson, with whom he was on good terms despite their different political convictions. The letter should be seen in the context of the political situation during the weeks following the Kansas City convention, when discussions within anti-imperialist circles about how they should vote were intense and heated. Hoar had declared his refusal to accept Bryan and he did not rest at that, but in a speech in the middle of July he made a sharp attack on the Democratic leader whom he accused of being responsible for the annexation of the Philippine Islands. Erving Winslow, secretary of the New England Anti-Imperialist League attacked Hoar in an open letter. Winslow recommended supporting Bryan and declared that backing McKinley would be a grotesque desertion, indicating lack of firmness in anti-imperialistic convictions.

Winslow's act met with approval in many quarters, mainly among Bryan's supporters, but Atkinson, who could not abide Bryan, went on to attack Winslow. In the ensuing conflict he went so far as to hand in his resignation as vice-president and member of the executive committee of the New England Anti-Imperialist League.[56]

Hoar and Atkinson were united by their uncompromising anti-imperialism and they shared a great mutual respect, even though they often had widely differing opinions on the tactics that the opponents of imperialism should employ. In one of his letters to Atkinson, marked "Highly Confidential," Hoar wrote:

"I am sorry and amazed that some of our worthy friends who resisted Imperialism seem inclined to support Bryan, although I am not amazed at the savageness with which some of them attack me for not agreeing with them. We had the treaty all beaten. The Senate was the West Point of the struggle. We needed only one-third, and we had almost a majority against it, when Bryan came to Washington and, in spite of the remonstrances of the wisest and shrewdest Democratic leaders, insisted that the treaty should bt ratified. I did not see him myself, although he has since written to me justifying his course.[57] I have every reason to suppose that my earnest remonstrances were conveyed to him. His course was as if some influential General in our Revolutionary War had surrendered West Point to the British, and then had induced the Continental Congress to pass a law to the effect that George III was the rightful Monarch, and the British Parliament the legislature for the Thirteen Colonies, justifying himself by the fact that he wanted to put a stop to strife, and that we would discuss later when we had an opportunity for a popular election the question whether the submission to them should continue or whether she should let us go.

Now at that time I had separated myself from every Republican in the Senate. I was being violently denounced by Republican newspapers all over the country. My political life in Washington had become solitude. My name was kept standing in the New York Sun, like a prominent advertisement, in a black list of 'traitors.' Now I do not fancy helping Mr. Bryan to get the prize of the Presidency in that way."

The personal bitterness toward Bryan shines through. But it was not only Bryan's past which made him unacceptable as the champion of anti-imperialism, but his attitude to the current situation in the Philippine Islands. The Democratic platform stated that the Filipinos should first have "a stable form of government" and then independence. Hoar transcribed this freely into "We will give them good government, and thereafter when it is practicable give them their independence." But "Government and Independence" were "birthrights" and not "gifts to be given," and Hoar could find no substantial or practical difference between Bryan's attitude and the attitude of the Republican imperialists. According to the stubborn Massachusetts senator, the only difference was that Bryan and his supporters talked anti-imperialism to push free silver and other issues dear to them. In a later letter he summed up his view of Bryan in these words: "I believe Mr. Bryan did what he knew was wrong for the sole purpose of securing his own political advancement, and I cannot, therefore, give him my confidence for the future. He will be worthless as an Anti-Imperialist. He will be thoroughly mischievous in every other respect."[58]

Hoar's attitude received the reception one might expect in the press. Democratic newspapers attacked the senator for what was described as treachery to the cause he had fought for. The Boston *Post* found "something pathetic in this humiliation."[59] The Republican press praised Hoar. His assurance that he would support McKinley and Roosevelt was of the greatest value and was widely exploited in campaign propaganda. The reaction of the Independent press varied in accordance with how each individual newspaper responded to the dilemma. Most of these papers treated Hoar's decision with respect and understanding.

Hoar was not alone in his views. Many other conservative anti-imperialist Republicans reacted in the same way. Among them were Senator Hale, the only Republican apart from Hoar who had voted against the treaty with Spain, and congressmen such as Littlefield and McCall, who were known for commitment to anti-imperialism.

There were other anti-imperialists who could not under any circumstances conceive of supporting Bryan, who preferred McKinley, but who could not bring themselves to give the Republicans their support. They considered the plans for launching a third party quite meaningless, if not harmful. They chose another way out: McKinley for president, but Democrats or at least anti-imperialists in the House of Representatives. Charles Francis Adams was an eloquent advocate of this line.

242

Adams' attitude to Bryan was negative and he had rejected the idea of supporting him. He was sceptical not only to Bryan but to the Bryan Democrats: "I have reason to believe that that party, South and West, is honeycombed with Imperialism," he wrote Schurz,[60] and in another letter written shortly after the convention in Kansas City, he expounded what he thought of Bryan. He said he was unable to decide whether Bryan was a knave or a fool. "If he really believes what he says, that the ratio of 16 : 1 is divinely ordained ... the man is distinctly a fool ... If however, with his tongue in his cheek, and a wink of the eye he takes the ground that this is merely put forward for consistency's sake ... then he is a knave."[61] But Bryan was obviously not a knave in this sense, nor did Adams believe him to be. He refused to support Bryan. He had no wish to launch a third ticket. He chose the solution that anti-imperialist Republicans should vote for McKinley, defeating Bryanism, but vote for Democratic candidates in the Congressional election, defeating imperialism.[62] Erving Winslow called this idea an absurdity and a foolish notion, but other prominent anti-imperialists, including Atkinson, reacted favorably.[63]

Adams continued to urge this plan, the more so after attempts to start a third party failed, forcing the anti-imperialists if they wanted to vote at all, to choose between McKinley and Bryan. In the middle of October he took the initiative in starting an open correspondence with Schurz, who at this point was supporting Bryan.[64] By arrangement with Samuel Bowles, publisher of one of the leading anti-imperialist newspapers, the Springfield *Republican*, two letters were published on October 31, one from Adams and one from Schurz in which they each argued for their respective opinions on how Independent anti-imperialists should vote in the election.[65] The letters were spread through Associated Press and appeared in several newspapers, including the New York *Times*, Boston *Herald*, Springfield *Union and Republican*. Schurz' arguments against Adams' idea was that it would be an ineffective method of defeating imperialism.[66] Schurz' and Adams' correspondence can hardly have had any noticeable influence on voters. John Hay, the Secretary of State, summed up the situation in a letter to McKinley: "Schurz thinks it will be best to elect a lunatic President, and trust a sane Congress to keep him in order. Adams thinks that the best way would be to elect a sane man President and have a lunatic Congress for him to control; and neither of them seems to realize that it makes not the slightest difference what both of them think."[67]

243

Even if distrust of Bryan was deeply rooted in many anti-imperialists there were many cases where people who had opposed Bryan, including Republicans, Mugwumps and Gold Democrats, were persuaded by commitment to anti-imperialism to give the Peerless Leader their support. They included Bourke Cockran, George Boutwell, and Richard Olney, all energetic opponents four years previously of "the silver-tongued orator."[68]

Special attention was attracted by the support given by Bourke Cockran, an ardent Gold Democrat who had fought Bryan with determination in the 1896 campaign. His return to the Democratic camp and his active contributions in support of Bryan in the campaign were a great source of satisfaction for the Democrats, while they caused him to be bitterly attacked by Bryan's opponents. In replying to a friend who reproached him for his standpoint, Cockran wrote:

"I am neither a Gold Democrat nor a Silver Democrat; a Bryan Democrat nor an anti-Bryan Democrat. I am simply a Democrat without limitation, qualification or hyphen. In 1896 I believed that loyalty to Democratic principles consisted in opposing the candidate of the Democratic Party and to give my vote its utmost efficiency in that direction I cast it for the Republican nominee. But in this contest a new and overshadowing issue has arisen—an issue which imposes on some of us the duty of making certain that the fruits of a war for humanity and civilization shall not be perverted by the Republican Party to a cruel, cowardly and treacherous policy."[69]

Cockran's anti-imperialism had a strong anti-British bias and the Irishman had been one of the harshest critics of the English in the campaign on the Boer question, underway all spring and summer. Cockran's attitude was that the silver issue was obsolete but that his own views on the subject had in no way changed. When asked by Charles H. Taney, publisher of the Wheeling *Register,* how he stood on the currency question, he telegraphed on October 11: "My abhorrence of the Chicago platform has not diminished. On the same issue my attitude today would be precisely the same as it was four years ago."

Cockran was a brilliant speaker and the Democratic campaign manager, Stone, put him to work both in the Middle West and in the Eastern states. The plan had been that he should undertake a trip to the Far West, but Stone thought it imperative that he should go to Connecticut, New York and Maryland, to persuade Democrats opposed to Bryan to vote Democratic. Cockran concluded with an important speech in Boston, a passionate declaration of anti-imperialistic belief. It was met with acclaim by all anti-imperialists, including those who refused to support Bryan.

The foremost aim in the campaign of anti-imperialists who had decided to back Bryan was to persuade the greatest possible number of Independents to cast their votes for him. At the beginning of September an action was started to collect signatures of prominent persons who had voted for McKinley in 1896, an appeal directed at "the Independent Voter," which attacked the McKinley administration and urged people to vote for Bryan. Prominent figures behind the appeal included Edwin Burrit Smith and Herbert Welsh, the latter a vice-president in the Anti-Imperialist League and the driving force of its Philadelphia section.

An effort was made to get Cleveland to sign, but he refused to do anything that might remotely be interpreted as support for Bryan. Hope was placed in several university presidents, in particular Eliot of Harvard and Hadley of Yale. Another man from Yale who was also counted on was William G. Sumner, a convinced anti-imperialist, one of the vice-presidents of the League who had signed the petition sent to the Senate on January 30, 1899, appealing to senators not to consent to the treaty. Sumner was approached and asked both to sign the appeal and to forward the same request to President Hadley. Sumner refused and explained that he did not intend to vote for Bryan.[70] A direct appeal to Hadley was negative.[71] Following Herbert Welsh's suggestion, Schurz wrote to Eliot, whom he knew well, but he refused. Eliot was critical of expansion—he too had signed the address to the Senate in January 1899—but considered that this was not sufficient reason for backing Bryan: "I prefer to take the chances with McKinley and his probable associates, rather than with Bryan and his probable associates."[72]

Other disappointments followed. A whole series of prominent anti-imperialists refused categorically to support Bryan, among them John G. Carlisle, Secretary of the Treasury in Cleveland's cabinet, Horace White, of the Evening Post, Robert Fulton, a New York financier, Carnegie, and Ottendorfer, all officers in the Anti-Imperialist League. They refused to sign the address and backed McKinley.[73] Carlisle took an active part in the campaign.[74]

Not all who were asked refused. By the beginning of November, over forty names had been collected, including George Boutwell, Senator Wellington, ex-Senator D. H. Chamberlain from Massachusetts, Dana Estes, William Lloyd Garrison, Edwin Godkin, Louis R. Ehrich, and Judson Harmon.

But Schurz was disappointed: "What a terrible burden Bryan is to our just cause," he sighed in a letter to Herbert Welsh.[75] If it proved impossible to collect more names and above all more weighty names, it would in his opinion be better to refrain from publishing the address, since it displayed weakness rather than strength.[76] Smith was satisfied with the list, however, and declared that it was to be published, with the result that Schurz refused to sign it himself.[77]

The congress in Indianapolis did not bring only disappointments for Bryan. He won the support of several prominent figures who earlier had hesitated or at least taken their time in declaring where they stood. Schurz was one, and the others included Richard Olney, Cleveland's Secretary of State, and the Republican senator from Maryland, George Wellington. These three men represented different political viewpoints, but they had a common denominator in that they had all fought Bryan in 1896 and were supporting him in 1900.

Henry Loomis Nelson, former editor of *Harper's Weekly*, had contacted both Cleveland and Olney to get statements about where they stood in the opening phase of the campaign. Cleveland refused, but Olney published an open letter, dated August 14 but not published until the beginning of September, in which he stated his reasons for supporting Bryan. Olney, who lived in Boston, was a confirmed opponent to silver and in no way involved in the anti-imperialist movement. His support for Bryan caused widespread comment.

Olney's views on foreign and colonial policy are of interest, partly because of his earlier position as Secretary of State, partly because they represented an important line of thought shared by many Democrats and Republicans. In the March issue of the *Atlantic Monthly* he presented his views. He started by condemning the policy of isolation, when the importance of maintaining a strong naval force had been ignored and both the navy and the merchant fleet allowed to fall into disrepair. He greeted with satisfaction the new insight into and will to accept America's role as one of the great nations. He saw behind this newly awakened awareness "above all that instinct in the line of national growth and expansion whose absence would be a sure symptom of our national deterioration."[78] Olney felt no hesitation in admitting that he was an expansionist. He rejoiced in the fact that the American people had opened their eyes "to the fact that they were one of the foremost powers of the earth and should play a commensurately great part in its affairs." This was not only a duty but a necessity, since the need for new markets emerged ever more clearly.

The new policy was inspired both by "duty" and by "interest". Olney went so far as to recommend further annexations in the Caribbean. Annexation of Cuba was for him the natural part of events and he regretted the over-hasty and unfortunate Teller resolution whereby Congress had guaranteed Cuba's independence.

Olney considered that a new, active foreign policy, backed by a strong army and navy, was essential for expansion, which in turn he was convinced was necessary for the United States. And apart from these aspects of interest," it was the duty of the United States to start acting like the great power it was.

Olney's attitude seems similar to that of wholehearted expansionists like Whitelaw Reid, but there was an important difference. Olney was no globalist but rather a hemispherist, and he devoted three-quarters of the article to an attack on the Republican administration's policy on the Philippine Islands. Unlike many anti-imperialists he did not deny the Government's right to acquire and rule new territories. However, he asserted that neither "duty" nor "national interest" required annexation of the Philippines. He rejected as "baseless and fantastic" the idea that Americans had some "solemn obligation to carry the blessings of good government and civilization to the inhabitants of the Philippine archipelago." He refuted the argument that annexation was necessary or advantageous for commerce. Trade in the Far East was hindered by annexation. America had left itself open to attack both politically and militarily, and placed itself in an impossible position by demanding an Open Door in China and at the same time refusing the same thing in the Philippines. "We are no longer an American Empire simply—we are become an Asiatic Empire also, environed by all the rivalries, jealousies, embarrassments and perils attaching to every Power now struggling to get commercial and political supremacy in the East."[79]

As has been shown, Olney diverged sharply from the anti-imperialists proper and ex-President Cleveland commented on the article in a letter, declaring that he could not share Olney's view, but was "so antiquated as to wish we were well back in our old place."[80]

In his open letter Olney explained that Bryan was not the candidate he would have wished and that in some respects his views were quite different to those expressed in the Kansas City platform. But he gave the arguments that had made him decide it was his duty to support Bryan and fight McKinley. His arguments were *against* McKinley rather than *for* Bryan. He described the McKinley administration as "a syndicated Presidency—

a Presidency got for the Republican party by the money of a combination of capitalists intent upon securing national legislation in aid of their particular interests." The Dingley Tariff was an example of exploitation. A large portion of the letter consisted of attacks on the policy in the Philipinnes. Olney's criticism was on the same lines as the article in the *Atlantic Monthly.* He considered annexation of the Philippine Islands as proof that the United States had become an "international landgrabber" like the other great nations while he criticized the failure to win Cuba, "the key and inspiration of the war," lying right at our door, "the key to the Gulf of Mexico and absolutely essential to our defense against foreign attack."

This policy, by means of which the United States "sets up in business as an Asiatic power," would not only bring upon them heavy economic burdens, but involve the nation in entangling alliances and international complications.

Olney's letter caused a stir. The Democratic Campaign Committee printed and distributed one million copies.[81] The New York *Telegram* declared it almost as great a sensation as if Cleveland had come out for Bryan. The press reacted mainly along party lines. The Baltimore *Sun* (Dem.) wrote that Olney's statement was convincing and should influence not only Gold Democrats but persuade every "thoughtful and patriotic man."[82] Republican newspapers were critical. The New York *Sun* (Rep.) found the letter "sadly lacking in the sane, intellectual qualities usually shown by Mr. Olney." Several newspapers insinuated that there were tactical, political motives lurking in the background. Olney was suspected of being interested in the Democratic presidential nomination in 1904.[83] In a private letter earlier during the year to S. B. Griffin, editor of the Springfield *Republican*, Olney had given a detailed account of his attitude to Bryan's renewed candidacy and counted even then on the possibility that he might support Bryan, despite differing opinions. In this letter Olney had pointed out how his views on foreign and colonial policy differed. Olney was critical of the McKinley administration's Philippine policy, but did not at all follow the same line as the anti-imperialists whom Bryan had joined.[84] Olney did not consider that the holding of colonies was against the Constitution. He was an expansionist but wanted to extend "the American Empire" primarily through annexation of Cuba. Mainly for political reasons, that is, by considering "national interest" and not for ideological reasons, he opposed what he called "an Asiatic Empire."

At the same time as Olney came out for Bryan, another almost equally

248

sensational declaration of the same kind appeared. In this case it was the Republican senator from Maryland, George Wellington, an intense anti-imperialist, driven by conviction to take the step of breaking with his party and backing the Democratic candidate. Wellington made his sensational announcement in a speech in Cumberland, Maryland. Bryan was present, and welcomed his new supporter in a passionate speech.

Wellington's change of heart was acclaimed by the Democratic press as an act of courage and integrity. Some newspapers took the opportunity to get at Senator Hoar, who was backing McKinley, "preferring the flesh-pots of party to the interests of the republic."[84a]

The Republicans condemned Wellington as a deserter and queried his "mental and moral condition." The Chicago *Evening Post* went so far as to suggest that the senator had "become erratic and hyperemotional through addiction to a dementalizing drug."[85]

6

If George F. Hoar, William Graham Sumner, John G. Carlisle, Presidents Hadley and Eliot, Horace White and others decided to vote for McKinley —despite everything, and men like Richard Olney, George Boutwell, William Lloyd Garrison and Louis R. Ehrich came out for Bryan—for lack of a better alternative, others could find neither the Democratic nor the Republican presidential candidate acceptable. Thus ex-President Grover Cleveland was disgusted with the Kansas City platform. However, he refused to give political advice, even if he "was pestered to death nearly with appeals to come out for Bryan."[86] In private letters to friends he expressed his distress and his total alienation from "the new Democracy," calling Bryan "the demagogue and insolent crusader."[87] Cleveland refused to support either Bryan or McKinley: "I suppose it is a case of being damned if I do and damned if I don't, but I have made up my mind that I am entitled to decline enlistment in the war between Bryanism and McKinleyism," he wrote in September 1900 in a confidential letter, answering a request from the Baltimore *Sun* for a statement in connection with Olney's open letter in support of Bryan.[88] The Democratic ex-president did not cast a vote in 1900.

The Kansas City platform naturally was a disappointment to the Gold Democrats who had hoped to be able to support their party again. But many leading anti-imperialist Gold Democrats had been pessimistic even before the convention. One of Donelson Caffery's associates, William Everett, had in the middle of May published a letter to the editor of the New York *Evening Post* under the heading, "The Duty of the Gold Democrats," in which he asserted that the Gold Democrats should set up their platform and nominate candidates as in 1896.[89]

Prominent Gold Democrats and anti-imperialists gathered in New York on July 18 to prepare for the important meeting to be held in Indianapolis a week later by the National Committee of the National Democratic Party, the official name of the Gold Democrats who had entered the election in 1896 with Palmer and Buckner as candidates. The meeting was dominated by such radical anti-imperialists as Thomas Osborne, William Everett, and J. J. Chapman. A declaration was passed in which both McKinley and Bryan were said to be unacceptable. Another resolution also passed on imperialism, far more radical than the Kansas City platform, which declared that not only Cuba and the Philippines but Puerto Rico and Hawaii had a right to independence. A vote for McKinley was a vote for imperialism, a vote for Bryan a vote for free silver and further debauching of the civil service. Those present were "ready and anxious" to join with others in a party which could adopt a platform presenting these issues.[90]

Press reaction to the meeting held in New York on the eighteenth was not encouraging. Regular Republican and Democratic newspapers were negative, though from different angles. Both sides pointed out the futility of such a measure, even if a third party were, against probability, to gain as many votes as the Palmer-Buckner ticket of 1896. The Gold Democratic newspapers, which had spoken out against the Kansas City platform, usually rejected the idea of a third ticket. The New York *Times* backed McKinley, while some others declared themselves in favor of Bryan.[91]

Even among Independent newspapers there were few who supported a third party. Most important were probably the Springfield *Republican,* the Philadelphia *Record* and the New York *Evening Post,* also the most important anti-imperialist papers.[92] Among newspapers wholly negative were the Brooklyn *Eagle* and the Washington *Star,* while others like the New Haven *Register,* which was Republican but which supported neither Bryan nor McKinley, spoke of the idea with amiable condescension as quite meaningless. The New Orleans *Times-Democrat* pointed out the weakness of the movement: no chance of winning over Gold Democrats, who were expansionists, or anti-imperialist Republicans who were also bimetallists. The remainder of the theoretically possible supporters would prefer Bryan or McKinley or simply take to the woods.[93]

The decision reached on July 18 had not been unanimous, and when the National Committee met a week later the majority of those present proved of a quite different opinion. In the resolution then adopted no mention was made of imperialism, and nomination of special candidates for the National Party was declared "unwise and inexpedient." The Kansas City platform was attacked, with the explanation that "we urge the voters not to be deceived by the plea that the money question has been finally settled." The result, in fact if not formally, was that supporters of the National Party were urged to vote Republican.

Voting for McKinley was a solution distasteful to many, not least the radical anti-imperialists who had been behind the resolution passed in New York on July 18. They preferred a third ticket and did not lack sympathizers among Independents. Many deprecated the fact that the Gold Democrats had not nominated candidates, who could have presented an alternative for the anti-imperialist Mugwumps and Republicans, for whom Bryan was unacceptable.

There is no doubt that Bryan's speech of acceptance converted and convinced many hesitant anti-imperialists and directly influenced the course of events at the Liberty Congress, which assembled a week later on August 14 in Indianapolis where Democratic notification ceremonies had taken place. While par example Edwin Burrit Smith had been enthusiastic over the Kansas City platform's anti-imperialist plank and tried in his turn to persuade Carl Schurz to abandon the idea of a third ticket, Schurz had in no way been convinced.[94] Restating of the silver plank of 1896 and omission of a civil service plank had confirmed his dislike of Bryan.[95] He was not alone. Among others, Moorfield Storey followed Schurz as before. After the Democratic candidate's acceptance speech, however, Moorfield Storey changed his mind. He was enthusiastic over Bryan's position on imperialism and had written immediately to Schurz, asking if he did not think there was reason to reconsider.[96] Schurz admitted the speech had been excellent, but did not trust Bryan and would still not give up the idea of a third ticket.[97]

Schurz wanted neither a Gold Democrat candidate nor a Mugwump, but "an old Republican."[98] He felt the same way as ex-Senator Henderson.[99] He would have been glad to see Henderson as the anti-imperialists candidate, but this was impossible for health reasons. Schurz placed his hope in the influential former Speaker in the House of Representatives, Thomas B. Reed, convinced anti-imperialist. If he could not be persuaded, Schurz had in mind the elderly General William Birney, formerly chairman

251

of the Anti-Imperialist League in Washington and one of the vice-presidents of the American Anti-Imperialist League.[100]

There was deep division among anti-imperialist Gold Democrats and Independents over a third ticket. The Philadelphia *Record* (Ind. Dem.), the New York *Evening Post* and the Springfield *Republican* at the beginning of August recommended that the Liberty Congress adopt a platform against imperialism and for the gold standard, and nominate their own candidates. The Springfield *Republican* mentioned as possible candidates ex-Senator John B. Henderson and George Boutwell, with Senator Donelson Caffery, William Everett from Massachusetts, or Louis R. Ehrich as conceivable vice-presidential candidates.

Among those who rejected the idea of a third ticket was Herbert Welsh, leading anti-imperialist in Philadelphia, and the secretary of the Anti-Imperialist League in Washington, W. A. Croffut.[101] "Third parties have always been marvelously successful in preventing the right man from being elected," Croffut wrote later to Henderson, who was skeptical of Bryan and would have preferred some other candidate nominated in Indianapolis.[102] As pointed out Erving Winslow shared Croffut's opinion and considered a third-party movement "futile and disastrous,"[103] while others hoped they would be able to unite around new candidates.

One group, described by Winslow as "wholly unmanageable and irreconcilable."[104] led by Osborne, Everett, Chapman and A. B. Farquhar, was particularly negative to Bryan.[105] These men had been behind the resolutions passed by a Gold Democratic committee in New York on July 18, and when the National Committee of the National Democratic Party refused to follow their recommendations Osborne and his sympathizers started agitating for a third party.

When delegates to the Liberty Congress assembled on August 14, however, the pro-Bryan faction proved to have a strong majority. A contributory factor had been the positive impression made by Bryan's speech of acceptance, made a week earlier. There was a further reason. The Congress proved a disappointment since only about 300 delegates turned up instead of the expected 800. That Bryan would be nominated at the congress was no secret to anyone who had followed the resolutions adopted by local anti-imperialist organizations. An exampel was one adopted by the anti-imperialists in Boston at a large Liberty Meeting at Faneuil Hall on August 7, which included this passage: "We believe that free silver is less serious than free slaughter; we deprecate the appeal to the pocket at home and to the cannon abroad; the doctrine that Americans can be made rich

252

by taxation and Filipinos righteous by force; and the practice of assimilation of lower races in Asia and the malevolent dissipation of higher ideas in America." Interest shown in the Congress by the Bryanites pointed in the same direction, as did backing from many prominent anti-imperialists even before the congress opened. Many of those to whom Bryan was unacceptable stayed away, and, despite the opposition of a small group, Bryan was endorsed.[106]

Schurz had still not abandoned the idea of a third-party movement, even though he found Bryan's speech of acceptance satisfactory from an anti-imperialist point of view. He had not been able to be present at the congress in Indianapolis for personal reasons—his youngest son had died—and even after the congress he was interested in a separate ticket for the anti-imperialists, to avoid having to vote for Bryan. Moorfield Storey was more impressed by Bryan's speech, but declared in a letter to Schurz of August 18 that if, despite what had happened in Indianapolis, Schurz still felt they should launch their own candidates, he was willing, if hesitant, to be a candidate.[107] During the weeks that followed, probes were made to find out the chances of a third party.

Edwin Burrit Smith naturally opposed every such attempt. In reporting to Schurz on the Indianapolis congress he emphasized that the committee on resolutions had consisted of ten men who had voted for McKinley in 1896, seven Gold Democrats who had voted for Palmer, and one who had not voted at all. There was no market whatsoever for a third ticket. After three-and-a-half hours debate Osborne and his sympathizers had only won the support of fifteen votes in the congress in their efforts to prevent endorsement of Bryan.[108]

Herbert Welsh of Philadelphia and Louis R. Erich of Colorado Springs were equally firm opponents of a third ticket.[109] Erich was a convinced goldstandard man, member of the Executive Committee of the National Sound Money League, but also an extremely active anti-imperialist. He was not only one of the vice-presidents of the American Anti-Imperialist League but a member of its executive and finance committees. In a letter to Schurz after the congress in Indianapolis he declared he could not under any circumstances back a third-party movement which would have a negative effect on Bryan's chances and deliver a blow to anti-imperialism, the cause they were fighting.[110]

Erich was also one of those who tried in vain to persuade Grover Cleveland to come out for Bryan.[111]

There were still others representing the opposite point of view. Apart

253

from Osborne, Everett and Chapman, such men as Everett V. Abbot, Isaac H. Klein and Oswald Garrison Villard (of the *Evening Post*) all tried to secure Schurz' support.[112] Schurz was invited to a meeting at Carnegie Hall on September 5, at which it was intended to nominate candidates and adopt a platform—in other words to organize a third-party movement.[113] Other anti-imperialists whose support they hoped for were ex-Senator Henderson and Samuel Bowles. The prospective candidates were Senator Donelson Caffery and Storey, or Caffery and Everett.[114]

By the end of the month it became obvious that the idea of a third ticket would not work. In letters to Henderson and Storey, Schurz expressed doubt that Osborne and his sympathizers had any prospects. They lacked backing and found it difficult to get people to cooperate. He asked Henderson and Storey to come to New York on September 4, to together decide what attitude to take on the fifth at the Carnegie Hall. But those he wrote to were even more negative than Schurz. Storey replied that there was not a chance of organizing a third party and he declined to be present at the meeting.[115]

Nor did ex-Senator Henderson, who had earlier recommended this solution, consider there was any longer a market for a third-party movement. The silver question was as out-of-date as "last year's bird nest."[116] On September 1, Schurz gave up. "The time for a third ticket has passed," he admitted in letters to Louis Ehrich[117] and Storey,[118] and despite pressure he refused to attend the meeting on September 5.

Osborne, Everett, Chapman, Farquhar and their sympathizers went through with the meeting as planned. A new "national party" was started. The recommendations decided upon by the committee on July 18 but rejected by the Gold Democrats' National Committee on the 25th of the same month were finally carried out.[119] A platform was adopted which was not only anti-imperialistic but which declared in favor of the gold standard, civil service reform, and abolition of all "corrupting special privileges" and all "trustbreeding tariffs."[120] Donelson Caffery of Louisiana was nominated as candidate for the presidency, and Archibald M. Howe of Massachusetts as vice-presidential candidate.

This attempt to create a third-party movement was a fiasco. Caffery and Howe refused to accept nomination, and nobody else was nominated in their place. Osborne and his fellows were criticized from different quarters. The *Ethical Record* published a debate between Osborne and William Lloyd Garrison under the heading, "What Shall the Perplexed Voter Do?" Osborne argued that anti-imperialists who did not share

Bryan's views on the silver question should support neither the Democrats nor the Republicans but "cast an honest vote." Garrison claimed that a third party would only be to the advantage of Mark Hanna and appealed to the anti-imperialists to back Bryan.[121] Others, for whom Bryan's silver demand was even more distasteful than McKinley's imperialism, said the attempt to start a third party would be to the advantage of Bryan and they should back the Republicans. Ex-Senator Palmer, presidential candidate for the "National Democratic Party," or the Gold Democrats, in 1896 argued on these lines.

As things had turned out, Schurz could not now avoid backing Bryan. A year earlier he had described the alternative as dreadful. He had, however, declared even then: ". . . if a cruel fate should force me to choose between McKinley and the imperialistic policy, and Bryan as the anti-imperialist candidate, I should consider it my duty—a horrible duty—to swallow all my personal disgust and to defeat—or, at least, try to defeat—imperialism at any cost. I do not see how I could act otherwise."[122] Schurz adhered faithfully to this line. Although they had fundamentally divergent views Olney was wrestling with the same problems as Schurz and he also expressed them in much the same way. In a letter written before the start of the campaign, he wrote that he was "wrestling with the problem whether duty, however, disagreeable, does not require me to vote for the only other candidate (Bryan) who has a chance of being elected."[123] Olney came to the same conclusion as Schurz, but much more rapidly. Schurz' support of Bryan came unwillingly and his contribution to the campaign was not so much backing Bryan as attacking McKinley. On September 28 he made a speech entitled "For Truth, Justice and Liberty" in Cooper Union in New York, at an anti-imperialistic mass meeting organized by the Greater New York Association of Anti-Imperialist Clubs.[124] This speech attracted a great deal of attention and was used frequently by the Democrats as a campaign document. Schurz refused, however, to become president of the National Association of Anti-Imperialist Clubs, an organization formed on the basis of cadres of the Anti-Imperialist League, for creating local organizations that could pursue Democratic election agitation.[125] It seems as if being active in this National Association was for Schurz much too openly pro-Bryan. He felt his position in the campaign was as he later expressed it, "a real martyrdom," something he accepted only because he felt it was his duty to fight imperialism. If he had refused to participate, he would have felt he was belying his whole moral existence.[126]

Schurz' reaction was not very different from that of, for example, Sterling Morton, a Gold Democrat and anti-imperialist, who despite his profound distaste for Bryan could not with a good conscience refrain from voting for him. "It is a choice between evils," he wrote to Grover Cleveland shortly before the election, "and I am going to shut my eyes, hold my nose, go home, and disinfect myself."[127]

Edward Atkinson could not conceive of backing either Bryan or McKinley. He had long been one of the most active anti-imperialists, above all in the production of anti-imperialist pamphlets. His distrust of Bryan was as deep as that of Charles Francis Adams, and in addition his belief that the issue overshadowed all else in importance had somewhat lessened.[128] He had no intention of joining senator Hoar in voting for McKinley. Instead he chose to concentrate on the election to Congress, to ensure anti-imperialist members of the House of Representatives.[129] In his view—and in that of Adams—an anti-imperialist majority there would be able to bring the imperialist policy to an end by refusing to appropriate funds. "I decline to vote either for the robber or for the receiver of the stolen goods," he declared, referring to Bryan's support of the peace treaty with Spain.[130]

Atkinson's method of tackling the problem was received with scepticism by most anti-imperialists. Erving Winslow described the idea as "a foolish notion" and "an absurdity," words reminiscent of John Hay's comment on the correspondence between Schurz and Charles Francis Adams.[131] Nevertheless, Atkinson followed his plan of action with enthusiasm and energy.

This was nothing new, but Atkinson relied on this line, rejecting both a third ticket and support of either of the two main candidates in the presidential election. He had started working along these lines much earlier than anyone else. He had suggested this method more than a year previously, and put it into practice in the state elections of 1899. He worked from the assumption that resources were limited and it was necessary to use them effectively. They should concentrate on "close" districts. In the preliminary phase Atkinson distributed a printed questionnaire to find out which districts were worth a bid.

Return to Edward Atkinson, Box 112, Boston, Mass.

1. Town or City .... State of ....
2. Number of Congressional District ....
3. Present Member of Congress ....

4. Party ....

5. Majority or Plurality last Election ....

6. Supposed Views on Tropical Expansion ....
   ....
   ....

7. General Character—Nationality etc. of the Voter—Urban or Rural—
   Agriculture—Mechanic Arts—Manufacturing, etc. ....
   ....
   ....
   ....

8. Principal Places where Bureaus of Information for distribution of
   documents, etc., may be established ....
   ....
   ....

9. Names and Addresses of persons in such places who may be ready to
   serve and to organize Anti-Imperialist Leagues or branches of Leagues
   now in force.
   ....
   ....

10. General suggestions for securing the election of Members of the next
    Congress who will oppose the Imperial Policy of Tropical Expansion,
    especially in the Districts in which the present member was elected to
    the present Congress by only a plurality or by a small majority.
    ....
    ....

                              Date ....
                              Name ....
                              Address ....

During the autumn of 1899, Atkinson was active in Ohio's First Congressional District which included Cincinnati and had a Republican Congressman, William B. Shattuc, a sixty-year-old conservative who had been a general in the Civil War. Like other members of Congress, Shattuc was on Atkinson's mailing list and received anti-imperialist pamphlets and the periodical, *The Anti-Imperialist*. Shattuc returned the *Anti-Imperialist* with a brief note: "Take my name off your list. I am no traitor to my country." Atkinson replied ironically that he would do his best to remove Shattuc's name from the list of congressmen after the next election. A violently polemical correspondence followed. Shattuc was certain that "not a precinct in the First Ohio Congressional District" would elect Atkinson or his likes "as a delegate to a convention to nominate a director for the County poorhouse." He directly challenged Atkinson to try to prevent his being nominated in September of the following year.

Shattuc published Atkinson's letter and his own reply in a Cincinnati newspaper. The polemics continued, and Atkinson in turn published the correspondence with his own comments in the *Anti-Imperialist*. He printed a special edition of 5000 copies of the newspaper for distribution in Shattuc's district, and organized the circulation of anti-imperialist literature there, not only in English but in German since German voters were an important group.[132]

Atkinson was not content and saw the situation as an opportunity for testing the line of action he was recommending. Ohio was an important state and Shattuc had identified himself with McKinley's foreign policy. Success here would reverberate afield. The situation was not too hopeful. In 1898, Shattuc had defeated his Democratic opponent with a plurality of over 6000 votes, from a total of 34,000. But Atkinson set up an anti-imperialist, or rather anti-Shattuc, operational center in Cincinnati, with a friend, Edward Stang, in charge. Their agitation had some effect, since Shattuc's position was thought to be weaker, and both Atkinson and Stang were convinced Shattuc would not be nominated for re-election.[133] Despite the efforts of Atkinson and the anti-imperialists, he was re-elected. The organisation of his opponent, John B. Peaslee, was feeble and poverty-stricken, and the election was a fiasco for Atkinson's line. Shattuc's share of the votes increased by over 6000; Shattuc's plurality went up to over 8000.

Atkinson and the other anti-imperialists worked in several other districts, and at the end of August 1899 he declared that "the work is now well under way in a large number of the districts in which the present incumbent has either a plurality or a small majority."[134] His goal was to acquire a balance of power in the Congress which was to be elected in the fall of 1900. Atkinson used the elections of 1899 as a testing ground. In Iowa, the Democrats based their campaign on anti-imperialism, in an attempt to win the German vote.[135] Some success was achieved on a local level but not much.[136]

The pattern of the election in Iowa foreshadowed that of the presidential election of 1900. The Democrats declared imperialism "the burning issue" and kept quiet on the currency question. The Republicans made systematic attempts to center the debate on the money issue. The Iowa platform contained no reiteration of 16 : 1, only a perfunctory reaffirmation of the Chicago platform. The Republicans published the silver plank of 1896 together with the Democrats' reaffirmation of 1899, to pin their opponents to the spot from which they were so discreetly trying to escape.

258

CHAPTER VIII

Campaigning

Organizing the Campaign: Methods, Strategies, Tactics

When Mark Hanna was placed at the head of the Republican National Committee in 1896 he declared that the management of a national political campaign was but a business matter.[1] His way of leading the Republican campaign bore him out and was epoch-making, both when it came to acquiring resources and in making use of them in the most effective way possible. It was a great advantage for the Republicans once again to have Hanna as Commander-in-Chief. As in 1896, the Republicans, like the Democrats, set up two headquarters, one in New York and the other in Chicago. Of the two, the one in Chicago became the most important for both parties, which was only natural considering that the most decisive battlegrounds of the campaign were in the Middle West.

The leader of the Executive Committee, also called the Campaign Committee, under Hanna, was Henry C. Payne of Wisconsin. The Secretary was Perry S. Heath of Indiana. The importance attached to Indiana can be seen from the fact that of the ten members of the Campaign Committee, yet another was a Hoosier, namely Harry S. New, the editor of the Indianapolis *Journal*. Three main methods of election propaganda were used: 1) public speaking, 2) the dissemination of documents, "literature," 3) the insertion of editorials and news articles in weekly and daily newspapers.

The men in charge of the Republican spellbinders were in Chicago, Major Henry C. Hedges of Ohio and in New York, Joseph H. Manley of Maine and Senator N. B. Scott of West Virginia. The Chicago division alone had at its disposal over 600 regular committee orators, not counting hundreds of volunteers. Among the Republican spellbinders were 50 Germans, 25 Swedes, 25 Norwegians, 6 Finns etc.[2] Towards the end of the

259

campaign, the Republican National Committee calculated that their speakers were making about 7000 speeches a day.[3]

Among the most expensive items in the work of the campaign were the production and distribution of leaflets, brochures, books, posters etc. The Republican Campaign Text-Book was ready in August, and, together with other printed matter, cost approximately a million dollars in production and distribution. About a hundred different documents were printed and disseminated to a total of one hundred million. Thus 6,500,000 copies of McKinley's Letter of Acceptance were printed in English and foreign languages, 500,000 in German, 250,000 in Swedish, 100,000 in Polish etc.[4] And of McKinley's acceptance speech no less than between forty and fifty million copies were printed and circulated.[5] This flood of literature was directed primarily towards the doubtful states, where their role was essential while safe Republican or Democratic states took second place. Special consideration was also paid to sectional prejudices, a factor that was of extreme importance in the election campaign of 1900, with its pronounced variations in attitude towards, for example, the silver issue and even expansion. The currency issue was particularly sensitive in the silver states Colorado, Wyoming, Utah and Idaho, and the procedure there was that the regular Republican campaign literature was edited by "a well-informed gentleman" in Denver to adapt it to the tastes of the Mountain States. The material was then distributed from Denver.[6]

More important than public speaking and the dissemination of literature, however, was the work carried out by the third division within the Campaign Committee, namely that which produced and distributed news, articles and editorials to weekly and daily newspapers. Different means of approach were used. One method was to supply country weeklies with "patent insides." About 200 newspapers were given stereotyped matter. This applied mainly to small provincial newspapers, while the more important were provided with proof-slips to be set up at the editor's discretion.

According to the estimations made by the Republican campaign leaders, about 2000 provincial newspapers had no other political news and discussion than that sent out by the Republican headquarters. The result of this production and distribution to the newspapers was fantastic. Something like 4000 newspapers published this political propaganda material regularly.[7]

The activities of the Republican National Committee under the leadership of Mark Hanna naturally cost far more money than any previous election campaign. But Hanna was the man to produce the money, too. The Republican Party was the party of big business and the rich and once Hanna had succeeded in rousing these wealthy groups from their apathy, by frightening them with the silver specter and Bryan's presumed extremism, there was no difficulty in getting large contributions. It was not so for the Democrats. Their needs were the same, but their resources far smaller.

The Democrats also understood the necessity of having a stream-lined, efficient, business-like organization. Willis J. Abbot, the manager of the National Democratic Press Bureau, put it into words when he said that if Mr. John D. Rockefeller applied to campaign management some of the methods that he had used in building up his Standard Oil Company, he might be an almost invincible chairman of a National Committee.[8] But although they realized their need, the Democrats did not have an organizer of Hanna's capacity and above all they did not have the financial resources that the Republican Campaign Committee had at its disposal. One result was that in the final phase of the campaign the Democrats could only produce 2500 speeches per day, compared to the Republicans 7000, and another that the distribution of literature had to be restricted. The number of different documents produced was as large as the Republicans', but the editions were smaller. Bryan's "Imperialism" speech, that is his Speech of Acceptance, was, however, printed in over 8,000,000 copies, including translations into Greek, Finnish and Yiddish.

Like the Republicans, a special effort was made with material for the newspapers and the same methods were used. The Democrats also made use of the fact that the smaller provincial newspapers to a considerable extent bought what was known as "plate matter," which was ready-set and furnished in the form of stereotype plates. They engaged firms which supplied the plate or "patent-inside" matter. Democratic copy was supplied to seven "patent-inside" houses, which in their turn served about 4000 different newspapers.

Both parties naturally also devoted a lot of their agitation to bringing direct pressure on the voters through local leaders. The chairman of the Democratic Campaign Committee, J. G. Johnson, had created a nationwide organization, in which there was to be in each precinct a special representative of the Democratic National Committee. These grassroot representatives were in a position to have a personal knowledge of doubting voters, to be able to supply them with pamphlets and other campaign material and to take polls and then report back, first to the county and then via the state committees to the National Campaign Committee.

For the Democrats in particular, it was necessary to economize with the resources available. The Democratic National Committee, and especially the Executive Committee, were forced to try to decide which states were safely Democratic, which were unmoveable Republican and which could be considered doubtful. All available resources were to be concentrated on this third category. The Democrats counted on holding the states that had given a majority to Bryan in 1896. In addition they normally reckoned with Maryland and Kentucky as fairly certain new gains. The states usually thought of as doubtful were New York, New Jersey, Delaware, West Virginia, Ohio, Indiana, Illinois, Wisconsin, Minnesota and California. In some of these cases, one must suspect an exaggerated wishful thinking or propagandistic adjustments, while in other cases the assessments were reasonable. In any event, the Democratic Executive Committee devoted most of its efforts and resources to four states: New York, Indiana, Ohio and Illinois. The situation was such that if Bryan won the states that were counted as being safe, New York or two of the three Middle West states just named could decide the election in Bryan's favor.

On the Republican side, there was really never any doubt about the victory. The economic trends were in their favor, they had superior economic resources and an extremely skilful campaign organization. By means of continual analyses, they followed developments in the various states and could in this way allocate resources where they would do most good. These predictions provide a good picture of the assessments that were made of the situation. They naturally contain an element of propaganda, since a part of them at least were intended for publication. But those that were made on behalf of the Executive Committee were nevertheless primarily intended for internal use and they also proved to be accurate to an amazingly high degree.

The first Republican survey still extant is dated March 1 and shows a noticeable element of caution.[9] No less than sixteen states, with a total of 139 electoral votes were described as doubtful, "probably Republican" or "probably Democratic." The states placed in the "safe" Republican group were California, Connecticut, Illinois, Indiana, Iowa, Maine, Massachusetts, Michigan, Minnesota, New Hampshire, New Jersey, North Dakota, Ohio, Oregon, Pennsylvania, Rhode Island, Vermont, and Wisconsin. What is most remarkable in this list is the absence of New York, which like Kansas, Washington, West Virginia and Wyoming was classified as probably Republican. Bryan was not conceded a single state as safe outside the South and even that was not considered absolutely certain. Alabama, Arkansas,

Florida, Georgia, Louisiana, Mississippi, South Carolina, Tennessee, and Texas were placed in the Democrats' safe column, while Colorado, Missouri, Montana, Nebraska, Nevada, Utah and surprisingly even North Carolina and Virginia were denoted as being probably Democratic. Finally those classified as doubtful were Delaware, Idaho, Kentucky, Maryland and South Dakota.

In a forecast from June, Kansas and Washington have been put in the safe column, while Indiana now is considered only "probably Republican." South Dakota is in the same column, while Nevada is labelled "doubtful" instead of "probably Democratic."

When the campaign got underway in the autumn, the number of analyses also increased. The situation was now judged somewhat differently than during the spring. New York was definitely placed in the column "safe Republican," like South Dakota, Washington and Kansas. Rather more uncertain were West Virginia and Wyoming, which occur sporadically as "probably Republican."[10] Indiana moved in the opposite direction. This state was described as safe in the spring despite the storm of opinion over the Puerto Rican tariff, undoubtedly because the survey had been made before the full effect of the protest reactions made itself felt. In the autumn, however, Indiana caused anxiety, even if the most frequent prediction was that it would go to McKinley. As far as the Democrats were concerned, Virginia and North Carolina were placed as "safe Democratic" in all the autumn's surveys.

At the beginning of September, a statement was published giving the forecast of the Republican managers for the presidential election. The man behind it was H. C. Payne, vice-chairman of the Republican National Committee and chairman of the Campaign Committee. It is of particular interest, since it reflects the Republican view of the situation at the start of the campaign proper. The forecast was as follows.

Certain for McKinley		*Conceded to Bryan*	
California	9	Alabama	11
Connecticut	6	Arkansas	8
Illinois	24	Colorado	4
Iowa	13	Florida	4
Kansas	10	Georgia	13
Maine	6	Idaho	3
Massachusetts	15	Louisiana	8

Michigan	14	Mississippi	9
Minnesota	9	Missouri	17
New Hampshire	4	Montana	3
New York	36	Nevada	3
North Dakota	3	North Carolina	11
Ohio	23	South Carolina	9
Oregon	4	Tennessee	12
Pennsylvania	32	Texas	15
Rhode Island	4	Utah	3
South Dakota	4	Virginia	12
Vermont	4	Total	145
Washington	4		
Wisconsin	12		
Wyoming	3		
Total	249		

Fighting ground

Delaware	3	West Virginia	6
Kentucky	13	Indiana	15
Maryland	8	Total	53
Nebraska	8		

Total vote 447
Necessary to elect 224

The states that are of the greatest interest are naturally those that are described as doubtful in different surveys or that turn up in varying columns. These are mainly Colorado, Idaho, Indiana, Kentucky, Maryland, Missouri, Montana, Nebraska, Nevada and Utah. There is a marked uncertainty over the Mountain States. It was partly connected with the hesitance about the importance of the silver issue but also with the complicated situation with regard to Populists and Silver Republicans. At the beginning of October, a number of Republican predictions appeared simultaneously, all reflecting the same uncertainty. In a survey conducted by Manley, member of the Republican Campaign Committee, Colorado was described as doubtful, together with Montana, Nevada and Utah.[11] An analysis made at the same time by Youngblood gave Bryan Colorado and Montana, while the other two, Nevada and Utah, were described as doubtful. Manley also had Idaho, Kansas, Missouri, and Nebraska in this column, while Youngblood had Idaho as probably Republican, Kansas as Republican, Missouri as Democratic and Nebraska as doubtful, while Manley saw it as safe Republican.[12] A third Republican assessor, Senator N. B. Scott from West Virginia, member of the Executive Committee of the Republican National Committee, had Idaho, Indiana, Kentucky, Maryland, Montana and Nebraska as doubtful.[13]

At the same time as Manley, Youngblood and Scott were making their predictions, a forecast was published in the New York *Herald*. Of the states discussed above, the *Herald* gave Maryland, Colorado, Missouri, Nebraska, Nevada and Utah to Bryan. Kentucky was conceded to McKinley, while Idaho, Indiana and Montana remained in the "doubtful" column.[14]

From the beginning of October, the situation had, according to the Republican assessors, became more stable. Indiana was now thought to be safe for McKinley, Maryland too. The uncertainty remained, however, with regard to the Mountain States, plus Idaho, Nebraska, Kentucky and Missouri. In the final survey which was made the day before the election, the Republican campaign leaders claimed to be certain of 294 electors. They had then not calculated with most of the states earlier denoted as doubtful: Colorado, Idaho, Missouri, Montana, Nebraska, Nevada, Utah.

If instead of taking the states individually, we look at the assessments as a whole, we obtain the following picture from the Republican side:

Date	Rep.	Prob. Rep.	Dem.	Prob. Dem.	Doubtful
1.3	207	59	101	49	31
4.9	249	20	139		39
6.9	249		145		53
3.10	266		112		54
9.10	261		136		50
18.10	281		133		33
24.10	281		131		35
29.10	302		112		33
(5.10)	294[15]				

Considering that McKinley received 292 electoral votes in the election, the Republican prediction must be said to be very good.[16] The same does not apply to the Democrats. Their surveys were neither as systematic nor as realistic as those of their opponents. There were very marked elements of propaganda in them and wishful thinking shone clearly through. As an example, it can be mentioned that in a prediction released by the Democratic National Committee three weeks before the election, not only had all the states considered by the Republicans to be "doubtful" been placed as "safe Democratic," but a number of states that the Republicans had not once queried during the autumn had also been treated in the same way. This applied, for example, to Kansas, New Jersey, New York, South Dakota and Washington. McKinley was only conceded seven states: Iowa, Maine, Massachusetts, New Hampshire, Pennsylvania, Rhode Island and Vermont, while California, Connecticut, Illinois, Michigan, Minnesota, North Dakota, Ohio, Oregon, Wisconsin and Wyoming were described as "doubtful." All these states were to vote Republican with a broad margin.[17]

The Two Duellists: Bryan and Roosevelt on the Stump

Although both parties had many spellbinders, the campaign was dominated by two men: Bryan on the Democratic side and Roosevelt for the Republicans. Both travelled enormous distances and made an incredible number of speeches. Bryan's stump-speaking, however, was probably somewhat less extensive than it had been in 1896. As the *Review of Reviews* noted, a repetition of that campaign "would seem scarcely possible for any man twice in a lifetime."[18] Nevertheless his effort was still impressive. One day he made no less than thirty-two speeches, which was said to be an all-time record even for Bryan.[19]

Bryan's speech of acceptance had been given a very favorable reception by the anti-imperialists and many of those who had previously been undecided had made up their minds to support him. It was not long, however, before discordant notes disturbed the harmony and once again it was the silver issue which caused the dissonance. One week after the Indianapolis meeting, Bryan initiated the campaign in his hometown, Lincoln, Nebraska. The themes he stressed above all were Imperialism, Trusts and Silver. Even though he did not allow the silver issue to dominate, it was usually included and to such an extent that the Chicago *Times-Herald* felt moved to declare in a headline: "Bryan reverts to silver."[20] This was not altogether correct, since in several of his speeches Bryan said very little on the question of coinage.[21] But what he did say was enough for his opponents. Bryan performed the same tightrope act in Kansas at the end of August, when he repeated in his speech of acceptance to the Fusionist faction of the Populists that imperialism was the paramount issue, also devoting plenty of space to trusts but not much to silver.

If Bryan's cautious inclusion of the silver question in his introductory

266

campaign at the end of August was enough to disquiet many gold-minded anti-imperialists, an article published by Gage, Secretary of the Treasury, was to revive "the silver scare" on a full scale, in the political agitation at least. Gage claimed that if Bryan was elected president, he would be able to order the Secretary of the Treasury to make payment in silver of all public debt payable in coin and for all current disbursements as well. The results could be catastrophic. Gage's article caused a sensation and was exploited to the last ounce by the Republicans. Carl Schurz counterattacked in the press and in a bitter exchange with Gage described his arguments as *greuel* propaganda, while at the same time pointing out that even the theoretical possibility of such measures being taken could easily be stopped by the vote of the Republican majority in Congress.[22] In this fight, Bryan showed a certain lack of tactical skill which his opponents were not slow to exploit. The New York *Herald* tried repeatedly to obtain a statement from Bryan concerning his reaction to Gage's article, but Bryan first refused to be interviewed and later only answered that he preferred to discuss the questions in his own way and in his own time.[23] In this way he left the field wide open for his opponents to concentrate the debate on the silver issue, a development that his own election strategists had done everything in their power to avoid.

Bryan's letter of acceptance, published September 18, had the same effect of stressing the ambivalence in his attitude towards the main content of the election campaign and shifting the emphasis from the paramount issue. Imperialism took second place to the other issues that Bryan had earlier stressed as being central and which had been taken up by the Kansas City platform. Great attention was paid to the trust issue, on which Bryan repeated the promise made by the platform of "an unceasing warfare against private monopoly in nation, state and city." Bryan also discussed the currency question in detail, again demanding explicitly free silver at a ratio of 16 : 1. Other questions were given less prominence.

The reception given to Bryan's letter followed the expected pattern. The Republicans and many Independents saw it as a blatant proof that all the talk of the silver issue no longer being important had been gravely misleading. Bryan was immovable on this point. He intended "to pull the props from under our entire system and precipitate repudiation and ruin," claimed the New York *Herald*.[24] "The whole letter emphasizes Bryan's position as a destructive public man," in the opinion of the Boston *Transcript*.[25] The Gold-Democratic newspapers were naturally equally

267

astringent in their comments. The Philadelphia *Record* recognized the voice of the Bryan of 1896 and described the Democratic standardbearer as "radical, persistent, resourceful, and eager to overturn the established order even though chaos may come."[26]

Even the newspapers that usually supported Bryan were noticeably restrained in their praise. Some chose to note that Bryan had not retreated from his commitment to anti-imperialism and that the paramount issue had not been given so much space simply because it had been allowed completely to dominate the acceptance speech. It emerges quite plainly, however, that many people were disappointed that Bryan had reiterated 16 : 1. "His infatuation got the better of his judgment," as the St. Paul *Pioneer Press* put it and the Washington *Post* emphasized that the letter was "far more pleasing to his political enemies than to his supporters in states without whose vote he cannot be elected."[27]

Among those who were seriously worried by what they saw as Bryan's shift of emphasis from anti-imperialism to the coinage issue were naturally Schurz and his supporters. "The silver scare is growing," he declared at the end of September and considered that Bryan's letter of acceptance was not one of the least reasons for this.[28] The Republican press had been forced on to the defensive on the issue of imperialism, but helped not least by Bryan's behaviour they had succeeded in bringing the money question to the foreground.[29] A number of prominent anti-imperialists who had just declared for McKinley were thought to have done so just because of the line taken by Bryan on the currency issue. This applied to Carnegie, Carlisle and Ottendorffer, among others.

Louis R. Erich tried with the help of James Jones, the chairman of the Democratic National Committee and leader of Bryan's campaign, to get Bryan to make a public statement that would put an end to the speculations, which Gage had set rolling and which frightened so many businessmen. Bryan steadfastly refused to do so, however. His attitude contributed considerably to the difficulties experienced, for example, in collecting signatures to the address to "the Independent Voter."[30]

Carl Schurz' recurrent complaint that Bryan had "strangely neglected" the paramount issue was based not only on Bryan's letter of acceptance, but also on the impression given in the many speeches that the Democratic presidential candidate had made so far. In a letter to Edwin Burrit Smith in the middle of October, Schurz exploded in exasperation: "Bryan has done himself irreparable harm by descending from the high level of his Indianapolis speech down to his letter of acceptance and his small talks

268

all over the country."[31] During the entire initial phase of the campaign, Bryan restricted his appearances to the West and the Middle West. Before starting his campaign tour in the Eastern states towards the middle of October, he had covered Missouri, North and South Dakota, Kansas, Nebraska, Minnesota, Wisconsin, Indiana, West Virginia and Ohio.

An examination of the newspaper accounts of these appearances suggests that even if Bryan did not neglect taking up what he described as the imperialism of the McKinley administration, it was nevertheless the trust issue and the trying conditions of the working classes that were given most space in the speeches. In the latter case, he often referred to the on-going miners' strike in West Virginia.[32] In the great majority of cases, Bryan also took up the silver question, usually relatively briefly. According to the newspaper reports, the audiences were not especially interested in this particular point.

A clear difference is noticeable when Bryan transferred his campaign to the Eastern states during the final phase of the election campaign. The trusts were still given their due share, but silver disappeared almost completely. Instead the paramount issue, imperialism, again came to the fore. The climax of the campaign in the East, and in the opinion of many observers the culmination of the entire Democratic campaign, came on October 16, when Bryan appeared before crowds of jubilant supporters in New York. He made four speeches that day, in Madison Square Garden, Tammany Hall, Cooper Union and at an Open Air meeting in Madison Square. The reports on the size of the audiences varied between 40,000 and 100,000,[33] but everyone was agreed that Bryan's reception was a manifestation of enthusiasm of a kind seldom seen.

Both Bryan's speeches in New York and the reaction to them provide a good picture of Bryan's tactics in the final stage of the campaign and of the part played by the controversial issue of foreign policy in this connection. Most detailed was the first speech, which was made to a packed Madison Square Garden. The Democratic presidential candidate opened with a bitter attack on his opponents, who had asserted that Bryan and the Democrats were against "honest wealth." They were completely wrong. On the contrary, the party was "the best friend of that wealth that represents ability of muscle or of mind employed in its accumulation." But Bryan differentiated sharply between honest wealth which was a just compensation for services rendered, and dishonest wealth. The Democratic Leader continued with an elegantly phrased attack on Mark Hanna's effective election slogan about the full dinner pail, and then went on to devote himself in caustic detail to the trust issue. The second half of the speech took up the threat of militarism and imperialism, which the policy of the Republican administration contained. Neither in this nor in any of the other three speeches he made that day, did Bryan mention the Kansas City platform's most controversial plank, the silver coinage and 16 : 1. This startling fact caused the Baltimore *Herald* to state indignantly: "There has been no more flagrant instance of campaign dodging in our political history." The reaction was similar in, for example, the New York *Times* and other sworn enemies of Bryan, while the Springfield *Republican* welcomed the omission as proof that Bryan had realized that the issue no longer had a place in current politics. The pro-Bryan press greeted the appearance of the Orator of the West with enthusiasm. The New York *Journal* declared: "It means much to the American people whether we have a jellyfish for a president or a man of character, strength and conviction. We have tried the jellyfish—now let us have the man." The New York *World* was also strongly positive, as were many other Democratic newspapers, such as the Philadelphia *Times* and the Boston *Traveler*. Some still reacted negatively, however. In addition to the New York *Times* mentioned before, Democratic press organs such as the Baltimore *News* and the Philadelphia *Record* were not convinced.[34]

A striking feature of both Bryan's speeches and the comments of his opponents is the extremely strong social nature of the antagonisms, amounting almost to a class struggle. Bryan attacked the trusts fiercely and continued to play on the theme of "the dollar and the man." His standpoint on silver was indeed felt by the opposing side to be a threat to the entire existing pattern of production, a destructive element. Despite this, it is still surprising to note the vehemence and rancour that was typical of many of the reactions of the anti-Bryan press. The highly-regarded New York *Tribune*, Whitelaw Reid's paper, claimed that Bryan was "the apostle of claptrap and appeals to ignorance," and asserted that he was even more dangerous than he appeared to be as the apostle of repudiation and the fifty-cent dollar in 1896.[35] There is throughout an insistence that Bryan was taking advantage of the emotions of the ignorant masses: "The larger the crowd and the hoarser the cry that greets Bryan the firmer and more general the determination grows that he must be overwhelmingly defeated," wrote the Philadelphia *Press*, and the Baltimore *Herald* expressed a similar opinion: "There was everything in the speech to please the unthinking crowd. There was nothing to arouse the confidence of thoughtful voters."[36]

And *Gunton's Magazine* commented on Bryan's New York appearance that he had built up his position almost exclusively on deliberate appeals to every sentiment and prejudice which makes for class hatred and social upheaval.[37]

By far the greater part of the press was against Bryan and he had been savagely run down many times since the 1896 election campaign. In a letter to Herbert Welsh, Elwood Corser wrote at the beginning of October that things had gone so far that even if an angel were to descend from heaven and assure these people that Bryan was not only above reproach in his personal character, but that he was also a man of great ability, of wide grasp of public questions, of most exceptional patriotic and inflexible purpose, this assurance would fall on ears closed against belief.[38] As shown above, this negative picture of Bryan had also influenced many anti-imperialistic mugwumps, who were undecided how to vote in the presidential election of 1900.[39]

The New York speeches, with the silver issue so completely pushed into the background as to be almost excluded and the main stress placed on attacks on the trusts and on the McKinley administration's foreign policy, on what was described as its imperialism, were typical of the majority of the speeches made by Bryan during the campaign in the East. His opponents did not fail to notice that he varied his message regionally. The close coverage given by the press of the appearances made by the main antagonists made it impossible for such adaptations to different geographical target groups to pass unnoticed. As a result the tactic lost some of its effectiveness and led to accusations of lack of principle and opportunism. Bryan found himself in a difficult dilemma. Without New York and preferably Indiana too, he could not win. The silver issue that was so dear to him and that he personally believed still gripped large numbers of voters in the Middle West and West, was completely impossible in the Eastern states. At the same time, the other main issue, which the platform had given pride of place, imperialism, was considered far from attractive in the West. The situation necessitated a certain straddling of the issues. It was difficult for Bryan to avoid attacks on this account.

The principal role in the Republican election campaign came to be played by Theodore Roosevelt. What he achieved was a real feat of strength. The vice-presidential candidate is said to have made 673 speeches in 24 states and to have covered over 21,000 miles.[40] "I am as strong as a bull moose and you can use me up to the limit," he assured Hanna before the start of the campaign, but when he saw the schedules that had been prepared even he was shaken.[41] At the beginning of September, his voice was badly strained and he appealed continuously for the number of appearances per day to be cut down and to be allowed to rest on Sundays.[42] He overcame this reaction, however, and was soon declaring again that he was "fit as a fighting cock."[43]

To start with, Roosevelt was sceptical about the organization of the campaign, which meant that he was to make a large number of whistle stop speeches daily. He did not want to appear to be "a second-hand Bryan" and wanted to avoid anything that could seem "undignified."[44] Payne and Hanna succeeded in calming him on this point, however, Roosevelt's campaign, above all in the West, had colorful, striking elements, which contributed to the popularity he gained. The Republican campaign officers exploited to the utmost Roosevelt's image from his time as a Rough Rider.

During the intensive campaign in Indiana in the middle of October, in which the Republicans staked all they had for the state that was considered "pivotal," the local campaign committees hired horses at a price of $2.50 each and paid men to act as Rough Riders.[45]

In Grand Rapids (Michigan),[46] South Bend (Indiana),[47] Fargo (North Dakota)[48] and a great number of other places in Colorado, Utah, Kansas, Nebraska etc., these demonstrations attracted attention. They were skilfully exploited by Roosevelt, both when he declared his expansionist message in heroic terms and when he made fun of Bryan's talk of the threat of militarism. As has been mentioned earlier, what worried the Republican campaign leaders most was the general political apathy and the Rough Riders under the command of Colonel Roosevelt were to be brought in to fight "General Apathy," the worst enemy they had to meet.[49]

Roosevelt's campaign can be easily followed by means of a detailed book of cuttings, with material from both larger newspapers and small local publications.[50] An analysis of these press notices, supplemented with manuscript material, gives a clear picture of the way in which Roosevelt's —and the Republicans'—tactics were drawn up in the campaign. In the Eastern states and parts of the Middle West, the New York governor declared that the main issue of the election was and remained the same as in 1896: silver or sound money. The question of the trusts was also taken up, and naturally foreign policy, the territorial expansion. In the last case, however, the tone was somewhat muted, the arguments on the whole defensive and playing on the idealistic-humanitarian line. The duty line predominated. During his wide campaign in the West, on the other hand, Roosevelt changed both the proportions and the emphasis in his speeches.

Silver was toned down and disappeared completely in, for example, Colorado. At the same time expansionism was made a positive campaign issue. It was presented with a rhetoric spiced with the romance of action and the striving for great deeds. The apologetic, humanitarian arguments of defence were replaced by claims of National Interest and aspirations to becoming a Great Power. At the same time the acrimony of the attacks on Bryan's anti-imperialism increased and the Republican candidate showed samples of the violent fighting spirit that caused the normally moderate Charles Towne to describe him as "an intellectual Comanche."[51]

Roosevelt started on September 6 in Detroit and after speeches in Michigan, Indiana and Wisconsin, the campaign moved West.[52] Between the 11th and the 16th, he covered South and North Dakota. The greater part of this time was spent in South Dakota. It had been decided to make an energetic effort there in order to defeat the sharp-tongued Senator Pettigrew, the special enemy of Mark Hanna.[53] After Dakota, it was the turn of Montana, Idaho, Utah, Wyoming and Colorado. The last-named state was also given an unusually large share of Roosevelt's time. An extra day was allowed for backing up Senator Wolcott "in his gallant fight."[54] From Colorado the campaign proceeded to Kansas. On October 1 we find Roosevelt in Bryan's home state and Nebraska was also given special priority for obvious reasons. After short visits to Iowa, Illinois and Missouri, the dynamic vice-presidential candidate continued to Indiana, where the Republicans and Roosevelt made a greater effort than in any other state apart from New York. Next in turn lay Kentucky, Ohio, West Virginia and Maryland, after which Roosevelt devoted practically the entire final stage of the campaign, from October 21, to his own home state.

After his return home from the campaign in the West, Roosevelt again changed the emphasis and proportions in his speeches. The silver issue was pushed to the fore, the more flowery, expansionist rhetoric eliminated. At the same time Roosevelt started to direct his arguments more immediately against Bryan's latest campaign speeches, which was noticeable not least in the East, where Roosevelt followed in Bryan's tracks.

Thus on September 6, Roosevelt initiated his campaign proper with an appearance in Detroit. The following day he spoke in Grand Rapids and on September 8 in South Bend, Indiana. The three speeches that he made these three days in a row contained, with minor variations, the main material that he used during the campaign. The manuscripts of the speeches have been preserved and deserve attention, since they demonstrate clearly the Republican campaign tactics, above all Roosevelt's own.[55]

The Detroit speech was called, "The Prophesies of Mr. Bryan." The introduction was at the same time a summary of the content:

"In this campaign the issue of overshadowing importance is whether we shall continue or abandon the governmental policy which has brought this country to the highest pitch of prosperity at home and which has kept the national honor unstained, both at home and abroad. To deliberately undo the work would be to dishonor the national reputation and to throw us into dreadful industrial chaos. The Kansas City platform deliberately commits our opponents to a policy which means material disaster and moral disgrace."

Roosevelt then went on to quote a scathing speech by Carl Schurz from the campaign of 1896 attacking the silver plank of the Chicago platform and made much of the fact that the Kansas City platform contained an explicit repetition of this silver plank. "If the American people are true to themselves they must in the most unequivocal manner repudiate the populistic and communistic doctrines enunciated in the Kansas City platform exactly as they repudiated them in '96'."

Roosevelt was using the very method that the leading Democratic tacticians had feared and that they had tried to prevent by their vain attempts to make Bryan agree not to reiterate 16 : 1. The main part of the Detroit speech painted a picture of the catastrophe that abandoning the "sound money" line would lead to, with constant variations on the prosperity theme and quotations to demonstrate how the favorable development had put Bryan's prophesies to shame. Towards the end of his speech, Roosevelt also touched on Bryan's and the Kansas City platform's statements on militarism and imperialism. All talk of the threat of militarism was waved aside as being incredibly ridiculous and with regard to expansion, Roosevelt declared his basic attitude clearly und unambiguously: "There is not a dividing line of any kind to be drawn between our methods of expansion in 1898 and 1899 and the methods of expansion under which we acquired Michigan, Illinois, Florida, Louisiana, Minnesota, Missouri, Oregon, California, Hawaii and Alaska ... The policy of expansion is America's historic policy."

The next speech, given in Grand Rapids, was called, "Free silver, trusts and the Philippines" and the content was thereby clearly declared.[56] The introduction was very similar to that of the Detroit speech: "There are several great issues at stake in this campaign, but of course the greatest issue of all is the issue of keeping the country on the plane of material well-being and honor to which it has been brought during the last four years." In a vehement attack on Bryan and the Democrats, Roosevelt declared that the paramount issue was free silver: "It is paramount, and the attitude of the populist democracy in trying to keep it out of sight East of the Mississippi, while insisting upon their adherence to it West of the Mississippi, is in itself enough to discredit them in the eyes of all good citizens, whether republicans or genuine democrats."

It is worth noting that Roosevelt's accusation against the Democrats during the campaign came to apply equally to his own behavior, although conversely. The "silver scare" was exploited to the full in the Eastern states and to a large extent in the Middle West, while at the same time the theme of expansion was more muted there and in some places in the East took on a more defensive style. In the West, on the other hand, the expansion motif was put forward as a positive issue and Roosevelt blossomed out into a rhetorical enthusiasm that came close to surpassing that of Albert Beveridge.

In his speech at Grand Rapids, Roosevelt also took up the question of the trusts. He tackled the subject by accusing Bryan and the Democrats of demagogy and hypocrisy and made skilful use of the Republicans' favorite arguments on this subject: the great Ice Trust scandal, which had been uncovered in New York and in which a number of prominent Tammany politicians had been involved.[57]

One interesting strategem used by Roosevelt in this speech was to compare the current campaign with that of 1864, in which Lincoln was re-elected. Roosevelt found striking analogies on a large number of points, in which McKinley was naturally given the role of Lincoln.

The last of the Grand Rapids speech was devoted to the Philippines. Roosevelt went into the subject in more detail than he had the previous day in Detroit, but there was also a difference in the content, since the arguments given noticeably followed the duty line, in other words were more defensive. He categorically denied that the Filipinos were capable of self-government. Any attempt to give them independence would result in a horrible confusion of tyranny and anarchy. To surrender the islands would mean bloodshed and misery. The only chance the islands had of getting peace and good government was under American rule, and it would be cruel and immoral of America to fail in her duty and desert her responsibility. It was a completely typical and consistent duty argument. When building up to his finale on the theme of the "white man's burden," Roosevelt also got entangled in the romance of action and willpower that was so typical of him:

"The man goes out to do a man's work, to confront difficulties and over-come them, and to train up his children to do likewise. So it is with the Nation. To decline to do our duty is simply to sink as China has sunk. If we are to continue to hold our heads high as Americans, we must bravely, soberly and resolutely front each particular duty as it arises, and it is because of the great truth contained in this principle that we appeal to every man, Northener and Southerner, Easterner and Westener, whether his father fought under Grant or under Lee, whatever political party he may have belonged to in the past,—to stand with us now, when we ask that the hands of President McKinley be upheld, and that this Nation instead of shrinking in unmanly terror from its duty, shall stride forward to use its giant strengt for the upholding of our honor and the interests of mankind in doing that part of the world work which Providence has allotted to us."

The day after Roosevelt's appearance in Grand Rapids, it was the turn of South Bend, Indiana. He started with a detailed and acrimonious attack on the Kansas City silver plank. After devoting almost half the speech to variations on this theme, he proceeded to the Philippine policy. He partly followed the same line as the previous day, but developed in particular one motif that had been present the day before but was now given much more space, namely *greuel* stories of the alleged cruelties of the Aguinaldo forces against their opponents and the civil population. The duty line recurs: it is the obvious duty of America to save the Philippine population from the atrocious terror of the rebellious bands of murderers.

One example of Roosevelt's tactics can be given from the relatively brief appearance he made on September 17 at Helena, Montana, where he limited his speech to a single theme: "the bogie of militarism." Referring to a speech made by Bryan a short time before in Chicago, Roosevelt called the Democratic presidential candidate's talk of the dangers of militarism both incredibly ludicrous and in addition an insult to the American soldier. His speech developed into a lofty panegyric over the brave, upright, self-sacrificing American soldiers, who were performing heroic deeds in the Philippines, "facing death by bullet at every step from a foe ten times as numerous as themselves, and if wounded and left behind, facing what was infinitely worse than death—the most dreadful torture."[58]

Even if Roosevelt for tactical reasons avoided taking up the silver issue in the silver states, it naturally happened that he or his fellow speakers were asked by the audience to express their views. In Montana Senator Carter had made a direct request that the currency issue should be excluded altogether. An amusing incident has been related by one of Roosevelt's colleagues during the campaign, a lawyer from New York by the name of John Proctor Clarke. He made a speech in Butte, Montana, and was foolish enough to ask for questions from the audience. "A big flannel-shirted man" stood on a chair and shouted: "Talk about silver"! The effect was as if the platform shook with the trembling of the knees of the local committee. The speaker was also on the point of losing his composure, but he recovered and cried: "Silver, silver, why, that's a dead issue, chloroformed by prosperity, why, not even Bryan is talking about it this year." According to Clarke, this answer was greeted by great applause, the danger was over, and Roosevelt could go on to speak of the Philippines.[59] The silver issue turned up on other occasions during the tour of the West however, and not always equally idyllically. At a meeting held in Colorado on September 27, Roosevelt was mobbed by miners, and other incidents also occurred, which showed that the silver issue still held a grip on some groups in these states.[60] On the whole, however, Roosevelt's exploitation of his heroic style was successful. He was effective, not least because of his personal popularity.

After his extensive tour of the West, Roosevelt swung towards the East once more. The contents of his speeches now changed insofar as the silver issue was brought out again, expansionism explained more according to the duty line and the trust question given more space. At the same time, the cowboy and Rough Rider image that had been so strongly accentuated in the West was toned down and the vice-presidential candidate adopted a more moderate, statesmanlike attitude. A typical example of this new style was given in the rather long speech he made on October 9 in St. Louis, called "National Honor and National Greatness."[61]

In the introduction Roosevelt made the same comparison between the current campaign and that of 1864, very briefly, but on the same lines as he had developed in more detail a month earlier.[62] He then declared: "It is a bit difficult to know what issue to discuss, because our opponents change the paramount issue so often." The first question that he took up, however, was not unexpectedly the silver coinage and as so often in the Republican propaganda a great deal was made of Gage's statement and Bryan's failure to give a straight answer. Roosevelt made skilful use of this millstone that had weighted the necks of his opponents ever since Kansas City.

More interesting was the trust issue, where Roosevelt once again made effective use of the Ice Trust scandal in New York and Van Wyck's and Croker's role in this. More important, however, was that the Governor of New York on this occasion presented his fundamental attitude on the question of the trusts, the attitude that was to be the hallmark of his policy even when as president he had managed to gain a reputation as a "trust-buster." He admitted that the trust system had its drawbacks, that improper practices and serious abuses occurred in some places. But all this was to be dealt with and cured and he pointed to what had already been achieved in this area during his period as Governor of New York. But Roosevelt also declared emphatically that developments had not been wholly negative. The whole development of a highly specialized and highly complex modern industrial civilization had tended to produce these great aggregates of corporate wealth. This form of consolidation involved risks, but was not altogether evil. More effective systems of production, better service, lower prices were all made possible by the trusts and the question was to make use of these advantages while at the same time stopping the abuses by control and legislation.

After dealing with the financial and economic questions, Roosevelt got on to his favorite message: the all-decisive importance both for the individual and for a nation of a fighting spirit, readiness to take action, persistence. In a sweep through the centuries, he recalled Marathon, Salamis, Thermopylae, the achievements of the Romans, the struggles of Holland and Switzerland for independence etc. "We Americans belong to a Republic infinitely greater than any that has been seen before, and it will indeed be an evil day for mankind if this republic shrinks back and fears to do its share in the world-work of the great world powers." This then developed into an eulogy on the virtues of the soldier and on the heroic efforts of the American soldiers throughout the ages, leading up to the conclusion of the speech: a relatively brief but energetic argumentation for the policy of the McKinley administration with regard to the Philippines. The stress is placed on the duty line, the responsibility of the victors. "Now what is our duty in the Philippines? It is a duty to govern those islands in the interest of the Islanders; not less than in accordance with our own honor and interest," claimed Roosevelt and declared that consequently they could under no circumstances abandon the population of the islands to "the leadership of a syndicate of inconceivably corrupt and cruel half-breeds." "Peace, peace and good-will, good government and a constantly increasing measure of self-government," all these were after all standard properties in the Republican state platforms, especially in the East.[63] The fact that Roosevelt now took this line so emphatically was a signal that the campaign was now moving East, to voters who did not easily fall for the more cynical or self-interested expansionism and who could not be expected to be beguiled by the flowery rhetoric that was appreciated in the West. But all the same Roosevelt concluded his speech by making an appeal to "the men and women of the mighty West," which was a resounding fanfare of typical Roosevelt brand, reminiscent of his popular appearance in June at the Republican National convention:

". . . surely you are not among those who tremble and shrink back and stand aside from the contest, to let stronger and braver peoples reach forward and take the rewards of the victories you have won. Surely, you will stand by your duty. And I ask you, my fellow countrymen, I appeal to you now, at the threshold of the new century, to declare once and for all in the face of the peoples of all mankind the doctrine that where once the American flag has been hoisted in honor, it shall never be hauled down in dishonor."

Roosevelt devoted the final phase of the campaign to his home state and the enormous effort he put into the election movement culminated, like Bryan's, in a triumphant appearance in Madison Square Garden. The meeting took place eleven days after Bryan's, on October 27, and the speech made by Roosevelt largely took the form of a direct attack on the Democratic presidential candidate.[64] As usual, Roosevelt suggested that Bryan represented "National Dishonor at home and abroad," and that the Commoner and his "Bryanized Democracy" had no right to claim one particle of heirship to the party founded by Jefferson and perpetuated by Jackson. Great play was also made of Bryan's connection with Croker.

Characteristically Roosevelt cast himself into the currency question first and developed this theme in roughly the same way as before in, for example, Detroit, Grand Rapids and South Bend.[65] But the attacks on Bryan were sometimes of a very personal nature. The Democratic presidential candidate was presented as a revolutionary, destructive and endangering law, peace and order. He "preaches the doctrine of envy, the doctrine of greed," "appeals to the worst, the basest passions in mankind," "seeks to sow seeds of malice and envy," and was said to be the follower not of Jefferson and Jackson but of Murat and Robespierre. Theodore Roosevelt's total unwillingness or inability to understand or respect political opponents was often expressed in striking terms. In a letter he described the Democrats outside the Solid South as being "the concentration of all the lunatics, all the idiots, all the knaves, all the cowards and all the honest people who are hopelessly slow-witted."

As in a number of his earlier appearances, Roosevelt spoke a lot about Bryan's fears of militarism in the United States. The reason is easy to see: most people felt that Bryan's and the anti-imperialists accusations on this point were violently exaggerated and Roosevelt found it easy to ridicule his opponent.[66] On the other hand, he was very brief on the subject of the paramount issue. At the end of the speech the question was taken up in a very few words, mostly taken direct from the speech made in St. Louis on October 9.[67] It was a straight declaration on the defensive duty line, with no expansionist overtones at all. "We are in the Philippines as a result of the Spanish war. We cannot get out either with honor to ourselves or with honor to the people who have trusted us ... They shall have such liberty as could never come to them under the rule of an unspeakably corrupt and unspeakably cruel syndicate of Malay bandits and Chinese half-breeds. They shall have liberty and they shall have it under the American flag."

The way in which Roosevelt marked Bryan as an instigator of social unrest and as a hate-monger, emphasizing the silver question as still being of crucial importance and simultaneously toning down of the expansionistic notes was characteristic of his and his fellow campaigners' tactics in New York. A plainly consistent line was being followed.

Pivotal States: Indiana and New York

1

From the outset, the two main parties had made a special effort in two states: Indiana and New York, both of which were allotted a greater proportion of the campaign material and speakers than other states.

The difficulties experienced by the Democrats in keeping up with the intensive Republican agitation in Indiana and New York depended not only on a lack of economic resources, but also on the circumstances that the Republicans held a clear advantage as far as the press was concerned. The situation is illustrated in the table shown below:

	Daily		Weekly		Daily and Weekly		
	N.Y.	Indiana	N.Y.	Indiana	N.Y.	Indiana	Total
Republican	57	54	241	164	298	218	516
Democratic	37	48	157	144	194	192	386
Independent	41	25	262	137	303	162	465
Non-partisan	22	16	210	127	232	143	375

280

Thus of 902 newspapers that themselves stated party color, 57 % were Republican. At the beginning of the campaign, the Republicans in fact controlled 66 % more dailies and weeklies in the ten doubtful states than the Democratic organization.[68] One method used by the Democrats to balance the superior resources of the Republicans with regard to the press, was to spread pamphlets and other political publications. Despite their limited resources, they distributed during the initial phase of the campaign 2,500,000 documents in Indiana and 4,000,000 in New York. Ohio, another battle ground, received 3,500,000.[69]

The two main contestants both made quite extraordinary efforts. Bryan visited Indiana three times, Roosevelt twice, each tour including a large number of appearances. In addition, as has already been mentioned, the Democrats placed their notification ceremonies in Indianapolis. The anti-imperialists also convened there and in September a National Convention of Democratic Clubs gathered in the city. New York on the other hand became the arena for the intensive efforts made by both parties at the climax of the campaign. Mass meetings were held at which Bryan and Roosevelt, with their respective assistant spellbinders, staked all the strength and energy they had left. This order of priorities was not surprising: success in New York was practically indispensable for a Democratic victory and they should preferably win in Indiana too.

An important question with regard to the election in Indiana was how the Populists would act. The antagonism remained between the Fusionist and the Middle-of-the-road factions of the People's Party and it proved impossible to bridge them. The most prominent Fusionists in the state, A. P. Hanna and John Medrat, tried to create a united Populist backing of Bryan. However, the state convention on February 22 was controlled by uncompromising Middle-of-the-roaders such as F. J. S. Robinson and C. M. Walter, chairman and secretary respectively of the People's Party's State Committee, and by S. W. Williams of Vincennes and Burkhart, who was nominated as the party's candidate for governor in the state.[70] Despite the efforts by the anti-Bryan faction, most of the Populists eventuelly voted for Bryan in the presidential election.

At Indiana's Democratic state party convention in June, it had emerged clearly that the Taggart faction was in control and in Kansas City, the Indiana delegation had fought hard to get 16 : 1 excluded from the plat-form.[71] Despite some resistance within the delegation, Thomas Taggart placed S. E. Morss, the editor of the Indianapolis *Sentinel*, on the Committee on Resolutions at the convention. Apart from Taggart and Morss, it was above all Menzies who dominated this conservative wing. The Silverites were not unrepresented. Foremost among them was George W. Ray, but he was forced to retreat. A short while before the convention, an attempt was made by the Democrats' Silver wing to promote Shively of South Bend, the Democratic candidate for Governor of Indiana in 1896, as Bryan's running mate, but his name was soon dropped. He did not even have the backing of the leading politicians among the Indiana Democrats.[72]

The outcome of the fight over the platform in Kansas City was naturally a great disappointment for the Taggart faction, who were fully convinced that silver was a very considerable hindrance in Indiana. Not unexpectedly, the line they chose to follow was to play down and minimize to the utmost the importance of the currency issue, while at the same time violently attacking the McKinley administration's "imperialism." All their efforts were concentrated on the paramount issue. An example of this is the gubernatorial candidate, Kern, who did not even mention the silver issue in the speeches he made during the summer. Nor did Morss take up the subject in the *Sentinel*.[73] During July and a large part of August, imperialism dominated almost wholly, while from the end of August the trust issue in particular also began to be given a large and increasing share of attention.

In the initial phase the Democratic tactics succeeded remarkably well. This can probably be partly explained, at least as far as Indiana is concerned, by the violent storm of opinion that had been stirred up during the spring by the Puerto Rican Tariff Bill. The reaction had not been less powerful among Republican voters and in the Republican press. For this reason, the Democratic accusations and attacks could not be ignored, and the Republicans were forced to go into battle on an issue that they had not chosen and would have preferred to avoid. The problem was not diminished by the fact that the Indianapolis *Journal* bitterly criticized the McKinley administration during the spring and now had to make its position clear. A striking example of the difficulties in which the *Journal* found itself, but also of the demagogic devices in which the electoral campaign abounded, is an editorial from August 4, headlined "Two kinds of expansion." A distinction is made between "expansion for expansion's sake" and "expansion for honor's sake." Expansion could be a question of National honor and National duty. This was the case in the United States' recent acquisition of territory. In contrast to this was placed expansion for National greed or partisan politics. After wending its way through a

282

tortuous line of arguments, the *Journal* arrived at the conclusion that "the Republican party favors expansion only as a matter of National honor and necessary adjunct of National duty, the Democratic party favors it for expansion's sake."[74]

In August the Republicans made a concerted effort to shift the emphasis of the political debate from foreign policy to above all the silver issue.[75] At the same time, Bryan's name was being linked both with radical populists such as Altgeld and with corrupt machine politicians, primarily the Tammany boss, Croker.[76] The notification ceremonies, however, and especially Bryan's speech of acceptance, enforced the retention of foreign policy as a main issue, as did the closely following anti-imperialist congress in Indianapolis.

The antagonisms that existed among the Democrats in Indiana weakened to some extent their campaign efforts, or at least diminished their effectivity. Relations were not as hearty as they might have been, neither between Taggart and the Silver Republicans in the state, who were led by VanVorhis, nor with the Populists. It is hardly surprising that Bryan's most enthusiastic supporters were to be found within the silver faction and that it was also they first and foremost who rallied round and cheered the Democratic presidential candidate at the anti-imperialists' "Liberty Congress" in Indianapolis in the middle of August.[77]

The Republican election propaganda repeatedly published reports about Democrats who had deserted Bryan and declared for McKinley. Much was made, for example, of Captain W. E. English, Charles Denby and Maurice Thompson. English, who had served in the war against Spain, gave as the reasons for his change of mind that he could not accept Bryan's populism and that he believed in sound money and expansion.[78] Denby from Evansville had been former Minister to China and was a firm believer in expansion. He attacked Bryan savagely, describing him as being cowardly and unpatriotic.[79] Thompson, a well-known writer, was also a bitter opponent of Bryan and a convinced expansionist.[80] Interviews with other Democrats who had abandoned Bryan appeared constantly. In general the reason given was that they believed in expansion and sound money and felt unable to follow Bryan's line on these issues. Although the Kokomo *News* spoke of a mass flight from the Democrats to the Republican party, it was naturally in fact only a relatively limited number of cases, but they were exploited to the full.[81]

Despite the efforts made by the Indiana Republicans in August to shift the campaign from foreign policy to other issues, above all to replace

283

expansion with prosperity and promote Mark Hanna's slogans, "the full dinner pail" and "let well enough alone," the Democrats managed to retain anti-imperialism as the paramount issue during the whole of August and part of September. A clear swing can be discerned around the middle of September. One reason was undoubtedly that the general public proved to be only moderately interested in both Republican expansionism and Bryan's anti-imperialism and therefore in the fight to win votes, both sides found it necessary to change the emphasis of the campaign on to issues that the common man felt to be more important. Another contributory factor was the widespread strike in the Pennsylvanian coalmines, which broke out at the beginning of September and which caused the Republicans great misgivings. But the main reason for the change in the campaign agitation in Indiana was that Bryan, as has been pointed out in another context, rearranged his tactics at this point.[82]

Towards the end of August, Bryan had started to bring up the silver issue again and at the same time to press the trust question strongly. The effects of this was soon apparent and was reinforced by the presidential candidate's letter of acceptance. In Indiana, however, the silver issue had little appeal and was avoided by most Democratic campaign speakers and newspapers. When, following Bryan's example, new issues were sought for, issues that could complement and perhaps even replace anti-imperialism, the trust question was pushed forward. The number of articles and editorials on this subject increased markedly in the *Sentinel* at the end of August and by the middle of September questions concerning financial policy and the trusts were dominating the campaign. This became particularly noticeable after the coal strike had broken out and in connection with a campaign tour made by Mark Hanna in Indiana at this point.[83] Throughout September, the *Sentinel* had a long series of articles in which different trusts were subjected to a critical examination.

The situation in Indiana at the end of September suggests that the Republicans—with Bryan's help—had succeeded in reviving the silver question in the campaign, that trusts and monopolies dominated the Democratic agitation with anti-imperialism in second place, while the Republicans embellished the theme of prosperity, with secondary attacks on "the 50 cent dollar" and "the bugaboo of imperialism." The Indianapolis *Journal* estimated that at least half of the Gold Democrats whom deserted Bryan in 1896 would not support him now either, while at least half of the Silver Republicans of that year were expected to return to McKinley.[84] The Gold Democrats also conducted a campaign against Bryan in the state, even if their activities were relatively limited.[85]

During the first half of October, the electoral campaign in Indiana reached a peak of very high intensity. At the beginning, the Democrats held the initiative, since the National Convention of Democratic Clubs held in Indianapolis gave rise to a burst of activity. Although the agitation had from the start been strongly influenced by anti-imperialism, it was the trust issue which markedly dominated the meeting in Indianapolis.[86] Throughout September, the *Sentinel*, supported by other Democratic news-papers in the state, had pressed this issue in editorials and special articles and this line was maintained. Anti-imperialism was not forgotten, however: one of the highlights of the Convention was a fiery speech made by Bourke Cockran. Bryan naturally made an appearance at the convention and took the opportunity of making a speaking-tour at the same time, in which he chiefly emphasized the trust and monopoly issues and in which the coal mining strike played a prominent part.

The Republicans were not slow to respond. So far Fairbanks and Beveridge had mainly been active outside the state, but they were now hurled into the intensified campaign in their home territory. They were backed up by Attorney General Taylor and Governor Mount, among others. Fairbanks spoke chiefly on the economic policy, relying on Mark Hanna's recipe for prosperity, while not unexpectedly Beveridge devoted much of his agitation to the theme of expansion. The climax of the campaign, however, was Roosevelt's tour of the state between October 10 and 12.

The leader of the campaign train and the man mainly responsible for arranging Roosevelt's tour was Harry S. New. On certain stretches, Senators Fairbanks and Beveridge also rode the campaign train, as did Governor Mount, a number of Indiana's Republican congressmen, members of the Republican state committee and other prominent men within the party. Captain W. E. English, and other converts from the Democratic party, were also taken along.[87]

Roosevelt's three-day campaign in Indiana covered 24 towns and naturally attracted great attention. According to the *Journal*, the Republi-can vice-presidential candidate drew enormous crowds: 40,000 in Fort Wayne, 30,000 in LaFayette, 10,000—15,000 in Frankfort etc. Roosevelt's appearances were accompanied by an intense press campaign. On October 10, the first day of the tour, the *Journal* published two editorials devoted to the main antagonists of the campaign, Roosevelt and Bryan. The former was glorified as a man of action, with force, honesty, ability. Bryan on the other hand was presented as a public enemy, a deadly threat to prosperity as a result of his hostile attitude to business interests and his silver madness. A couple of days later, another violent attack was made on the Democratic leader. The key adjectives were "unscrupulous and dishonest."[88] These leading articles clearly signified an increasingly apparent trend in the Republican agitation, namely vicious personal attacks on Bryan. At the same time it was very plain that the expansion theme had had to retire to the background and make way for the prosperity arguments. The labor votes were those aimed at and now and then the specter of silver was aired. Mark Hanna used the same tactics when he toured Indiana in the final phase of the campaign. In his appearances in Fort Wayne, South Bend, Elkhart, Goshen and Warshaw, the main organizer of the Republican campaign addressed himself in particular to the working-class voters and played on variations of his basic theme: "the full dinner pail" and "let well enough alone." Beveridge varied the theme in a new way when he declared that expansion was necessary to ensure the full dinner pail.

The Republican tactics in Indiana were summed up splendidly in an editorial in the Indianapolis *Journal* in the final phase of the campaign: "A vote for Mr. Bryan against McKinley, or for a Democratic candidate for Congress against a Republican, is a vote to substitute souphouses for factories and empty dinner pails for full ones."[89]

Meanwhile the Indianapolis *Sentinel* continued its campaign on the trust issue. Mark Hanna was attacked particularly bitterly, but Roosevelt did not escape. He was described as "a mountebank," and his nomination as Republican vice-presidential candidate was declared "a national scandal," the election of him would be "a national disgrace."[90] The attacks on the McKinley administration were also complemented during the final stage of the campaign with acrimonious charges of alleged corruption within the Republican county administrations.[91] At the same time the paramount issue was again taken up. For the finale of the campaign, Bryan returned to Indiana and made about ten appearances at which he largely listed once more the usual array of arguments.[92]

The efforts made by both parties in Indiana demonstrate both the importance assigned to the state and the fact that it was considered uncertain. Both sides claimed throughout the campaign that they were convinced of victory, but as late as October, Indiana was still being placed in the "doubtful" column in Republican forecasts.[93] At the turn of the month, September—October, the Hoosier state was described as doubtful by John Hay, Secretary of State,[94] an opinion that was shared at the local level by e.g. Hilton U. Brown, manager of the Indianapolis *News* (Rep.).[95]

286

Towards the end of the month, the state was admittedly classified as "safe," but even on November 2, the Indianapolis *Journal* only estimated the expected Republican majority at 12,000—15,000, which must be seen as an indirect admission that the result could in no way be considered certain.

2

The New York delegation had played an important part in the tactical manoeuvres around the convention in Kansas City, and its large population also made this state of special interest in the campaign. As before, the situation was made more complicated by the intense power struggle between the Tammany boss, Croker, and Hill.[96] As Democratic candidate for governor, Hill backed Bird S. Coler, comptroller of New York City, a man with a very solid reputation, not least among independent voters. The Platt machine in its turn nominated Odell as the Republican candidate, a man who despite these connections received the wholehearted support of Theodore Roosevelt.[97] Roosevelt, however, had from the beginning had misgivings about Odell's chances of winning and would have preferred to see Elihu Root as the gubernatorial candidate, if it had been possible to persuade him to accept the candidacy.[98] Coler was felt also by many other Republicans to have very good chances, representing a clear threat to the election of Odell. It was a relief to the Republicans, therefore, that Coler, who was unacceptable to Tammany, was defeated at the nominations. Croker proved to be stronger than Hill and his candidate, John B. Stanchfield, defeated Hill's candidate with 294 votes to 154, a result that led *Public Opinion* to declare that the Democratic state convention marked the ascendancy of Croker as state boss.[99]

The split between the Croker and Hill factions in New York was obviously a very serious handicap for the Democrats. Croker's actions at the state convention and the nomination of Stanchfield was said by the New York *World* to be certain to have "a necessarily disastrous effect upon the anti-imperialistic national Democratic ticket." And the New York *Evening Post* was even more pointed: "There has never been in the history of political parties a case where the personal preferences of delegates and the obvious advantage of the party were so ruthlessly overborne by a boss as when Croker insists that the Democratic convention shall not nominate Comptroller Coler, of New York City, for governor." The New York *Press* spoke of "the flattest and most uncompromising denial of a

287

popular demand." Stanchfield did not receive unreserved support from many newspapers, although he was endorsed by e.g. the New York *Times,* Brooklyn *Citizen* and Albany *Argus.*[100] "Crokerism" was not supported anywhere outside New York and in many places the reaction to the Tammany Tiger's move was extremely negative. The Nashville *American* called Croker "a vulgar, ignorant, overbearing, political charlatan," and even the newspapers that were more restrained in their criticism voiced great fears of the effect this would have on the Democratic party's chances in New York and consequently in the election as a whole.[101]

The situation in New York was naturally problematic for Bryan. In August Senator James K. Jones still believed that Bryan had a fair chance of carrying New York. However, he noted that there was a disposition to fall into the Republican program of making the financial question the leading issue, which made the Democrats lose to some extent, and in his opinion they would also lose some votes on the question of imperialism.[102] Bryan adapted to the circumstances as best he could, among other things by almost totally ignoring the silver issue in his speeches, which was clearly a concession to the Hill faction. Both Hill and Croker made a show of giving Bryan their wholehearted support. This was, however, a considerably qualified truth.[103] Croker's actions at the Democratic state convention showed quite plainly that he placed the importance of having a gubernatorial candidate loyal to Tammany higher than the party's chances of winning the election. In the same way, Hill's activity in the campaign was rather desultory, a fact which is not surprising considering both his relations to the candidate for governor backed by Croker and his completely negative attitude towards Bryan's populist tendencies and his policy on the currency issue. Neither Hill's supporters, nor the conservative Democrats as a whole were particularly pleased by Bryan's increasingly open fraternization with the Croker faction in the final stage of the campaign. In connection with the appearances made in New York by the Democratic presidential candidate on October 16, an incident occurred, which attracted a great deal of attention and was exploited for a vicious attack on Bryan personally. At the beginning of the speech that Bryan made in the Cooper Union, he said: "I am prepared to say that great is Tammany and Croker is its prophet."[104]

The Bryan wing of the Democrats found it difficult to assert themselves during the campaign. Willis Abbot placed the responsibility on Croker,[105] but an equally important factor was the attitude of the conservative Democrats towards "Bryanism." While such men among the conservative

New York Democrats as Edward H. Shepard and Bourke Cockran actively worked for Bryan, a large number of others, such as Abram S. Hewitt, Charles S. Fairchild, Oswald Ottendorffer, George Foster Peabody and Alexander E. Orr refused to give their support to the Democratic ticket.[106]

Although the Democrats never went so far as to classify New York as safe, many of them believed that a victory was possible, despite the problems that existed. One such person was James McGuire, chairman of the executive committee of the Democratic state committee, and another Congressman Amos J. Cummings.[107] Others among the optimistic assessors were Charles H. Jones, main author of both the Chicago and the Kansas City platform,[108] and,—at least during the early stages of the campaign— James K. Jones, the Democratic national chairman.[109]

The outcome in New York was not easy to assess. Croker controlled New York City, and there Bryan's victory was assured. But if he was to have any prospects of a gain in the state, the majority in New York City had to be conclusive. The Republicans had a solid majority in New York outside New York City and Bryan's grip on the Democrats there was for reasons well-known relatively weak. The state also had a not unimportant number of independent voters. They were strongly critical of the Republican Platt machine, but had on the other hand even less sympathy for Croker and Tammany. "Stick to imperialism, militarism and trusts," was a typical piece of advice given to Bryan by a New York Democrat, who also declared emphatically: "We cannot make headway here in the east on the money question. Not one in five-hundred has the slightest comprehension of it; neither are they disposed to be interested in it or to study it."[110] Bryan tried to follow this line, but the Republicans naturally did everything in their power to keep the silver issue alive and thereby feed the suspicion towards the Democratic presidential candidate felt by mugwumps and conservative Democrats. And these tactics did not fail in their effect.

Even though the Republicans found it on the whole difficult to believe in defeat in New York, and though the state had never even been placed in the "doubtful" column in their official predictions, a certain amount of uncertainty remained for some time in some quarters. One of those worried by the situation in New York was Whitelaw Reid.[111] This was above all the case prior to the settling of the coal miners' strike in Pennsylvania. The strike stands out as the most worrying feature of the campaign from the Republican point of view and the only time that Joseph H. Manley, member of the Republican National Committee and specially concerned with the predictions that were made regularly, was uncertain about New

York. He referred to the possible effects of a continued strike as the reason. Towards the end of the campaign, however, he became convinced of a victory in New York with a clear majority, an assessment shared by most Republicans.[112]

CHAPTER IX

Election and the Issues

1

The outcome of the election demonstrated with brutal clarity that the Democrats' hopes and predictions of a victory for Bryan had been nothing but daydreams.

In 1896 McKinley had won convincingly with a plurality of about 700,000 votes and a majority of 95 electors. In many states, however, the election had been very even and a swing of less than 30,000 votes, suitably distributed, would have been enough to give Bryan California, Delaware, Indiana, Kentucky, North Dakota, Oregon and West Virginia, which would have given him the victory.[1] This accounted for the optimism felt by many Democrats. Reality proved to be different. McKinley obtained 292 electoral votes, against 155 for Bryan. Instead of closing the gap, Bryan had lost a further 150,000 votes to McKinley. While the President increased the absolute total of his share of the votes by over a hundred thousand, the Democrats fell back slightly. Since the electorate must have increased by something like a million since 1896, this showed a clear reduction in the poll, confirming the apathy that had often been noted during the campaign. Bryan had been less successful than the Republicans in mobilizing these new voters. Another partial explanation of this relative decrease in the voting figures can also be that the 1896 campaign had been abnormally heated and that voters on both sides who had been activated then did not feel this election to be so vital. Participation in the voting was also noticeably low in the Southern states, which was attributed to the lack of support in the South both for Bryan himself and for his platform.[2]

Although the assessments of the election prospects that were published prior to the election by the Democrats' campaign committee partly owed their strong optimism to the requirements of propaganda, it is obvious that they really did count on there being a chance of victory. Many people were completely convinced that Bryan would win, others thought that it would at least be an even fight. The result was clearly a shock for many of them. James K. Jones admitted in a letter to Bryan: "I was so completely stunned, so overwhelmed by the result that I have not yet fully recovered from it."[3] And J. G. Johnson, vice-chairman of the Executive Committee, described himself as being "heart sick over the outcome of our campaign."[4] William Sulzer, Democratic congressman from New York and one of those who had striven to become Bryan's running mate, wrote that when the returns came in he was "simply dozed."[5]

Leading Republicans had hardly ever doubted during the campaign that McKinley would win. Further proof of the excellent, smoothly functioning organization that Hanna and his colleagues had built up is provided by the fact that the predictions they published, though cautious, gave a very realistic view of the political situation. In fact if anything, their estimations were somewhat under-dimensioned and compared to the rose-colored visions of the Democrats, the sense of reality and grasp of the actual situation shown by the Republicans is extremely impressive

In Republican quarters the victory was therefore accepted as being relatively self-evident, even though the magnitude of McKinley's victory was surprising. The comments made often reveal a total lack of respect for the bearer of the Democratic banner and satisfaction over what was seen—prematurely—as his political demise. Thus Whitelaw Reid spoke of the election result in a letter to Cushman Davis as "the final elimination of such a pestilent growth in place of what ought to be a legitimate and useful opposition."[6]

Mugwumps and reformists, who shared Bryan's anti-imperialistic ideas, often regarded his defeat with equanimity, sometimes even with satisfaction. Thus after the election Charles J. Bonaparte of the Civil Service Reform League wrote: "I cannot say that it awakens in me any very great enthusiasm, but I have a feeling of relief at being rid of Bryan, certainly for four years, and I hope forever."[7]

The first comments from the Democratic side expressed not only disappointment, but also bewilderment. What had caused the defeat, or rather how could they suffer so great a defeat, when they had previously come to the conclusion that a great victory was possible for Bryan? Different assumptions and attempts at explanation were bandied about. Several commentators pointed out that they had obviously misjudged the working-class voters. M. F. Tarpey, the Californian representative on the Democratic National Committee, wrote a report to Bryan immediately before the election, in which he assured him that the prospects for California going

	Total vote		Counties[8]	
	1896	1900	1896	1900
UNITED STATES	13,899,857	13,964,567	2,738	2,748
Democratic	6,379,830	6,356,734	1,551	1,340
Republican	7,098,474	7,218,491	1,163	1,385
Other	421,553	389,342	8	2
New England	896,674	907,764	67	67
Democratic	242,947	336,983	—·	2
Republican	615,672	539,003	67	65
Other	48,055	31,778	—	—
Middle Atlantic	2,989,245	3,122,253	148	149
Democratic	1,112,169	1,267,502	15	21
Republican	1,769,505	1,756,385	132	128
Other	107,571	98,366	—	—
East North-Central	3,732,292	3,817,831	435	435
Democratic	1,650,316	1,658,141	131	113
Republican	2,018,366	2,058,740	299	322
Other	63,610	100,950	—	—
West-North-Central	2,225,724	2,277,552	581	583
Democratic	1,075,835	1,008,860	292	151
Republican	1,117,655	1,210,596	289	430
Other	32,234	58,096	—	—
South Atlantic	1,377,826	1,295,677	514	519
Democratic	725,772	700,113	350	375
Republican	627,142	572,594	161	143
Other	24,912	22,970	—	—
East South-Central	1,028,155	959,924	356	356
Democratic	575,198	528,447	255	252
Republican	427,503	411,315	100	104
Other	25,454	20,162	—	—
West South-Central	780,285	618,277	360	357
Democratic	568,801	402,713	303	307
Republican	219,245	190,419	48	30
Other	92,239	25,145	1	2
Mountain	379,285	470,468	154	156
Democratic	307,264	250,782	141	88
Republican	68,698	210,702	13	68
Other	3,323	8,984	—	—
Pacific	490,371	494,821	123	126
Democratic	221,528	203,193	61	31
Republican	234,688	268,737	54	95
Other	34,155	22,891	7	—

Democratic were good. One of the reasons given was that, according to the information received, organized labor would vote Democratic to an extent that it had not done for many years.[9] After the election Tarpey wrote an apologetic letter, in which he explained that the reason for his total misjudgement was that "the working classes have deceived us as to their position." The story was the same elsewhere in the country.[10] The same explanation, that "the laboring man" had let them down, often recurred, not least from anti-imperialists, who sometimes clothed their bitterness in a tone of aggression. The workers have "joyfully fitted their necks to the yoke," explained W. A. Croffut and asked: "Is there any hope for such people"?[11] "I am losing my sympathy for the laboring man and the small merchant ... When laboring men get so low as to wish the continuance of the shooting down of the poor Philippines in order to put a few more cents in their pockets, it shows that no reason will reach him except through sever punishment," wrote another active anti-imperialist in California to Bryan. Even a man like Senator Pettigrew expressed doubt as to the labor vote.[12] "The average workingman cannot, or will not, think beyond a full belly," claimed a disappointed anti-imperialist, who was a member of the People's Party National Committee.[13] The theme is varied in many ways, but the best and most laconic summing-up came from a bankman from Nebraska: "The full dinner pail has won."[14]

In actual fact there had been active anti-imperialist elements on the labor side. Samuel Gompers was one of the vice-presidents of the Anti-Imperialist Leaugue.[15] The Knights of Labor followed a consistently anti-imperialistic line in the *Journal of the Knights of Labor*.[16] The great mass of working men played a waiting game, however, with the exception of the unions that felt directly threatened.[17] The loss of the full dinner pail was feared more than imperialism.[18]

The bitterness and disappointment felt by many anti-imperialists over the outcome of the election was particularly marked. They had not only looked upon the fight against the policy of the McKinley administration as being the all decisive issue, but had also turned it into a question of moral values. It had come to represent a trial of strength between good and evil, between the hydra of imperialism and the defenders of liberty and justice. Many leading anti-imperialists had awaited the results of the election with a degree of optimism. Thus immediately prior to the election, Edwin Burrit Smith, chairman of the Executive Committee of the Anti-Imperialist League, wrote to Carl Schurz that he was taking an increasingly hopeful view of their prospects in the election. He thought admittedly that it would be a close fight, but saw some indications of a landslide for Bryan.[19] And the day before the election Elwood S. Corser wrote to Bryan that he was fully convinced of a victory.[20] So the result was a shock:

"Lord God of our fathers, and of our children, how can these things be! The very stones of the streets should cry out against our Philippine infamy ... We seem to have become a people without moral conviction," wrote Corser to W. A. Croffut, secretary of the Washington section of the Anti-Imperialist League. He went so far as to say that he considered "this nation doomed to decadence and to perish in a night."[21]

Croffut's letter to Bryan also gives a typical expression of the bitterness and disappointment felt by the anti-imperialists. "It seems now as if the country was given over to carnage and plunder ... to blood and ashes. That there is a few thousand who have not bowed the knee to Baal is a slight consolation. The worst of it all is that the American people have deliberately become partners in the great crimes we are committing and have brutally ordered that they be continued."[22] Croffut regarded the election result as a mandate on imperialism and he was by no means alone in this view.

Other anti-imperialists, although disappointed, did not react with the pessimism and defeatism shown by Croffut and Corser. Erving Winslow, secretary of the New England Anti-Imperialist League, pointed out that the Republicans' majority in New England had decreased by more than half a million votes and he attributed this to the anti-imperialist agitation. There was every reason to continue the fight and he regarded the situation in a relatively optimistic light. Other prominent anti-imperialists in New England, such as William Lloyd Garrison, Moorfield Storey and Albion A. Perry had a similar attitude.[23]

In many of his speeches and arguments Bryan had embroidered on the theme that the fight was between "the Dollar and the Man." The Dollar had won. This was the most frequent interpretation given by Democratic commentators. "The Almighty Dollar rules the country absolutely," wrote the secretary of the State Executive Committee in Georgia.[24] Often these explanations of the outcome of the election were combined with accusations against the Republicans of bribery, vote-purchasing and corruption. More level-headed and responsible Democrats rejected these charges that dishonest methods should have affected the result of the election, however, even though they stressed at the same time the superior resources available to the Republicans for financing their campaign.

Otherwise there was enormous variation in the explanations given of the huge defeat of Bryan and the Democrats. Sometimes the blame was placed on influential machine-politicians, who were said to have let Bryan down.[25] Some pointed to Croker, others to David B. Hill.[26] Boss Harrison of Illinois, McLean of Ohio and ex-Senator Gorman of Maryland were also among those often seen as villains.[27] Sometimes—and often—Bryan's revival of the silver issue was said to have been fatal. "A great issue was weighted down by free silver and business timidity," complained one typical letter-writer.[28] There were also those, however, who were of the opinion that it was a mistake not to push the question of bi-metallism harder.[29] The anti-imperialist agitation of the Democrats was seen as a handicap by some, while other commentators claimed that regionally at least it had had a clearly positive effect.

Bryan himself gave an account of what he felt about the outcome of the election and the reasons behind it. His analysis led to the conclusion that three factors had been decisive: "money, war and better times."[30] By "money" he meant the superior financial resources enjoyed by the Republicans during the campaign. Even if Bryan hinted at an illegitimate use of money, he did not state that as being the most important point, but instead the opportunities his opponents had had of conducting a campaign of maximum efficiency without financial obstacles.

The efforts made by the Democrats to force the voters to take a stand against imperialism by voting for Bryan were in his opinion neutralized by the fact that the war was still in progress, which favored the sitting administration due to the feeling that "it is not safe to swap horses while crossing a stream." Apparently the voters had also accepted the Republicans' assertion that the Philippine question could not be tackled until the revolt had been suppressed.

It was, however, the third factor, "better times", that Bryan saw as being the most important contributory reason for his defeat. The decisive influence was quite simply "fear of change." The voters still had a vivid memory of the deep depression that had afflicted them a few years earlier and the Republicans had skilfully exploited to the utmost the fear of the working classes that these bad times could return. On the other hand Bryan denied categorically that the Democrats' defeat was in any way connected with the demand for free silver coinage.[31] He admitted that this was an issue that developments had relegated to a subordinate position.[32]

2

During the previous summer, when the two parties had drawn up the main outlines for their campaigns, the Democrats had given foreign policy a central position as the paramount issue, formulating it as a fight for and against territorial expansion of the type exemplified by the acquisition of the Philippines. It has been shown that the campaign did in fact follow this strategy to a considerable extent. But did this issue affect the outcome of the election? Modern research has shown that the question of which concrete factors have caused the voter to decide one way or the other is utterly complicated. In elections that are dominated by a number of important national issues, but that are at the same time personal elections of a local nature, it is obviously extremely hazardous to isolate and try to determine the effect of a single issue that has been debated during the campaign. A regional survey of the election results can nevertheless provide certain indications.

The Democrats could mark up more than marginal successes in the Eastern states in the actual number of votes. This applied above all in New England, where the increase in Democratic votes approached 100,000, while the Republicans suffered a total loss of about 75,000 voters there. In the Middle Atlantic States, too, Bryan increased his share, while the Republicans largely held the numbers gained in 1896. In both cases, however, it was a question of safe Republican territory and had no effects.[33]

The Democratic successes in New England, which were quite clear although without significance for the final outcome of the election, were greatest in Massachusetts, but substantial in all the states. The reason was that many of those who had bolted in 1896 had come back to the party, their return being eased by the efforts made by Bryan and the Democrats to play down the silver issue in the East. At the same time, anti-imperialism was most strongly rooted in just this region, and had tended to split the Republicans there. As a result some of them had probably stayed at home. Boston, where McKinley had won by 18,000 in 1896 but which was something of a Mecca of anti-imperialism, turned in a plurality of 10,000 votes for Bryan, thus returning to the Democratic column.[34]

The fact that anti-imperialism actually influenced voters in New England, above all in Massachusetts, can also be substantiated in other ways. Thus Congressman McCall of Massachusetts ran no less than 3300 votes ahead of McKinley in his district. As was mentioned previously, McCall had played a leading role in the fight against the Puerto Rican tariff in

Total Vote for Electors by Sections and by States

	1896	1900
NEW ENGLAND	896,674	907,764
Democratic	242,947	336,983
Republican	615,672	539,003
Other	38,055	31,778
Maine	118,419	107,694
Democratic	34,587	37,822
Republican	80,403	66,413
Other	3,429	3,459
New Hampshire	83,670	92,364
Democratic	21,271	35,489
Republican	57,444	54,799
Other	4,955	2,076
Vermont	63,847	56,213
Democratic	10,179	12,849
Republican	51,127	42,659
Other	2,541	795
Massachusetts	401,568	414,804
Democratic	105,711	156,997
Republican	278,976	238,866
Other	16,881	18,941
Rhode Island	54,780	56,548
Democratic	14,459	19,812
Republican	37,437	33,784
Other	2,884	2,952
Connecticut	174,390	180,141
Democratic	56,740	74,014
Republican	110,285	102,572
Other	7,365	3,555

the spring. He not only led the Republican revolt on this occasion in the House of Representatives, but also followed a clearly anti-imperialist line in other contexts. McCall's success was all the more remarkable, since Henry Cabot Lodge and his lieutenants, in particular George H. Lyman, had systematically worked to undermine McCall's position.[35] There is no reason to doubt the validity of a comment made on the election results in Massachusetts, which pointed out that in 1896 the Democratic machine knifed Bryan for all it was worth and supported him in 1900. But in addition it is undeniable that anti-imperialism also played a part.[36]

Mention was made above of the disappointment felt by Bryan's supporters

	1896	1900
MIDDLE ATLANTIC	2,989,245	3,122,253
Democratic	1,112,169	1,267,502
Republican	1,769,505	1,756,385
Other	107,571	98,366
New York	1,423,876	1,548,043
Democratic	551,369	678,462
Republican	819,838	822,013
Other	52,669	47,568
New Jersey	371,014	401,000
Democratic	133,675	164,808
Republican	221,367	221,707
Other	15,972	14,485
Pennsylvania	1,194,355	1,173,210
Democratic	427,125	424,232
Republican	728,300	712,665
Other	38,930	36,313

over the working man's vote. Pennsylvania, "the workshop state," gave the Republicans an overwhelming plurality of almost 300,000. This in itself was nothing new, since the result had been almost identical in 1896. Bryan had, however, obviously failed to win the working class voters, despite his attempt to appeal to them with his "Dollar and the Man" theme. In West Virginia, Ohio and Indiana, all states with large wage-earning populations, the Republican majority increased on the figures of 1896. The prosperity factor neutralized Bryan's anti-trust agitation.

The strike among the coal miners that had worried the Republicans had been settled in good time before the election by means of a ten per cent increase in wages. The credit for this was largely Mark Hanna's. He was extremely well-informed about conditions in the coal industry and considered that the claims of the miners were highly justified. In addition he naturally realized how important it was from a tactical point of view to get the strike settled, not least because the Republicans' main weapon was the general satisfaction with the good times. Charles G. Dawes, who was a discerning man, went so far as to say that the settling of the strike was Hanna's "most remarkable accomplishment" during the entire campaign.[37] The effect was also reflected in the election figures. The counties in which the strike had taken place, Luzerne, Lackawanna and Schuylkill, all gave heavy Republican pluralities. The county of Schuylkill had incidentally given a plurality of 1800 to the Democrats in 1896.[38]

It is more doubtful whether the election results in New York and Chicago, cities with large numbers of working-class voters, can be interpreted in the same way. Tammany's usual majority was greatly reduced and in the normally Democratic Chicago, Republican candidates gained several pluralities. On the other hand, the election in both these cities was influenced by machine-political complications, which makes it difficult to come to any conclusions at all about how far the national issues affected the outcome there.

The result of the election in the Middle West was a sore blow to the Democrats. In the East North-Central area, the Democrats had a worse election than 1896 everywhere, with the exception of Illinois. The absolute voting figures had not changed noticeably, but the relationship between Democratic and Republican counties changed from 134 : 299 to 113 : 322. The situation was much worse in the West North-Central section. A Democratic majority of three in counties was changed to a Republican majority of no less than 279. South Dakota, Nebraska and Kansas had voted Democratic in 1896. All now landed in the Republican column, like the rest of the area.[39] The Republican plurality rose from a little over 40,000 to about 200,000 in the West North-Central section, where the greatest swing took place, while the East North-Central section formed a transitional stage to the results in the Eastern states, with a small increase for the Democrats in the absolute number of votes and a somewhat larger, but very moderate increase for the Republicans.

Earlier we have followed the political contest in Indiana with particular attention, since it was regarded by both parties as a pivotal state and came to be perhaps the hottest battlefield during the campaign. It is therefore a matter of special interest to look a little more closely at the election results there. As was pointed out in another context, Indiana is particularly suited for a case-study, because of its political, social, economic and demographic structure. The results in the state did in fact reflect the election results as a whole in the nation.[40] The number of votes for Bryan in Indiana increased by about four thousand. To no avail, however, as the Republicans gained even more ground, with over 11,000 additional votes. The Democrats held their four districts nevertheless and the only individual change in Indiana's congressional delegation was that the Republican George W. Faris retired in favor of Elias S. Holliday, Brazil.

As far as the counties are concerned, the Republicans made a net gain of three and increased their plurality from 49—43 to 52—40. They won seven and lost four. Three of the Democratic gains, Perry, Floyd and Clark, lay in the third district and one, Bartholomew, in the fourth. This meant that the Democrats had consolidated their position in the southern part of the state. Senator Fairbanks' reports from just these districts at the beginning of the year had each and all been extremely optimistic. Three factors had been emphasized in many of them: the absence of silver sentiment among the Democrats, the insignificance of anti-imperialism as a political issue and the general satisfaction with prosperity and good times.[41] Despite this, the Democrats had succeeded in holding and even strengthening their positions in the three southernmost congressional districts, the first, second and third. In the other districts, however, a certain amount of success for the Republicans could be noted. Martin county, which had given a clear Democratic majority in 1896, now voted Republican. There was also a marked increase in the number of Republican votes in the adjoining or neighboring counties, Sullivan, Davies and Monroe, in the second district and Orange in the third. It can be noted that it was in these areas that powerful pro-expansionist currents were reported at the beginning of the year.[42]

Otherwise the main Republican advance lay in central Indiana, primarily in the eighth and ninth districts, where Jay, Fountain and Clinton counties landed in the Republican column, while considerable gains in votes were made in a number of other counties. The Republicans also gained some ground in the adjoining tenth and eleventh districts.

Did then "the paramount issue" influence the outcome of the election in Indiana? It was mentioned above that the Republicans had had some success in counties from which reports had been received of a positive response to McKinley's foreign policy. Any suggestion of there being a causal connection here is contradicted, however, by the fact that Sullivan, Knox, Green and Crawford counties, from which similar reports had been received, showed unchanged or even somewhat improved figures for the Democrats.[43] It also emerges clearly that the attempts to win over the German voters with the help of anti-imperialist agitation had failed. It is possible that the reduction of the Republican plurality by 3000 votes in Marion county (Indianapolis) to some extent depended on the support of German voters, like a similar Democratic advance in Allen county (Fort Wayne), but on the other hand the Democrats had stood still or lost ground in other areas with a concentration of German voters. Here as elsewhere, the retention of the demand for free silver had been exploited to the utmost by the Republicans, closely connected with the most effective of all arguments, the prosperity line.

To summarize, it can be seen from the results in Indiana that the Republican success was quite clear-cut but achieved with a very moderate rise in the number of votes. There is every reason to believe that the advance stemmed from the same factors that determined the outcome of the election in most of the country. The opposition had not been able to convince the voters that there was a large important issue and in the prevailing boom and with memories of the earlier depression still fresh in people's minds, it was easy for the Republicans to exploit the fear of uncertain, hazardous changes. "Prosperity" and "the full dinner pail" weighed heaviest.

The South Atlantic section showed no essential changes compared to 1896. The voting figures fell for both parties, obviously because of voter apathy, especially noticeable in the South. Quite naturally, the only places in which there had been a real fight, were Delaware and Maryland. In Maryland above all, the Democrats had really exerted themselves, partly with the support of the Republican Senator George Wellington, the fierce anti-imperialist who came out for Bryan. The Democratic polling total increased by nearly 20,000 votes, while the Republicans slipped back slightly. The swing was not enough to ensure a victory, however.[44]

The South-Central sections voted safely Democratic, which was only to be expected. The polling figures were nevertheless lower than in 1896 for both parties and the Democrats in particular felt the effects of the voters' apathy. The only change was in Kentucky, which in 1896 had been won by the Republicans by a handful of votes, but which now gave Bryan 8000 votes plurality.

	Total vote		Counties	
	1896	1900	1896	1900
MOUNTAIN	379,285	470,468	154	156
Democratic	307,264	250,782	141	88
Republican	68,698	210,702	13	68
Other	3,323	8,984	—	—
Montana	53,149	63,641	23	24
Democratic	42,469	37,146	21	13
Republican	10,494	25,373	2	11
Other	186	1,122	—	—
Idaho	29,686	57,981	21	21
Democratic	23,189	29,414	21	12
Republican	6,324	27,237	—	9
Other	173	1,330	—	—

	Total vote		Counties	
	1896	1900	1896	1900
Wyoming	21,093	24,646	13	13
Democratic	10,376	10,164	5	—
Republican	10,072	14,482	8	13
Other	645	—	—	—
Colorado	186,924	220,930	56	57
Democratic	158,821	122,705	54	39
Republican	26,379	92,622	2	18
Other	1,724	5,603	—	—
Utah	78,119	93,074	27	27
Democratic	64,607	45,006	26	10
Republican	13,491	47,139	1	17
Other	21	929	—	—
Nevada	10,314	10,196	14	14
Democratic	7,802	6,347	14	14
Republican	1,938	3,849	—	—
Other	574	—	—	—
PACIFIC	490,371	494,821	123	126
Democratic	221,528	203,193	61	31
Republican	234,688	268,737	54	95
Other	34,155	22,891	7	—
Washington	93,583	107,601	34	36
Democratic	51,646	44,823	25	9
Republican	39,153	57,456	8	27
Other	2,784	5,322	—	—
Oregon	97,414	84,216	32	33
Democratic	46,739	33,385	17	5
Republican	48,779	46,526	15	28
Other	1,896	4,305	—	—
California	299,374	303,004	57	57
Democratic	123,143	124,985	19	17
Republican	146,756	164,755	31	40
Other	29,475	13,264	7	—

The drop in votes for the Democrats in the East and West South-Central sections was about two and half times as great as that for the Republicans. Thus about a third of the votes from 1896 were lost in Louisiana, a quarter in Alabama and a fifth in Arkansas. There were also other contributory reasons for this, but it can be noted that the attempt made by the Democrats to make opposition to the McKinley administration's expansion policy the main issue of the campaign was anything but popular in large parts of the South, where on the contrary expansionism had prominent advocates both in the press and among politicians.

For those who had believed that the silver issue could be useful for the Democrats in the election, the result was a crushing blow. The outcome in a number of the mining states shows how completely this question had lost every ounce of appeal for the voters. In Colorado, Bryan had won in 1896 with a majority of 132,000. This was now reduced to 30,000. The refusal of the Democrats to nominate Charles Towne as vice-presidential candidate had alienated some. Others had returned to the Republican fold after losing faith in the overshadowing importance of the silver issue. Further, the situation had been complicated by the fact that convinced silver men, such as Senator Henry Moore Teller, were at the same time pronounced expansionists. The fusion between Democrats, Silver Republicans and Populists in Colorado had also been undermined by powerful personal antagonisms. The fusion ticket won eventually, but with greatly reduced majorities.[45]

Nevada, which in the past had been almost exclusively identified with the silvermining industry, went for Bryan 4 : 1 (7802 for Bryan and 1938 for McKinley) in 1896. In 1900 the majority was reduced to about 2500. One typical example of the swing was that Senator Stewart, one of the chief founders of the free-silver movement, was working energetically for McKinley, while in 1896 he devoted all his efforts to Bryan. Of a majority of 17,000 in Idaho only a couple of thousand remained and the most flagrant example came in Utah, where a Democratic majority of 51,000 was transformed into a Republican victory by 2000 votes.

Altogether in the Mountain states, the Democratic majority diminished by about 200,000 votes, and if we look at the distribution of the counties, the figures have been changed from 141 : 13 to 88 : 68 in favor of the Democrats. There had been no lack of indications that things could go disastrously wrong for Bryan in the silver states. In addition to Senator Stewart of Nevada, ex-Senator Mantle of Montana and no less than six of the eight Colorado delegates who had bolted from the Republican National Convention in 1896 had come out for McKinley.[46] The swing in the Mountain states could also be seen in the press. In Denver the *Times* and the *Republican*, both of which had supported Bryan in 1896, had gone over to McKinley, and the Denver *Post* also turned against Bryan. In Butte, Montana, to take another example, Bryan was opposed now by both the *Inter Mountain* and the Montana *Journal*.

The great losses suffered by the Democrats in these states were obviously primarily the result of the death of the silver issue. This indifference to Bryan and his silver plank was considered, probably rightly, to have been reinforced by a very positive sentiment in favor of "expansion."[47] It can be assumed that this feeling had an even greater influence on the voters in the Pacific states, where a direct interest in possible trade expansion in the Pacific was often expressed and probably contributed to the large increase in the Republican pluralities in California and Oregon and to the fact that Washington, which in 1896 had voted Democratic with a plurality of over 12,000, now gave the Republicans an even greater plurality. The Republican majority in teh Pacific states rose from 13,000 to 65,000. The change was even more striking if we consider the distribution of the counties. In 1896 the Democrats had won in 61, as opposed to 54 for the Republicans. In 1900 only 31 voted for Bryan, while McKinley won in no less than 95 counties.[48]

3

The Republican victory was quite clear-cut, but the frequent talk of a landslide does not give a fair picture of the situation. It has been shown here that McKinley lost about 8000 votes in the Middle Atlantic states, where Bryan increased his share by over 150,000. And in one group of particularly disputed states, Connecticut, Delaware, Illinois, Indiana, Maryland, New Jersey, New York and West Virginia, the Republican losses totalled more than 200,000 votes. These were states with a total of 131 electoral votes. At the same time it can be noted that over a quarter of a million of McKinley's gained votes came from states that only commanded 44 electoral votes.[49]

The Republicans, as was only to be expected, interpreted the election result as a clear repudiation of Bryan, and all that he and the Democrats stood for, and a corresponding endorsement of the Republican platform and policies. This applied also to the policy of expansion. Editorials in the Republican press used phrases such as, "We do not wish to be a hermit nation"; we have "upheld the foreign policy in a way that cannot be misunderstood"; we have declared "in favor of the expansion of the American nation to include territory other than that on the North American continent"; we "recognize the manifest destiny of this nation to be one of the greatest of modern world powers, and assert that that which is called Imperialism is but the indication of a healthy growth, properly termed expansion." "The people have decided, after deliberation, that it is not desirable that the Constitution follows the flag."[50] The New York *Tribune*, which had denied during the campaign that Imperialism was the issue and had instead played untiringly on the currency question, declared after the election that the Republican victory indicated that the voters had come down clearly on the side not only of gold, but also of expansion.[51]

In the same way, the result was said to show an acceptance of protection, the gold standard and the party's trust policy. This was obviously not true. President McKinley himself listed soon after the election half a dozen factors that had contributed to the Republican victory: 1) "Our splendid party" 2) "The Gold Democrats" 3) "The Silver Republicans" 4) "The almost unbroken column of mechanics and agricultural laborers" 5) "The home influence" 6) "The business interest."[52] If we exclude the party, it is quite plain that no consensus existed between the five named contributories on any one central issue. There was only one common denominator, but it was decisive: "They voted for *Prosperity* and against change," as William Allen put it.[53]

Tariffs played no part in either the campaign or the election results. This issue was given no more than three lines in the Kansas City platform. The reformation of the tariff had become the identification label of the Democratic party, just as the protective tariff had become that of the Republican party. But the issue was no longer of any importance. In fact, the election can be seen as confirming that the parties were turning into clans, held together by emotional attachments, rather than devices to attain certain economical and social goals. Party loyalty of an emotional nature was decisive, rather than ideological commitment. The publicist Albert Shaw wrote in an article in the *Contemporary Review* on the subject of the 1900 election that the politicians were "sincerely loyal to the party name, just as one man may be a tenacious Baptist without having the slightest reason for not being, like his neighbor, a tenacious Methodist, except that he was born into a Baptist instead of a Methodist family."[54]

The 1896 presidential election campaign had to some extent been an exception, with more clearly defined, objective disputes and an ideological revitalization. The silver issue, which had served as a focal point, was now obsolete, however, and to a large extent the voters returned to their old allegiances. As has been emphasized earlier, the silver issue had proved to be near enough stone dead when it came to attracting the voters in the presidential election of 1900. One should nevertheless not forget that the silver question had had a certain role to play in making it possible to present Bryan as a threat to the newly-won prosperity, to appeal to the sentiments that lingered from 1896. The silver issue can also have had a negative effect on the attitudes of the German voters and contributed to their failure to respond as the Democrats had hoped. The negative reactions of the German-language press to the Kansas City platform with its silver plank had admittedly provided a pointer, but the Democrats had still had great hopes of breaking through here with the help of "the paramount issue." Newspapers such as the *Westliche Post* (St. Louis), the Cincinatti *Volksblatt* and not least the New York *Staats-Zeitung* greeted Bryan's defeat with great satisfaction. All were anti-imperialistic, but as another German newspaper, *Germania* (Milwaukee), put it, when faced with a choice between silver and imperialism, they "regarded free silver as the greater evil."[55] Democratic German-language newspapers, which supported Bryan, claimed that the Democrats would have had a good chance of winning if Bryan had been willing to relinquish silver.[56]

Another issue that had been important earlier played as little part as the tariff question in the 1900 election, namely the Southern race question, which Albert Shaw described as "almost the only question entitled to be regarded as of the first political magnitude that had heretofore divided the Republican and Democratic parties."[57] The Democrats had an uncontested hold of the South, but that which had been called "bloody shirt politics" had totally disappeared. The race question had been eliminated from national party politics.

Thus, the two issues, race and tariff, which had previously been those that had primarily divided the parties, had hardly featured at all in the 1900 election campaign. "It is quite as novel a thing for the American citizen of mature years to go through a Presidential campaign without hearing the tariff question mentioned as to hear little or nothing of a controversial sort about the political and social status of the Southern negroes," remarked Albert Shaw in the article mentioned above.[58]

4

If then it was not the tariff, race or silver questions that decided the outcome of the election, was it after all "the paramount issue," that is, imperialism or the American colonial policy? This question has already been answered above, but it must once again be emphasized that the answer is negative.[59]

When the Democrats planned their campaign, there were a number of open or potential opponents to the re-election of McKinley outside their own party. These were Populists, both Fusionist and Middle-of-the-Road, Gold Democrats, Silver Republicans, Prohibitionists and Socialists (two different parties). Together they represented a substantial number of votes. Populists, Prohibitionists and Gold Democrats had together gathered considerably more than half a million votes in 1896. In addition to these groups, there was in some quarters of the Republican party strong opposition to McKinley. It was based on his civil service record, his trust policy, and not least the administration's Philippine policy. The strength of this opposition had been demonstrated in the fight over the Puerto Rican tariff in the spring.

In order to have any prospects of victory, Bryan and the Democrats had to win and retain Populists and Silver Republicans and at the same time break into the ranks of the Independents and if possible win back the groups that had bolted in 1896. In addition, if possible, the oppositional element within the Republican party should be won over. They were obviously heterogeneous groups, however, and the convention in Kansas City proclaimed as "the paramount issue" the only issue on which these elements that were opposed to McKinley were united, imperialism, and it was to this issue that Bryan also devoted almost his entire acceptance speech.

Yet it was not imperialism but prosperity that came to occupy the central position and finally to decide the outcome. Champ Clark, the well-known Democratic congressman from Missouri, tells a story about his experience on the campaign trail in 1900. He was speaking to an audience of farmers on imperialism when an old farmer called out: "Well, I guess we can stand it as long as hogs are twenty cents a hundred." In Clark's opinion arguments like that carried the Mississippi Valley for McKinley.[60] Since it was this "prosperity," "the full dinner pail," that formed the common base for the different pro-McKinley and anti-Bryan factions, the outcome was obvious. There is little doubt that Bryan's retention of the demand for free silver coinage had facilitated the shift made by the Republicans from imperialism to the prosperity line. In their deliberate use of scarifying tactics to make Bryan appear a threat to employment and prosperity, the Republicans had also received useful help from many employers and businessmen. It emerged that firms had informed their employees that the business would close down the day after Bryan's election. Contracts of employment and business contracts had been provided with a clause making them invalid if Bryan won in the election. In a thousand ways the voters had been given the impression that a vote for Bryan meant risking economic chaos and depression, while the re-election of McKinley would ensure continued good times.

Thus the presidential election of 1900 was more an election "for prosperity and against change" than a referendum on the new foreign policy and the status of the newly-acquired territories. It would be a mistake, however, to believe that the prominent part played by the question in the campaign and the violent and intensive debates it produced passed without a trace. On the contrary, the campaign came to have important and lasting consequences. The problems of the new expansionism had been illuminated and debated with an intensity that was highly educational. And one of the two great parties was on record as a categoric opponent to an imperialistic policy, that is to new colonial acquisitions of the type represented by the Philippines.

It has been clearly shown that tactical considerations played what was perhaps a decisive role in the process wereby the Democratic party worked out its stand for anti-imperialism. This does not alter the fact that, once the party line had been settled by adoption of the platform, it had immediate effects. These could be plainly observed in press opinion, where the Democratic newspapers adjusted to the party line in preparation for the election campaign. Since party identification was of considerable strength, this formulation of a party line against expansionism had direct consequences for the development of opinion among the Democrats, especially as it was proclaimed as the main issue during the campaign.

McKinley won the election. He and the Republicans gained about 52 per cent of the votes. It was a clear victory for the party that represented expansion. It was a well-known fact, however, that there were numerous independent and also Republican anti-imperialists, who could not bring themselves to support Bryan in the election because of his silver heresy and his populist leanings.

A negative opinion is much more powerful than a positive one. Here was a party with more than 45 per cent of the votes, which had backed a radical anti-imperialist line. The same attitude was to be found among a large proportion of the independent groups, which were traditionally considered to decide the outcome of elections. In such a situation there was no clear basis for an active expansionist foreign policy. It simply did not lie within the frame of opinion. Also, the differences that existed between the attitudes of Republicans and Democrats to foreign policy should not be exaggerated. The radical Republican expansionists as well as their counterpart, the extreme anti-imperialists, soon lost ground as their ideas and theories became obsolete and anachronistic.

The position of expansionism was weakened by another factor. In planning the line they were to take, the Democrats had simply appropriated the arguments and viewpoints which the radical anti-imperialist organizations had long expounded. This meant that humanitarian-idealistic and moral arguments predominated. This in turn meant that the Republicans had been driven to defend their expansionistic policy with arguments of the same kind—in other words, the "duty" line. Strategic and commercial-economic justifications became secondary. The annexations were presented as a task, a duty to humanity and civilization, which America had no right to shirk: a variation on the theme of the White Man's Burden. Such a position was vulnerable and was disasterously undermined by two factors. The first was the opposition shown by the people of the Philippines towards their American "liberators" and their refusal to show gratitude for the planned annexation, which was to pour blessings upon them. The second factor was the involvement of Great Britain in the Boer War, which released a strong anti-British reaction among ethnic groups such as the Germans and the Irish, and which became a difficult encumbrance for those Americans who dreamed of building an empire on the British model.

For such reasons then—the strength of the Democrats and the independents who were against imperialism, the unlovely spectacle in the Philippines, Britain's unattractive fight against the Boers—public opinion in the United States henceforth proved insufficiently powerful to allow an active policy of expansion.

A further important aspect must, however, be added to these. It has already been mentioned that an important role had been played in American expansionism by a dynamic group of politicians and publicists with powerful political ambitions for America as a Great Power. Following the victory over Spain, they had received support from the business world and groups with financial interests, who shared their belief in the threat of over-production at home and saw territorial expansion as one stage in the struggle for necessary new markets. But the era of colonial empires of the traditional type was in fact already over when the United States entered the race and the men of business and finance soon realized that commercial expansion did not at all necessitate territorial annexations, that these could on the contrary create new problems, not least with regard to the sacrosanct American tariff system.

310

Without the support of the business interests, and with several of the earlier most enthusiastic expansionists feeling considerably disillusioned by the Philippine adventure, the driving force of American imperialism in the traditional sense seeped away. At the same time, organized anti-imperialism also lost ground and the question that had been so violently controversial for almost three years was pushed into the background. The anti-imperialists were looking backwards to a society that no longer existed, the imperialists to a future world that never developed in the way they had prophesied. Neither side was any longer capable of mobilizing public opinion in support of a program of action.

Notes

Introduction

[1] J. A. Hobson, *Imperialism: A Study* (1902).
[2] V. J. Lenin, *Imperialism: The Highest Stage of Capitalism* (1917).
[3] Charles A. Beard, *The Idea of National Interest: An Analytical Study in American Foreign Policy* (1934).
[4] Marcus M. Wilkerson, *Public Opinion and the Spanish-American War: A Study in War Propaganda* (1932).
[5] Joseph E. Wisan, *The Cuban Crisis as Reflected in the New York Press, 1895—1898* (1934); George W. Auxier, "Middle-Western Newspapers and the Spanish-American War," 1895—1898 (in the *Mississippi Valley Historical Review XXVI*, 1940).
[6] Julius W. Pratt: "American Business and the Spanish-American War" (in *Hispanic American Historical Review, XIV,* 1934).
[7] Julius W. Pratt, *Expansionists of 1898: The Acquisition of Hawaii and the Spanish Islands* (1936). Cf. also Pratt, *America's Colonial Experiment* (1951).
[8] Dexter Perkins, *The Monroe Doctrine 1867—1907* (1937). Also *The American Approach to Foreign Policy* (1951).
[9] Thomas A. Bailey, *A Diplomatic History of the American People* (1950).
[10] Samuel Flagg Bemis, *A Diplomatic History of the United States* (1936).
[11] Robert E. Osgood, *Ideals and Self-Interest in America's Foreign Relations* (1953).
[12] Louis J. Halle, *Dream and Reality: Aspects of American Foreign Policy* (1959).
[13] Richard Hofstadter, "Manifest Destiny and the Philippines" (in Daniel Aaron, ed., *America in Crisis*, 1952).
[14] Selig Adler, *The Isolationist Impulse* (1957).
[15] Howard K. Beale, *Theodore Roosevelt and the Rise of America to World Power* (1956).
[16] Foster Rhea Dulles, *America's Rise to World Power, 1898—1954* (1954). Cf. also, Dulles, *Prelude to World Power* (1965).
[17] Oscar Handlin, *Chance or Destiny: Turningpoints in American History* (1945).
[17a] William A. Leuchtenburg, "The Needless War with Spain." In *Times on Trial,* ed. by Allan Nevins (1958).
[18] Nancy Leonore O'Connor, "The Spanish-American War: A Re-evaluation of Its Causes" (in *Science and Society*).
[19] William A. Williams, *The Tragedy of American Diplomacy, 1750—1955* (1959).
[20] William A. Williams, *The Contours of American History* (1961).
[21] William A. Williams, *The Roots of the Modern American Empire. A Study of the Growth and Shaping of Social Consciousness in a Marketplace Society* (1969). Cf. also, Robert Levin, "An Interpretation of American Imperialism" (in *Journal of Economic History* 32, 1972).
[22] Charles Vevier, "American Continentalism: An Idea of Expansion, 1845—1910" (in *American Historical Review* 65, 1960).

[23] Walter LaFeber, *The New Empire: An Interpretation of American Expansion, 1866—1898* (1963).

[24] Thomas J. McCormick, "A Fair Field and No Favor": American China Policy during the McKinley Administrations, 1897—1901 (Ph.D. diss., Univ. of Wisconsin 1960); and *China Market: America's Quest for Informal Empire, 1893—1901* (1967).

[25] Charles S. Campbell, Jr., "American Business Interest and the Open Door" (also in Campbell, *Special Business Interests and the Open Door Policy*, 1951).

[26] Paul A. Varg, *The Making of a Myth: The United States and China, 1897—1912* (1968).

[27] Marilyn Blatt Young, *The Rhetoric of Empire: American China Policy, 1895—1901* (1968). Also, "American Expansion 1870—1900: The Far East" (in *Towards a New Past*, ed. by Barton J. Bernstein, 1968).

[28] William J. Pomeroy, *American Neo-Colonialism: Its Emergence in the Philippines and Asia* (1970).

[29] Philip S. Foner, *The Spanish-Cuban-American War and the Birth of American Imperialism, I—II* (1972). Also Foner, "Why the United states Went to War with Spain in 1898" (in *Science and Society*, 32, 1968).

[30] Ernest R. May, *Imperial Democracy: The Emergence of America as a Great Power* (1961). Cf. also, May, *American Imperialism. A Speculative Essay* (1968).

[31] Harold U. Faulkner, *Politics, Reform and Expansion, 1890—1900* (1959).

[32] Frank Freidel, *The Splendid Little War* (1958).

[33] Margaret Leech, *In the Days of McKinley* (1959).

[34] H. Wayne Morgan, *William McKinley and His America* (1963). Cf. also Morgan, *America's Road to Empire* (1965).

[35] Richard W. Van Alstyne, *The Rising American Empire* (1960). Cf. also Frederick Merk, *Manifest Destiny and Mission in American History. A Reinterpretation* (1963).

[36] Robert H. Ferrell, *American Diplomacy: A History* (1959).

[37] Alexander DeConde, *A History of American Foreign Policy* (1963).

[38] Richard W. Leopold, *The Growth of American Foreign Policy* (1962).

[39] Daniel M. Smith, *The American Diplomatic Experience* (1972).

[40] David Healy, *U.S. Expansionism: The Imperialist Urge in the 1890's* (1970).

[41] John A. S. Grenville and George Berkeley Young, *Politics, Strategy, and American Diplomacy: Studies in Foreign Policy, 1873—1917* (1966).

[42] Osgood, *op. cit.*

[43] *Op. cit.*

[44] Ernest R. May, *op. cit.*

Chapter I

[1] Charles A. Beard, *The Idea of National Interest. An Analytical Study in American Foreign Policy* (1934), p. 50 ff. Over the years Manifest Destiny came to have varying implications and was cited in justification of the most widely differing programs. Cf. above all Albert K. Weinberg, *Manifest Destiny. A Study of Nationalist Expansionism in American History* (1935, pb. 1963).

[2] The New York *World*, Aug. 27, 1898.

[3] The *American Grocer*, Sept. 24, 1898.

[4] Cf. below, p. 34 f.

[5] Cf. Grenville and Young, *Politics, Strategy and American Diplomacy* (1966), p. 229 f. The planned canal between the Atlantic and Pacific Oceans provided the

expansionists with arguments which they often exploited. They stressed the importance of the U.S. being able to control the approaches to the canal both in the East and the West, and in addition to Cuba, other islands such as Santo Domingo and St. Thomas were also mentioned. Julius Pratt, *Expansionists of 1898,* p. 151 f.

[6] H. Cabot Lodge, "Our Blundering Foreign Policy," the *Forum* XII, 1895, p. 8 f. On Lodge see John A. Garraty, *Henry Cabot Lodge. A Biography* (1953), p. 144 ff.

[7] Albert Shaw to Andrew Carnegie, Andrew Carnegie Papers, LC.

[8] The *Arena*, Vol. XXIII: 4, April 1900, p. 337 ff.

[9] Elmer Ellis, *Henry Moore Teller: Defender of the West* (1941), p. 308.

[10] *Op. cit.,* p. 312 f.

[11] Frederick Merk, *Manifest Destiny and Mission in American History. A Reinterpretation* (1963), p. 221 ff.

[12] Cf. Pratt, *op. cit.,* p. 223 f.

[13] The Chicago *Journal*, Sept. 8, Cincinnati *Enquirer*, October 13, New York *Times,* October 13, 1900.

[14] The Jacksonville *Times-Union*, July 9, 1898.

[15] M. Halstead to W. McKinley, March 12, 1900. McKinley Papers, LC.

[16] Grenville and Young, however, warn quite rightly against stressing too strongly the influence of Lodge and Roosevelt prior to the war. *Op. cit.,* p. 268 ff. Cf. also Theodore Roosevelt's review of Captain Mahan's *The Influence of Sea Power upon History, 1660—1783. The Writings of Theodore Roosevelt* (1967), ed. by William H. Harbaugh, p. 36 ff.

[17] Congr. Record, 55th Congress, 3rd session, p. 959; cf. Pratt, *op. cit.,* p. 345 ff.

[18] Among these were the Atlanta *Constitution* and its editor Clark Howell, and the Indianapolis *Journal* (cf. below, p. 104) and others.

[19] Cf. below, p. 80 ff.

[20] Cf. D. Healy, *U.S. Expansionism; The Imperialist Urge in the 1890's* (1970), p. 52 ff.

[21] From a speech by Whitelaw Reid in Chicago, Feb. 13, 1899. R. I. Fulton and Thomas C. Trueblood (ed.), *Patriotic Eloquence Relating to the Spanish-American War and Its Issues* (1900), p. 232 f.

[22] On Reid and foreign policy, cf. Ernest R. May, *American Imperialism: A Speculative Essay* (1967), p. 59 ff.

[23] From a speech by Henry Cabot Lodge in Boston, Oct. 30, 1899. *Patriotic Eloquence,* p. 194 f. Among those who just as firmly fought the integrationists were also Senator William Lindsay from Kentucky. Speech Aug. 28, 1899. *Patriotic Eloquence,* p. 187 f.

[24] Walter LaFeber, *The New Empire. An Interpretation of American Expansion, 1860—1898* (1963), p. 24. Cf. W. A. Williams, *The Roots of the Modern American Empire. A Study of the Growth and Shaping of Social Consciousness in a Marketplace Society* (1969), p. 432 ff.

[25] F. Emory, *op. cit.*

[26] On Albert Beveridge, cf. below, p. 110 ff.

[27] R. Van Bergen, "Expansion Unavoidable." *Harper's Weekly*, XLIV (1900), p. 885 ff.

[28] David Healy, *op. cit.,* p. 178 ff. On Denby cf. also below, p. 77 and 283. Another enthusiastic expansionist with a similar background to Denby was John Barrett, former American minister to Siam. In articles such as "The Philippines, Our Approach to Asia" (*Harper's Weekly*, July 1900) and "A McKinley Doctrine for Asia" (the *North American Review*, Aug. 1899) he energetically advocated American commercial expansion in the Far East.

[29] The *Age of Steel*, May 21, 1898. Cf. Pratt, *op. cit.,* p. 269 f.

[30] Charles A. Conant, "The United States as a World Power." I. "The Nature of the Economic and Political Problem" (The *Forum*, July 1900); II. "Her Advantage in the Competition for Commercial Empire" (*ibid.*, Aug. 1900). — In a letter to Richard Olney, Conant summarized his view of the motive for the annexation of the Philippines: "/The Philippines/ will afford openings for the investment of American surplus capital." Conant to Richard Olney, March 21, 1900. Richard Olney Papers, LC.

[31] The *Forum*, Aug. 1900.

[32] *The Republican National Convention 1900. Proceedings.*

[33] Cf. W. A. Williams, *op. cit.*

[34] The overall role played by commercialism, economic expansionism, has been stressed by a number of writers, most recently, for example, by Thomas J. McCormick, *China Market. America's Quest for Informal Empire, 1893—1901* (1967), and Williams, *op. cit.*

[35] Cf. W. A. Williams, *op. cit.*, p. 432 ff.

[36] Charles A. Conant, The *Forum*, July 1900.

[37] The Chicago *Inter-Ocean*, Aug. 27, 1900.

[38] A. H. Mahan, "Sea Power and Expansion," The *Engineering Magazine*, Jan. 1900.

[39] Frederick Jackson Turner, "The Problem of the West," *Atlantic Monthly*, Sept. 1896, p. 289 ff. LaFeber, *op. cit.*, p. 70. For Turner on Expansionism, see also Williams, *op. cit.*, p. XII ff.

[40] Brooks Adams, *The Law of Civilization and Decay: An Essay on History* (1895). Arthur F. Beringause, *Brooks Adams: A Biography* (1955), p. 129 ff., LaFeber, p. 80 ff. For Brooks Adams' view of contemporary developments in world politics, cf. also e.g. Osgood, p. 63 ff., Healy, p. 101 ff. and Richard Hofstadter, *Social Darwinism in American Thought* (1944), p. 186 ff.

[41] Brooks Adams to Henry Cabot Lodge, June 26, 1900. Henry Cabot Lodge Papers, Mass. Hist. Society, Boston.

[42] Henry Cabot Lodge to W. McKinley, Oct. 22, 1900. McKinley Papers, LC.

[43] James C. Fernald, *The Imperial Republic* (1898), p. 64.

[44] The Indianapolis *Journal*, Sept. 20, 1900.

[45] The Indianapolis *Journal*, May 25, 1900.

[46] Cf. below, p. 246 ff.

[47] An excellent presentation of Mahan's ideas and his influence on Lodge and Roosevelt is given in John A. S. Grenville and George Berkely Young, *Politics, Strategy and American Diplomacy* (1966), p. 201 ff. On Roosevelt and Mahan see also e.g. Howard K. Beale, *Theodore Roosevelt and the Rise of America to World Power* (1956), p. 14 ff. Cf. also Robert E. Osgood, *Ideals and Self-Interest in America's Foreign Relations. The Great Transformation of the Twentieth Century* (1953), p. 32 ff.

[48] On Mahan see also e.g. Pratt, *op. cit.*, p. 12 ff.

[49] Whitelaw Reid, *Problems of Expansion*.

[50] Below, p. 246 f.

[51] Chicago, Oct. 16, 1898. *Patriotic Eloquence*, p. 290 f.

[52] Chicago, Oct. 18, 1898. *Ibid.*, p. 167 f.

[53] E. R. May, *Imperial Democracy*, p. 19 f.

[54] The New York *Herald*, June 2, 1898. Watterson had yet another argument in favor of expansion: "We escape the menace and peril of socialism . . . by a policy of colonialization and conquest." *Ibid.*

[55] Robert E. Osgood, *Ideals and Self-Interest in America's Foreign Relations* (1953), p. 1 ff.

[56] Peter F. Dunne, The Chicago *Journal*, The *Literary Digest*, Dec. 17, 1898.

315

[57] Thomas A. Bailey, *The Art of Diplomacy: The American Experience* (1968), p. 160.

[58] E.g. George R. Peck, Dec. 15, 1898. *Patriotic Eloquence*, p. 243 f.

[59] E.g. Cushman K. Davis, Senator from Minnesota, Chairman of the Committee on Foreign Relations, in a speech on Feb. 22, 1900. *Patriotic Eloquence*, p. 106 f.

[60] E.g. McKinley, Oct. 19, 1898. *Ibid.*, p. 218 ff.

[61] Charles Kendall Adams, "Colonies and Other Dependencies." The *Forum*, March 1900.

[62] F. H. Giddings, "Imperialism." *Political Science Quarterly*, Feb. 1899.

[63] Chicago *Tribune*, Sept. 18, 1898.

[64] Quoted by Albert K. Weinberg, *Manifest Destiny. A Study of Nationalist Expansionism in American History* (1935), p. 259.

[65] On this circle of motives, see the thorough and fundamental study by Weinberg, named above.

[66] *Op. cit.*, p. 270 ff.

[67] Orville H. Platt, Senator from Connecticut, quoted in Louis A. Coolidge, *An Old-fashioned Senator; Orville H. Platt* (1910). Cf. Healy, *op. cit.*, p. 131.

[68] Robert E. Osgood, *Ideal and Self-Interest in America's Foreign Relations* (1953), p. 35 ff.

[69] The *Outlook*, 1898.

[70] Cf. below, p. 48.

[71] The Baltimore *Sun, Public Opinion*, Jan. 18, 1900.

[71a] J. G. Schurman, "Our duty in the Philippines." Address delivered before the Union League of Philadelphia, Nov. 25, 1899. *Gunton's Magazine*, Jan. 1900. Cf. also J. G. Schurman, "The Problem of Territorial Expansion." The *Rieview of Reviews*, Oct. 1899.

[71b] The *Outlook*, Sept. 1898.

[72] The Chicago *Times-Herald*, July 1898.

[73] The *American Grocer*, Sept. 24, 1898.

[74] According to an estimate made by the First Philippine Commission, there were about 6.5 million Christians on the Philippines. Report, Senate Document No. 138. 56th Congress, 1st Sess., p. 107. On the view taken by the American Catholics of the policy of expansion, cf. Frank T. Reuter, *Catholic Influence on American Colonial Policies, 1898—1904*.

[75] Robert E. Speer, *Mission and Modern History* (1904).

[76] On the attitudes of various Christian bodies to the policy of expansion, cf. e.g. Frank T. Reuter, *op. cit.*; William J. Pomeroy, *American Neo-Colonialism. Its Emergence in the Philippines and Asia* (1970), p. 47 f.; Julius W. Pratt, *Expansionists of 1898. The Acquisition of Hawaii and the Spanish Islands* (1935), p. 279 ff.

[77] Cited by E. R. May, *Imperial Democracy: The Emergence of America as a Great Power* (1961), p. 248.

[78] *Patriotic Eloquence*, p. 21 ff.

[79] *Op. cit.*, p. 11 ff.

[80] In July 1900 the Boston *Herald* made a poll of fifteen cities and found that in all the cities concerned, it was the clergymen who were the most enthusiastic supporters of an expansionist policy. Marylin Blatt Young, *The Rhetoric of Empire*, p. 143.

[81] The *Journal of Social Science*, Nov. 37. Sept. 1899, p. 99 ff.

[82] The Chicago *Times-Herald*, Oct. 20, 1900.

[83] *Patriotic Eloquence*, p. 1 ff.

[84] *Ibid.*, p. 122 ff. Cf. also e.g. Henry Watterson, Editor of the Louisville *Courier-*

Journal, ibid., p. 337 f.

[85] *Patriotic Eloquence*, p. 304 ff.

[86] On Social Darwinism, see primarily Richard Hofstadter, *Social Darwinism in American Thought* (1945), p. 170 ff.

[87] Congressional Record, 55th Congress, 2nd session, p. 5766 ff. On anti-imperialists and the racial issue, cf. Christopher Lasch, "Anti-Imperialists, the Philippines, and the Inequality of Man." The *Journal of Southern History* XXIV, 1958.

[88] James M. Griggs, "Speech in Home District 1898." Scrapbook 1898. James M. Griggs Papers, Southern Historical Collection, Chapel Hill. On the racial question and American imperialism, see further Rubin Francis Weston, *Racism in U.S. Imperialism. The Influence of Racial Assumptions on American Foreign Policy, 1893—1946* (1972).

[89] *The Banker's Magazine*, Sept. 24, 1898.

[90] The *Forum*, July 1900.

[91] The Detroit *Tribune*, July 9, 1898.

[92] Robert E. Speer, *Mission and Modern History* (1904).

[93] Theodore Marburg, *Expansion* (1900, Reprinted from The *American*). Cf. D. Healy, *U.S. Expansionism*, p. 28 f.

[94] Josiah Strong, *Our Country: Its Possible Future and Its Present Crisis* (1885), p. 208 ff. On Strong see e.g. LaFeber, p. 72 ff.

[95] John Fiske, "Manifest Destiny." *Harper's New Monthly Magazine*, LXX (1885), p. 578 ff. Cf. Julius Pratt, *Expansionists of 1898* (1936), p. 3 ff., and E. R. May, *Imperial Democracy* (1961), p. 8.

[96] John W. Burgess, *Political Science and Comparative Constitutional Law*, I (1890), p. 30 ff. J. Pratt, *op. cit.*, p. 6 ff.

[97] See e.g. Howard K. Beale, *Theodore Roosevelt and the Rise of America to World Power*, p. 26 ff. and Richard Hofstadter, *Social Darwinism in American Thought*, p. 170 ff.

[98] "I hope that every man who strives to be efficient and moral will realize that it is for the interest of mankind to have civilization go forward, to have the higher supplant the lower life," stated Roosevelt in a speech made in the fall of 1898. Address by Theodore Roosevelt at the New England Dinner in Brooklyn, The *Outlook*, Dec. 31, 1898. In his book *The War with Spain*, published 1899, Henry Cabot Lodge claimed that the annexations in the Pacific "came from the instinct of the race, which paused in California only to learn that its course was still westward, and that Americans, and no one else, must be masters of the cross-roads of the Pacific," p. 235. On Lodge and America's destiny, cf. also Richard E. Welch, Jr., "Opponents and Colleagues: George Frisbie Hoar and Henry Cabot Lodge, 1898—1904." The *New England Quarterly*, p. 192 ff.

[99] The Chicago *Tribune*, May 3, 1898.

[100] J. T. Hudson, "Evolution and the Spanish-American War"; The *National Magazine*, Feb. 1899.

[101] The Boston *Transcript*, Jan. 21, 1899.

[102] H. H. Powers, "The Ethics of Expansion," *The International Journal of Ethics*, X, April 1900. Cf. Osgood, *op. cit.*, p. 65.

[103] H. H. Powers, "The War as a Suggestion of Manifest Destiny." *Publication of the American Academy of Political and Social Science*, No. 235, Oct. 4, 1898.

[104] The Boston *Transcript*, Nov. 22, 1898.

[105] Congressional Rec., 56th Congress, 1st session, p. 2621.

[106] Albert Beveridge to John Temple Graves. Jan. 26, 1900 (copy). Albert Beveridge Papers, LC. On Beveridge's concept of race, cf. Daniel Levine, "The Social Philosophy of Albert J. Beveridge," *Indiana Magazine of History*, June 1962.

[107] W. Reid, *Problems of Expansion*.

[108] Cf. below, p. 221 ff.

[109] William McKinley, Speech at Banquet of the Ohio Society of New York, March 3, 1900. *Speeches and Addresses of William McKinley* (1900), p. 363 ff. McKinley had expounded the same ideas earlier, e.g. in a speech on Dec. 15, 1898. He then described the war against Spain as "a supreme duty," which in its turn created new duties which should not be shirked. *Patriotic Eloquence*, p. 218 ff.

[110] The *Outlook*, Dec. 31, 1898.

[111] The *Literary Digest*, Nov. 6, 1899.

[112] *Patriotic Eloquence*, p. 211.

[113] Charles S. Olcott, *The Life of William McKinley*, II (1916), p. 110 f. Cf. Charles A. Beard, *The Idea of National Interest*, p. 254 ff.

[114] E. R. May, *Imperial Democracy*, p. 252 f.

[115] Washington Gladden, "The Issues of War," The *Outlook*, July 16, 1898.

[116] Quoted in Walter Millis, *The Martial Spirit. A Study of Our War with Spain* (1965, 1 ed. 1931), p. 408.

[117] See below, p. 200 f.

[118] The Indianapolis *Journal*, June 22, 1900.

[119] Speeches 1900. Theodore Roosevelt Papers, LC. Roosevelt romanticized the war. His declaration that "no triumph of peace is quite the same as the supreme triumphs of war" has often been quoted. In 1889 he had hoped for "a bit of a spar with Germany." In 1895, in the conflict over Venezuela, he looked forward to a war against Great Britain: "Let the fight come if it must . . . I don't care whether our sea coast cities are bombarded or not; we would take Canada," he wrote to Cabot Lodge. Theodore Roosevelt to H. Cabot Lodge, Dec. 20, 1895. Cit. from Beale, *op. cit.*, p. 51. And Roosevelt was naturally very enthusiastic over the war against Spain. "In strict confidence, . . . I should welcome almost any war, for I think this country needs one," he wrote to a friend six months before war broke out. Theodore Roosevelt to Francis V. Greene, Sept. 23, 1897. Beale, p. 37. On Roosevelt's attitude to the war, cf. also e.g. Osgood, p. 45 f., and Healy, p. 119.

[120] E. Berkeley Tompkins, "The Old Guard: A Study of the Anti-Imperialist Leadership." *The Historian*, XXX: 3 (1963), p. 386 f.

[121] The Chicago *Times-Herald*, July 9, 1898. Cf. Walter Millis, *The Martial Spirit. A Study of Our War with Spain* (1931), p. 317. The Chicago *Tribune*, Sept. 27, 1899.

[122] Richard Hofstadter, "Manifest Destiny and the Philippines" (in *America in Crises*, ed. by D. Aaron [1952]), p. 173 ff. Cf. also Marylin Blatt Young, *The Rhetoric of Empire: American China Policy, 1895—1901* (1968), p. 4 f. On social unrest as a breeding ground for imperialism, cf. also Thomas J. McCormick, *China Market. America's Quest for Informal Empire, 1893—1901* (1967), p. 21 ff.

[123] Franklin Giddings, *Political Science Quarterly*, Feb. 1899.

Chapter II

[1] Cf. above, p. 25 ff.

[2] Above, p. 32 f.

[3] On the Insular Commission and the efforts made by the Puerto Ricans to gain a hearing for their demand for free trade, see Edward J. Berbusse, *The United States in Puerto Rico, 1898—1900* (1966), p. 111 ff.

[4] Cf. below, p. 70 ff.

[5] Pomeroy, *op. cit.*, p. 25.

[6] *Op. cit.*, p. 105.

[7] A. L. Lowell, "The Colonial Expansion of the United States," The *Atlantic Monthly*, Feb. 1899, p. 145 ff. The debate continued the following year with two contributions, John Gorham Palfrey, "The Growth of the Idea of Annexation and Its Bearing upon Constitutional Law," *Harvard Law Review* (HLR), XIII, Jan. 1900; Alexander Peter Morse, "The Civil and Political Status of Inhabitants of Ceded Territories," *Harward Law Review*, XIV, Dec. 1900 p. 262 ff.

[8] *Harvard Law Review*, XII: 5, Jan. 1899, p. 291 ff. The essay is dated Dec. 11, 1898.

[9] *Ibid.*, p. 314 f. Cf. also C. F. Randolph, "Notes on the Law of Territorial Expansion" (1900), and "The Law and Policy of Annexation" (1901).

[10] George Wharton Pepper, "Our National Constitution as Related to National Growth. A Consideration of Certain Aspects of Our War with Spain." *Annual Address, June 6, 1898.*

[11] Simeon E. Baldwin, "The Constitutional Questions Incident to the Acquisition and Government of the United States of Island Territory," *Harvard Law Review*, Feb. 1899, p. 404 ff.

[12] *Ibid.*, p. 415 f.

[13] On Burgess, cf. above, p. 50 f.

[14] John W. Burgess, "How May the United States Govern Its Extra-Continental Territory?" *Political Science Quarterly*, Vol. XIV: 1, March 1899, p. 1 ff.

[15] John W. Burgess, "The Relation of the Constitution of the United States to newly acquired Territory," *Political Science Quarterly*, XV, Sept. 1900, p. 381 ff.

[16] Ernst Freund, "The Control of Dependencies through Protectorates," *Political Science Quarterly*, XIV, March 1899, p. 19 ff.

[17] Harry Pratt Judson, "Our Federal Constitution and the Government of Tropical Territories," The *Review of Reviews*, Jan. 1899, p. 67 ff.

[18] C. C. Langdell, "The Status of Our New Territories," *Harvard Law Review*, XII, Feb. 1899, p. 365 ff. The sheet is dated Jan. 25.

[19] See above, p. 61 f. and p. 64.

[20] The text is taken from a lecture held on Jan. 9. James Bradley Thayer, "Our New Possessions," *Harvard Law Review*, XII, March 1899, p. 464 ff.

[21] Abbot Lawrence Lowell, "The Status of Our New Possessions.—A third View." *Harvard Law Review*, XIII, Nov. 1899, p. 155 ff. Cf. also Julius W. Pratt, *America's Colonial Experiment* (1950), p. 159 f.

[22] A further variation in interpretation of the term "United States" was made by Carl Becker in the 1900 November issue of the *Annals of the American Academy of Political and Social Science*. According to Becker, this question could not be answered on the basis of the Constitution, since the term was used there sometimes in a more limited sense and sometimes in a wider one. If one instead went to the Supreme Court, it could be seen that the expression was there taken as meaning the *States and the territories,* while Congress had usually defined the *United States* as meaning the states alone. This emerged from the fact that when a new territory had been acquired and a civil government established, Congress had by specific legislative action extended to it the constitution and laws of the United States. However, in practice Congress had never exceeded the constitutional bounds of its own power as stated in the Constitution. Thus the line that Becker considered to apply was in fact the one that had been followed, namely that Congress had in the territories all legislative power not specifically denied to it by the Constitution. Carl Becker, "Law and Practise of the United States in the Acquisition and Government of Dependent Territory", *Annals of the American Academy of Political and Social Science*, Vol. XVI, Nov. 1900 (essay dated June), p. 404 ff.

[23] Cf. Whitney T. Perkins, *Denial of Empire. The United States and Its Dependencies* (1962), p. 116.

[24] H. K. Carroll, *Report on Puerto Rico. Its Population, Civil Government, Commerce, Industries, Productions, Roads, Tariff and Currency, with Recommendations.* Submitted Oct. 6, 1899 (1899).

[25] The *Forum*, XXVIII, Nov. 1899, p. 257 ff.

[26] The *Forum*, Nov. 1899, p. 263 f.

[27] See above, p. 67. Cf. Perkins, *op. cit.*, p. 117.

[28] *Report of the United States Insular Commission to the Secretary of War,* and The *Forum*, Dec. 1899, p. 403 ff.

[29] Richard W. Leopold, *Elihu Root and the Conservative Tradition* (1954), p. 25 ff., Margaret Leech, *In the Days of McKinley* (1963), p. 394 f.

[30] Cf. Worthington C. Ford, "Trade Policy with the Colonies," *Harper's Monthly Magazine*, July 1899, p. 293 ff. In some quarters the possibility was also entertained of the Philippines being admitted into the American tariff area. Cf. e.g. the Indianapolis *News*, April 18, 1899.

[31] The New York *Press*, Dec. 7, 1899.

[32] The New York *World*, Dec. 10, 1899.

[33] The *Literary Digest*, Dec. 16, 1899.

[34] Hearings: Senate Committee on Pacific Islands, 56th Congress 1st Session, Document No. 147. Cf. Berbusse, på 155 ff. Oxnard had supported the Anti-Imperialist Movement long before the Puerto Rican tariff crisis. E. Winslow to Edward Atkinson, Jan. 19, 1899. Edward Atkinson Papers, Mass. Hist. Society, Boston.

[35] *Ibid.* Also Cong Record, 56th Congress, 1st Session, Feb. 19, 1900, p. 2041. Cf. *The Democratic Campaign Handbook 1900*, p. 170 f.

[36] Cf. E. Berkeley Tompkins, "The Old Guard": A Study of Anti-Imperialist Leadership." The *Historian*, XXX: 3 (May 1963), p. 369. Herbert Myrick had like Henry Oxnard long supported the anti-imperialists. Edward Atkinson to Senator Hoar, Dec. 19, 1900; to E. B. Smith, Dec. 29, 1900. Edward Atkinson Papers, Mass. Hist. Society, Boston. Cf. also Schirmer, *op. cit.*, p. 150 and 208.

[38] Appel, *op. cit.*, p. 230 ff.

[39] The *Review of Reviews*, Vol. 21, Jan. 1900.

[40] The New York *Press*, Jan. 25, 1900.

[41] On Reid, se above, p. 33.

[42] Reid to J. B. Foraker, Feb. 5, 1900 (copy). Whitelaw Reid Papers, LC.

[43] Reid to John Hay, Feb. 9, 1900 (copy). Cf. Hay to Reid, Feb. 2, 1900, *ibid.*

[44] Cf. Reid's letters to John Hay, Feb. 7, Sept. 1 and Sept. 20, 1900, *ibid.*

[45] Reid to C. Davis, March 12; April 23, 1900, cf. Reid to Albert Beveridge, March 12, *ibid.*

[46] C. Davis to Reid, March 20 and April 7, 1900, *ibid.*

[47] Congr. Record, 56th Congr., 1st session, pp. 702, 1010.

[48] On the Foraker Act see Gordon K. Lewis, *Puerto Rico. Freedom and Power in the Carribean* (1968), p. 48 ff. Lewis shows that the Foraker Act in fact was far less liberal than the Spanish Autonomy Charter of 1897.

[49] Charles G. Dawes, *A Journal of The McKinley Years* (1950), p. 217.

[50] House Report No. 249, 56th Congress, 1st Session, Feb. 8, 1900. It is misleading to state as Braeman does, that McKinley reversed his stand and supported the bill. The Committee acted in agreement with the administration from the start. John Braeman, *Albert J. Beveridge: American Nationalist* (1971), p. 47.

[51] Senate Report No. 249, 56th Congress, 1st Session. Cf. Whitney Perkins, *Denial of Empire. The United States and Its Dependencies* (1962), p. 119 f.

[52] The importance of racial fears as a factor in the opposition to free trade for

Puerto Rico is stressed by Rubin Francis Weston, *Racism in U.S. Imperialism. The Influence of Racial Assumptions on American Foreign Policy, 1893—1946* (1972), p. 192 f.

[53] Congressional Record, 56th Congress, 1st Session, pp. 2073 f.

[54] *Ibid.*, p. 2079 f.

[55] *Ibid.*, p. 1951 ff.

[56] Cf. above, p. 68.

[57] Littlefield made a speech on Feb. 23 against the proposed measure.

[58] The *Outlook*, March 17, 1900.

[59] Speech of J. B. Foraker in the Senate, Jan. 11, 1900. *Speeches of J. B. Foraker*, II, No. E 660, L. C. Berbusse, p. 161. Cf. W. Mason to Edward Atkinson, March 12, 1900, E. Atkinson Papers, Mass. Hist. Society, Boston.

[60] Ross spoke in favor of this resolution. *The Republican campaign book for the Presidential election*, p. 379—389.

[61] See above, p. 66.

[62] *Ibid.* Cf. also Joseph B. Foraker, *Notes of a Busy Life*, II (1916), p. 77 ff.

[63] Cf. above, p. 66 ff.

[64] Speech of J. B. Foraker in the Senate, March 8, 1900.

[65] Joseph B. Foraker, The *North American Review*, April 1900.

[66] Cf. Foraker in *"Notes of a Busy Life*, II" (1916), p. 66 ff.

[67] R. Proctor to Elihu Root, March 30, 1900. Elihu Root Papers, LC. A powerful speech was also made by Senator Chauncey Depew, one of the most articulate globalists, with market expansion as its main argument (cf. above, p. 37). Chauncey Depew Papers, Washington University Library, Washington, D.C. Also in Chauncey M. Depew, *Orations, Addresses and Speeches*, Vol. VII (1910), p. 15 ff.

[68] See below, p. 118.

[69] Below, p. 122.

[70] Extracts from the *Campaign Handbook 1900*, p. 175 ff.

[71] Cited in the *Democratic Campaign Book*, p. 194.

[72] Cf. below, p. 98 ff.

[73] The Chicago *Times-Herald*, Minneapolis *Journal*. The expressions are common.

[74] H. M. Lewis to John C. Spooner, March 23, 1900; John K. Parish to Spooner, March 31, 1900. John C. Spooner Papers, LC.

[75] The *Literary Digest*, March 3, 1900.

[76] Other determined opponents to the bill were the Salt Lake *Tribune*, the Portland *Oregonian*, the San Francisco *Chronicle*, the Milwaukee *Sentinel et al.*

[77] In an article "The Constitution and the Flag," The *Forum*, May 1900. Denby, a conservative Democrat and expansionist, was himself a colonialist. Cf. above, p. 35.

[78] Contrary to Lowell, however, Mr. Justice White established that incorporation could be accomplished only with the express or implied consent of Congress, not by the treaty-making power alone.

[79] Cf. Julius W. Pratt, *America's Colonial Experience*, p. 216.

[80] Quoted in Beisner, *op. cit.*, p. 216.

[81] P. F. Dunne, *Mr. Dooley's Opinions* (1901), p. 26.

[82] Cf. Reid to Beveridge, March 12, 1900. Whitelaw Reid Papers, LC. Reid to Cushman K. Davis, April 23, 1900 (copy), *ibid.*

[83] Cf. below, p. 104 f.

[84] The fact that these two newspapers both followed the "flag line" is naturally not surprising, but on a previous occasion they had actually expressed the opposite view. The question of whether or not Congress when legislating for the territories was bound by the Constitution had in the summer of 1898 been tested by a court of law,

in a test case before the United States circuit court of appeals in San Francisco. The case concerned a decision by Congress that forbade the sale of alcoholic drinks to Alaska without special permission. The case was handled by Judge Morrow, who maintained in his decision "the now well established doctrine that the territories of the United States are entirely subject to the legislative authority of Congress. They are not organized under the Constitution nor subject to its complex distribution of the powers of government as the organic law, but are the creation, exclusively, of the legislative department, and subject to its supervision and control." The decision roused special interest since it was thought to decide the matter also for possible new acquisitions, Puerto Rico, the Philippines etc. Among the newspapers that then clearly backed the principle declared by Judge Morrow were both the New York *Evening Post* and the Springfield *Republican*. Thus they swung later during the intensified fight between expansionists and anti-imperialists.

Chapter III

[1] New York, Pennsylvania, Illinois and Ohio. Massachusetts had the same number as Indiana.

[2] Cf. below, p. 234 f. Also Flavius J. Van Vorhis, Chairman of the Indiana Silver Republican Committee, to Senator Marion Butler, April 10, 1900. Marion Butler Papers, Southern Historical Collection, Chapel Hill.

[3] John D. Barnhart and Donald F. Carmony, *Indiana. From Frontier to Industrial Commonwealth*, II, p. 433.

[4] Barnart and Carmony, *op. cit.*, p. 299. Indiana had a population of 2.52 million. 55.2 % were strictly rural and 44.8 urban, including small towns. S. S. Visher, *Economic Geography of Indiana*, p. 46.

[5] Evansville with 59,000 followed by Fort Wayne 45,000, Terre Haute 37,000 and South Bend 36,000. O. Dee Morrison, *Indiana "Hoosier State,"* I (1958), p. 44.

[6] Harvey L. Carter, "Indiana—Hell Bent for Election. Some Notes on Hoosier Politics." *Indiana Magazine of History*, XLI (1945).

[7] Mark Sullivan, *Our Times. The United States 1900—1925*, I (1926), p. 3 f.

[8] Smith, W. H., *The Life and Speeches of Hon Charles Warren Fairbanks* (1904), p. 97.

[9] On Beveridge see above, p. 44 and below, p. 110 ff.

[10] Charles Warren Fairbanks Papers, Lilly Library, Bloomington, Ind.; Albert J. Beveridge Papers, Library of Congress (LC).

[11] *Gunton's Magazine*, Nov. 1900, p. 418 f.

[12] The Indianapolis *Journal*, Jan. 11, 1900.

[13] See below, p. 118.

[14] See above, p. 52 and below, p. 118.

[15] The Pike County *Democrat*, Jan. 12, 1900.

[16] The Brownstone *Banner*, Feb. 6, 1900.

[17] The Decatur *Democrat*, Jan. 11, 1900.

[18] S. E. Morss to W. J. Bryan, May 29, 1899. W. J. Bryan Papers, LC. Also R. C. Bell to W. J. Bryan, June 20, 1899, *ibid.*

[19] The Peru *Evening Journal*, Jan. 10, 1900.

[20] The Salem *Democrat*, Jan. 17, 1900.

[21] The Rushville *Republican*, Jan. 16, 1900.

[22] E.g. the resolution adopted by the Democrats in Cass county. The Logansport *Pharos*, Jan. 6, 1900.

23 The *Hoosier State* /Newport/, Jan. 2, 1900.

24 The Winamac *Republican*, March 1, 1900; The Rushville *Republican*, Feb. 6, 1900; The Auburn *Dispatch*, Feb. 8, 1900.

25 The Columbus *Evening Republican*, Jan. 25, 1900.

26 The Mitchell *Commercial*, Jan. 11, 1900.

27 The Goshen *Democrat*, Jan. 14, 1900.

28 Herbert J. Rissler, *Charles Warren Fairbanks: Conservative Hoosier* (Ph. D. diss. 1961), p. 79.

29 Cf. Leonard D. White, *The Republican Era. A Study in Administrative History, 1869—1901* (1965), p. 264 f.

30 Thus six reports were received from the following counties: Clark (Borden, Charlestown, Henryville, Memphis, Ohio Falls, and Sellersburg), Greene (Jasonville, Lyons, Newark, Switz City, Scotland and Worthington), and Sullivan (Carlisle, Dugger, Merom, Pleasantville, Shelburn and Fagle). Both Harrison and Dubois sent five each and Knox, Decatur, Steuben and De Kalb four each.

31 A. Shaw to Charles W. Fairbanks, Osgood, Jan. 10, 1900. Fairbanks Papers, Lilly Library, Bloomington, Ind. (from now on referred to as LLB).

32 The election figures in 1896 were Dem. 4349, Rep. 3480. E. E. Robinson, *The Presidential Vote 1896—1932* (1934), p. 189.

33 A. C. Nicholson to Fairbanks, Wheatland, Jan. 9, 1900, Fairbanks Papers, LLB.

34 A. L. Osterhage to Fairbanks, Freelandville, s.d. LLB.

35 A Shaw to Fairbanks, Osgood, Jan. 9, 1900, LLB.

36 W. A. Morris to Fairbanks, Youngs Creek, Jan. 9, 1900, LLB.

37 John S. Miller to Fairbanks, Clarksburg, Jan. 10, 1900, LLB.

38 Walter P. Sparks to Fairbanks, Merom, Jan. 9, LLB, R. S. Quellen, Dugger, Jan 13, LLB.

39 H. I. Dickinson to Fairbanks, Jan. 10, 1900, LLB.

40 E. E. Mory to Fairbanks, South Milford, Jan. 5, 1900, LLB.

41 S. Sines to Fairbanks, Burns City, Jan. 11, 1900, LLB.

42 E. I. Ingles to Fairbanks, Scotland, Jan. 15, 1900, LLB.

43 Lincoln Golloway to Fairbanks, Zenas, Jan. 16, 1900, LLB.

44 J. D. Lucas to Fairbanks, Freetown, Jan. 20, 1900, LLB.

45 Walter P. Sparks to Fairbanks, Merom, Jan. 9, 1900.

46 E. I. Ingles to Fairbanks, Jan. 15, 1900, LLB.

47 E. E. Mory to Fairbanks, Jan. 5, 1900, LLB.

48 H. I. Dickinson to Fairbanks, Jan. 10, 1900, LLB.

49 I. A. Wilson to Fairbanks, Jan. 10, 1900, LLB.

50 H. I. Dickinson to Fairbanks, Epsom, Jan. 10, 1900, LLB.

51 David M. Leard to Fairbanks, Ray, Jan. 31, 1900, LLB.

52 C. N. Simmons to Fairbanks, Schnellville, Jan. 11, 1900, LLB.

53 Election figures from 1896, Dem. 3005, Rep. 1215. Robinson, *op. cit.*, p. 187.

54 Cf. Fred H. Harrington, "The Anti-Imperialist Movement in the United States, 1898—1900," *The Miss. Valley Hist. Review* 1935, p. 211 ff.

55 According to e.g. J. A. McCollough, delegate from Indiana at the Democratic Convention in Kansas City, *Proceedings, Dem., 1900,* p. 106. E. A. Baeker, Justice of the Peace at Vincennes in Knox county and contributor to Louisville *Anzeiger,* the only daily German-language newspaper published south of Ohio River, was of the same opinion. E. A. Baeker to W. J. Bryan, May 14, 1900, Bryan Papers, LC.

56 *The Twelfth Census of the United States, 1900, Population L,* p. 686 ff. Cf. J. D. Barnhard/D. F. Carmony, *Indiana, From Frontier to Industrial Commonwealth,* II, p. 290 ff.

57 S. Winkler to Fairbanks, Emison, Jan. 10, 1900, LLB.

[58] D. E. McCullum to Fairbanks, Leavenworth, Jan. 10, 1900, LLB.

[59] Election figures for Crawford 1896 were: Dem. 1655, Rep. 1490. Robinson, *op. cit.*, p. 186.

[60] B. Gooden to Fairbanks, Newark, Jan. 12, 1900, LLB.

[61] G. Gilbert to Fairbanks, Pleasant Lake, Jan. 10, 1900, LLB.

[62] "I am an Imperialist," declared e.g. H. I. Dickinson from Epsom, and professed himself an adherent of "an Imperial Republic." Dickinson to Fairbanks, Jan. 10, 1900, LLB. A similar declaration was made by G. H. Forkner from Auburn, who formulated a laconic platform: "McKinley, Protection, Expansion, Golddollar and Antitrusts." Forkner to Fairbanks, Auburn, Jan. 10, 1900, LLB. J. I. Duckwall, Muncie, went into the most detail, taking up a concrete discussion of the entire current situation with regard to the new territorial acquisitions. He was a convinced expansionist and urged among other things the annexation of Cuba. J. I. Duckwall to Fairbanks, Muncie, Jan. 7, 1900, LLB.

[63] W. P. Sparks to Fairbanks, Merom, Jan. 9, 1900, LLB.

[64] S. Sines to Fairbanks, Burns City, Jan. 11, 1900, LLB.

[65] L. Golloway to Fairbanks, Zenas, Jan. 16, 1900, LLB.

[66] W. Lucas to Fairbanks, New Haven, Jan. 12, 1900, LLB.

[67] W. A. Morris to Fairbanks, Young Creek, Jan. 9, 1900, LLB.

[68] S. Winkler to Fairbanks, Epsom, Jan. 10, 1900, LLB. D. E. McCullum to Fairbanks, Leavenworth, Jan. 9, 1900, LLB. E. E. Mory to Fairbanks, South Milford, Jan. 5, 1900, LLB.

[69] Cf. below, p. 105 ff.

[70] Cf. below, p. 122.

[71] J. Bennet Gordon to Beveridge, March 7 and March 14, 1900, Beveridge Papers, LC. In addition to the districts named above can also be mentioned the tenth, where the Chicago press played an important role.

[72] The Indianapolis *Journal*, Jan. 1, 2, 22, 30, Feb. 12, 1900, *et passim*.

[73] *Ibid.*, Feb. 19, 1900.

[74] Cf. above, p. 90.

[75] The Indianapolis *Journal*, Jan. 31, 1900.

[76] *Ibid.*, Jan 13, 1900.

[77] *Ibid.*, Jan. 31, 1900.

[78] *Ibid.*, Jan. 13, 1900.

[79] *Ibid.*, Feb. 18 and March 1, 1900.

[80] *Ibid.*, Feb. 20, 1900.

[81] *Ibid.*, Feb. 26 and Feb. 27, 1900.

[82] Cf. above, p. 80 ff.

[83] The Indianapolis *Journal*, March 6, 1900.

[84] *Ibid.*, March 7, 1900.

[85] *Ibid.*, March 13, 14, 15, 22, 26 and 27, 1900.

[86] *Ibid.*, March 27 and 30, 1900.

[87] *Ibid.*, April 2, 1900.

[88] Se above, p. 102 f.

[89] W. H. Hart to Fairbanks, March 1, Fairbanks Papers, LLB.

[90] R. A. Brown to Fairbanks, March 3, LLB.

[91] Harry S. New to Fairbanks, March 1, *ibid*. Other estimations of the number of Republicans that were opposed to the Puerto Rico tariff usually varied between 75 % and 98 %.

[92] John Braeman, "The Rise of Albert Beveridge to the United States Senate." *Indiana Magazine of History*, LIII, Dec. 1957, p. 371.

[93] Hawkins to Fairbanks March 3, 1900, Fairbanks Papers, LLB.

94 W. Campbell to Fairbanks, March 2, LLB.
95 E.g. A. A. Young, C. C. Binkley, W. C. Dull, John F. Dye, Wilson Root.
96 M. M. Hugg to Fairbanks, March 1, 1900, Fairbanks Papers, LLB.
97 N. C. Butler to Fairbanks, March 6, 1900, LLB.
98 V. H. Lockwood to Fairbanks s.d., LLB.
99 Frank Littleton to Fairbanks, Feb. 28, 1900, LLB.
100 R. W. McBride to Fairbanks, Feb. 28, 1900, LLB.
101 C. E. Everett to Fairbanks, March 2, 1900, LLB.
102 Frank Littleton to Beveridge, March 5, 1900, Beveridge Papers, LC.
103 Cf. below, p. 131.
104 R. O. Hawkins to Fairbanks, March 3, 1900, Fairbanks Papers, LLB.
105 Harry S. New to Fairbanks, March 1, 1900, LLB.
106 Harry S. New to Fairbanks, March 3, 1900, LLB.
107 Charles W. Moore to Fairbanks (tel.), March 1, 1900, LLB.
108 C. E. Everett to Fairbanks, March 2, 1900, LLB.
109 J. A. Woodhull to Beveridge, March 12, 1900, Beveridge Papers, LC.
110 H. G. Murphy to Beveridge, ibid.
111 Russel M. Seeds, History of the Republican Party of Indiana, p. 56 ff. John Braeman, "The Rise of Albert Beveridge to the United States Senate," Indiana Magazine of History, LIII, Dec., 1957, p. 358 ff.
112 The position of the parties in the Senate became: Dem. 14, Pop. 3, Rep. 33 and in the House: Dem. 39, Pop. 9, Rep. 52.
113 John Braeman, op. cit., p. 370 ff. and also Albert J. Beveridge, American Nationalist (1971), pp. 26 ff. Cf. Rissler, p. 100 ff.
114 Charles F. Remy, "The Election of Beveridge to the Senate," Indiana Magazine of History, XXXVI (1940), p. 125 ff. Braeman (1957), pp. 370 ff., John A. Coffin, "The Senatorial Career of Albert J. Beveridge," Indiana Magazine of History, XXIV: 3, Sept. 1928, p. 149 ff.
115 Edwin Burrit Smith to Edward Atkinson, Sept. 30, 1899, E. Atkinson Papers, Mass. Hist. Society, Boston.
116 Cf. above, p. 80.
117 H. Warrum to W. J. Bryan, Jan. 12, 1900, W. J. Bryan Papers, LC.
118 Beveridge to Paul Dana, J. C. Shaffer, H. H. Kohlsaat and others, March 7, 1900 (copy), Beveridge Papers, LC.
119 See above, p. 72 f.
120 Albert Shaw to Beveridge, March 20, 1900, Letterbox, Albert Shaw Papers, N.Y. Public Library.
121 Hilton U. Brown to Beveridge, March 17, 1900, Beveridge Papers, LC.
122 J. Parmenter to Beveridge, March 5, 1900, ibid.
123 L. Whitcomb to Beveridge, March 9, 1900, Beveridge Papers, LC. In a later letter, Whitcomb energetically supported Beveridge in his opposition to the bill. Whitcomb to Beveridge, March 26, 1900, ibid.
124 Frank Littleton to Beveridge, March 5, 1900, ibid.
125 Frank Littleton to Beveridge, March 13, 1900, ibid.
126 Joss was one of the group including Whitcomb and Littleton that had backed Beveridge from the very start.
127 Frederich Joss to Beveridge, March 13, 1900, ibid.
128 E. H. Hart to Beveridge, March 12, 1900, ibid.
129 N. W. Gilbert to Beveridge, March 25, 1900, ibid.
130 H. W. Bennet to Beveridge, March 28, 1900, E. O. Roose, editor of the Angola Magnet to Beveridge, March 13, ibid.
131 Harry S. New to Beveridge, March 17, 1900, from Hilton U. Brown s.d., from

Frank Payne, April 2, 1900, Beveridge Papers, LC.

[132] Morris Ross to Beveridge, Feb. 28, 1900, *ibid.*

[133] Fred L. Pussly to Beveridge, April 7, 1900, *ibid.*

[134] Charles G. Dawes, *A Journal of the McKinley Years* (1950), p. 214.

[135] *Op. cit.*, p. 219.

[136] Claude G. Bowers, *Beveridge and the Progressive Era* (1932), p. 127. Bowers has misunderstood the background to Beveridge's proposition. He thinks that it originated in a letter from Beveridge's friend, Chaffer, and fails to notice that this is in reply to the circular letter from the beginning of the month that is dealt with above and that Bowers has missed.

[137] Rotschild to Beveridge, March 19, 1900, Beveridge Papers, Bowers, *op. cit.*, p. 128.

[138] Faris in the 5th district had not been present at the vote but declared that he would have voted against it.

[139] H. W. Bennet to Beveridge, March 28, 1900, Beveridge Papers, LC.

[140] Bowers, *op. cit.*, p. 128. Naturally critical voices were also heard. E.g. Dana Estes of Boston thought that the speech was "very silly and inconsiderate." Dana Estes to Herbert Welsh, Jan. 30, 1900. Herbert Welsh Papers, Penn. Historical Society, Philadelphia.

[141] Cf. Coffin, *op. cit.*, p. 170 f.

[142] Dawes, *op. cit.*, p. 219. Cf. Bowers, *op. cit.*, p. 128 f.

[143] John Braeman, *op. cit.* (1972), p. 50.

[144] C. R. Lane to Fairbanks, March 4, 1900, Fairbanks Papers, LLB.

[145] Elmer Crocket to Fairbanks, March 8, 1900, *ibid.*

[146] G. W. Farrell to Fairbanks, s.d., *ibid.*

[147] C. DeWitt to Fairbanks, s.d., *ibid.*

[148] Fairbanks to New, March 15, 1900 (copy), Fairbanks Papers, LLB. Fairbanks discussed with New what could be done to reach a solution and at the same time maintain harmony in the party, and although New could not accept Fairbanks' line, they were in close contact the whole time. In addition, they were in complete agreement on another of the questions in the news at that time, the ship subsidy bill, that both were opposed to. The *Journal* had backed it earlier, but the anti-trust feelings had become so violent in connection with the Puerto Rico bill that the Ship Subsidy bill, which was also considered by its critics to be inspired by the trust interests, had been renamed "the Ship Subsidy Steal" and had become extremely unpopular. "— — — it were better for us to have a millstone tied about our necks and thrown into the sea than to take it /the bill/ up at this time," wrote New to Fairbanks, and he assured New that he was working for the rejection of the bill. New to Fairbanks, March 1, 9 and 12, 1900, Fairbanks to New, March 15, *ibid.*

[149] T. I. McCoy to Fairbanks, March 17, 1900 (tel.), Fairbanks Papers, LLB.

[150] E. Leonard to Fairbanks, s.d. (tel.), *ibid.*

[151] E. Crocket to Fairbanks, March 16, 1900 (tel.), *ibid.*

[152] W. Bigler to Fairbanks, s.d., *ibid.*

[153] Fred A. Sims to Fairbanks, March 17, 1900 (tel.), *ibid.*

[154] G. A. Cunningham (tel.), March 17, G. W. Self (tel.), March 16 and D. V. Miller, March 17, 1900 respectively, *ibid.*

[155] Thomas McNutt to Fairbanks, March 17, 1900, *ibid.*

[156] Theodore Shockney to Fairbanks, March 27, 1900, *ibid.*

[157] Charles Hernley to Fairbanks, March 16 and March 17 (tel.), *ibid.*

[158] Charles W. Fairbanks to John Connor, March 17, 1900. Cf. David J. Rothman, *Politics and Power. The United States Senate, 1869—1901* (1966), p. 107.

[159] See e.g. Harry New to Fairbanks, March 3 and 12, 1900, Fairbanks Papers, LLB,

McIntosh to Beveridge, March 10, 1900, Beveridge Papers, LC, The Indianapolis *Journal*, March 5, 1900.

[160] Cf. above, p. 80.

[161] Above, p. 118.

[162] Above, p. 78 f.

[163] Above, p. 70 f.

[164] The Indianapolis *News*, March 29, 1900.

[165] The material also includes some Gold Democrats who had voted for McKinley in 1896.

[166] See below, p. 125.

[167] The very high number of Republicans answering "Doubtful" in Evansville included some Gold Democrats who were considering returning to the Democratic party.

[168] Cf. above, p. 94.

[169] This point of view is to be found not only in the Indianapolis *Sentinel* and Fort Wayne *Sentinel*, but also in the Hartford City *Telegraph*, Columbus *Herald* and Plymouth *Democrat*, and others.

[170] For example, the Evansville *Journal* and to some extent also the Terre Haute *Express*, Kokomo *Dispatch*, Richmond *Palladium*, Goshen *Times*, Noblesville *Ledger* and others.

[171] J. M. McIntosh to Beveridge, April 2, 1900, Beveridge Papers, LC.

[172] L. G. Rotschild to Beveridge, April 17 and May 5, 1900, *ibid*.

[173] Fairbanks received many letters and telegrams immediately after the publication of his speech. R. O. Hawkins, who had been very worried earlier (cf. above, p. 106) expressed the relief generally felt. He wrote, "The speech of the Junior Senator fell flat here," and went on to assure Fairbanks of the enormous effect his speech had had. The critics were silenced and the ranks had closed again. R. O. Hawkins to Fairbanks, April 2, 1900 (tel.), Fairbanks Papers, LLB.

[174] The Indianapolis *Journal*, April 1—10, 1900.

[175] Frank Payne to Beveridge, April 2, 1900. Beveridge Papers, LC.

[176] Cf. Fred L. Pussly to Beveridge, April 7, 1900, *ibid*.

[177] Charles Hernley to Fairbanks, April 1 (tel.), Fairbanks Papers, LLB. LLB.

[178] See e.g. Miles K. Moffet, April 3, Frank L. Littleton, Frederick A. Miller, Charles H. Neff et al., April 4, 1900, *ibid*.

[179] Fairbanks to Charles Hernley, April 7, 1900 (copy), W. D. Page to Fairbanks, April 30, 1900, *ibid*.

[180] The Indianapolis *Journal*, April 3, 1900.

[181] W. H. Smith to Fairbanks, April 20, 1900, Fairbanks Papers, LLB.

[182] Joseph Kealing to Fairbanks, May 15, 1900, *ibid*.

[183] Francis D. Merrill to Fairbanks, April 14, 1900, *ibid*.

[184] Kealing to Fairbanks, April 18, 1900, *ibid*.

[185] *Ibid*.

[186] The Evansville *Courier*, March 15, 1900.

[187] The Indianapolis *Sentinel*, May 6, 1900.

[188] The Michigan City *Evening News*, Feb. 19, 1900, The Winamac *Democrat-Journal*, March 9, 1900.

[189] Cf. above, p. 76.

[190] Harry S. New to Fairbanks, March 3, 1900, Fairbanks Papers, LLB.

[191] Harry S. New to Fairbanks, March 12, 1900, *ibid*. Cf. Indianapolis *Journal*, March 9, 1900.

[192] McCoy, chairman of the Republican District Committee, declared this to be the case.

[193] The Indianapolis *News*, April 7, 1900.

[194] *Ibid.*, April 13 and 14, 1900.

[195] The Indianapolis *Journal*, April 26, 1900.

[196] The Indianapolis *Press*, April 14, 1900.

[197] The La Fayette *Sunday Times*, April 25, 1900.

[198] E.g. The Elkhart *Review*, Richmond *Palladium*, Madison *Courier*, South Bend *Tribune*, Wyandot County *Republican* and others.

[199] The Indianapolis *Journal*, April 19—21, 1900.

[200] Harry S. New to Fairbanks, May 18 and 25, 1900. Fairbanks Papers, LLB.

[201] Joseph Kealing to Fairbanks, May 28, 1900, LLB. See also the Indianapolis *News*, April 7 and 14, the *Sentinel*, April 15, the *Journal*, April 20, Columbus *Herald*, s.d., 1900.

[202] See above, p. 111.

[203] Fairbanks wrote to his close friend, D. W. Henry, about Hanly in January: "Frank Hanly has always been a friend of mine and is a true and generous friend now. There is no confidence that I would not repose in him. I can say to you personally that he has in the fullest manner possible expressed his desire to co-operate with me." Fairbanks to D. W. Henry, Jan. 2, 1900, D. W. Henry Collection, Indiana State Library, Indianapolis.

[204] Landis' speech was not on the program, "but the delegates would not let him escape," according to the Washington *Post*, April 26, 1900 and the Indianapolis *Journal*, April 26, 1900. Landis' speech was met with considerable interest because in it he proposed Senator Fairbanks as a presidential candidate in 1904. There had long been general talk of the possibility of Fairbanks running as vice-presidential candidate in the coming election, but his friends advised him against this, meaning that it would be better for him to aim at getting the first place on the ticket in 1904, something which would be made more difficult if he now let himself be maneuvered into the political dead end that the post of vice-president was by tradition. The Indianapolis *Press*, April 28, 1900, the Attica *Ledger*, May 5, 1900.

[205] The Indianapolis *Journal*, April 27, 1900.

[206] The Washington *Post*, from Associated Press, April 26, 1900.

[207] As governor, Durbin worked in close co-operation with the Fairbanks machine. During the very first days after he took office, there were items in the press to the effect that he and the senior Senator were planning to prevent Beveridge from being re-elected and make Durbin senator. The Indianapolis *Sentinel*, Jan. 4, 1901.

[208] R. A. Brown to Fairbanks, May 10; R. O. Hawkins to Fairbanks, May 19, 1900, LLB.

[209] Cf. above, p. 95.

[210] Rissler, *op. cit.*, p. 105.

[211] Cf. below, p. 162 f.

[212] The Indianapolis *Journal*, April 26, 1900.

[213] The Washington *Post,* April 30, 1900.

[214] Cf. above, p. 90; 98.

[215] The Laporte *Argus*, March 15, 1900.

[216] The Indianapolis *News*, March 24, 1900.

[217] The Indianapolis *Sentinel*, April 4, 1900, Columbus *Herald*, April 6, Delphi *Times*, April 3, 1900.

[218] The Indianapolis *Sentinel*, May 2 and 3, 1900.

[219] The Indianapolis *Journal*, April 28, Chicago *Times-Herald*, April 25, Laporte *Argus*, April 26, 1900.

[220] The Indianapolis *News*, April 25, 1900.

[221] J. Maurice Thompson to William Hayes Ward, March 5, 1900. Maurice Thomp-

son Papers, LLB.
²²² Thompson to Ward, March 5 and 13, 1900, *ibid.*
²²³ Thompson to Ward, March 13, 1900, *ibid.*
²²⁴ *A History of Indiana Democracy, 1816—1916*, pp. 383.
²²⁵ Claude G. Bowers, *The Life of John Worth Kern* (1918), p. 130.
²²⁶ The Indianapolis *News*, June 7, 1900.
²²⁷ The Terre Haute *Gazette*, July 3, 1900.
²²⁸ S. E. Morss to W. J. Bryan, July 11, 1900. W. J. Bryan Papers, LC.
²²⁹ W. E. Henry, *State Platforms of the Two Dominant Political Parties in Indiana, 1850—1900* (1902), p. 115 ff.
²³⁰ See below, p. 206 ff.

Chapter IV

¹ Cf. above, p. 22 f.
² Main sources used for the various platforms have been *The Tribune Almanac* 1901, The Chicago *Daily News Almanac* 1901 and the press.
³ On New York state convention, cf. below, p. 180 f.
⁴ The fact that idealistic and humanitarian planks, with "duty" and "responsibility" as their key-words, dominated in, for example, Massachusetts should be considered in the context of the dissension that prevailed among the Republicans there. The senators that represented them were George Frisbie Hoar, leading anti-imperialist, and Henry Cabot Lodge, one of the foremost advocates of globalism. Cf. Richard E. Welch, "Opponents and Colleagues: George Frisbie Hoar and Henry Cabot Lodge, 1896—1904." *New England Quarterly* 1963, p. 188.
⁵ The wording of New Hampshire's platform is also typical: "We glory in the triumphs of the Spanish war, both those on land and those on sea. We are proud of the splendid records of our naval and military heroes."
⁶ The neutral, uncommitted attitude displayed by the Michigan Republicans in their platform on the question of expansion is further illuminated by the fact that it contains one of the very few Republican platforms which expresses sympathy for the Boers. Only three Republican state party platforms have a pro-Boer declaration. No less than twenty-five Democratic platforms had such a declaration.
⁷ Cf. above, p. 128 ff.
⁸ The Indianapolis *Journal*. April 19, 1900. The Indianapolis *Sentinel* (Dem.) insinuated that Mark Hanna had written the Republican platform. The Indianapolis *Sentinel*, April 25, 1900.
⁹ See below, p. 205.
¹⁰ Charles G. Dawes, *A Journal of the McKinley Years*. Ed. by Bascom N. Timmons (1950), p. 224 f.
¹¹ Cf. above, p. 222 f.
¹² The Indianapolis *Journal*, April 25, 1900.
¹³ The conventions were held on May 10 and May 16—17, 1900 respectively.
¹⁴ Cf. William Appleman Williams, *The Roots of American Imperialism* (1970).
¹⁵ April 24 (Indiana), April 26 (Massachusetts) and May 9 respectively. Cf. above, p. 142 f.
¹⁶ Cf. below, p. 148 ff.
¹⁷ See below, p. 213.
¹⁸ E. W. Winkler, *Platforms of Political Parties in Texas, Bulletin of the University of Texas*, 1916: 53, p. 412.
¹⁹ The former platform also contained a declaration of sympathy for the Boers, one

of the few included in Republican state platforms. Thus such a declaration was not incompatible with an otherwise clearly pro-expansionist plank.

[20] The conventions were held April 24 and May 10 respectively.

[21] Cf. above South Carolina's platform, p. 145.

[22] On the New York Republican state convention, cf. below, p. 180 f.

[23] There was, however, a minority of delegates at the convention who wanted to retain the Philippines.

[24] The Hay-Pauncefote Treaty, cf. above, p. 102.

[25] Cf. above, p. 81 f.

[26] Cf. above, p. 141 ff.

[27] Cf. below, p. 185. The foreign policy plank was as follows: "In its platform of 1860 the republican party declared that the maintenance of the principles promulgated in the declaration of independence and embodied in the federal constitution, viz., that all men are created equal; that they are endowed with unalienable rights; that governments are instituted to secure their rights and that governments derive their just powers from the consent of the governed, is essential to the preservation of our republican institutions: but the republican party, under its present leadership, is endangering the preservation of republican institutions by placing the dollar above the man in the construction of government and by violating the principles that it once declared to be essential. We condemn the Puerto Rican tariff bill, recently passed by a republican house of representatives, as a bold and open violation of the nation's organic law and a flagrant breach of good faith. We assert that the constitution follows the flag and denounce the doctrine that an executive or a congress, created and limited by the constitution, can exercise lawful authority beyond that constitution or in violation of it. Believing that a nation cannot long endure half republic and half empire, we oppose wars of conquest and colonial possessions. The Filipinos cannot be citizens without endangering our civilization; they cannot be subjects without endangering our form of government, and as we are not willing to surrender our civilization or to convert a republic into an empire, we favor an immediate declaration of the nation's purpose to give to the Filipinos, first, a stable form of government; second, independence, and, third, protection from outside interference, as it has for nearly a century given protection to the republics of Central and South America. We favor the expansion of trade by every legitimate and peaceful means, but we are opposed to purchasing trade at the cannon's mouth with human blood; neither do we believe that trade secured and held by force is worth the price that must be paid for it. We are in favor of extending the nation's influence, but we believe that that influence should be extended, not by force and violence, but through the persuasive power of a high and honorable example. We oppose militarism. It imposes upon the people an unnecessary burden and is a constant menace. A small standing army and a well-equipped state militia are sufficient in time of peace; in time of war the citizen soldier should be a republic's defense. We believe, with Jefferson, in peace, commerce and honest friendship with all nations and entangling alliances with none, and we regard with apprehension the doctrine advocated in some quarters that this nation should in its dealings or diplomacy show partiality toward any of the European nations."

[28] The New York *World*, Philadelphia *Times*, Baltimore *News*, Kansas City *Star*, Hartford *Times*, Detroit *Free Press, et al.*

[29] The Indianapolis *Sentinel*, March 29, 1900.

[30] Cf. above, p. 81.

[31] See above, p. 149. Cf. also e.g. the Illinois platform, above, p. 150.

[32] Cf. above, p. 150 f.

[33] Cf. above, p. 83.

330

[34] Winkler, *op. cit.*, p. 4216. The Austin *Statesman* 21 and 22 June.
[35] The conventions were held on May 10 and 16 respectively, and May 17.
[36] See below, p. 159.
[37] The *Outlook*, 60, Dec. 24, 1898. The heading of the article is "Expansion: One step at a Time." Cf. Healy, *op. cit.*, p. 127.
[38] Robert A. Levine, *The Arms Debate* (1963), p. 27.
[39] Cf. below, p. 197 ff.
[40] Cf. below, p. 212 ff.
[41] Above, p. 150 f.
[42] This demand was made in the following Democratic platforms: Alabama, California, Florida, Georgia, Illinois, Louisiana, Maryland, Mississippi, Missouri, Montana, Nebraska, New Jersey, Oregon, Pennsylvania, Tennessee, Vermont. And in the Republican platforms from: Arkansas, California, Indiana, Maine, Maryland, Massachusetts, Mississippi, Missouri, Nevada, Oregon, Texas, Vermont.
[43] Se below, p. 189 ff.

Chapter V

[1] Cf. Merle Curti, *Bryan and World Peace*. Smith College Studies in History, p. 120.
[2] Cf. E. Berkeley Tompkins, "The Old Guard: A Study of the Anti-Imperialist Leadership." *The Historian* XXX: 3, (May 1963), p. 376 ff.; Fred Harrington, "The Anti-Imperialist Movement in the United States, 1898—1900." *The Mississippi Valley Historical Review*, XXII (1935).
[3] Below, p. 240 ff.
[4] Cf. J. Rogers Hollingsworth, *The Whirligig of Politics. The Democracy of Cleveland and Bryan* (1963), p. 158 ff.; Tompkins, *op. cit.*
[5] Hollingsworth, *op. cit.*, p. 160 ff.
[6] Charles B. Spahr to Carnegie March 12 and April 26, 1900. Carnegie Papers LC.
[7] J. Thompson, ed. of the Washington *Chronicle*, to Carnegie, January 23, 1900, H. Vallard, the New York *Evening Post*, to Carnegie, January 27, 1900, *ibid.*
[8] For Carnegie's views on Bryan. Cf. A. Carnegie, *Autobiography of Andrew Carnegie* (1920), p. 363 f.
[9] R. F. Pettigrew, *Imperial Washington* (1922), p. 320 ff. Pettigrew's account is followed by Daniel B. Schirmer, *Republic or Empire: American Resistance to the Philippine War* (1972), p. 189.
[10] Erwing Winslow, March 22, 1900. W. A. Croffut Papers, LC.
[11] Henderson to W. A. Croffut, March 19, 1900, *ibid.*
[12] Schurz to Moorfield Storey, March 2, to Edwin Burrit Smith, March 11, 1900. Schurz Papers, LC.
[13] Schurz to Edwin B. Smith, March 26, 1900 (copy), *ibid.*
[14] Samuel Bowles to Schurz, March 2, 1900, *ibid.*
[15] Moorfield Storey to Schurz, March 14 and March 24, 1900, *ibid.*
[16] Cf. below, p. 242 f.
[17] E. B. Smith to Schurz, March 17, March 24, 1900; Schurz to same, March 19 (copy), *ibid.*
[18] E. Winslow to Schurz, March 21, March 27; to Horace White (the *Evening Post*), March 22, Schurz to Winslow March 20, March 28, 1900 (copies). Haskins to Schurz, March 29, 1900, *ibid.*
[19] Dana Estes to Edward Atkinson, Dec. 22, 1898. Edward Atkinson Papers, Mass. Hist. Society, Boston.

[20] Schurz to Charles Francis Adams, March 2, 1899 (copy), Schurz Papers, LC.

[21] L. R. Ehrich to Edward Atkinson, July 16, 1899. Edward Atkinson Papers, Mass. Hist. Society, Boston. Cf. also Ehrich to W. J. Bryan, March 27, 1899. Bryan Papers, LC.

[22] David Starr Jordan, *Imperial Democracy* (1899). Theodore M. Etting to Herbert Welsh, Nov. 18, 1899. Herbert Welsh Papers, Pennsylvania Historical Society, Philadelphia.

[23] E. B. Smith to Schurz, March 17, 1900 (a copy of Jordan's letter to Bryan was sent to Schurz). Schurz Papers, LC.

[24] David Starr Jordan to W. J. Bryan, Feb. 7, 1900, W. J. Bryan Papers, LC. Copy among David Starr Jordan Papers, Stanford Univ. Library.

[25] Bryan to Jordan, Feb. 17, 1900. Jordan Papers (copy), Stanford University Library.

[26] David Starr Jordan to Bryan, March 7, 1900. W. J. Bryan Papers, LC.

[27] David Starr Jordan, "The Blood of a Nation." Boston *Evening Transcript*, March 17, 1900.

[28] Charles Darwin, *The Descent of Man*. Cf. David Starr Jordan, *The Days of Man, Being Memoirs of a Naturalist, Teacher and Minor Prophet of Democracy*, I (1922), p. 618 f.

[29] See e.g. Elwood Corser to W. A. Croffut, Jan. 18 and April 23, 1900. Croffut Papers, LC.

[30] Corser to K. Sniffen, Feb. 14, 1900. Herbert Welsh Papers, Pennsylvania Historical Society, Philadephia.

[31] Corser to Marion C. Butler, Feb. 5, 1900. Marion Butler Papers. Southern Historical Collection. University of North Carolina Library, Chapel Hill.

[32] B. Smith to Schurz, March 15, 1900. Schurz Papers, LC.

[33] Corser met Schurz on the occasion of the great anti-imperialist congress which was held in Philadelphia Feb. 22—23, and at which Schurz was one of the main speakers. Corser to Schurz, Feb. 23, 1900. Schurz Papers, LC.

[34] George G. Mercer to Schurz, Feb. 26, 1900. Schurz Papers, LC.

[35] E. B. Smith to Corser s.d. (copy). Schurz Papers, LC.

[36] Cf. Tompkins, "The Old Guard," p. 383.

[37] Edwin B. Smith to E. S. Corser, Feb. 26, 1900 (copy). Bryan Papers, LC.

[38] Elwood S. Corser to James K. Jones, Feb. 27, 1900 (copy), *ibid*.

[39] E. S. Corser to Bryan, March 8, 1900, *ibid*.

[40] E. B. Smith to Corser, March 7, 1900, *ibid*.

[41] E. B. Smith to Bryan, June 30, 1900, *ibid*.

[42] *Ibid*. The proposals were also sent to Elwood Corser.

[43] Charles J. Bonaparte agreed with the Anti-Imperialists in severely condemning McKinley. He had, however, declined to become one of the many honorary vice-presidents of the Anti-Imperialist League, since he considered "their course injudicious and calculated to defeat its own purposes." Charles J. Bonaparte to Lucius B. Swift, May 27, 1899. Lucius B. Swift Papers, Indiana State Library, Indianapolis.

[44] E. Osgood Brown to W. J. Bryan, July 18, 1900. Bryan Papers, LC.

[45] According to what Baumgarten wrote in a letter to Bryan, May 3, 1900, he wrote down Pulitzer's statement immediately after the conversation. Bryan Papers, LC.

[46] W. R. Hearst to W. J. Bryan, June 1899, *ibid*.

[47] A. Brisbane to Bryan, Feb. 6, 1900, *ibid*. Cf. also Paolo E. Coletta, *William Jennings Bryan I. Political Evangelist, 1860—1908* (1964), p. 249.

[48] W. R. Hearst to Bryan (tel.), May 20, 1900. Bryan Papers, LC.

[49] Cf. below, p. 224.

[50] James Creelman (N.Y. *Journal*) to Bryan, May 24, 1900. Bryan Papers, LC.

[51] Creelman to Bryan, June 2, 1900, *ibid.*

[52] On this see e.g. Alexander Stanwood, *Four Famous New Yorkers. The Political Careers of Cleveland, Platt, Hill and Roosevelt* (1923), p. 338 ff.

[53] On Croker cf. L. Stoddard, *Master of Manhattan*, p. 217 ff., and Louis W. Koenig, *Bryan. A Political Biography of William Jennings Bryan* (1971), p. 303 ff.

[47] Willis Abbot, *Watching the World Go By*, p. 204. Paul W. Glad, *The Trumpet Soundeth*, p. 67 f.

[55] John Girdner to Bryan, June 21, 1900, *ibid.* Cf. Coletta, *op. cit.*, p. 250 f.

[56] See below, p. 207 f.

[57] J. Creelman to Bryan, April 22, 1900. Bryan Papers, LC.

[58] James K. Jones to Bryan, Feb. 4, 1900, *ibid.*

[59] On Norman E. Mack, se below, p. 209.

[60] Girdner to Bryan, April 21, May 29 and June 16, 1900. Bryan Papers, LC.

[61] Girdner to Bryan, April 23 and June 16, 1900, *ibid.*

[62] On the platform see further above, p. 149.

[63] John S. Seymour to Bryan, March 23, 1900. Bryan Papers, LC.

[64] E.g., V. M. Jordan (ed. of the Gold Dem. *Press Post*, Columbus, Ohio) to Bryan, April 2, 1900, *ibid.*

[65] Cf. e.g. letter from Gov. Charles Thomas, Colorado, to Bryan, April 10, 1900, *ibid.*

[66] L. G. Bohmerich to Bryan, June 25, 1900, *ibid.*

[67] Louis W. Koenig, *op. cit.*, p. 300.

[68] Bryan to Merrill, April 26, 1900. Bryan Papers (copy), LC.

[69] S. B. Martin to Bryan, May 24, 1900, *ibid.*

[70] Geo Fred Williams to W. J. Bryan, April 24, 1900, *ibid.*

[71] Th. Malony, Secretary of the Dem. State Central Committee, to Bryan, Feb. 9, 1900, *ibid.*

[72] W. J. Gaynor to Bryan, June 29, 1900. Bryan Papers, LC.

[73] See e.g. Fred T. Dubois to Senator Teller, March 29, 1900 (copy). C. I. Thomas to Bryan, April 2, 1900, *ibid.*

[74] E.g. Pettigrew to Bryan, April 9, 1900, *ibid.* Cf Pettigrew, *Imperial Washington*, p. 320 ff.

[75] E.g. E. Corser to W. A. Croffut, April 23, 1900. Croffut Papers, LC.

[76] Cf. above, p. 168 ff.

[77] J. K. Jones to J. G. Johnson, May 3, 1900. Bryan Papers, LC.

[78] Publicly Senator Jones denied that he was trying to talk Bryan into dropping the 16 : 1 issue. Indianapolis *Journal*, June 12, 1900.

[79] Adopted at the convention on March 26. Cf. above p. 151.

[80] Charles H. Jones to Bryan, June 26, 1900. Bryan Papers, LC.

[81] Bryan had also discussed the platform with others than those named here. One was J. H. Ralston in Washington, D.C., with whom he discussed what should be said on the Philippines. Ralston to Bryan, June 11, 1900. Bryan Papers, LC.

[82] In the Kansas City platform: "any attempt by corporations to interfere with the public affairs of the people or to control the sovereignty which creates them, should be forbidden under such penalties as will make such attempts impossible."

[83] Cf. below, p. 213.

[84] See above, p. 151 f.

[85] W. J. Stone to J. K. Jones, June 25, 1900. Bryan Papers, LC.

[86] W. J. Stone to Bryan, June 25, 1900, *ibid.*

[87] C. H. Jones to Bryan, June 26, 1900, *ibid.*

[88] Bryan to W. J. Stone, June 30, 1900, *ibid.*

[89] James Jones, Johnson, Stone, Campau and Guffey to Bryan, July 1, 1900, *ibid.*
[90] Cf. Coletta, *op. cit.*, p. 256.

Chapter VI

[1] G. Wallace Chessman, "Theodore Roosevelt's campaign against the Vice-Presidency," *Historian* XIV. Cf. Theodore Roosevelt's own account, *Theodore Roosevelt. An Autobiography* (1926), p. 308 f.
[2] A well-informed account of the nomination of candidates is to be found in *Public Opinion*, July 5, 1900.
[3] Cf. Karl Schriftgiesser, *The Gentleman from Massachusetts. Henry Cabot Lodge* (1944), p. 184 ff.
[4] Thomas A. Bailey, "Was the Presidential Election of 1900 a Mandate for Imperialism?" The *Miss. Vall. Hist. Rev.* XXIV, 1937. Cf. also Margaret Leech, *In the Days of McKinley* (1959), p. 529 ff.
[5] *Official Proceedings of the Twelfth Republican National Convention held in the city of Philadelphia, June 19, 20 and 21, 1900* (1900) (cit. *Proceedings, Rep.*), p. 37.
[6] *Proceedings, Rep.*, p. 47.
[7] *Ibid.*, p. 47.
[8] *Ibid.*, p. 89.
[9] Indianapolis *Sentinel*, June 21, 1900.
[10] See above, p. 53.
[11] *Proceedings, Rep.*, p. 103 ff.
[12] On Roosevelt's nomination, see also Ralph G. Martin, *Ballots and Bandwagons* (1964), p. 17 ff.
[13] See above, p. 177 f.
[14] *Proceedings, Rep.*, p. 116.
[15] *Ibid.*, p. 118.
[16] *Ibid.*
[17] Cf. above, p. 41 f.
[18] *Proceedings, Rep.*, p. 124.
[19] *Ibid.*, p. 126.
[20] *Living Issues of the Campaign of 1900* (ed. L. F. Prescott), p. 189.
[21] *Proceedings, Rep.*, p. 134.
[22] Cf. above, p. 228 f. Cf. Chauncey M. Depew, *My Memories of Eighty Years* (1922), p. 166.
[23] Porter, *Party Platforms*, p. 122.
[24] The New York *Times*, June 22, 1900.
[25] The Philadelphia *Press*, June 23, 1900.
[26] The New York *Journal of Commerce, The Literary Digest*, July 5, 1900.
[27] In a letter to Scott C. Bone, editor of the Washington *Post*, Charles Warren Fairbanks suggested that Grosvenor's vexation could be connected with his disappointment over the fact that no ship subsidy plank was included. C. W. Fairbanks to S. C. Bone (copy), C. W. Fairbanks Papers, Indiana Historical Society Library, Indianapolis. In a letter to McKinley, Mark Hanna in his turn commented sardonically: "Grosvenor has got Fairbanks crazy about the platform. It was an outrage the way that document was emasculated, but I am sorry the way it has been advertised. Foraker and Fairbanks have got their wind up for 1904, so I can see a little fun ahead." M. A. Hanna to McKinley, June 26, 1900. McKinley Papers, LC.

Cf. also C. H. Grosvenor to Charles Emory Smith (copy), July 2, 1900, *ibid.*

[28] Margaret Leech, *op. cit.,* p. 542. The *Public Opinion,* July 5, 1900. The *Nation* s.d.

[29] The *Public Opinion,* July 5, 1900. The same opinion is to be found in the Democratic publication *New World.*

[30] N. Butler to Charles W. Fairbanks, June 9, 1900. Charles Warren Fairbanks Papers, Indiana Historical Society, Indianapolis.

[31] D. B. Hill to Bryan, June 29, 1900 (tel.). Bryan Papers, LC.

[32] Hill to Bryan, July 1, 1900 (tel.), *ibid.*

[33] Above, p. 210.

[34] The *Outlook,* July 17, 1900.

[35] E. E. Crandall to Bryan, July 14, 1900. Bryan Papers, LC.

[36] N. E. Mack to Bryan, July 11, 1900, *ibid.*

[37] *Ibid.*

[38] On Croker at the convention, cf. e.g. Poultney Brigelow, "What I saw at Kansas City." *Contemporary Review,* July 1900. Also Alexander Stanwood, *Four Famous New Yorkers. The Political Careers of Cleveland, Platt, Hill and Roosevelt* (1923), p. 339 ff.; also Rogers Hollingworth, *op. cit.,* p. 168 f.

[39] Stanwood, *op. cit.,* p. 343 f.

[40] Robert Lee Dunn, "Making Presidents by Photography," *Appleton's Magazine,* Sept. 1907. The photograph is also reproduced there.

[41] E. McClanahan to W. J. Bryan, July 23, 1900. W. J. Bryan Papers, LC. Cf. also Coletta, p. 259.

[42] Brigelow, *op. cit.*

[43] Cf. below, p. 150 f.

[44] *The Memoirs of William Jennings Bryan. By Himself and His Wife Mary Baird Bryan* (1925), p. 125 f.

[45] Cf. above, p. 213.

[46] N. Mack to Bryan, July 11, 1900. Bryan Papers, LC.

[47] *Official Proceedings of the Democratic National Convention, Held in Kansas City, on July 4, 5 and 6, 1900* (cit. *Proceedings, Dem.*), p. 42.

[48] *Proceedings, Dem.,* p. 57 ff.

[49] *Ibid.,* p. 117 f.

[50] The *Outlook,* June 23, 1900.

[51] *Proceedings, Dem.,* p. 111 ff.

[52] *Ibid.,* p. 107.

[53] *Ibid.,* p. 101 ff.

[54] Cf. above, p. 253 f.

[55] *Proceedings, Dem.,* p. 120.

[56] W. J. Stone to Bryan, May 13, 1900. Bryan Papers, LC.

[57] Stone suggested mottoes on the flag, and his suggestions appeared unchanged or with minor alterations on the giant flag unfurled. Stone's original suggestions were a) Governments derive their just powers from the consent of the governed, b) The constitution and the Flag, One and Inseparable, Now and Forever, c) This is the Flag of the Republic—Not an Empire, d) It shall wave over States not provinces— over Freemen, not vassals. He sent the suggestions to Bryan, James Jones and J. G. Johnson and they changed the wording slightly.

[58] Two very brief planks expressed in 1896 support for the Monroe Doctrine and sympathy for Cuba. Porter, *National Party Platforms 1840—1960,* p. 99 ff.

[59] Porter, *op. cit.,* p. 112.

[60] See above, p. 170.

[61] Porter, *op. cit.,* p. 113.

[62] The *Nation*, July 12, 1900.
[63] Porter, *op. cit.*, p. 113. On the use of the Monroe Doctrine in anti-expansionistic arguments, cf. Dexter Perkins, *A History of the Monroe Doctrine* (1941, pb 1963), p. 198 f.
[64] See above, p. 162.
[65] Se above, p. 148 ff.
[66] Porter, *op. cit.*, p. 115.
[67] *Proceedings, Dem.*, p. 126 f.
[68] *Ibid.*, p. 133.
[69] See above, p. 210.
[70] *Proceedings, Dem.*, p. 105.
[71] The *North-American Review*, June 1900, p. 753 ff.
[72] Cf. below, p. 234.
[73] Cf. below, p. 304.
[74] *Proceedings, Dem.*, p. 165.
[75] E.g. W. J. Stone, *ibid.*, p. 167 f.
[76] *Ibid.*, p. 182 f. Stanwood, *op. cit.*, p. 64, has slightly different figures.
[77] The absence of a civil service plank has sometimes been blamed on the influence of Tammany Hall and Croker. E.g. Chicago *Evening Post,* July 10.
[78] The *Outlook*, July 14, 1900.
[79] Cf. Koenig, *op. cit.*, p. 324.
[80] Cf. also Walter Wellman, "The Kansas City Convention", the *Review of Reviews,* July 1900.

Chapter VII

[1] *Proceedings, Rep.*, p. 145.
[2] McKinley's Letter of Acceptance, *Living Issues of the Campaign of 1900* (1900), p. 191 ff.
[3] See above, p. 204 ff.
[4] *Proceedings, Rep.*, p. 150.
[5] *Ibid.*, p. 161.
[6] *Ibid.*, p. 164.
[7] *Ibid.*, p. 173.
[8] See above, p. 197 f.
[9] See above, p. 200 f.
[10] *Proceedings, Rep.*, p. 178 f.
[11] The *Literary Digest*, Sept. 22, 1900; *Public Opinion*, Sept. 20, 1900.
[12] The New York *Tribune*, Sept. 17, 1900, The *Nation*, Sept 20, 1900.
[13] Cf. above, p. 177 f.
[14] W. A. Swanberg, *Citizen Hearst. A Biography of William Randolph Hearst* (1961), p. 216 ff. Cf. also Rogers Hollingsworth, *op. cit.*, p. 175 f.
[15] The *Public Opinion*, Sept. 20, 1900.
[16] The *Literary Digest*, Sept. 22, *Public Opinion*, Sept. 20, 1900.
[17] *Proceedings, Rep.*, p. 187.
[18] *Ibid.*, p. 188.
[19] John P. Altgeld to W. J. Bryan, July 7, 1900. W. J. Bryan Papers, LC.
[20] W. A. Croffut to W. J. Bryan, July 7, 1900, *ibid.*
[21] F. Feigel to W. J. Bryan, July 16, 1900, *ibid.*
[22] E.g. The Cincinnati *Enquirer*, Atlanta *Journal*, Dallas-Galveston *News* and others.

The *Public Opinion*, July 26 and the *Literary Digest*, July 14, 1900.

[23] Koenig, *op. cit.*, p. 322.
[24] The *Literary Digest, Review of Reviews, Public Opinion*, July—August 1900.
[25] Cf. above, p. 210 f.
[26] Statement made by Dr. Pretorius in an interview in the Brooklyn *Eagle*, Aug. 12 1900.
[27] The *Public Opinion*, July 5, 1900.
[28] The *Public Opinion*, July 5, 1900, the *Literary Digest*, July 28, 1900.
[29] Theodore Roosevelt to Bartlett Johnson, Aug. 9, 1900 (copy). Theodore Roosevelt Papers, LC.
[30] The *Washington Post*, July 22, 1900.
[31] The *Public Opinion*, July 5, 1900.
[32] The Brooklyn *Eagle*, July 11, 12, 1900.
[33] The nineteen German-American newspapers in the Middle West included in the Brooklyn *Eagle's* poll were the following: *Republican: Republikaner* (Chicago), Dakota *Freie Presse* (Yankton, S.D.), *Freie Presse* (Cincinnati, O.); *Independent Republican: Westliche Blätter* (Cincinnati, O.); *Independent: Abendpost* (Chicago), *Freie Presse* (Chicago), *Germania* (Milwaukee, Wis.), *Volksfreund* (Appleton, Wis.), *Duluth-Superior Volksfreund* (Duluth, Minn.), *Journal* (Terre Haute, Ind.), *Germania* (Grand Rapids, Mich.), Kansas *Telegraph* (Topeka, Kan.), Missouri *Staats-Zeitung* (Kansas City, Mo.) and *Westliche Post* (St. Louis, Mo.). *Independent Democratic: Anzeiger und Herold* (Grand Island, Neb.), Michigan *Volksblatt* (Detroit, Mich.), Iowa *Staats-Anzeiger* (Des Moines, Ia.) and *Demokrat* (Evansville, Ind.); *Democratic: Demokrat* (Plonia, Ill.). A study of other German-language newspapers confirms the picture given by the *Eagle's* poll.
[34] W. J. Bryan to W. A. Croffut, July 14, 1900. W. A. Croffut Papers, LC.
[35] Richardson, U.S. Representative from Tennessee, had been Permanent Chairman in Kansas City.
[36] *Proceedings, Dem.*, p. 199.
[37] There were exceptions, cf. above, p. 213.
[38] *Speeches of W. J. Bryan, Revised and arranged by Himself*, Vol. 2 (1911), p. 208.
[39] *Proceedings, Dem.*, p. 208. Bryan, *Speeches* 2, p. 21 f., *Living Issues of the Campaign of 1900* (1900), II, p. 1 ff.
[40] Cf. Merle Curti, *Bryan and World Peace*. Smith College Studies in History, 1931, p. 122 ff.
[41] The *Memoirs of William Jennings Bryan. By Himself and His Wife Mary Baird Bryan* (1925), p. 120 f. Cf. also Paola E. Coletta, "Bryan, Anti-imperialism and Missionary Diplomacy," *Nebraska History* 44: 3 (1963), p. 170.
[42] On Bryan and the ratification of the peace treaty, cf. W. Stull Holt, *Treaties Defeated by the Senate. A Study of the struggle between President and Senate over the Conduct of Foreign Relations* (1933), p. 165 ff., and Paolo E. Coletta, "Bryan, McKinley and the Treaty of Paris," *Pacific Historical Review*, XXVI (May, 1957), pp. 131—146.
[42] *Proceedings, Dem.*, p. 211.
[43] *Ibid.*, p. 214 ff.
[44] *Proceedings, Dem.*, p. 225 has by mistake *Cuban* instead of Filipinos.
[45] See above, p. 213.
[46] *Proceedings, Dem.*, p. 227.
[47] *Living Issues of the Campaign of 1900*, II, p. 23 ff.
[48] Donelson Caffery to E. Atkinson, May 18, 1900. Edward Atkinson Papers, Mass. Hist. Society, Boston.
[49] W. Winslow to Horace Boies, June 2, 1900 (copy), Atkinson Papers, *ibid*.

[50] See above, p. 168 ff.
[51] Carl Schurz to Welsh, June 7, 1900 (copy), E. B. Smith to Schurz, June 9, 1900, *ibid*, E. B. Smith to E. Atkinson, June 16, 1900. Atkinson Papers, Mass. Hist. Society, Boston.
[52] E. B. Smith to E. Atkinson, June 16, 1900, *ibid*.
[53] Thomas Osborne to E. Atkinson, June 28, 1900, *ibid*.
[54] Cf. below, p. 252 f.
[55] G. F. Hoar, *Autobiography of Seventy years* (1903), p. 322 f.
[56] E. Winslow to Atkinson, July 17, 1900, Atkinson Papers, Mass. Hist. Society. Another of Winslow's critics was Thomas Osborne, who declared in a letter to Atkinson that Winslow "has undoubtedly done more damage to the cause than can easily be repaired." Osborne to Atkinson, Aug. 9, 1900, *ibid*.
[57] W. J. Bryan wrote to Hoar and Hoar answered with a letter in which he put forward the same points of view as in the letter to Atkinson, and called the failure to prevent the ratification of the peace treaty "the greatest single disappointment of my public life." He also explained that he could not help regarding Bryan as the man most responsible, next President McKinley, for the ratification of the odious treaty. Hoar to Bryan, May 15, 1900. Bryan Papers, LC. On Hoar, cf. Richard E. Welch, Jr., *George Frisbie Hoar and the Half-Breed Republicans* (1971), p. 254 f.
[58] G. F. Hoar to E. Atkinson, Aug. 14, 1900. Atkinson Papers, Mass. Hist. Society. Hoar steadfastly maintained this standpoint and defended it also in his autobiography. G. F. Hoar, *Autobiography of Seventy Years* (1903), II, p. 323.
[59] The Boston *Post*, May 30, 1900; *Public Opinion,* July 5, 1900. Cf. also Daniel B. Schirmer, *Republic or Empire: American Resistance to the Philippine War* (1973), p. 140 ff.; Welch, *op. cit*., p. 268 ff., and "Opponents and Colleagues: George Frisbie Hoar and Henry Cabot Lodge 1898—1904." *New England Quarterly* 19, p. 200 ff. Beisner, *op. cit*., p. 161 f.
[60] Charles F. Adams to Carl Schurz, Oct. 18, 1900. Schurz Papers, LC.
[61] Charles F. Adams to Carl Schurz, July 14, 1900, *ibid*.
[62] Charles F. Adams to Carl Schurz, July 27, 1900, *ibid*.
[63] Erwing Winslow to W. A. Croffut, July 17, 1900. Croffut Papers, LC.
[64] Schurz and Adams had been closely associated for many years. Cf. Charles F. Adams, *Autobiography*, p. 184.
[65] Charles F. Adams to Carl Schurz, Oct. 17, Oct. 29 and Nov. 7, 1900; Schurz to Adams, Nov. 5 (copy); Samuel Bowles to Schurz, Oct. 27 and 31, 1900, Schurz Papers, LC.
[66] The New York *Times*, Oct. 31, 1900. Cf. Edwin B. Smith to Schurz, Nov. 3, 1900. Schurz Papers, LC.
[67] Cf. W. R. Thayer, *Life and Letters of John Hay,* II, p. 257. Hay used almost identical words in a letter to Henry Adams, Robert L. Beisner, *Twelve against Empire. The Anti-Imperialists, 1898—1900* (1968), p. 129.
[68] Old George Boutwell made an active contribution during the 1900 campaign. On October 18 he made a big anti-imperialistic speech in Salem (Mass.), which took the form of an excellent summary of the anti-imperialistic arguments put forward by him and his sympathizers. The speech has been printed in Boutwell's memoirs, *Reminiscences of Sixty Years in Public Affairs,* II (1902), p. 322 ff.
[69] The letter, sent to Treadwell Cleveland, is quoted from James McGurrin, *"Bourke Cockran. A Free Lance in American Politics"* (1948), p. 204.
[70] Schurz to E. B. Smith, Oct. 4, 1900 (copy). Schurz Papers, LC.
[71] H. Welsh to Schurz, Sept. 25, 1900. Moorfield Storey to Schurz, Oct 2, 1900, *ibid*.
[72] Schurz to Moorfield Storey, Oct. 3, 1900; to Welsh same date (copies). Charles

Eliot to Schurz, Oct. 4, 1900, *ibid.*

[73] Fulton Cutting to H. Welsh, Oct. 2, 1900 (copy). Schurz Papers, LC. Horace White to Welsh same date (copy), *ibid.* Schurz to E. B. Smith, Sept. 30, 1900 (copy), *ibid.*

[74] Schurz to E. B. Smith, Sept. 30, 1900 (copy), *ibid.*

[75] Schurz to Welsh, Oct. 5, 1900 (copy), *ibid.*

[76] Schurz to E. B. Smith, Oct. 4, and 13, 1900 (copy), *ibid.*

[77] Schurz to E. B. Smith, Oct. 18 (copy), *ibid.*

[78] Cf. above, p. 50 f.

[79] Richard Olney, "Growth of our foreign policy," The *Atlantic Monthly,* Vol. LXXXV, March 1900, p. 289 ff.

[80] Grover Cleveland to Richard Olney, March 20, 1900 (copy). Cleveland Papers, LC.

[81] H. L. Nelson to R. Olney, Sept. 9, 1900. Richard Olney Papers, LC.

[82] The *Literary Digest,* Sept. 15, 1900, p. 304.

[83] See e.g. The Boston *Transcript* (Rep.) and New York *Press* (Rep.), *ibid.* Olney had no such plans. He was, however, for tactical reasons nominated as presidential candidate by the Democratic state convention in Massachusetts in 1904. Henry James, *Richard Olney and his Public Service* (1923), p. 177 f.

[84] Olney to S. B. Griffin, 1900, published as appendix to H. James, *Richard Olney and his Public Service* (1923), p. 308 ff. Cf. Olney to Griffin, Sept. 9, 1900 (copy). Richard Olney Papers, LC.

[84a] The Baltimore *Sun* (Dem.). Similar statements in e.g. the Washington *Times* and Chicago *Chronicle* (both Dem.).

[85] The *Literary Digest,* Sept. 15, 1900, p. 304.

[86] G. Cleveland to D. H. Dickinson, Oct. 12, 1900 (copy). Cleveland Papers, LC. Robert McElroy, *Grover Cleveland. The Man and the Statesman* (1923), II, p. 288 f

[87] *Op. cit.,* p. 219 f.

[88] *Ibid.*

[89] The New York *Evening Post,* May 18, 1900.

[90] The *Public Opinion,* July 26, 1900. Cf. E. Stanwood, *A History of the Presidency from 1897 to 1909* (1912), p. 68 f.

[91] The *Literary Digest,* July 14, 21, Aug. 4, 1900.

[92] The *Public Opinion,* July 26, 1900, *Literary Digest,* Aug. 4, 1900.

[93] *Ibid.*

[94] E. B. Smith to Carl Schurz, July 20, 1900. Schurz Papers, LC.

[95] C. Schurz to Moorfield Storey, July 22, 1900; Schurz to E. Winslow, July 22, 1900 (copies), *ibid.*

[96] Moorefield Storey to Schurz, Aug. 10, 1900, *ibid.*

[97] Schurz to Moorefield Storey (copy), Aug. 11, 1900, *ibid.*

[98] Schurz to Edwin B. Smith, July 30, 1900 (copy), *ibid.*

[99] Schurz to Henderson (copy), July 31, 1900, *ibid.*

[100] Schurz to W. B. Smith (copy), Aug. 9, 1900, *ibid.*

[101] At this point Croffut left his post within the organization as a result of a conflict between himself and the chairman, O'Farrell. The dispute had arisen in connection with the arrangements made for the Boer delegates who had recently visited the United States.

[102] Croffut to J. B. Henderson, Aug. 11, 1900, Henderson to Croffut, Aug. 14, 1900. W. A. Croffut Papers, LC.

[103] Cf. above, p. 240 f.

[104] Erwing Winslow to Edwin B. Smith, Aug. 8, 1900. W. A. Croffut Papers, LC.

[105] See above, p. 239; 250 f. Cf. William Everett in the New York *Evening Post,* May 8, 1900.

[106] See e.g. the Indianapolis *Journal,* Aug. 15—16, 1900.

[107] Moorefield Storey to Schurz, Aug. 18, 1900. Schurz to Moorefield Storey, Aug. 20, 1900. Schurz Papers, LC.

[108] E. B. Smith to Schurz, Aug. 18, 1900, *ibid.*

[109] H. Welsh to E. B. Smith, March 3, June 18, Sept. 25, Oct 5, 1900. Herbert Welsh Papers, Penn. Hist. Society, Philadelphia.

[110] Louis R. Erich to Schurz, Aug. 21, 1900. Schurz Papers, LC.

[111] "To me it is utterly incredible how any man who has looked into the heart of our Philippine imbroglio and who, in the slightest degree, realizes the influence which a colonial policy must exert on the future of a republic can hesitate in opposing the McKinley administration," he wrote to Grover Cleveland, Aug. 20, 1900. Grover Cleveland Papers, LC.

[112] Everett V. Abbot to Schurz, Aug. 20, 1900. I. H. Klein to Schurz, Aug. 28, 1900. O. G. Villard to Schurz, Aug. 29, 1900. Schurz Papers, LC.

[113] E. V. Abbot to Schurz, Aug. 20, 1900, *ibid.*

[114] Thomas Osborne to Schurz, Aug. 29, 1900, *ibid.* Cf. also Osborne, Chapman *et al.* to Donelson Caffery, Dec. 28, 1900. Donelson Caffery Papers, Southern Historical Collection, Chapel Hill.

[115] M. Storey to L. R. Ehrich, Sept. 1, 1900 (copy), *ibid.*

[116] Henderson to Schurz, Aug. 28, 1900, *ibid.*

[117] Schurz to L. R. Ehrich, Sept. 1, 1900 (copy), *ibid.*

[118] Schurz to M. Storey, Sept. 1, 1900 (copy), *ibid.*

[119] Cf. above, p. 250. Also A. B. Farquhar, "The New Movement," Address, Sept. 5, 1900. E. Atkinson Papers, Mass. Hist. Society, Boston.

[120] *Ibid.*

[121] *The Ethical Record,* Vol. II, Oct.—Nov. 1900.

[122] Schurz to Charles F. Adams, Nov. 5, 1899 (copy). Schurz Papers, LC.

[123] Richard Olney to D. R. Francis, June 15, 1900 (copy). Richard Olney Papers, LC. Cf. Olney to Grover Cleveland, June 15, 1900 (copy), *ibid.*

[124] Claude M. Fuess, *Carl Schurz, Reformer,* p. 364. Cf. also D. M. Osborne to Moorfield Storey, Sept 25, 1900. Moorfield Storey Papers, LC.

[125] See below, p. 259 ff.

[126] Quoted from F. Bancroft and W. Dunning, *A Sketch of Carl Schurz's Political Career 1869—1906,* in the *Reminiscences of Carl Schurz,* III, p. 477 (N.Y. 1908).

[127] E. Berkeley Tompkins, *Anti-Imperialism in the United States: The Great Debate 1890—1920* (1970), p. 234.

[128] Cf. Beisner, *op. cit.,* p. 103.

[129] Cf. Harold Francis Williamson, *Edward Atkinson. The Biography of an American Liberal, 1827—1905* (1934), p. 230 f.

[130] E. Atkinson to Hoar, Aug. 13, 1900 (copy). Atkinson Papers, Mass. Hist. Society.

[131] E. Winslow to W. A. Croffut, July 17, 1900. Croffut Papers, LC. Cf. above, p. 243. Atkinson's methods and his virulent language had dismayed many anti-imperialists almost from the beginning of the movement. Cf. Robert L. Beisner, *Twelve against Empire. The Anti-Imperialists, 1898—1900* (1968), p. 98 ff. E. Berkeley Tompkins, *Anti-Imperialism in the United States, 1890—1920* (1970), p. 289 f.

[132] E. Atkinson to Shattuc, Aug. 15, 29, 31, Sept. 6, 1899 (copies), W. B. Shattuc to Atkinson, Aug. 10, 25, Sept. 2, Atkinson Papers, Mass. Hist. Society.

[133] E. Atkinson to E. Stang, Nov. 17, 1899, Stang to Atkinson, Oct. 10, Nov. 22, 1899, *ibid.*

[134] E. Atkinson to W. B. Shattuc, Aug. 31, 1899 (copy), *ibid.*

[135] C. W. Walsh, member of the Democratic National Committee, to Atkinson, Oct. 9, 1899, *ibid.*
[136] Dem. County Central Committee, Ringold County, Iowa, to Atkinson, Nov. 20, 1899, *ibid.*

Chapter VIII

[1] See e.g. Perry S. Heath, "The Lessons of the Campaign," The *Forum*, Dec. 1900.
[2] The *Review of Reviews*, Nov. 1900.
[3] *Ibid.* Cf. William H. Allen, "The Election of 1900." *Annals of the American Academy of Political and Social Science*. No. 292, Dec. 1900.
[4] Perry S. Heath to Cortelyou, Oct. 1, 1900. McKinley Papers, LC. Cf. The *Review of Reviews*, Nov. 1900.
[5] Coletta, *op. cit.*, p. 281.
[6] The *Review of Reviews,* Nov. 1900.
[7] The *Review of Reviews*, Nov. 1900; *Public Opinion*, Nov. 8, 1900. According to information obtained from an employee of the Republican National Committee, over 5000 newspapers were supplied with material and 125,000,000 copies of documents were issued. In addition 21,000,000 Postal Cards were distributed from Philadelphia. C. R. Berckland to Albert Shaw, Nov. 2, 1900. Albert Shaw Papers, New York Public Library. Perry S. Heath has stated that the newspaper service covered no less than about 6000 newspapers. Perry S. Heath to Cortelyou, Sept. 27, 1900. McKinley Papers, LC.
[8] Willis J. Abbot, "The Management of the Democratic Campaign." The *Review of Reviews*, Nov. 1900.
[9] Responsible for the prediction was H. C. Payne, General Correspondence, Vol. 44, McKinley Papers, LC.
[10] Wyoming was even classified on one occasion as dobutful.
[11] Joseph H. Manley to Cortelyou, Oct. 3, 1900, McKinley Papers, LC.
[12] Youngblood to Cortelyou, Oct. 5, 1900, *ibid.*
[13] N. B. Scott to Cortelyou, Oct. 9, 1900, *ibid.*
[14] The New York *Herald*, Sept.
[16] Cf. below, p. 291.
[17] Cf. below, p. 293.
[18] The *Review of Reviews*, Sept. 1900, p. 392. Cf. E. Stanwood, A History of the Presidency from 1897—1909, p. 72 ff.
[19] Wayne C. Williams, *William Jennings Bryan,* p. 234. Cf. also J. R. Johnson, "Imperialism in Nebraska, 1898—1904," *Nebraska History* 44: 3 (1963), p. 158.
[20] The Chicago *Times Herald,* Aug. 22, 1900.
[21] As e.g. in Wahoo, Nebraska, Aug. 21, Omaha, Aug. 26 and Dakota City (Neb.), Aug. 28.
[22] The *Outlook*, Sept. 8 and 15, 1900.
[23] The *Nation*, Sept. 6, 1900.
[24] The New York *Herald* (Ind.), Sept 19, 1900. The Philadelphia *Ledger* (Ind. Rep.) expressed a similar opinion on the same date.
[25] The Boston *Transcript* (Rep.) quoted in *Public Opinion*, Sept. 27, 1900.
[26] The Philadelphia *Record* (Dem.) quoted in *Public Opinion*, Sept 27, 1900.
[27] The St. Paul *Pioneer Press* (Rep.), Sept. 19, 1900. In the same way The *Outlook* assured its readers: "Mr Bryan could hardly please the administration better than by shifting his campaign to the silver and trust issues," The *Outlook*, Oct. 1900.
[28] Schurz to Edwin Burrit Smith, Oct. 13, 1900. Schurz Papers, LC.

[29] Schurz to Moorefield Storey, Oct. 1, 1900 (copy), *ibid.* Schurz to Herbert Welsh, same date (copy), *ibid.*

[30] See above, p. 245.

[31] Schurz to Edwin Burrit Smith, Oct. 13, 1900 (copy). Schurz Papers, LC.

[32] Cf. below, p. 300.

[33] The *Outlook*, Oct. 27, 1900. *Public Opinion* gives the figures as 60,000, *Public Opinion*, Oct. 25, 1900.

[34] A detailed survey of press opinions can be found in *Public Opinion*, Oct. 25, 1900.

[35] The New York *Tribune*, Oct. 18, 1900.

[36] The Philadelphia *Press* (Rep.) and Baltimore *Herald* (Ind.) quoted in *Public Opinion*, Oct. 27, 1900.

[37] *Gunton's Magazine*, Nov. 1900, p. 387.

[38] Elwood S. Corser to Herbert Welsh, Oct. 8, 1900. Herbert Welsh Papers, The Hist. Soc. of Pennsylvania, Philadelphia.

[39] Cf. above, p. 240 ff.

[40] The New York *World*, Nov. 5, 1900. Roosevelt himself put the figure at 681. Roosevelt to Edward North Buxton, Nov. 19, 1900 (copy). Roosevelt Papers, LC.

[41] Roosevelt to M. A. Hanna, June 27, 1900. Roosevelt Papers, LC. If Roosevelt compared himself with "a bull moose," the critical Edward Atkinson came to think of a different animal: "a bulldog with confused ideas." Edward Atkinson to W. A. Croffut, Aug. 15, 1900. E. Atkinson Papers, Mass. Hist. Society, Boston.

[42] Roosevelt to H. C. Payne, Sept. 6, 16, 17, 1900 (draft). Roosevelt Papers, LC.

[43] Roosevelt to H. C. Payne, Sept. 16, 1900 (copy), *ibid.*

[44] Roosevelt to Hanna, June 27, 1900 (copy), *ibid.*

[45] The Cincinnati *Enquirer*, Oct. 13, 1900.

[46] The Grand Rapids *Morning Democrat*, Sept. 8, 1900; Chicago *Daily News*, same date.

[47] The South Bend *Tribune*, Sept. 10, 1900.

[48] The New York *Sun*, Sept. 17, 1900.

[49] H. C. Payne to Roosevelt, Aug. 22, 1900. Roosevelt Papers, LC.

[50] Vol. 7, Clippings 1900: Aug. 10—Dec. 31, 1900, *ibid.* There is also some material of interest in Lindsay Denison, "Campaigning by Special Train," *Everybody's*, Aug. 1904, and in J. A. Swisher, "Theodore Roosevelt in Iowa," The *Palimpsest*, Oct. 1932, pp. 397 ff.

[51] The New York *Herald*, Aug. 28, 1900. Minneapolis *Tribune*, Sept. 12, New York *Press*, Sept. 19, 22, Cheyenne *Leader*, Sept. 24, Cincinnati *Enquirer*, Oct. 13, Salt Lake City, Sept. 22, 1900.

[52] Detailed itineries of Roosevelt's campaign are to be found in the Roosevelt Collection, Harvard University Library.

[53] H. C. Payne to Roosevelt, Aug. 22, 1900. Roosevelt Papers, LC.

[54] *Ibid.*

[55] Series 5 A, Speeches 1899—1901. Roosevelt Papers, LC.

[56] "Free silver, trusts and the Philippines." Speeches 1899—1901, Roosevelt Papers, LC.

[57] Cf. above, p. 189.

[58] "The Bogie of Militarism," Speeches 1899—1901, Series A 5, Roosevelt Papers, LC.

[59] John Proctor Clarke, "Random Recollections of campaigning with Col. Roosevelt." Manuscript, 333.2 C 5, Roosevelt Collection, Harvard University Library.

[60] Clippings Aug.—Dec. 1900. Vol. 7. Roosevelt Papers, LC. Cf. Elmer Ellis, *Henry Moore Teller, Defender of the West* (1941), p. 333.

[61] "National Honor and National Greatness." Speeches 1899—1901, Series A 5, LC.

[62] Cf. above, p. 275.

[63] Cf. above, p. 141 ff.

[64] Address at Madison Square Garden, Oct. 27, 1900. (Manuscript.) Speeches 1899—1900, Roosevelt Papers, LC.

[65] Cf. above, p. 139 f.

[66] One technique used by Roosevelt during his campaign in the West was that, after quoting Bryan's speech about imperialism leading to a large standing army, with the threat of militarism and oppression, he would cry to the large audience: "Let the soldiers stand." When perhaps half a dozen soldiers stood up, Roosevelt would point to them dramatically: "There are your oppressors." Wayne C. Williams, *William Jennings Bryan*, p. 234.

[67] See above, p. 277.

[68] "The Election of 1900." The *Annals of the American Academy of Political and Social Science*, No. 293, Dec. 1900.

[69] Willis J. Abbot, "The management of the Democratic Campaign." The *Review of Reviews*, Nov. 1900.

[70] C. M. Walter to Marion Butler, March 2, 1900. Marion Butler Papers, Southern Historical Collection, North Carolina University Library, Chapel Hill. Cf. I. H. Tibbles to Marion Butler, March 9, 1900, *ibid.*

[71] See above, p. 139.

[72] The Indianapolis *Journal*, Feb. 2, July 3 and 4, 1900. The Indianapolis *Sentinel*, July 1 and 3, 1900.

[73] The Indianapolis *Journal*, July 16, The Indianapolis *Sentinel*, July 7, 11, 13, 22 and 24, 1900.

[74] The Indianapolis *Journal*, Aug. 4, 1900.

[75] The Columbus *Republican*, April 2, 1900; The Indianapolis *Journal*, Aug. 8; The Terre Haute *Tribune*, Aug. 8; Wabash *Plain Dealer*.

[76] The Indianapolis *Journal*, Aug. 14.

[77] *Ibid.* Aug. 16, 1900.

[78] The Indianapolis *Journal*, Aug. 24, 1900.

[79] *Ibid.* Aug. 27, 1900.

[80] *Ibid.* Aug. 29, 1900.

[81] The Kokomo *News*, Sept. 10, 1900. The Indianapolis *Journal*, Sept. 1, 4, 7, 1900.

[82] Cf. above, p. 267 f.

[83] The Indianapolis *Journal*, Sept. 15, 16, 1900.

[84] The Indianapolis *Journal*, Sept. 20, 1900. At the same time Van Vorhis, the Silver Republican leader in Indiana, believed in a Democratic victory.

[85] *Ibid.* Sept. 28, 1900.

[86] The Indianapolis *Sentinel*, Sept. 3—7, 1900. The Indianapolis *Journal*, same date.

[87] The Indianapolis *Journal*, Sept. 29.

[88] *Ibid.* Oct. 10, 13, 1900.

[89] *Ibid.* Oct. 20. Cf. also the Mishawaka *Enterprise*, Oct. 19, 1900.

[90] The Indianapolis *Sentinel*, Oct. 29, 1900.

[91] *Ibid.* Oct. 26 and Nov. 2, 1900.

[92] The Indianapolis *Journal*, Nov. 2 and the *Sentinel*, same date.

[93] The New York *Times*, Oct. 3, 1900. Prediction, Oct. 4, 1900. McKinley Papers, LC, N. B. Scott, Oct. 9, 1900, *ibid.*

[94] John Hay to Samuel Mather, Sept. 28, 1900. William Roscoe Thayer, *Life and Letters of John Hay*, II (1908), p. 253.

[95] H. U. Brown to Albert Beveridge, Sept. 20, 1900. Albert Beveridge Papers, LC.

[96] Koenig, *Bryan*, p. 337 f., Coletta, *op. cit.*, p. 271.

[97] Roosevelt to Cabot Lodge, Aug. 27, 30, 1900. *Selections from the Correspondence*

of *Theodore Roosevelt and Henry Cabot Lodge, 1884—1918*, Vol. I (1925), p. 474 f. Roosevelt to T. C. Platt, Aug. 20, 1900 (to Seth Low, Aug. 3, 1900). Theodore Roosevelt Papers. Copies of Letters 1888—1903, LC.

[98] Theodore Roosevelt to D. B. Sickels, Aug. 23, 1900 (copy). Elihu Root Papers, LC.

[99] *Public Opinion*, Sept 9, 1900.

[100] Also e.g. the Philadelphia *Ledger*.

[101] *Public Opinion*, Sept. 20, 1900.

[102] James K. Jones to W. J. Bryan, Aug. 4, 1900. Bryan Papers, LC.

[103] Willis J. Abbot gave in his reports to Bryan lively descriptions of the bitter fight between Hill and Croker and of their attitudes to Bryan. He summed up thus: "The interesting thing to me was that both factions, while showing the bitterest antagonism to each other, were one in professed support of you and the Chicago platform. Between us I lay some emphasis on the word professed." W. J. Abbot to W. J. Bryan, Oct. 25, 1900. Also Sept. 18, 1900. Bryan Papers, LC.

[104] The *Outlook*, Oct. 27, 1900.

[105] "I think the Chicago Platform Democracy in New York will go to pieces. Croker's attitude has cut the ground from under our feet," Abbot wrote to Bryan at the end of October. W. J. Abbot to W. J. Bryan, Oct. 25, 1900. Bryan Papers, LC.

[106] The *Nation*, Aug. 23, 1900.

[107] Amos Cummings to W. J. Bryan, Aug. 9, and Oct. 15, 1900. James McGuire to Bryan, Aug. 3, 1900. Bryan Papers, LC.

[108] C. H. Jones to W. J. Bryan, Oct. 29, 1900, *ibid.*

[109] James K. Jones to W. J. Bryan, Aug. 4, 1900, *ibid.*

[110] P. S. Bennet to W. J. Bryan, Aug. 9, 1900, *ibid.*

[111] W. E. Chandler to Albert Beveridge, Sept. 24, 1900. Beveridge Papers, LC. Whitelaw Reid to Theodore Roosevelt, Sept. 21, 1900. Roosevelt Papers, LC, and Aug 18, 1900 (copy). Whitelaw Reid Papers, LC.

[112] Joseph H. Manley to Cortelyou, Oct. 3 and Oct. 23, 1900; to McKinley, Oct. 24, 1900. McKinley Papers, LC.

Chapter IX

[1] W. J. Stone, "The Campaign of 1900 from a Democratic Point of View," The *Forum*, Sept. 1900.

[2] The Philadelphia *Press*, The Florida *Times Union* and *Citizen*. The *Literary Digest*, Dec. 29, 1900.

[3] James K. Jones to W. J. Bryan, Dec. 1, 1900. Bryan Papers, LC.

[4] J. G. Johnson to W. J. Bryan, Nov. 19, 1900, *ibid.*

[5] W. Sulzer to W. J. Bryan, Nov. 14, 1900, *ibid.*

[6] W. Reid to Cushman Davis, Nov. 11, 1900. Whitelaw Reid Papers, LC.

[7] Charles J. Bonaparte to Lucius B. Swift, Nov. 7, 1900. Lucius B. Swift Papers, Indiana State Library, Indianapolis.

[8] Figures taken from E. E. Robinson, *The Presidential Vote, 1896—1932* (1934).

[9] M. F. Tarpey to W. J. Bryan, Nov. 2, 1900. Bryan Papers, LC.

[10] M. F. Tarpey to W. J. Bryan, Nov. 9, 1900, *ibid.*

[11] W. A. Croffut to W. J. Bryan, Nov. 7, 1900, *ibid.*

[12] R. I. Pettigrew to W. J. Bryan, Nov. 13, 1900, *ibid.*

[13] W. M. Deisher to W. J. Bryan, 1900, *ibid.*

[14] G. A. Linckhart to W. J. Bryan, Nov. 10, 1900, *ibid.*

[15] R. H. Harvey, *Samuel Gompers: Champion for the Toiling Masses* (1935).

[16] John C. Appel, *The Relationship of American Labor to United States Imperialism, 1895—1905* (diss., typewritten, 1950), p. 181 f.

[17] Cf. above, p. 70 f.

[18] Appel, *op. cit.*, p. 187 et al. On Gompers and the issue of imperialism cf. also Daniel B. Schirmer, *Republic or Empire: American Resistance to the Philippine War* (1972), p. 139, and William Pomeroy, *American Neo-Colonialism. Its Emergence in the Philippines and Asia* (1970), p. 99 ff.

[19] E. Burrit Smith to Carl Schurz, Nov. 3, 1900. Schurz Papers, LC.

[20] E. S. Corser to W. J. Bryan, Nov. 5, 1900. Bryan Papers, LC.

[21] E. S. Corser to W. A. Croffut, Dec. 8, 1900. Croffut Papers, LC.

[22] W. A. Croffut to W. J. Bryan, Nov. 7, 1900. Bryan Papers, LC.

[23] Erwing Winslow to W. A. Croffut, Nov. 8 and 19, 1900. Bryan Papers, LC. Cf. Edwin Burrit Smith to Moorfield Storey, Nov. 16, 1900. Moorfield Storey Papers, LC.

[24] J. W. Goldsmith to W. J. Bryan, Nov. 10, 1900. Bryan Papers, LC.

[25] A. J. Elias to W. J. Bryan, Nov. 9, 1900, *ibid.*

[26] Melvin G. Palliser to W. J. Bryan, Nov. 26, 1900, *ibid.*

[27] Thomas D. Watkins to W. J. Bryan, Nov. 9, 1900, William Sulzer to W. J. Bryan, Nov. 14, G. E. Doying to W. J. Bryan, Nov. 18, 1900, *ibid.* J. S. Corbin to W. J. Bryan, Nov. 8, 1900, *ibid.* As head of the Chicago delegation at the convention in Kansas City, the influential Carter Harrison had worked hard to prevent the silver plank of 1896 being reiterated. Cf. Harry Barnard, *Eagle Forgotten. The Life of John Peter Altgeld* (1962, 1st ed. 1938), p. 424.

[28] Henry W. Richmond to H. Welsh, Nov. 10, 1900. Welsh Papers, Penn. Hist. Society, Philadelphia. Cf. also Edwin Burrit Smith to Carl Schurz, Nov. 7, 1900. Schurz Papers, LC.

[29] E.g. F. J. Van Vorhis to W. J. Bryan, Nov. 14, 1900. Bryan Papers, LC.

[30] The *North American Review*, Dec. 1900.

[31] Cf. also Paul W. Glad, *The Trumpet Soundeth*, p. 60.

[32] Cf. *The Memoirs of William Jennings Bryan*, p. 125.

[33] E. E. Robinson, *The Presidential Vote, 1896—1932*, p. 59.

[34] K. Schrifftgiesser, *The Gentleman from Massachusetts. Henry Cabot Lodge* (1944), p. 194 f.

[35] Richard E. Welch, "Opponents and Colleagues," p. 198 f.

[36] Francis C. Lourke to Theodore Roosevelt, Oct. 24, 1900. Theodore Roosevelt Papers, LC. The Hartford *Times* claimed that the swing to the Democratic column was caused by the work of the anti-imperialists. Cf. Schirmer, *op. cit.*, p. 220.

[37] Charle G. Dawes, *A Journal of the McKinley Years*, p. 252.

[38] Cf. *Gunton's Magazine*, Dec. 1900, p. 483 f.

[39] In South Dakota Mark Hanna and the Republican campaign committee had made a special effort to ensure the defeat of Senator Pettigrew, Hanna's bitter enemy. R. F. Pettigrew, *Imperial Washington* (1922), p. 291 ff.

[40] Cf. above, p. 293; 298 f.

[41] Cf. above, p. 95 ff.

[42] Cf. above, p. 96.

[43] Cf. above, p. 97.

[44] Robinson, *op. cit.*, p. 185 f.

[45] *Ibid.*, p. 50 f.

[46] Cf. Elmer Ellis, *Henry Moore Teller: Defender of the West* (1941), p. 325 ff.

[47] The *Outlook*, Sept. 1, 1900.

[48] Cf. e.g. *Gunton's Magazine*, Dec. 1900, p. 481 ff.

[49] Robinson, *op. cit.*, p. 63 f.

[50] Cf. William H. Allen, "The Election of 1900." *Annals of the American Academy of Political and Social Science,* No. 293, Dec. 25, 1900.

[51] Harry W. Baer, *The New York Times since the Civil War,* p. 264.

[52] McKinley in a speech before the Union League, Philadelphia, Nov. 24, 1900, Allen, *op. cit.,* p. 62.

[53] *Ibid.,* p. 63.

[54] Albert Shaw, "The American Presidential Election," The *Contemporary Review,* Vol. LXXVIII (1900), p. 609.

[55] The *Literary Digest,* Nov. 24, 1900. Cf. above, p. 230 ff.

[56] The New York *Morgen Journal,* the Baltimore *Deutsche Correspondent* (both Dem.), et al. In the same way, e.g. the Chicago *Abendpost* (Ind.).

[57] Shaw, *op. cit.,* p. 611.

[58] *Ibid.,* p. 621.

[59] On the election as a mandate on expansion, cf. George H. Mayer, *The Republican party* (1967), p. 270, also Thomas A. Bailey, "Was the Presidential Election of 1900 a Mandate on Imperialism?" The *Mississippi Valley Historical Review,* XXVI (June 1937) and Julius W. Pratt, *America's Colonial Experiment. How the United States Gained, Governed and in Part Gave Away a Colonial Empire* (1950), p. 80 ff. Hollingsworth, *op. cit.,* p. 184 f.

[60] Wayne C. Williams, *William Jennings Bryan,* p. 236.

Bibliography

PRIMARY MATERIALS

Manuscript Sources

Library of Congress, Washington, D.C.
    Albert J. Beveridge Papers
    William Jennings Bryan Papers
    Andrew Carnegie Papers
    Grover Cleveland Papers
    George B. Cortelyou Papers
    William A. Croffut Papers
    John Hay Papers
    William McKinley Papers
    Richard Olney Papers
    Whitelaw Reid Papers
    Theodore Roosevelt Papers
    Elihu Root Papers
    Carl Schurz Papers
    John C. Spooner Papers
    Moorfield Storey Papers
Harvard University Library, Cambridge, Massachusetts
    Theodore Roosevelt Collection (Widener Library)
    Thomas Wentworth Higginson Manuscripts (Houghton Library)
Indiana Historical Society, Indianapolis, Indiana
    Charles Warren Fairbanks Papers
Indiana State Library, Indianapolis, Indiana
    William Dudley Foulke Papers
    D. W. Henry Collection
    Benjamin S. Parker Papers
    Lucius B. Swift Papers
Lilly Library, Indiana University, Bloomington, Indiana
    Charles Warren Fairbanks Papers
    Maurice Thompson Papers
Massachusetts Historical Society, Boston, Massachusetts
    Edward Atkinson Papers
    Henry Cabot Lodge Papers
New York Public Library
    Albert Shaw Papers
University of North Carolina, Chapel Hill, North Carolina
    Southern Historical Collection

Marion Butler Papers
Donelson Caffery Papers
Arthur P. Gorman Papers
James M. Griggs Papers
Historical Society of Pennsylvania, Philadelphia, Pennsylvania
Herbert Welsh Papers
Stanford University Library, Palo Alto, California
David Starr Jordan Papers
Washington University Library, Washington, D.C.
Chauncey Depew Papers

Official Documents and Related Materials

American Imperialism and the Philippine Insurrection. Testimony Taken from Hearings on Affairs in the Philippine Islands before the Senate Committee on the Philippines, 1902. Ed. by Henry F. Graff. Boston, 1969

The Battle of 1900. An Official Hand-Book for Every American Citizen. New York, 1900.

Congressional Record. 55th and 56th Congress

Democratic Campaign Book, 1900

Congressional Directory, 56th Congress. 1900

Hearings: Senate Committee on the Pacific Islands. 56th Congress, 1st Session. Document No. 147

Historical Statistics of the United States. Colonial Times to 1957. Washington, D.C., 1960

Legislative and State Manual of Indiana for 1899 and 1900. Compiled from Official Records by William E. Henry. Indianapolis, 1900

National Party Platforms. Ed. by Kirk H. Porter. New York, 1924

Official Proceedings of the Democratic National Convention, Held in Kansas City on July 4, 5, and 6, 1900. Chicago, 1900

Official Proceedings of the Twelth Republican National Convention 1900. Philadelphia, 1900

Petersen, Svend, A Statistical History of Our Presidential Elections. 1963

Platforms of Political Parties in Texas. Ed. by E. W. Winkler. Bulletin of the University of Texas, 1916: 53

Prescott, Lawrence F., Living Issues of the Campaign of 1900. Its Men and Principles. Chicago, 1900

The Records, Briefs, and Arguments of Counsel in the Insular Cases of the October Term, 1900, in the Supreme Court of the United States. Compiled by Albert H. Howe. 1901

Report on the Island of Porto Rico: Its Population, Civil Government, Commerce, Industries, Productions, Roads, Tariff, and Currency. Oct. 6, 1899. By Henry K. Carroll, Special Commissioner for the United States to Porto Rico. 1900

Reports on Industrial and Economic Conditions of Puerto Rico. By Geo. W. Davis. Oct. 1899. Printed 1900.

Republican Campaign Text-Book, 1900. Philadelphia, 1900

Robinson, Edgar E., The Presidential Vote, 1896—1932. Stanford, California, 1934

State Platforms of the Two Dominant Political Parties in Indiana, 1850—1900. Ed. by William E. Henry. Indianapolis, 1902

United States Supreme Court. Opinions Delivered in the Insular Tariff Cases. Washington, D.C., 1901

Books, Articles, and Pamphlets

Adams, Brooks, *America's Economic Supremacy*. New York, 1900
— *The Law of Civilization and Decay*. New York and London, 1896
Adams, Charles Kendall, "Colonies and Other Dependencies." *Forum*, 27, 1899
Allen, William H., "The Election of 1900."*Annals of the American Academy of Political and Social Sciences*, No. 292. Dec. 1900
Atkinson, Edward, *The Anti-Imperialist*. Brookline 1899
— *The Cost of National Crime*. Boston, 1898
Baldwin, Simeon E., "The Constitutional Questions Incident to the Acquisition and Government of the United States of Island Territory." *Harvard Law Review*, XII, Feb. 1899
Barret, J. "A McKinley Doctrine for Asia." *North American Review*, Aug. 1899
— "The Philippines, Our Approach to Asia." *Harper's Weekly*, July 1900
— "Our Interests in China—A Question of the Hour." *American Review of Reviews*, Jan. 1900
Becker, Carl, "Law and Practice of the United States in the Acquisition and Government of Dependent Territory." *Annals of the American Academy of Political and Social Science*, VII, Nov. 1900
Bigelow, Poultney, "What I Saw at Kansas City." *Contemporary Review*, 72, July, 1900
Boutwell, George, S., *Republic or Empire?* Boston, 1900
— *Party or Country?* Boston, 1900
— *The Crisis of the Republic*. Boston, 1900
— *Bryan or Imperialism?* Boston, 1900
— *The Presidents Policy of War and Conquest Abroad*. Chicago, 1900
Brooks, Francis A., *An Examination of the Scheme for Engrafting the Colonial System of Government upon the United States Constitution*. Boston, 1900
Bryan, William Jennings, "The Issue of the Presidential Election." *North American Review*, 170, July 1900
— "The Election of 1900." *North American Review*, 171, Dec. 1900
— *Republic or Empire? The Philippine Question*. Chicago, 1899
Burgess, John W., "How May the United States Govern Its Extra-Continental Territory?" *Political Science Quarterly*, XIV, March, 1899
— *Political Science and Comparative Constitutional Law*. Boston and London, 1893
— "The Relation of the Constitution of the United States to Newly Acquired Territory." *Political Science Quarterly*, XV, Sept. 1900
Carroll, H. K., "How Shall Puerto Rico Be Governed?" *Forum*, Nov. 1899
Cochran, Bourke, *In the Name of Liberty*. Boston, 1900
Conant, Charles A., "The United States as a World Power. 1—2." *Forum*, July-Aug., 1900
Creelman, James, "Bryan the Man." *The Independent*, 52, 1900
Curtis, H. G., "The Status of Puerto Rico." *Forum*, Dec. 1899
Davenport, Homer, *The Dollar or the Man?* Boston, 1900
Denby, Charles, "The Constitution and the Flag." *Forum*, May 1900
Denison, Lindsay, "Campaigning by Special Train." *Evereybody's*, Aug. 1904
Dunn, Robert Lee, "Making Presidents by Photography." *Appleton's Magazine*, Sept. 1907
Dunne, Finley Peter, *Mr. Dooley's Opinions*. New York, 1900
"The Election of 1900". *Annals of the American Academy of Political and Social Science*, No. 293, Dec. 1900
"Expansion not Imperialism." *Outlook*, 60, 1898

Fernald, James C., *The Imperial Republic*. New York, 1898
Fiske, John, "Manifest Destiny." *Harper's New Monthly Magazine*, 70, 1885
Ford, Worthington Chauncey, "Trade Policy with Colonies." *Harper's New Monthly Magazine*, July 1899
Freund, Ernst, "The Control of Dependencies through Protectorates." *Political Science Quarterly*, XIV, March 1899
Giddings, Franklin Henry, *Democracy and Empire*. New York and London, 1900
— "Imperialism." *Political Science Quarterly*, XIV, Feb. 1899
Gladden, Washington, "The Issues of War." *Outlook*, July 16, 1898
Griggs, James M., *Speech in Home District*. 1898
Halstead, Murat, "American Annexation and Armament." *Forum*, 24, 1897
Heath, Perry S., "The Lessons of the Campaign." *Forum*, Dec. 1900
Henderson, John B., *The Newly-Acquired Islands and the Constitution*. Philadelphia, 1900
Henry, Guy V., "Our Duty in Porto Rico." *Munsey's Magazine*, Nov. 1899
Hudson, J. T., "Evolution and the Spanish-American War." *National Magazine*, Feb. 1899
Jordan, David Starr, *The Blood of the Nation*. Boston, 1902
— *The Human Harvest*. Stanford, California, 1906
— *Imperial Democracy*. New York, 1899
— *"Lest We Forget."* 1898
— *War and the Breed*. New York, 1915
Judson, Harry Pratt, "Our Federal Constitution and the Government of Tropical Territories." *American Review of Reviews*, Jan. 1899
Langdell, C. C., "The Status of Our New Territories." *Harvard Law Review*, XII, Feb. 1899
Lodge, Henry Cabot, "Our Blundering Foreign Policy." *Forum*, 12, 1895
— *The War with Spain*. Boston, 1899
Lowell, Abbot Lawrence, "The Colonial Expansion of the United States." *Atlantic Monthly*, Feb. 1899
— "The Status of Our New Possessions.—A Third View." *Harvard Law Review*, XII, Nov. 1899
Mahan, Alfred Thayer, *The Interest of America in Sea Power*. Boston, 1897
— *Lessons of the War with Spain*. Boston, 1899
— *The Problem of Asia and Its Effect upon International Conditions*. Boston, 1900
— "Sea Power and Expansion." *The Engineering Magazine*, Jan. 1900
Marburg, Theodore, *Expansion*. New York, 1900
Masters, Edgar Lee, *The Constitution and Our Insular Possessions*. 1900
Morse, Alexander Peter, "The Civil and Political Status of Inhabitants of Ceded Territories." *Harvard Law Review*, XIV, Dec. 1900
Olney, Richard, "Growth of Our Foreign Policy." *Atlantic Monthly*, 65, March, 1900
Opper, *Willie and His Papa, and the Rest of the Family*. New York, 1900
Palfrey, John Gorham, "The Growth of the Idea of Annexation and Its Bearing upon Constitutional Law." *Harvard Law Review*, XIII, Jan. 1900
Parrish, Samuel L., "American Expansion Considered as a Historical Evolution." *Journal of Social Science*, 37, 1899
Parkhurst, Charles H., *Guarding the Cross with Krupp Guns*. New York, 1900
Patriotic Eloquence Relating to the Spanish-American War and Its Issues. Ed. by R. I. Fulton and Thomas Trueblood. New York, 1900
Pepper, George Wharton, *Our National Constitution as Related to National Growth*. 1898

Powers, H. H., "The Ethics of Expansion." *The International Journal of Ethics,* X, April 1900
— "The War as a Suggestion of Manifest Destiny." *Publications of the American Academy of Political and Social Science,* No. 235, Oct. 1898
Randolph, Carman F., *The Law and Policy of Annexation.* New York, 1901
— *Notes on the Law of Territorial Expansion, with Especial Reference to the Philippines.* New York, 1900
— "The Insular Cases." *Columbia Law Review,* Nov. 1901
Reid, Whitelaw, *Our New Interests.* New York, 1900
— *Problems of Expansion, as Considered in Papers and Addresses.* New York, 1900
Rowe, L. S., "The Supreme Court and the Insular Cases". *Annals of the American Academy of Political and Social Science,* Sept. 1901
Schurman, Jacob G., "Our Duty in the Philippines." *Gunton's Magazine,* Jan. 1900
— "The Problem of Territorial Expansion." *American Review of Review,* Oct. 1899
— *Philippine Affairs.* New York, 1904
Schurz, Carl, *American Imperialism.* Chicago, 1899
— *The Policy of Imperialism.* Chicago, 1899
Shaw, Albert, "The American Presidential Election." *Contemporary Review,* 78, Nov. 1900
Smith, Edwin Burritt, *Republic or Empire?* Chicago, 1900
— "The Constitution and Inequality of Rights." *Yale Law Journal,* Feb. 1901
— *National Expansion under the Constitution.* 1898
Smith, Howard L., *Some Aspects of Territorial Expansion.* Chicago 1898
Speer, Robert E., *Mission and Modern History.* 2 vols. New York and London, 1904
Stillman, James W., *Republic or Empire? An Argument in Opposition to the Establishment of an American Colonial System.* Boston, 1900
Strong, Josiah, *Our Country. Its Possible Future and Its Present Crisis.* New York, 1885
Sumner, William Graham, *The Conquest of the United States by Spain.* Boston, 1899
Thayer, James Bradley, "Our New Possessions." *Harvard Law Review,* XII, March 1899
Turner, Frederick Jackson, "The Problem of the West." *Atlantic Monthly,* Sept. 1896.
Van Bergen, R., "Expansion Unavoidable." *Harper's Weekly,* 44, 1900
Von Holst, Hermann, *The Annexations of Our Spanish Conquests.* 1898
— *Some Lessons we Ought to Learn.* Chicago 1899
Wellman, Walter, "The Kansas City Convention." *American Review of Reviews,* July 1900

Published Papers, Memoirs, and Autobiographies

Abbot, Willis, *Watching the World Go By.* Boston, 1933
Adams, Charles Francis, *An Autobiography.* Boston, 1916
Beveridge, Albert, *The Meaning of the Times and Other Speeches.* Indianapolis, 1908
Boutwell, George, *Reminiscences of Sixty Years in Public Affairs.* 2 vols. New York, 1912
Bryan, William Jennings, *The Memoirs of William Jennings Bryan. By Himself and His Wife Mary Baird Bryan.* Chicago, 1925
— *The Second Battle, or the New Declaration of Independence.* Chicago, 1901
William Jennings Bryan, *Selections.* Ed. by Ray Ginger. Indianapolis, 1967

— *Speeches of William Jennings Bryan. Revised and Arranged by Himself.* 2 vols. New York and London, 1911—1913

Carnegie, Andrew, *The Autobiography of Andrew Carnegie.* Boston and New York, 1920

Clark, Champ. *My Quarter Century of American Politics.* 2 vols. New York, 1921

Cleveland, Grover, *Letters of Grover Cleveland, 1850—1908.* Selected and ed. by Allan Nevins. Boston, 1933

Dawes, Charles G., *A Journal of the McKinley Years, 1893—1913.* Chicago, 1950

Depew, Chauncey M., *My Memories of Eighty Years.* New York, 1922

— *Orations, Addresses and Speeches.* Vol. 7. New York, 1910

Dunn, Arthur W., *From Harrison to Harding: A Personal Narrative, Covering a Third of a Century, 1888—1921.* 2 vols. New York and London, 1922

Fairbanks, Charles Warren, *The Life and Speeches of Hon. Charles Warren Fairbanks.* Indianapolis, 1904

Foraker, Joseph B., *Notes of a Busy Life.* 2 vols. Chicago, 1916—1917

Foulke, William Dudley, *A Hoosier Autobiography.* Oxford, 1922

Hoar, George Frisbie, *Autobiography of Seventy Years.* 2 vols. New York, 1903

Jordan, David Starr, *The Days of A Man. Being Memoirs of a Naturalist, Teacher, and Minor Prophet of Democracy.* 2 vols. New York, 1922

Kohlsaat, H. H., *From McKinley to Harding: Personal Recollections of Our Presidents.* New York, 1923

La Follette, Robert M., *La Follette's Autobiography: A Personal Narrative of Political Experiences.* Madison. 1913

Lodge, Henry Cabot, *Speeches and Addresses, 1884—1909.* Boston, 1909

McKinley, William, *Speeches and Addresses of William McKinley. From March 1, 1897 to May 30, 1900.* New York, 1900

Pettigrew, R. F., *Imperial Washington. The Story of American Public Life from 1870 to 1920.* Chicago, 1922

Roosevelt, Theodore, *An Autobiography.* New York, 1913

— *The Letters of Theodore Roosevelt.* Ed. by Elting Morison. 8 vols. Cambridge, Massachusetts, 1951—1954

— *Selections from the Correspondence of Theodore Roosevelt and Henry Cabot Lodge, 1884—1918.* 2 vols. New York and London, 1925

— *The Writings of Theodore Roosevelt.* Ed. by William H. Harbaugh. Indianapolis, 1967

Schurz, Carl, *Reminiscences.* Vol. 3. Continued by F. Bancroft. New York, 1908

— *Speeches, Correspondence and Political Papers of Carl Schurz.* Ed. by Frederick Bancroft. 6 vols. New York 1913

Stoddard, Henry L., *As I Knew Them. Presidents and Politics from Grant to Coolidge.* New York, 1927

White, William Allen, *Autobiography of William Allen White.* New York, 1946

Newspapers and Periodicals

Albany Argus
American Grocer
American Review of Reviews
*Annals of the American Academy of
   Political and Social Science*
Appleton's Magazine
Arena
Atlanta Constitution

Atlanta Journal
Atlantic Monthly
Attica Ledger
Auburn Dispatch
Austin Statesman

Baltimore Herald
Baltimore News

Baltimore Sun
Banker's Magazine
Birmingham News
Bloomfield Germania
Boston Advertiser
Boston Anzeiger
Boston Herald
Boston Journal
Boston Post
Boston Record
Boston Transcript
Boston Traveler
Brooklyn Citizen
Brooklyn Eagle
Brownstone Banner
Buffalo Times
Buffalo Volksfreund
Butte Inter-Mountain

Charleston News and Courier
Chattanooga Times
Cheyenne Sun Leader
Chicago Abendpost
Chicago American
Chicago Chronicle
Chicago Daily News
Chicago Evening Post
Chicago Inter-Ocean
Chicago Journal
Chicago News
Chicago Record
Chicago Republikaner
Chicago Staats-Zeitung
Chicago Times-Herald
Chicago Tribune
Cincinnati Enquirer
Cincinnati Freie Presse
Cincinnati Times-Star
Cincinnati Volksblatt
Cincinnati Westliche Blätter
Cleveland Leader
Cleveland Plain Dealer
Cleveland Wächter und Anzeiger
Clinton Republican
Columbia City Weekly Mail
Columbia City Post
Columbia Law Review
Columbus Biene
Columbus Herald
Columbus Press-Post
Columbus Republican
Commercial and Financial Journal

Contemporary Review
Cosmopolitan Magazine

Dakota Freie-Presse
Dallas News
Dallas-Galveston News
Davenport Demokrat
Decatur Democrat
Delphi Times
Denver News
Denver Republican
Denver Times
Detroit Free Press
Detroit Tribune
Duluth-Superior Volksfreund

Elkhart Review
Engineering Magazine
English News
The Ethical Record
Evansville Courier
Evansville Journal
Everybody's Magazine

Fairmount Weekly News
Farm and Home
Fort Wayne Sentinel
Florida Times-Union and Citizen
Forum
Fountain Warren-Democrat

Goshen Daily Democrat
Goshen Times
Grand Island Anzeiger
Grand Rapids Morning Star
Greencastle Star-Press
Gunton's Magazine

Hamilton County Ledger
Harper's Monthly Magazine
Harper's Weekly
Hartford City Telegram
Hartford Courant
Hartford Times
Harvard Law Review
Hoosier State Weekly
Huntingburg Argus
Huntington Herald

The Independent
Indianapolis Journal
Indianapolis News

Indianapolis Press
Indianapolis Sentinal
Indianpolis Sun
International Journal of Ethics

Jacksonville Times-Union and Citizen
Jasper Courier
Journal of Commerce and Commercial
    Bulletin
Journal of the Knights of Labor
Journal of Social Science

Kansas City Star
Kansas Telegraph
Kokomo Dispatch
Kokomo News
Kokomo Tribune

LaFayette Times
LaFayette Journal
Laporte Argus
Laporte Bulletin
Laporte Herald
Lincoln Freie Presse
Lincoln Staats-Anzeiger
Literary Digest
Logansport Pharos
Louisville Anzeiger
Louisville Courier-Journal
Louisville Dispatch

Macon Telegraph
Madison Courier
Manchester Union
Marion Chronicle
Marion News
Memphis Commercial-Appeal
Michigan City Dispatch
Michigan City News
Milwaukee Germania
Milwaukee Sentinel
Minneapolis Journal
Minneapolis Tribune
Mitchell Commercial
Mishwaka Enterprise
Montana Journal
Montgomery Advertiser
Muncie Morning Star
Muncie Times
Munsey's Magazine

Nashville Evening Banner

Nashville American
Nation
National Magazine
Nationale Prosperität
Nebraska Post
New Albany Public Press
New Albany Tribune
New Haven Register
New Orleans Deutsche Zeitung
New Orleans Picauyne
New Orleans Times-Democrat
New York Evening Post
New York Evening Telegram
New York Herald
New York Mail and Express
New York Press
New York Morgen Journal
New York Staats-Zeitung
New York Sun
New York Times
New York Tribune
New York World
Noblesville Ledger
North American Review

Omaha Bee
Omaha World-Herald
Outlook
Overland Monthly

Peru Evening Journal
Philadelphia Bulletin
Philadelphia Inquirer
Philadelphia Ledger
Philadelphia North American
Philadelphia Press
Philadelphia Record
Philadelphia Times
Pike County Democrat
Pittsburg Post
Platte River Zeitung
Plymouth Democrat
Political Science Quarterly
Portland Oregonian
Public Opinion

Richmond Dispatch
Richmond Evening Item
Richmond Palladium
Richmond Sun-Telegram
Richmond Times

Rockville Tribune
Rushville Republican

Salem Democrat
St Louis Westliche Post
Salt Lake Tribune
San Fransisco Chronicle
St Louis Globe-Democrat
St Louis Post-Dispatch
St Paul Pioneer-Press
Shelby Democrat
South Bend Courier
South Bend Times
South Bend Tribune
Springfield Republican
Springfield Union
Tammany Times
Tell City News
Terre Haute Express

Terre Haute Gazette
Terre Haute Journal
Terre Haute Tribune
Tipton Advocate

Vevay Reveille
Vincennes Commercial
Vincennes Daily Sun
Wabash Plain Dealer
Washington Post
Washington Star
Washington Times
Wheeling Register
Winamac Democrat-Journal
Winamac Republican
Winchester Democrat
Worthington Times

Yale Law Journal

SECONDARY MATERIALS

Books and Articles

Adler, Selig, *The Isolationist Impulse. Its Twentieth-Century Reaction.* New York, 1957

Alexander, D. A. S., *Four Famous New Yorkers: The Political Careers of Cleveland, Platt, Hill, and Roosevelt.* New York, 1923

Appel, John C., *The Relationship of American Labor to United States Imperialism, 1895—1905.* Unpublished PhD thesis. Univ. of Wisconsin, 1950

Auxier, George W., "Middle-Western Newspapers and the Spanish-American War", 1895—1898. *Mississippi Valley Historical Review,* XXVI, 1940

Bailey, Thomas A., *The Art of Diplomacy: The American Experience.* New York, 1968

— *A Diplomatic History of the American People.* New York, 1950
— *The Man in the Street.* New York, 1948
— "Was the Presidential Election of 1900 a Mandate for Imperialism?" *Mississippi Valley Historical Review,* XXLV, 1937

Bancroft, F., & Dunning W., *A Sketch of Carl Schurz's Political Career 1869—1906.* In *The Reminiscences of Carl Schurz.* 3. New York, 1908

Barnhard, Harry, *Eagle Forgotten. The Life of John Peter Altgeld.* New York, 1938

Barnhart, John D., & Carmony, Donald F., *Indiana. From Frontier to Industrial Commonwealth.* II. New York

Beale, Howard K., *Theodore Roosevelt and the Rise of America to World Power.* Baltimore, 1956

Beard, Charles A., *The Idea of National Interest. An Analytical Study in American Foreign Policy.* Chicago, 1934

Beisner, Robert L., *Twelve Against Empire.* New York, 1968

Bemis, Samuel Flagg, *A Diplomatic History of the United States.* New York, 1936

Berbusse, Edward J., *The United States in Puerto Rico, 1898—1900.* Chapel Hill, North Carolina, 1966

355

Bernstein, Barton J., and Leib, Franklin A., "Progressive Republican Senators and American Imperialism, 1898—1916." *Mid-America,* July 1968

Beringause, Arthur F., *Brooks Adams: A Biography.* Boston, 1955

Bowers, Claude G., *Beveridge and the Progressive Era.* Boston, 1932

— *The Life of John Worth Kern.* Indianapolis, 1918

Braeman, John, *Albert J Beveridge: American Nationalist.* Chicago, 1971

Braeman, John, "The Rise of Albert Beveridge to the United States Senate." *Indiana Magazine of History,* LIII, Dec., 1957

Callcott, W. H., *The Caribbean Policy of the United States, 1890—1920.* Baltimore, 1942

Campbell, Charles, S., *Anglo-American Understanding, 1898—1903.* Baltimore, 1957

— *Special Business Interest and the Open Door Policy.* New Haven, Connecticut, 1951

Carter, Harvey L., "Indiana—Hell-Bent For Election. Som Notes on Hoosier Politics." *Indiana Magazine of History,* XLI, 1945

Chessman, G. Wallace, "Theodore Roosevelt's Campaign against the Vice Presidency." *The Historian,* XIV.

Coffin, John A., "The Senatorial Career of Albert J Beveridge." *Indiana Magazine of History,* XXIV, Sept., 1928

Coletta, Paola E., "Bryan Anti-imperialism and Missonary Diplomacy." *Nebraska History,* 44: 3, 1963

— "Bryan, McKinley and the Treaty of Paris." *Pacific Historical Review,* XXVI, May, 1957

— *William Jennings Bryan:* I. *Political Evangelist, 1860—1908.* Lincoln, Nebraska, 1964

Coolidge, Louis A., *An Old-fashioned Senator: Orville H Platt.* New York, 1910

Croly, Herbert, *Marcus Alonzo Hanna, His Life and Work.* New York, 1912

Curti, Merle E., *Bryan and World Peace.* In *Smith College Studies in History.* Vol. XVI. Northampton, 1931

DeConde, Alexander, *A History of American Foreign Policy.* New York, 1963

Dulles, Foster R., *America's Rise to World Power, 1898—1954.* New York, 1954

— *The Imperial Years.* New York, 1956

— *Prelude to World Power. American Diplomatic History, 1860—1900.* New York, 1965

Eseray, Logan, *A History of Indiana From 1850 to the Present. Vol. II.* Indianapolis, 1918

Faulkner, Harold U., *Politics, Reform and Expansion, 1890—1900.* New York, 1959

Ferrell, Robert H., *American Diplomacy: A History.* New York, 1959

Foner, Philip S., *The Spanish-Cuban-American War and the Birth of American Imperialism, 1895—1902.* 2 vols. New York, 1972

— "Why the United states Went to War with Spain in 1898." *Science and Society,* 32, 1968

Freidel, Frank, *The Splendid Little War.* New York, 1958

Fuess, Claude M., *Carl Schurz: Reformer.* Port Washington, New York, 1932

Garraty, John A., *Henry Cabot Lodge. A Biography.* New York, 1953

Ginger, Ray, *Altgeld's America. The Lincoln Ideal Versus Changing Realities.* Chicago, 1958

Glad, Paul W., *Mc Kinley, Bryan and the People.* Philadelphia, 1964

— *The Trumpet Soundeth: William Jennings Bryan and His Democracy.* Lincoln, Nebraska, 1960

Grenville, John A. S., & Young, George Berkeley, *Politics, Strategy, and American Diplomacy.* New Haven, Connecticut, 1966

Griswold, A. Whitney, *The Far Eastern Policy of the United States.* New Haven, Connecticut, 1938

Handlin, Oscar, *Chance or Destiny: Turning Points in American History.* Boston, 1954

Halle, Louis J., *Dream and Reality: Aspects of American Foreign Policy.* New York, 1959

Harrington, F. H., "Literary Aspects of American Anti-Imperialism, 1898—1902." *New England Quarterly,* X, 1937

— "The Anti-Imperialist Movement in the United States, 1898—1900." *Mississippi Valley Historical Review,* XXII, 1935

Harvey, R. H., *Samuel Gompers: Champion for the Toiling Masses.* 1935

Hays, Samuel P., *The Response to Industrialism, 1885—1914.* Chicago, 1957

Healy, David, *US Expansionism. The Imperialist Urge in the 1890's.* Madison, Wisconsin, 1970

Hobson, J. A., *Imperialism: A Study.* London, 1902

Hofstadter, Richard, "Manifest Destiny and the Philippines." In *America in Crises,* ed. by D. Aaron. New York, 1952

— *Social Darwinism in American Thought.* Boston, 1955

Hollingsworth, Rogers J., *The Whirligig of Politics. The Democracy of Cleveland and Bryan.* Chicago, 1963

Holt, W. Stoll, *Treaties Defeated by the Senate. A Study of the Struggle between President and Senate over the Conduct of Foreign Relations.* Baltimore, 1933

James, Henry, *Richard Olney and His Public Service.* Boston, 1923

Johnson, J. R., "Imperialism in Nebraska, 1898—1904." *Nebraska History,* 44: 3, 1963

Johnson, J. R., *Nebraska in the Spanish-American War and the Philippine Insurrection. A Study in Imperialism.* Unpublished PhD thesis, University of Nebraska, 1937

Johnson, Walter, *William Allen White's America.* 1947

Kennan, George F., *American Diplomacy, 1900—1950.* New York 1952

Koening, Louis W., *Bryan: A Political Biography of William Jennings Bryan.* New York, 1971

La Feber, Walter, *The New Empire. An Interpretation of American Expansion, 1860—1898.* Ithaca, 1963

Lasch, Christopher, "The Anti-Imperialists, the Philippines, and the Inequality of Man." *Journal of Southern History, XXIV,* 1958

Leech, Margaret, *In the Days of McKinley.* New York, 1959

Lenin, V. I., *Imperialism the Highest Stage of Capitalism. A popular Outline.* New rev translation. New York, 1939

Leopold, Richard W., *Elihu Root and the Conservative Tradition.* Boston, 1954

— *The Growth of American Foreign Policy.* New York, 1962

Leuchtenburg, William, "The Needless War with Spain", in *Times of Trial,* ed. by Allan Nevins. New York, 1958

— "Progressivism and Imperialism. The Progressive Movement and American Foreign Policy, 1898—1916." *Mississippi Valley Historical Review,* XXXIX, 1952

Levin, Robert, "An Interpretation of American Imperialism." *Journal of Economic History,* XXXII, 1972

Levine, Daniel, "The Social Philosophy of Albert J Beveridge." *Indiana Magazine of History,* June 1962

Levine, Lawrence W., *Defender of the Faith. William Jennings Bryan: The Last Decade 1915—1925.* London, 1965

Levine, Robert A., *The Arms Debate.* Cambridge, Massachusetts, 1963

357

Lewis, Gordon K., *Puerto Rico. Freedom and Power in the Carribean.* 1968

Long, J. C., *Byan, The Great Commoner.* New York, 1928

Mc Call, Samuel W., *The Life of Thomas Brackett Reed.* Boston, 1914

Mc Cormick, Thomas, "Insular Imperialism and The Open Door: The China Market and the Spanish American War." *Pacific Historical Review, XXXII: 2,* 1963

— *China Market. America's Quest for Informal Empire, 1893—1901.* Chicago, 1967

Mc Elroy, Robert, *Grover Cleveland. The Man and the Statesman.* 2 vols. New York, 1925

Mc Gurrin, James, *Bourke Cockran. A Free Lance in American Politics.* New York, 1948

Mc Kee, D. L., "Samuel Gompers, the A F of L and Imperialism, 1895—1900." *The Historian, XXI,* 1959

Maxwell, Robert S., *La Follette and the Rise of the Progressives in Wisconsin.* Madison, Wisconsin, 1956

May, Ernest R., *American Imperialism: A Speculative Essay.* New York, 1968

— *From Imperialism to Isolationism, 1898—1919.* New York, 1964

— *Imperial Democracy. The Emergence of America as a Great Power.* New York, 1961

Mayer, George H., *The Republican Party, 1854—1964.* New York, 1964

Merk, Frederick, *Manifest Destiny and Mission in American History. A Reinterpretation.* New York, 1963

Merrill, H. S., *Grover Cleveland and the Democratic Party,* 1957

Millis, Walter, *The Martial Spirit. A Study of Our War with Spain.* Boston, 1931

Morgan, H. Wayne, *William McKinley and His America.* Syracuse, New York, 1963

O'Connor, Nancy Leonore, "The Spanish-American War: A Reevaluation of Its Causes." *Science and Society,* 1958

Olcott, Charles S., *The Life of William McKinley.* 2 vols. Boston, 1916

Osgood, Robert Endicott, *Ideals and Self-Interest in America's Foreign Relations. The Great Transformation of the Twentieth Century.* Chicago, 1953

Pelling, Henry, *American Labor.* Chicago, 1960

Perkins, Dexter, *The American Approach to Foreign Policy.* Cambridge, Massachusetts, 1953

— *The Evolution of American Foreign Policy.* New York, 1948

— *A History of the Monroe Doctrine.* Boston, 1941

— *The United States and the Carribean.* Cambridge, Massachusetts, 1947

Perkins, Whitney, *Denial of Empire. The United States and Its Dependencies.* 1962

Pollack, Norman, *The Populist Response to Industrial America. Midwestern Populist Thought.* Cambridge, Massachusetts, 1962

Pomeroy, William J., *American Neo-Colonialism: Its Emergence in the Philippines and Asia.* New York, 1970

Porter, Glenn, *The Rise of Big Business, 1860—1910.* New York, 1973

Pratt, Julius W., *America's Colonial Experiment. How the United States Gained, Governed and in Part Gave Away a Colonial Empire.* New York, 1950

— "American Business and the Spanish-American War." In *Hispanic American Historical Review, XIV,* 1934

— *Expansionists of 1898. The Acquisition of Hawaii and the Spanish Islands.* Chicago, 1936

— "The Large Policy of 1898." The *Mississippi Valley Historical Review, XIX,* 1932

Reuter, Frank T., *Catholic Influence on American Colonial Policies, 1898—1904.* Austin, Texas, and London, 1967

— *The Emergence of America as a Great Power.* 1901

Rissler, Herbert J., *Charles Warren Fairbanks: Conservative Hoosier.* Unpublished Ph. D. thesis, Indiana University, 1961

Rothman, David J., *Politics and Power: The United States Senate, 1869—1901.* Cambridge, Massachusetts, 1966

Schirmer, Daniel B., *Republic or Empire. American Resistance to the Philippine War.* Cambridge, Massachusetts, 1972

Schriftgiesser, Karl, *The Gentleman from Massachusetts: Henry Cabot Lodge.* Boston, 1944

Seeds, Russel M., *History of the Republican Party of Indiana.* Indianapolis, 1899

Smith, Daniel M., *The American Diplomatic Experience.* Boston, 1972

Stanwood, Alexander, *Four Famous New Yorkers. The Political Careers of Cleveland, Platt, Hill, and Roosevelt.* New York, 1923

Stanwood, Edward, *A History of the Presidency from 1897 to 1909.* New York, 1912

Stoddard, L., *Master of Manhattan: The Life of Richard Croker.* New York, 1931

Sullivan, Mark, *Our Times: The United States 1900—1925. I. The Turn of the Century.* New York, 1926

Swanberg, W. A., *Citizen Hearst. A Biography of William Randolph Hearst.* New York, 1961

Swisher, J. A., "Theodore Roosevelt in Iowa." *The Palimpsest,* Oct. 1932

Taussig, F. W., *The Tariff History of the United States.* New York, 1964

Thayer, William Roscoe, *The Life and Letters of John Hay.* 2 vols. Boston, 1915

Tompkins, E. Berkeley, "The Old Guard: A Study of the Anti-Imperialist Leadership." *The Historian,* XXX: 3, 1968

— *Anti-Imperialism in the United States: The Great Debate, 1890—1920.* Philadelphia, 1970

Tuchman, Barbara W., *The Proud Tower. A Portrait of the World before the War, 1890—1914.* New York, 1966

Varg, Paul A., *The Making of a Myth: The United States and China, 1897—1912.* East Lansing, Michigan, 1968

Vevier, Charles, "American Continentalism: An Idea of Expansion, 1845—1910." *American Historical Review,* LXV, 1960

Visher, S. S., *Economic Geography of Indiana.* New York, 1922

Weinberg, Albert K., *Manifest Destiny. A Study of Nationalist Expansionism in American History.* Baltimore, 1935

Welch, Jr., Richard E., *George Frisbie Hoar and the Halfbreed Republicans.* Cambridge, Massachusetts, 1971

— "Motives and Policy Objectives of Anti-Imperialists 1898." *Mid-America,* LI, 1969

— "Opponents and Colleagues: George Frisbie Hoar and Henry Cabot Lodge, 1898—1904." *The New England Quarterly,* XXXIX, 1966

Weston, Rubin Francis, *Racism in U.S. Imperialism: The Influence of Racial Assumptions on American Foreign Policy, 1893—1946.* Columbia, South Carolina, 1972

White, Leonard D., *The Republican Era: A Study in Administrative History, 1869—1901.* New York, 1958

Whittaker, William G., "Samuel Gompers, Anti-Imperialist." *Pacific Historical Review,* XXXVIII, 1969

Wilkerson, Marcus M., *Public Opinion and the Spanish-American War: A Study in War Propaganda.* Baton Rouge, Louisiana, 1932

Williams, Wayne C., *William Jennings Bryan.* New York, 1936

Williams, William Appleman, *The Contours of American History.* Chicago, 1961

— *The Roots of the Modern American Empire. A Study of the Growth and Shaping of Social Consciousness in a Marketplace Society.* New York, 1969

— *The Tragedy of American Diplomacy.* New York, 1959

Williamson, Harold Francis, *Edward Atkinson. The Biography of an American Liberal, 1827—1905.* Boston, 1934

Wisan, Joseph E., *The Cuban Crisis as Reflected in the New York Press, 1895—1898.* New York, 1934

Woodward, C. Vann, *Tom Watson: Agrarian Rebel.* New York, 1938

Young, Marilyn Blatt, "American Expansion, 1870—1900: The Far East." In *Towards a New Past,* ed. by Barton J. Bernstein. 1968

— *The Rhetoric of Empire. American China Policy, 1895—1901.* Cambridge, Massachusetts, 1968

Index

Strong, Josiah 30
Sullivan, Mark 88
Sulzer, William 180, 181, 292
Sumner, William Graham 245, 249

Taft, William Howard 88
Taggart, Thomas 88, 91, 137, 139,
  281—283
Taney, Charles H. 244
Tarpey, M. F. 292
Taylor, Robert S. 285
Teller, Henry Moore 28, 184, 215
Thayer, James Bradley 65, 66
Thomas, Charles S. 184, 209
Thompson, Maurice 137, 138, 283
Thurston, John M. 48
Tillman, Benjamin R. 211, 212
Tompkins, Arthur S. 76
Towne, Charles A. 174, 184, 215, 217,
  218, 273, 304
Turner, Frederick Jackson 39
Turpie, David 110

Valentine, John J. 171
Van Bergen, R. 35
Van Voorhis, John 283
Van Wyck, Augustus 169, 208, 209, 277
Van Wyck, Robert 179, 181

Vest, George G. 32, 77
Villard, Oswald Garrison 254
Vorhees, Daniel W. 110

Wallace, Lew 137
Walter, C. M. 281
Washington, George 235
Watson, James E. 76, 112, 121, 132, 136
Watterson, Henry 42
Weinberg, Albert 44
Wellington, George 79, 80, 245, 246,
  249, 302
Welsh, Herbert 169, 175, 245, 246, 252,
  253, 270
Whitcomb, Larz A. 111, 114, 118
White, Edward Douglas 82
White, Horace 175, 249
Williams, S. W. 281
Williams, George Fred 181, 183, 184
Williams, James R. 210
Wilson, Charles B. 106
Winslow, Erving 169, 170, 234, 239, 241,
  243, 252, 256, 295
Wolcott, Edward O. 45, 197, 198, 200,
  201, 203, 220, 222, 273

Youngblood 264, 265

365